# THREE-POINTED STAR

Karl Benz and family pictured with that great motoring pioneer, Baron von Liebig. (*Mercedes-Benz*)

# THREE-POINTED STAR

## The Story of Mercedes-Benz

**DAVID SCOTT-MONCRIEFF**

Revised and updated edition

GENTRY BOOKS
LONDON

This revised edition first published 1979.
ISBN 0 85614 058 9


Published by Gentry Books Limited,
16 Regency Street, London SW1.
Distributed in the U.S.A. by

Printed in Great Britain by
Billing and Sons Limited, Guildford.

To

MY MOTHER

who drove a Gottlieb Daimler-engined
car, before the turn of the century

# CONTENTS

The drawings reproduced at the beginning of each chapter are by Carlo Demand and are taken from *The Big Race* by Ernst Rosemann and Carlo Demand (published 1955 by Nest Verlag GmbH, Frankfurt a. M.)

# FOREWORD

DIFFERENT cars fascinate different people. There are few of us who do not bear in our hearts some secret allegiance, often formed in childhood, for one particular make. Some are partisans for the blood-red Alfa-Romeos, carrying, like a blazon of chivalry, the viper of Milan; others, for those that bear on their broad foreheads the letter B, set between the wings of Osiris. Yet others, though this historic name is now no more than the symbol of a glorious past, are heart and soul for trim horizon-blue Bugattis. And soon a new generation will grow up to revere the black stallion on a yellow shield of Ferrari. Only very few of these fanatical partisans ever drive, let alone own, the makes of their choice; they are content to worship from afar.

There is another famous marque—a three-pointed star, a star that has been carried by the great white Mercedes cars on the roads of the world. It is a proud emblem, worthy of the cars it adorns, and worthy of the history of those who built them and those that preceded them. So we are glad to have the opportunity to chronicle, in English for the first time, the history of this great make that shares with Panhard the honour of being one of the first to race and still be racing.

We should like to express our thanks to the many people who have so gladly given us their help and advice in the preparation of this book.

Firstly to Mr. Edward L. Mayer, the doyen of English Mercedes enthusiasts, who provided many photographs from his private collection and inestimable assistance from his memory and records. To Mr. George Monkhouse for the numerous photographs he has allowed us to reproduce, and his helpful criticism whilst this book was in proof. To Mr. Laurence Pomeroy, Technical Editor of *The Motor*, who has been a mine of information which never failed us, and to the Secretary of the R.A.C., who extended to us the full facilities of the Club library. Mr. Hermann Scott, too, deserves our thanks for cheerfully translating the mass of contemporary German records we set before him.

We wish also to acknowledge the kindness of the editors and proprietors of *The Autocar*, *The Motor* and *Motor Sport*, who not only supplied us with photographs, but allowed us to reproduce extracts from many articles appearing in their publications of the last half-century. In tracing the story of Mercedes-Benz, we found these journals an invaluable and fascinating supplement to the official records.

Lastly, we pay our debt of gratitude to the Daimler-Benz Company. Without them there would have been no three-pointed star: without their readiness to give all the assistance we asked of them, there might well have been no book.

# FOREWORD TO NEW EDITION

It is a matter of considerable pride that *Three-Pointed Star*, which I wrote in the early nineteen fifties, has been running even longer than 'Coronation Street'. As before, I have had tremendous help in preparing this latest edition, particularly with the greatly expanded selection of illustrations. Help has come here from two major sources. Since I wrote the book, my friend Edward Mayer has died. His priceless collection of Mercedes photographs in the early days of this century was bequeathed to the Mercedes-Benz Club. Much gratitude is due to Kenneth J. Clark of Malmesbury, now custodian of the collection, who allowed me full access to it. And, of course, the parent company, Daimler-Benz A.G., were as unstinting, beyond the call of duty, as ever, with their help. When I first wrote *Three-Pointed Star* a quarter of a century ago, the Mercedes historic photographs were all stored unsorted in a cellar, and finding anything was very much a lucky dip. Now they have a superbly efficient photo filing system. It is now possible to put a finger on what one requires in seconds rather than minutes. My friend Artur Keser is no longer with us, but Bernd Harling looked after me in his place. Bernd is a wonderful chap to work with, and not only does he speak perfect English, but he understands my German. Working together, we got through a week's work in two long hard days. And, for good measure, he took me to lunch at a Stuttgart restaurant which serves nothing but asparagus! So, with the aid of Messrs. Clark and Harling we have been able to re-illustrate this book with a bigger selection of pictures, virtually all hitherto unpublished. And, of course, as always, Erik Johnson, of Mercedes-Benz (U.K.) Ltd., has been a tower of strength, ready and willing to give help whenever called upon. Finally, as before, I am indebted to Peter Hull, the late St. John Nixon and Clarence Paget for their invaluable contributions to the earlier editions of this book.

# I
# A STAR IS BORN 1900

*'Von hier aus wird ein Stern aufgehen, und ich will hoffen, dass er uns und unseren Kindern Segen bringt.'*

'A star shall arise from here, and I hope that it will bring blessings to us and to our children.'

*Gottlieb Daimler,* circa 1880, *when questioned about the star painted on the wall of his house.*

Werner steering the first Mercedes to victory in the Nice–Salon–Nice race, 1901. (*Carlo Demand: The Big Race*)

# KARL BENZ

IN 1900, the Daimler Motoren Gesellschaft made a motor-car which they christened Mercedes* after the daughter of Emile Jellinek, Consul in Nice for the old Austro-Hungarian Empire, and a Director of the Credit Lyonnais. The new sporting Mercedes model was such an instantaneous success, after the usual teething troubles had been overcome, that from the year mentioned the products of this Company, reorganized in 1926 as the Daimler-Benz Aktiengesellschaft, were known throughout the world by that name.

The early work of both Benz and Daimler is the seed from which the Mercedes car germinated, and therefore it is right that this narrative should start with some brief account of these two engineers.

The world into which Benz and Daimler were born was very different from the world of today. Prior to the Bismarck epoch, the Germany of the early nineteenth century was a series of kingdoms, principalities and duchies. It was a world of caste and privilege, but underlying it all was the age-long German respect for hard work, learning and fine craftsmanship. In addition, there was an excellent higher educational system available to all who were competent, irrespective of class or purse. Such, very briefly, was the Kingdom of Württemberg in 1844.

There is a striking similarity between the early years and struggles of our own George Stephenson and those of Karl Benz, who was destined to revolutionize travel as completely as did Stephenson. Both were sons of humble mechanics, both their fathers perished in the course of their work, and both had to fight, in grim poverty, every step of their way to success. The only difference was that Benz had the benefit of a good system of cheap education which was not to be seen in Britain for many years, and was certainly non-existent in the early days of George Stephenson.

On November 25, 1844, Josephine Benz, the wife of Johann Georg Benz, an engine-driver on the Karlsruhe railway,

* Accents were used in the normal way, an acute on the second 'e' and a grave on the third 'e', until 1909.

presented her husband with a son who was duly given the name of Karl. The wife's father, an unwilling conscript in Napoleon's army, met his death in tragic circumstances during the abortive march against Moscow.

Two years after the boy's birth, a pointsman on the line between Karlsruhe and Heidelberg made a mistake which resulted in a slow-moving engine running off the rails for a short distance before coming to a halt. All the employees nearby hastened with blocks of wood and crowbars, to re-rail the engine before the consequences of the pointsman's mistake could be noticed by a senior official. Sweating and straining with his companions to save the unfortunate pointsman from trouble, Johann Benz contracted pneumonia and died within a few days. His widow, who received a frugal pension of six gulden, twenty-four kreutzer per month, was determined that her young son should have a sound education irrespective of the sacrifice entailed. She had hopes that one day he might secure a post in the Civil Service.

She and the boy lived in a nice little house in the small town of Mühlberg near Karlsruhe, but to further her plans for her young son, Frau Benz moved into the town of Karlsruhe so that she might supplement her small income somewhat in turning to account a fine art at which she was outstandingly good—cookery.

After passing his examination, young Benz entered the Karlsruhe Lyceum, which might be compared to an English Grammar School. This institution was celebrated for its instruction in the natural sciences, and of the thirty hours spent on actual classes each week, no fewer than four were devoted to the teaching of physics, which soon became Karl Benz's favourite subject.

It is interesting to record that the annual fees for this school were equivalent to two months' pension allowed to Frau Benz. She, good woman, scraped and saved every penny that she could so that her son could establish a small laboratory in the attic of their trim little home.

Karl then graduated to Karlsruhe Polytechnic. Once again, Germany preceded us by a number of years in the establishment of subsidized colleges for higher technical education. Here it was possible for a young man, irrespective of his means, to study to an advanced stage the subject in which he was interested. Life, however, was not easy for either mother or son. The boy was earning nothing, and his mother took in boarders to help feed and clothe him, and pay his fees. Karl did what little he could to help her and occasionally added to the family's income by repairing watches.

At the Polytechnic, Karl Benz had an outstandingly fine teacher, Ferdinand Redtenbacher, who had done considerable research, both theoretical and practical, into the internal combustion engine, as then in its infancy, with a view to industrial use. Redtenbacher and the professor who succeeded him, Franz Grashof, seem to have been working along much the same lines as Lenoir, who produced the first practical working gas engine in 1860.

It was in this atmosphere that Karl Benz, a star pupil and protégé of Ferdinand Redtenbacher, grew up. It was therefore not surprising that at the back of his fertile young brain there was always the idea of an alternative power to steam. In 1861, a Lenoir engine was installed in the machine-tool works of Max Eyth at Stuttgart. Young Benz was allowed to assist with this. It is on record that although this early gas engine was very under-powered, it worked remarkably well.

Benz graduated from the Polytechnic in 1864, and went off to get practical experience. For a short time he worked for a locksmith, for his mother was ill and he wished to be near her. Later he signed on as a fitter at the Karlsruhe Maschinenbaugesellschaft. This factory, large for those days (800 employees), turned out every kind of foundry-work and machinery from locomotives and turbines to immense industrial boilers. The working-hours were 6 a.m. to 7 p.m., and it was here that the twenty-year-old Benz nearly met his death. He and another workman were lying on their backs fitting a newly-forged piece to a railway engine raised from the ground on a wooden scaffold, when a splintering crash was heard and the wooden beams began to sag under the great weight. Benz managed to get his head and chest out before he was pinned down. In the meantime, every man in the erecting shop had seized blocks and crowbars and struggled to free them. By a miracle, both youths were rescued, shaken but unhurt.

For two years Benz worked as a fitter, gaining valuable experience. The work was hard and the hours long, but the hardships he sustained were not too high a price to pay for the engineering lessons he learnt. He went on to the Karl Schenk works, first working in the shops and then, after a few months, in the office. After two years he obtained a better position with Benckiser Brothers, a large firm of engineers and ironfounders in Pforzheim. In the spring of 1870, his gallant mother, who had worked so hard and had made such sacrifices for her son's education, died. Karl Benz was now twenty-five, and he stood alone in the world.

After his mother's death, he took a job with a firm of structural engineers in Pforzheim who specialized in bridge-building. Here he met his future wife, Berta Ringer, but owing to the uncertainty of employment due to the outbreak of the Franco-Prussian war, they delayed their marriage until July 1872, when he was twenty-seven and his fiancée twenty-three. A year prior to their marriage, Benz went to Vienna in the hope of making progress in the world so that he could marry in better circumstances, but he was disappointed with what awaited him; the opportunities for an enthusiastic young engineer appeared to be rather worse than they were in Germany. After a month he returned to Mannheim, where he started a small workshop on his own account in partnership with a man named August Ritter.

The small firm of 'Benz and Ritter; Mechanische Werkstätte' did not prosper sufficiently to support both partners, so Benz, with the help of his wife's small capital, paid Ritter back the sum he had put into the business, and thus became the sole proprietor.

Eugen, the first of the Benz children, was born on May 1, 1873. His birth was greeted by the chill wind of what economists call a 'commercial recession', and referred to by normal human beings as a slump. This lasted for some years, and during this period a second son, Richard, was born on October 21, 1874.

Benz's financial position went from bad to worse. A friend in Pforzheim who had lent him money for his business suddenly asked for its return. The only possible way in which this demand could be met was by selling up the struggling little business; at the last moment, however, the bank came to the rescue with a guarantee that saved the actual workshop building, but all the contents, including the machine-tools, had to go.

Benz and his wife put up a gallant fight. During the winter of 1878, he managed to make some small progress with his first two-stroke engine. By that time, the four-stroke engine had been patented, and the popular opinion was that it would soon oust the two-stroke, but with fanatical single-mindedness and with his wife always helping him, the young engineer continued with what few hand tools were left to him.

On New Year's Eve of 1880, they were almost penniless and had not sufficient money to purchase an evening meal, but the engine on which so much time and energy had been expended was running satisfactorily under its own power, and the sound of each explosion was a veritable *Ohrenschmaus* to both of them.

But engines do not sell themselves, and purchasers were not easy to find; funds continued to be very low until a photographer, for whom Benz had carried out some work in a highly satisfactory manner, and which had defied the efforts of other engineers, put up a small amount of capital to enable Benz to continue his research work and development.

Difficulty with the Patent Office was also experienced. Benz's application for a patent was refused on the grounds that the patent specification was couched in too general terms, and this refusal resulted in a dispute which lasted some fifteen months.

During this time, Benz began to make a few two-stroke gas engines. In the official commercial register of Mannheim for 1881, he had the honour of seeing his small business described as the Mannheimer Gasmotorenfabrik, but further difficulties were in store. He had entered into a contract with a man named Otto Schmuck to act as agent for the sale of the goods he was manufacturing. Schmuck was a failure, and being pressed for money, he was persuaded to turn his business into a company with nine shareholders; its official title was the Gasmotorenfabrik of Mannheim. This was in October 1882, but further difficulties arose which culminated in Benz cutting himself adrift from the business and making a fresh start on his own account. He was almost penniless, with a wife and four children to support, and to add to his troubles he was involved in a law case with his late partners in respect of a gas engine of his own design. He lost the action and was at his wits' end how to provide for the common necessities of life. Everything appeared to be working against him when suddenly his luck changed in a manner which had an appreciable influence on his designing and manufacturing the first practical petrol-driven motor-car the world ever saw.

Two business friends, Max C. Rose and Friedrich W. Esslinger, offered to finance him in a new company to be formed called Benz und Cie; Rheinische Gasmotorenfabrik of Mannheim, and during the winter of 1883–4 he was free to develop his ideas without the constant fear of financial troubles arising. Patents were taken out in both France and in the U.S.A., and the usual lamp-type of ignition on gas engines was replaced by an electric ignition system.

Let us take a brief glance at the first car Benz made, and while doing so, keep in mind the fact that every part of this vehicle had to be designed out of his own head and made with his own hands. He had to decide whether it should have three wheels or four, whether it should be driven by the front wheels or by the back; whether it should be steered by the front or rear wheels, how the power should be carried from the engine to the wheels or to one wheel, whether the engine should be placed in front, amidships or at the rear, and how the vehicle should be controlled.

1885 Benz, the first production car in the world. Top speed 18 k.p.h. at 400 r.p.m. (*Mercedes-Benz*)

Benz had never seen a motor vehicle in his life; neither had he any knowledge of the form the few wholly unsuccessful experiments before him had taken. The genius of the man only comes home to us if we try to picture what our thoughts would be if we were given a gas engine and were told to attach it to some form of road vehicle so that the one propelled the other

—and we had never seen a self-propelled vehicle in our lives.

The illustrations, and the description of Benz's first car in Appendix II, will show how he solved all these involved problems. His first attempt was necessarily primitive, but in the circumstances in which this machine was designed is there an engineer today who would have done better or as well? Let us also bear in mind another highly interesting fact; this first car had at least four features common to nearly every car on the roads today: a water-cooled engine, electric ignition, a differential gear (of extraordinarily modern design), and a mechanically-operated inlet valve. For fully fifteen years after 1885, inlet valves were of the automatic type.

The precise date on which this first car was tested has never been definitely established. It is beyond dispute that this epoch-making event took place during the spring of 1885 on private ground surrounding Benz's workshop. It is established further that in the autumn of the same year, it covered 1000 metres at a speed of 12 km. per hour on the public highway and that during the summer of 1886 it was used fairly extensively in the streets of Mannheim, but each time the car was taken out it created such a sensation that Benz feared police intervention. Quite often it had to be pushed back to the workshop, but Benz was determined that it should cover a lengthy distance unaided, and to do so he had to take it out after dark.

He set himself the task of driving it, unaided, round two circles in Mannheim. From his workshop, up the Waldhof-strasse as far as Waldhof, and back again via Kaeferthal. The larger circle took him as far as Sandhofen.

Time after time he set out, but only to be pushed back by his passenger and anyone else who would help. The distances covered began to increase, and on one never-to-be-forgotten night, he made a non-stop run of both circles; from that moment, the spread of the motor-car throughout the world began, and no amount of special pleading on behalf of others who were before Benz will ever overcome the fact that Karl Benz designed, manufactured and drove in 1885 the first successful petrol-driven road vehicle the world ever saw. His predecessors, such as de Rivaz, Lenoir, Marcus, Butler, Delamare-Deboueville et Malandin and others, all made highly praiseworthy efforts to build a successful road vehicle propelled by an internal combustion engine, but they all failed, and had none of these been born, the development of the motor-car would not have been retarded in point of time by a single hour, nor in point of development by an inch. Karl Benz succeeded, whereas the efforts of those who came before him led to nothing at all. Save Daimler, and one or two experimentalists who achieved nothing, not a hand in Europe was at work on the automobile when Benz was designing his first car.

The first press notice in the paper *Neue Badische Landeszeitung* lauded the car's performance, but men of influence and money belittled it and ridiculed Benz's efforts. Even experienced engineers said that this 'mad obsession' would ruin the stationary-engine business which he had built up so courageously. Nevertheless, improvements were effected almost daily, and nightly after the children were in bed Frau Benz charged the accumulator for the ignition by treadling away at her sewing-machine stand, to which a little dynamo had been attached.

Karl Benz encountered the fanatical opposition which all the other pioneers of motoring had to face. Horses shied furiously as his car approached, and an old woman in Odenwald who heard the machine approaching, dashed screaming into her house declaring that the Old Gentleman was positively on her doorstep.

But Benz's courage and his faith in the future of the motor-car never failed him. When he attended the Munich Exhibition in 1888 he badgered the Munich Authorities into allowing him to drive his car through the streets. They consented reluctantly, providing that he made himself responsible for any damage he caused. The car was received with enthusiastic commentary in the Munich press. The reporters were particularly impressed by the fact that the car would run for an hour on one litre of fuel. Benz was awarded the Gold Medal of the Exhibition.

But in spite of these non-remunerative encouragements, scarcely a car was sold. In later years Benz recalled a singularly bad omen. Almost his first customer was removed to a lunatic asylum shortly after having taken delivery. Doubtless, anti-motorists of that period applied the much-abused phrase, *Post hoc ergo propter hoc.*

During 1888 Frau Benz, that fine and remarkably energetic woman, had an historic adventure. At 5 a.m. one morning, while her husband was still asleep, she piled her two eldest boys, aged fourteen and fifteen, into the car, and with Eugen Benz at the tiller, drove from Mannheim to Pforzheim. Frequent stops were necessary for various reasons, and much manual assistance had to be given at the hills, but they reached their goal, and to the undying glory of the female sex let it be recorded that this first long journey by car was accomplished by a middle-aged housewife supported only by her two young sons. Truly, the spirit of Joan of Arc, Florence Nightingale and Lady Godiva had not waned appreciably in 1888.

Five days later, the return journey was undertaken by the

courageous trio. Karl Benz was naturally proud of his family's achievements. But, apart from welcoming the publicity, it was typical of Benz that he realized the journey proved a lower gear for hill-climbing to be necessary, and this was incorporated in his future productions.

When it had been shown that long journeys could be made by car, Benz found himself thoroughly embroiled with local authorities who bedevilled him with petty restrictions and nonsensical regulations as thoroughly as any bureaucrats of today. He was permitted to circulate on the roads of the State of Baden 'provided that the specification of the vehicle was the same as that shown on the plans in the office at Mannheim' and 'provided that he gave audible warning of his approach with a loud bell' and observed other restrictions.

The many petty restrictions plus a lack of faith in the automobile held back buyers, and wide publicity was given to an article in a scientific journal written by no less a panjandrum than the librarian of the Imperial Patent Office, in which he stated pontifically: 'The internal combustion engine has as little future as steam for motivating road vehicles.'

On the other hand, *Leipziger Illustrierte* envisaged the motor-car replacing the horse. But the fact remained that the cars were not selling, and the two co-directors of Karl Benz grew increasingly discouraged.

Benz, like Ettore Bugatti a quarter of a century later, always liked to produce in his own factory all the components that he possibly could. By 1887 his heart and soul were in the development of the motor-car and he was in the factory from early morning until late at night supervising every detail. In 1889 he exhibited at the World's Fair in Paris, but with practically no success: indeed, the French, still smarting from the Franco-Prussian war, were most unwilling to buy anything bearing a German name. Emile Roger, a French cycle manufacturer, bought a car and took up the Benz agency for France. The cars were known as the Roger-Benz cars and a number were sold. The two co-directors of Benz, however, were dissatisfied with the amount of time and money being spent on the development of motor-cars, and they refused to sanction any further expenditure.

After some stormy scenes, the two sceptical directors withdrew and once again Karl Benz had a remarkable stroke of good fortune. Two men of ability and foresight, F. von Fischer and Julius Ganss, offered to support Benz financially. Although the business was still mortgaged to the two late directors, good progress was made and Karl Benz was given a free hand in connexion with automobile development, von Fischer supervising the internal administration, and Julius Ganss the sales.

Julius Ganss proved himself to be a very capable salesman; indeed he appears to have been one of those rare individuals who could sell anything, and the readiness with which he opened up markets for Benz cars in such important centres as Berlin, Paris, London, Brussels, St. Petersburg, Moscow, Vienna, the South American capitals and elsewhere suggests that to sell refrigerators to reluctant Eskimoes would have been child's play to him.

Benz, on the other hand, was essentially an inventor, an engineer and a technician, with but little gifts for administration and none at all for common salesmanship, but with von Fischer and Ganss at the helm, the business made sound progress.

From 1890 onwards the firm concentrated on the production of petrol-driven stationary engines which had a good sale in places where town gas was not available. But, at the same time, this remarkable team was laying down the foundations of a motor-car business.

The first Benz cars were three-wheelers. For some considerable time Benz had felt that this was not a satisfactory arrangement, but had been too hard pressed in other directions to develop a four-wheeled car. He experimented during 1891, and in 1892 the first one was on the road. From 1893 onwards, the flourishing stationary-engine business made less and less demands on him, and he was able to spend most of his time in the department which he had established expressly for motor-car construction.

It was about this time that he was joined on the technical side by an able collaborator named August Horch, who saw at an early date that the cars being produced in the Benz factory were under-powered. Benz was very hostile towards making faster cars, so Horch approached Ganss, and laid his suggestion before him. Ganss appreciated the thought and a more powerful engine was soon being designed. In due course, Horch presented Benz with a *fait accompli* in the form of an engine yielding an additional horse power. Benz, in spite of his earlier opposition, took it in good part and incorporated the Horch modified engine in his next car, thus adding five miles per hour to its speed.

The decade had now arrived when the motor-car, from being the laughing-stock of the multitude, became a practical proposition. Benz, like others, was making progress. In 1888 he abandoned the horizontal flywheel, and followed this by introducing a starting handle to replace the earlier method of pulling the flywheel over by hand, although this did not go into general production until considerably later. In 1897 he made his first twin-cylinder engine, the predecessor of the 5-h.p. and 8-h.p. two-cylinder Benz engines that became so well known. The metal rod-spoked wheels of the early three-wheeler cars were replaced by wooden wheels contracted out to a firm of wheelwrights, but the metal wheels remained in considerable production till well after the turn of the century.

Here let us quote from a contemporary motor journal, and a British one to boot. In its first number, dated November 1896, *The Automotor and Horseless Vehicle Journal* gives the following account of one of Karl Benz's productions.

THE BENZ MOTOR-CARRIAGE

A Bradford correspondent writing of this vehicle—which is the invention of Mr. Benz of Mannheim, and is being introduced into this country by the Arnold Motor-Car Company of East Peckham—gives an interesting account of a ride which he recently enjoyed. He states that by the courtesy of the local agent, Mr. James E. Tuke, Aldermansbury, he was initiated into the mysteries of the horseless carriage, riding with Mr. Tuke in a small car of 1½ h.p. from Otley to Bradford, the time occupied being an hour and twenty minutes exactly. The day was very unsuitable owing to the heavy condition of the roads, and the success of the ride under such adverse circumstances showed how great the scope of the invention must be. At present the machine is hardly out of the experimental stage, but on the flat a good speed was attained. One fine feature of the machine is the ease with which the speed is regulated, without having recourse to the brake. Hollings Hill can be descended, either fast or slow, simply by setting the indicator, or, if economy be aimed at, the gearing may be shifted, and the wheels allowed to revolve downhill under the control of the brake. It appears that a car of 1½ h.p. is not quite equal to carrying two people up the Yorkshire hills in bad weather, but an addition of '½ h.p.' would probably be ample. The little carriage now in Mr. Tuke's possession is one of the smallest made, and its value is about £130. No particular mechanical knowledge is required to understand the working of the car, and when once charged with oil and electricity it will run for 150 miles. The sensation of travelling by this new and convenient method is precisely that of cycling, with the exception of the labour involved by the latter. All that is needed for motor-car riding is a hand for steering and a head to restrain one's natural inclination for racing on the public road. Of the utility and general merit of the horseless carriage there cannot be any doubt. For doctors the novelty appears to offer immediate advantages, but a general adoption of the vehicle by tradespeople and others will naturally be a work of time, and must depend upon the further development of the invention itself. These motors have found much favour in France and Germany, and will doubtless obtain a fair measure of success in this country.

Benz was very much opposed to the early pneumatic tyres made first for bicycles by the brothers André and Edouard

Michelin in France, and introduced by them in the 1896 Paris–Marseilles motor race. He fought against their use until as late as 1901, when he was forced to adopt them on practically all his cars. He did fit them earlier to some of his cars, but it was very much against his inclinations.

At about this time Karl Benz pioneered a major improvement, a ball-bearing back axle. This needed considerable courage, for ball bearings were not to become, for a couple of decades, either reliable, cheap, or trouble free.

Some hundreds of these early Benz cars were sold; by 1898 two hundred had been sold in England and a further two hundred in France. Ganss, pioneer of so much sales technique, must surely have been the first manufacturer to employ a journalist who was also a qualified engineer to 'write' his publicity for him. This did not at all meet with the approval of Benz who, on the grounds that 'good wine needs no bush', held that the merits of a car were sufficient advertisement without any form of newspaper advertising.

There are alive today one or two old men who were taught to drive by Karl Benz. Whenever he tested a car on the road he would take one or more pupils with him for instruction.

The 1899 Benz *Ideal* was the best-selling car of its day. (*Mercedes-Benz*)

Those still living recall that Benz drove very slowly and courteously, making them always stop the engine for approaching horses lest they should take fright.

The factory was now in full production; Benz and his colleagues had built up a first-class team of technicians and mechanics who took a pride in their work. The favourite among them was Hans Thum, who goes down to history as the man who was instrumental in having the four-miles-per-hour speed limit rescinded. He was sent one day to collect some high-ranking government officials from the railway station. These august worthies were shocked to see a horse-drawn milk float about to pass them and one asked Thum if the car could go faster. Thum replied that it could go very much faster, but to do so was '*streng verboten*'. So they ordered him to drive as fast as he could, and Hans Thum rattled the delighted officials up to eighteen or twenty miles an hour with perfect safety. The four-miles-an-hour limit was immediately repealed. Benz used to recall with a chuckle, in his old age, that he had an understanding with the driver of the milk float!

Benz was now building quite a diversity of models. There was the *Victoria*, a luxury carriage costing about 4,000 marks (about £1,000) and a similar, lighter, less elaborate, and cheaper version called the *Velo*. Even more expensive was the *Phaeton*. There was an omnibus carrying eight people and propelled by a 5-h.p. motor and a six-seater landau on a similar chassis. In 1897, the popular 5-h.p., pneumatic-tyred four-seater *Dos-à-Dos* appeared. Specimens of this exist today. The following year the engine was increased to 9-h.p. and the car, with three speeds and reverse, could attain the thrilling speed of over twenty-five miles an hour!

The *Velo* developed into the *Comfortable* with two seats and a small front seat for a child. Its maximum speed was scarcely 17 m.p.h., but its reliability was outstanding for those days, and it climbed the Brenner and other Alpine passes. Public opinion held that it was the best car Benz had ever made and the sales were fairly brisk.

King Leopold II of Belgium ordered a car, and Benz set out to build his *Royale*, which he called the *Duc*. It was a two-seater with a basketwork seat for a servant. Top speed was about 22 m.p.h. He also built his first racing car of 16 h.p. to special order for Fritz Held, his sales concessionaire in Mannheim.

The year 1899 saw even more models. There was a super-luxury car called *Mylord*, of 8 h.p., increased later to 10 h.p. Then at the Paris Exhibition of 1900 came the 9-h.p. *Spider* with four speeds and reverse. A fairly successful attempt was made to capture the cheap market with the 3½-h.p. Benz *Ideal*, but they soon became out of date, and many of the 265 built remained unsold.

Nevertheless, interest in the Benz *Ideal* was very considerable at that time, and in the correspondence columns of the motor press owners aired their opinions constantly, and on the whole favourably. Here is a letter taken at random from *The Autocar* of September 24, 1898. Incidentally, nobody liked the tyres fitted by Mr. Benz. All changed to Connelly's, which apparently never gave any trouble.

> We are . . . indebted to Mr. Campbell for the following details of the . . . Benz Ideal, purchased through Mr. H. Hewetson, of 59 Mark Lane, London, in February last, since which date it has run 2520 miles. A seat has been fitted to the rear of the car with footboard, making a double dogcart, and very much improving its appearance. The front wheels are 26 in. in diameter, and the back wheels 36 in. The driving wheels have been recently fitted with Connelly's 'Ideal' wired tyres, which have proved most satisfactory. The car is beautifully upholstered in chocolate morocco and spring-seated cushions; the wings are wide, and on the most muddy roads keep the car absolutely clean. The motor is a single-cylinder horizontal Benz, and every part is easily get-at-able for adjustment, etc. The cylinder is 4½ in. bore by 5 in. stroke, developing on the brake 3 h.p. Power is transmitted by belts; there are two speeds, the low speed takes the car with three people up a gradient of one in eight, while on the high speed the car has run from Derby to Uttoxeter, eighteen and three quarter miles, nearly all dead level, in fifty minutes, with two people, and it ran from Derby to Llandudno, 135 miles, in nine hours. The gearing is by roller chains, which, with the exhaust, are practically noiseless, and even when travelling at full speed the occupants can converse in ordinary tones, except when passing a horse-drawn vehicle. The brakes are five in number, viz. two in the wheel rims, two band brakes, and, the most powerful of all, the piston of engine working against a cushion of air in the cylinder, the supply of gas being cut off. The engine is practically a gas engine, the impulse being produced by a compressed mixture of gas and air in the proportion of ten parts of gas to ninety of air, this mixture being ignited behind the piston by an electric spark, the gas being produced as wanted, automatically, from the evaporation of deodorized, steam-treated naphtha from the Anglo-American Oil Co., one gallon of which, at 7d. a gallon, will run the car thirty miles. The electric spark is obtained through an electric coil from two two-volt accumulators in series which are charged from a Boron battery at a cost of 3½d., one charge running the car 350 miles. Up to the present time the motor-car has been running better and better every month, and after the 2520 miles, neither car nor engine show the slightest signs of wear, not a nut or bearing has worked loose, nor has any bearing required adjusting, yet there is not the least play between the working parts. The bearings are very long, and this has a great deal to do with the excellent way both journals and brasses are wearing.

In March 1899, *The Autocar* records the arrival of a new model, apparently a 3½ h.p., though this fact is not mentioned.

The famous Crypto gear, however, provides the clue and this gadget kept correspondents in the motor papers happy for some time to come.

> Hearing that Messrs. Benz's latest production had made its appearance in London, we took the opportunity of a spare hour last week to look up Mr. Hewetson [the Benz agent] and found him up to the eyes in business, but not too busy to accord us that courtesy which is one of his characteristics, and he very readily acceded to our wish to try the new pattern vehicle, and we were soon, with Mr. Coles in charge, gaily motoring away in the direction of Hornsey Rise. The new vehicle ran with very little noise, and with an extremely small amount of vibration, indeed, the improvement in these two respects over the earlier Benz cars which made their appearance in this country is remarkable. The principal feature, however, of the new pattern is the addition of a third, or hill-climbing, speed, which consists of the fitting within the low-speed-driven pulley of what is known to cyclists as a Crypto two-speed gear. The striker of this is attached to the steering port, which in the Benz vehicles carries the belt-shifting gear as well, and by raising the lever the reducing gear at once comes into action, bringing the speed down to somewhere about 2 m.p.h. Of course, as our readers know, the question of hill-climbing is purely one of relation of speed to power, and by a suitable reduction in the gearing a car can be made to go up anything, and practically this is what the new Benz will do within reason, thus removing one of the greatest drawbacks to the Benz carriages of the past—that they would not ascend hills. . . .

Hitherto, all Benz cars had had their engines at the back. Benz brought out three with the engine mounted horizontally in front, the *Tonneau*, the *Elegant Tonneau*, and the *Charrette*, which was a lighter and cheaper edition of the other two. All of these three were unsuccessful. By 1900 the day of the horizontal engine was passing rapidly, and the Benz business began to fall off seriously.

Then there were the goods vehicles. In 1896 the Automobile Club de France inaugurated an international competition for goods vehicles carrying 100 kilos. Of fifteen entrants only eight reached the starting line and they were all steam-propelled! A few years later, however, the Benz petrol-driven trucks were rapidly ousting the steamers from the market. It is interesting to record that the first Benz delivery van sold in France was delivered to Bon Marché of Paris.

Although the company was doing reasonably well, a new and very disturbing factor was appearing, in the form of motor racing. Benz, like the late Sir Henry Royce, was fundamentally opposed to racing, for he held that quality was of more importance than mere speed. Sales were being lost in all directions to manufacturers who indulged in the early continental classic races. At the 1900 World Exhibition in Paris, Benz exhibited a four-seater racing car of 14 h.p. capable of 40 m.p.h. But this gesture was not enough. The unpalatable fact remained that the firm of Benz et Cie was fast losing ground, and the firms who raced were forging ahead to capture a rapidly expanding market.

However much the energy, bull-dog determination and faith in the coming of the automobile of Karl Benz is admired, there is no disguising the fact that he was a pig-headed man, who refused to see in his early work the writing on the wall, which appeared so soon and so clearly. The early business he built up by his own hands fell a victim to his nature. He refused to have his eyes opened to the fact that his early efforts were but stepping stones towards better things. In his view, something approaching finality in motor-car design had been reached by the turn of the century. The slow-running, heavy, unresponsive horizontal engine was the correct design, so he told himself, and for some years he made a desperate effort to swim against the tide of progress until his own business began to collapse over his head, and he was forced to abandon the unequal contest.

When one takes stock of the circumstances in which the automobile was invented, some very striking instances are disclosed of inventors having crippled their own efforts by some unfortunate mental characteristic. The German Jew, Siegfried Marcus, was undeniably a greater engineering genius than Benz, and had he only been imbued with Benz's grit and determination and not flitted, butterfly-like, from one invention to another before each one had even emerged from the early experimental stage, we should have been proclaiming him today the inventor of the automobile, instead of Benz. An examination of the construction and general lay-out of the Marcus car of 1877 discloses a degree of genius which Benz did not possess, but it was Marcus's effervescent nature that killed his efforts and has caused him to become one of the many 'might-have-beens'.

## GOTTLIEB DAIMLER

It is never difficult to start an argument about 'who built the first motor-car'. If, by the term 'motor-car', a self-propelled road vehicle is implied, the answer is Cugnot with his steam carriage built for the transport of artillery rather than for carrying passengers, although it is possible that future research may show that he was considerably antedated by Verbiest, a Jesuit priest accredited to the Court of the Emperor Chien Lung of China. Chien Lung was more or less contemporary with Louis Quatorze and Charles II. Attached to his Court was a College of Jesuits, for he seriously considered embracing the Christian religion, which would have been quite a triumph for the Jesuits, because, under the etiquette of old China, had the Emperor become a Christian, so, automatically, would his four hundred million subjects! Chien Lung, like the late King Pradjihipok of Siam, had a passion for mechanical gadgets, and both were men of learning and culture.

The good fathers spent, therefore, much time in their charming little Baroque College, destroyed, alas, by European soldiers half a century ago, devising fresh mechanical novelties to hold Chien Lung's interest. These were not toys—for many of the fathers were men of considerable scientific achievement—but contrivances many years ahead of their time, and of great interest. A number of them survived, until recently, in the Winter Palace at Pekin, but not among them, unfortunately, Father Verbiest's steam carriage. Verbiest was really an astronomer, and the fact that he did build this steam carriage is recorded, but little more is known; not nearly enough on which to base a claim. There are, however, in the archives of the Vatican, a large quantity of chests of despatches and reports from this Jesuit mission which have not been opened for at least two centuries. So it is within the bounds of possibility that one day evidence may be discovered that will put Father Verbiest in Cugnot's place.

So much for carriages with steam as the motive power, but if we restrict the question to vehicles propelled by internal combustion engines, the field narrows and the controversy becomes more acute. It has been shown already that Karl Benz had a very conservative nature and gave far too much attention to the present and far too little to future progress in design.

Gottlieb Daimler and his inseparable friend, Wilhelm Maybach, on the other hand, always advocated progress and fluidity of design. Credit might be given to Benz for building the automobile and to Daimler for laying down the tradition that one must be constantly building something better. A fitting motto for Daimler would have been the nickname of Jenatzy's electric-powered world record car, *Jamais Content.*

Let us for a moment contrast the background of the two men. Benz, as was shown in the last chapter, came from working-class stock; Daimler, on the other hand, was born in better surroundings. But in spite of this, Daimler, with true Teutonic passion for work, laboured just as hard as Benz, and his death at the relatively early age of sixty-six was largely due to overwork.

For many centuries, the Daimler family had been well-to-do tradespeople in the pretty little Swabian town of Schorndorf. Johannes Daimler was the proprietor of a bakery. Gottlieb, born on March 17, 1834, was the second of four children. He, like Benz, was born into a world more akin to the eighteenth century than our own, for it was not until he was already eighteen months old that the first railway in Germany (from Nürnberg to Fürth) was built. There is little to say of his schooldays except that at first his principal interest was in history, particularly the Thirty Years' War. Later, however, he became very fond of mathematics and geometry, winning, to the delight of his father, a number of prizes for the latter.

Johannes Daimler would have liked his son to enter the Civil Service, but in the spring of 1848 there were revolutions all over Europe, and the Kingdom of Württemberg hurriedly raised an army. The quick-witted father, who foresaw a threat of war and consequent armament, decided that it would be much more profitable to apprentice his son to a gunsmith. So young Gottlieb was duly articled to Hermann Raithel, a flourishing and old-established gun-maker.

Daimler was not the type of man who made friends easily; perhaps he was too seriously-minded and preferred the company of himself and books to that of young people of his own age. Nevertheless, F. R. Simms, who knew Daimler intimately, always said that he had a very lively sense of humour. His chief hobbies were singing and Schiller. He had an extensive collection of Swabian folk songs, and he took great pleasure in going to Stuttgart to see performances of Schiller's *Don Carlos* and similar works by the master.

The medieval test of making a complete article, carrying out every process one's self, before being admitted as a tradesman, persisted up to quite recent times. Young Daimler's *chef d'œuvre* on the conclusion of four years' apprenticeship was a pair of double-barrelled pistols with fine walnut butts and superbly chased barrels. Raithel was delighted and wanted his pupil to complete his second four years with him, but the young man went to what would be the equivalent of our Polytechnic to study theoretical technical subjects.

Here he met a man, much older than himself, named Ferdinand Steinbeis, who was to have considerable influence on his life. Steinbeis was a man of remarkable ability who, in later years, was to become Chief of the Civil Service of the Kingdom of Württemberg. He took Daimler under his wing and persuaded him to work for a scholarship and study at a large engineering works, which was associated with a technical training college in Alsace. This was some eighteen years before the Franco-Prussian War, so Alsace was at that time part of France.

Daimler won the scholarship, and in January 1853, started work at the Werkzeug Maschinenfabrik, at Grafenstadt, near Strasbourg.

Here, young Daimler seems to have made good progress. The managing director, J. F. Messner, was anxious to develop young engineers to their best advantage, and wisely balanced practical work in the shops with classes in theory and design. It was a hard school; they often worked from 5 a.m. to 11 p.m., but some magnificent engineers were produced. Daimler, helping some labourers move a heavy iron sheet, met with a nasty accident, for a piece of boiler plate was dropped on his left hand and crushed it badly.

In 1856, the works started to build locomotives. Daimler did not think his technical knowledge of locomotive construction justified his staying on and asked Messner for his release, in order that he could continue his theoretical studies. The managing-director was loth to lose such a promising young man, but gave him a glowing testimonial. Daimler went off to the Stuttgart Polytechnic for a two years' advanced course-His curriculum was ambitious; among other things, he studied machine construction, freehand drawing, English, practical geometry, and general and specialized mechanics.

By 1859 he had graduated in all these subjects, and having acquired excellent testimonials from his teachers, he returned home for a brief vacation. The Germans always regard the Swabians as the Scots of Germany, and indeed there is some similarity between the two in their shrewdness, infinite capacity for hard work coupled with tenacity, and their singleness of purpose and frugal living. After his holiday, Daimler went back to work for Messner at Grafenstadt, in Alsace.

He had become convinced that steam power was outmoded and that alternative methods should be tried. He went to Messner and asked for time and resources with which to build experimental engines. Messner rejected this proposition on the grounds that his factory was now laid out for locomotive production and the steam engines to drive the plant did everything required of them. Daimler stayed on for a time because he felt he owed Messner a debt of gratitude, but being a Swabian he was not so easily turned from his purpose.

The wealthy and influential friend Steinbeis, now Dr. Steinbeis, persuaded Daimler to go to Paris and examine the Lenoir gas engines. This proved a disappointment, for he found that they were so thoroughly protected by patents that little or no development could be done by anyone outside the Lenoir organization; and in any case, Daimler was not impressed by the engine.

Steinbeis, who was a man of considerable wisdom, recognized that the young Daimler was a gifted engineer, and to broaden his mind and develop his technical knowledge, he persuaded Daimler to go to England for a couple of years. Steinbeis was a wealthy man and he probably subsidized his protégé's journey. Daimler always said that the experience he gained in England was of great value to him. For a time he was with Armstrong Whitworth, with Roberts & Co. in Manchester, and also in Coventry. He learned the most up-to-date production methods; he perfected his English and became thoroughly acquainted with the British patent system. This proved very useful to him in later life. Shortly after visiting the World's Fair in London in 1862 he returned to Germany.

By this time it was not only Steinbeis who recognized in Gottlieb Daimler a gifted young engineer. His talent was becoming known in engineering circles, and on his return from England his friend Heinrich Straub offered him the position of chief engineer at the Straub & Sons metalworks, Geislingen, a very large and important concern. He proved himself a first-class administrator as well as a clever engineer, but Straub, who firmly believed in steam and water power as the only possible sources, refused to expend any time or money on the internal combustion engine. Daimler was equally obstinate, and so they parted company in the summer of 1865. Another appointment was immediately offered to, and accepted by Daimler: the management of the Bruderhaus engineering works at Reutlingen, which was organized on unusual lines.

This business was owned and run by a man named Gustav Werner, a wealthy social reformer who attempted to control it on the lines of the Fabian Society, which might have been adequate in theory but certainly did not work out in practice. Here, by stepping up production and expanding the factory, Daimler was able to show a good profit. Whether it was due to Werner's horror at Daimler doing anything so incompatible with doctrinaire Socialism as showing a profit, or whether Daimler could not tolerate Werner's fabian fancies, history does not relate, but in July 1869, Daimler resigned.

In the meantime, some important events had taken place. In Reutlingen Daimler met his future wife, Emma Pauline Kurz, whom he married on November 9, 1867. He worked with the first of his great technical collaborators, Emile Kessler, who was also of Bruderhaus. Unfortunately this partnership of two brilliant men did not last long, for Kessler died some months before Daimler's wedding.

But it was during the time he was at Reutlingen that he formed a friendship which continued until the day of his death, and which had a supreme influence not only on his life but on automobilism of the world; he met for the first time Wilhelm Maybach, the designer of the first Mercedes car, a vehicle that revolutionized motor-car design the world over.

Wilhelm Maybach was born on February 9, 1846. He was the second of five sons of a master cabinet-maker in Heilbron. After the early death of both his parents, Maybach came to Reutlingen when he was only ten and lived with and was cared for by Gustav Werner at the Gustav-Werner Stiftung in that town. At the age of fifteen he became an apprentice, and as he showed some aptitude for drawing, he worked in the drawing-office attached to the Gustav-Werner factory. Later, at an evening college for advanced students, he studied languages and general engineering.

A great deal will be heard in subsequent chapters of this book about Wilhelm Maybach and his close association with Daimler.

On July 1, 1869, Daimler left Reutlingen and accepted an appointment of some importance with the Maschinenbaugesellschaft of Karlsruhe. The firm were large manufacturers of locomotives, steam engines and the like. He was quickly promoted to the position of technical director, and it is interesting to record that the railway bridge between Kehl and Strasbourg was built by the firm.

On September 13, 1869, Daimler's first son, Paul Friedrich was born, and this event was followed two years later by the birth of a second son, Wilhelm Adolf. Daimler had not been long in Karlsruhe when Maybach followed him from Reutlingen. Daimler saw in Maybach an engineer of outstanding ability with whom he hoped to co-operate when his ideas developed. While he was at Karlsruhe his thoughts were already turning towards a light, fast-running internal combustion engine, but he had little opportunity for research work and development in that direction.

In 1872, Daimler was appointed technical director of the recently-established Deutz Gas Engine Works of Otto & Langen. Otto was one of the pioneers of the four-stroke engine, and he and Daimler worked together reasonably well for a time, but discord subsequently broke out. Langen was a non-technical man who provided most of the capital with which to start the business, and for a long time he endeavoured to pour oil on the troubled water in which both Daimler and Otto were floundering. Langen recognized Daimler's brilliance as an engineer and it was he who had persuaded Daimler to leave Karlsruhe and become the technical director of the Deutz Gas Engine Works.

At the outset Daimler made it clear that he wanted a free hand in the technical administration and workshop routine, and was to be allowed to engage or dismiss whom he liked. One of his first acts, after appointment, was to engage Wilhelm Maybach as chief draughtsman.

It is possible that the hostility between Otto and Daimler was caused by a certain degree of tactlessness on the part of the latter. Although production under his administration made good progress, there was almost constant bickering between him and Otto; Langen, as Otto's original partner, usually took sides with him, although there was no denying the improvements Daimler effected.

Hard work was the breath of life to Daimler; he never took a holiday. His working hours were without limit and it was common practice for him to get up from his bed and go into the workshop in the middle of the night to see how things were progressing while the night-shift were on duty. He drove everyone as hard as he drove himself, and he annoyed them by thriving on it.

After joining Otto & Langen he proceeded to select the best men from the various firms where he had worked, gather them into a team and regard them as a single unit of labour; many of the men he employed came from his native Swabia.

One of Daimler's chief tasks, when re-organizing the labour, was to instil in each man the vital importance of absolute precision and care, so necessary for the construction of satisfactory internal combustion engines. He instituted a system of inspection of all work done, basically similar to the practice adopted in the Mercedes-Benz factory today. By October of his first year, an engine a day was being built. At the beginning of 1874 production was increased to fifty per month, two engines per day by the end of that year, and three per day by the following February! Wilhelm Maybach was living up to all Daimler's hopes, and he was promoted from chief engineer draughtsman to chief designer. Daimler also introduced what might be termed nowadays a system of 'service after sales', which proved of value to clients: and all the time he was indefatigable in developing and improving the original engines of Otto & Langen.

His singleness of purpose and merciless drive not only brought him into conflict with his colleagues and his workmen, but also with his co-directors. Gottlieb Daimler does not appear to have been a harsh man, or a slave driver, but he was imbued with an overpowering love for work, and was quite unable to understand anyone else not sharing this feeling.

The rock on which he and the other directors invariably split was research and development. Otto, as tactless as Daimler himself, was allergic to his constant search for technical improvement and, to a certain extent, Langen supported his partner. A temporary truce was declared when a rival firm produced a better engine which sold in some quantity. Daimler was given a free hand to go ahead with the production of something that would compete with it. A separate department to build this new engine was formed. Here, under Daimler, a new four-stroke engine, built under licence from the American patentee, George Brayton, made its début. This proved successful, and the directors showed their appreciation of Daimler's services by presenting him with a large block of shares in the company. By this time his work was beginning to enjoy world-wide recognition, wherever the gas engine was in use. But such was his energy, that in spite of all the other work he was doing, he managed to indulge in a certain amount of experimental work on a light, fast-running power unit, which he still had in view.

While his new four-stroke gas engine was making good progress, he continued research work on an 'atmospheric gas and petroleum engine' which was the forerunner of the petrol engine as we know it today. When Wilhelm Maybach was experimenting with this in the presence of Otto and Daimler, an explosion occurred which might have been serious, but fortunately, no one was injured.

This small explosion touched off a bigger one, the smouldering quarrel between Daimler, who wanted to go on experimenting, and Langen, who desired increased production of the successful new, Daimler-designed, four-stroke industrial gas engine. Fuel was added to the flames by Otto wishing to have this engine called after him, on the rather unfair basis that he held more shares in the company than Daimler. The directors supported this suggestion but Daimler refused to yield. The atmosphere between them all was sultry in the extreme, but oil was thrown on the troubled waters by the suggestion that Daimler should take a trip to Tsarist Russia, an untapped market of vast potential wealth, to explore the possibilities there.

From an historian's point of view, Daimler's comments on the journey that he made in the autumn of 1881 are most illuminating, for he was a widely travelled man of considerable culture, and an acute observer. He travelled by way of Hanover, Berlin, Frankfort-on-Oder, Warsaw, and Moscow. He was greatly impressed by the beauty of St. Petersburg and the glorious architecture of the Scotsman Cameron, as well as by the Imperial Ballet he saw. The technical development taking place in that city made a strong appeal to him, and he remained there a short time giving technical advice to certain German firms. He was amazed by the fantastic and utterly feudal differences in Holy Russia between the upper and lower classes. It was marked enough in the Germany of his day, but under the Tsars it was immeasurably greater.

From St. Peterburg he went to Riga, the capital of Latvia, in which city he wrote a report emphasizing the vast potential wealth and commercial potentialities of the Russian Empire. Returning via Kharkov and the Ukraine, Kiev and Odessa, he went to Vienna, where he visited a recently established branch of the Deutz factory making his gas engines. Throughout his long journey, he saw almost limitless possibilities for a fast-running, light internal combustion engine for use on land and sea.

During Daimler's absence, matters had reached a climax in Deutz. Otto had written an official letter, still preserved in the archives, to Eugen Langen to say that he found co-operation with Daimler no longer possible. In this connexion, we must discount Langen's hostility towards Daimler, for the competition in the gas-engine world was increasing, and it would be disastrous to lose Otto and the patents he held to a rival firm. So Langen was forced to decide that Daimler must be the one to go, an act which the directors sugared by offering him the management of a branch factory to be opened in St. Petersburg.

It is not difficult to imagine Daimler's feelings when he was virtually dismissed from an organization on which he had spent fourteen hours per day, seven days per week, for ten years, to develop. Being essentially a fair-minded man, he started to investigate the possibilities of establishing a factory for Otto & Langen in St. Peterburg, but the treatment he had received could not be overlooked and the position he had held was filled by Hermann Schumm whom Daimler had engaged during his term of office.

After some negotiations, he was able to retain the shares he held in Otto & Langen; although by no means a wealthy man, he was not embarrassed by financial difficulties. Nevertheless, he realized that he was abandoning a certainty for an uncertainty, but his wife encouraged him to do so as she already saw signs of his health breaking down if he continued working at such high pressure; she was anxious too for him to devote more time to the education of his children.

For these reasons they moved from Deutz to Cannstatt in his native Swabia. Cannstatt was a pleasant little town, well known as a health resort and spa. By July 1882, the family were comfortably installed in a large house at 13 Taubenheimstrasse, which was surrounded by tall trees and shrubs, and in the large garden there was a summer-house which Daimler could convert into a workshop for research and experimental purposes.

One of Daimler's first moves was to induce Wilhelm Maybach to join him in the experimental work he intended to carry out. Maybach demurred at first because, as chief designer for Otto & Langen, he was holding an important position which held out good prospects for advancement in the gas-engine world, but his close friendship with Daimler overcame these thoughts, and eventually an agreement was drawn up between them in the terms of which Maybach became Daimler's right-hand man in the field they set out to cover. This might be summarized as follows:

The invention and development of a different system of ignition which would be self-timing, and would need no slide or other type of valve for its proper operation. This was considered by Daimler to be a *sine qua non* for any high-speed engine.

The design of a high-speed combustion engine having either one or two cylinders which would run on spirit.

Construction of a road vehicle equipped with such an engine, as well as a boat, etc.

There is an impression in some quarters that the German word *Benzin* (meaning petrol) was coined in honour of Benz, but this is not so. The spirit was chemically determined by

Michael Faraday in 1825: eight years later, before Karl Benz was born, a professor of chemistry at Berlin University gave it its name.

Daimler was also not the first man to make use of petrol as a motive power. An Englishman named William Barnett, of Brighton, was among the first to experiment with it for this purpose, several decades earlier. Moreover, the word 'petrol' was not first coined in England. It was used by Eugen Langen in a letter he wrote to his friend, Adolf Schmidt of Liege, Belgium, dated September 28, 1876, which disposes of the highly-coloured reports about the word having been coined here.

Daimler was fortunate in his choice of a workshop. Undoubtedly the summer-house in the garden of 13 Taubenheimstrasse influenced his purchase of the house. It was a fair-sized shed erected by the previous owner. There was a space near the entrance which accommodated his secretary, Karl Link, and a room well lighted by three windows where Daimler had his simply-equipped workshop. The drawing office consisted of a spare room in Maybach's own house in another part of Cannstatt.

Frau Daimler's hopes that after moving to Cannstatt her husband would relax somewhat were never realized. For twelve months, he and Maybach continued their research work all day and often far into the night, and these nocturnal excursions into the workshop together with the noise they made aroused the suspicions of a gardener in Daimler's employ. The fact that nobody was allowed into this secret workshop seemed to lend colour to the suspicions in his mind that some form of illegal work was going on, so he informed the local police authorities.

In the course of years, a picturesque story has accumulated about the local police breaking into Daimler's workshop and demanding to see this, that and the other 'in the name of the law', but investigation into the true facts suggests that much imagination has been exercised. According to the authoritative account of the late Paul Siebertz, this is what happened: After the gardener had reported his suspicions to the police at Cannstatt, he was asked to take an impression of the key of the workshop door; this he did and a key was made from it by the police. Then, on a particular day, very early in the morning, he was requested to tie up Daimler's dog; the police then made their visit to the workshop without anyone, save the gardener, being any the wiser. They found nothing which suggested the making of false coinage that they had in their minds, so they retired as gracefully as possible. As far as is known, neither

Daimler nor Maybach heard of the incident until some time later.

The workshop Daimler had equipped in his garden suited his purpose for a short time but it soon became apparent that something larger would be required if he developed the idea of horseless carriages and engines for boats upon which he was so determined.

On July 5, 1887, he purchased for some 30,200 marks a small factory which had been occupied by Zeitler and Missel at 67 Ludwigstrasse, Seelberg in Cannstatt. The spacious rooms and ample floor-space provided far better accommodation for research work, construction and testing, and the move in question signified the first step towards a properly-equipped factory for manufacturing Daimler products.

The main obstacle Daimler had to overcome, before a high-speed engine could be produced, was the ignition. By 1883 Daimler had invented 'hot-tube' ignition which he had then more or less perfected and patented. Three light, fast-turning engines were built, the first in the world, and forerunners of the petrol engine of today. This design had, of course, the hitherto unknown advantage that it carried its own fuel in a small tank and was, for the first time, an independent unit which did not need to be coupled up to the gas mains.

When the prototype had been perfected, so certain was Daimler of its success as a mobile power unit for industrial purposes that, regardless of past quarrels, he offered it to his old firm of Otto & Langen of Deutz. He even offered to come back as technical director to supervise its being put into production. Langen placed his offer before the directors, who declined it on the grounds that they thought Daimler's new engine of little value!

Gottlieb Daimler was a man of many advanced ideas. One of these was to provide personal transport for the man in the street who desired to have some kind of a vehicle of his own but whose means were insufficient to purchase a carriage. It was with this idea in his mind that he applied his talents to designing the first motor-bicycle the world ever saw. In after life, he always said he regretted not developing the idea into cheap transport for the masses. One wonders today what his thoughts would be if he could see the highways positively littered with motor-bicycles, of which he was undeniably the father.

Daimler's first and only motor-bicycle was necessarily primitive, because at that time the diamond-framed 'safety' bicycle was almost a novelty. It was constructed of wood and iron and resembled the hobby-horse of our forefathers. The tyres consisted of heavy iron bands shrunk on to the wooden wheels;

the $\frac{1}{2}$-h.p. engine was mounted amidships and the rider sat on what might be described as a horse-saddle above the engine.

In some quarters it is thought that this motor-bicycle must have been incapable of being steered or balanced; such a thought is incorrect. It is definitely established that Daimler's son Paul drove the machine in question on November 10, 1885, a distance of three kilometres from Cannstatt to Untertürkheim and back; there is other, although less definite, evidence that Maybach also used it on a number of occasions. Daimler protected it by the necessary patents, but he never developed the design; instead of doing so, he began experiments with a boat on the Neckar fitted with one of his own engines. As people were afraid it might explode, he fitted the hull with a number of porcelain knobs so that passengers might think it was propelled by electricity.

Other activities continued through the winter of 1885–6; Daimler and Maybach tested one of their engines in a sleigh on the frozen surface of Lake Cannstatt, but without much success. Almost at the same time, these two engineers began work on the first successful four-wheeled petrol-driven motor-

A reproduction of Gottlieb Daimler's 1885 motorcycle. The original was destroyed by fire. (*The Edward Mayer Collection*)

Daimler's 1886 rear-engined motor carriage with tube ignition. (*The Edward Mayer Collection*)

car the world ever saw.

One's faith in Seneca's phrase '*Nullum magnum ingenium sine mixtura dementiae*' is appreciably strengthened when it is recorded that Daimler anticipated all horse-drawn vehicles one day being converted to motor-driven when his engine became popular; a road vehicle specially designed for self-propulsion had not occurred to him at that time.

With this thought in mind, he purchased an ordinary horse-drawn carriage from a firm of coach-builders in Cannstatt, explaining that he wanted to give it to his wife as a birthday present. Numerous alterations were made to the carriage to make it strong enough to take the engine that was to be installed, and in due course it was pushed round to his workshop after dark by the coachbuilder's son, and was manhandled into the workshop by Daimler's gardener and the servant-girl. After he and Maybach had completed the necessary drawings and calculations, it was again pushed round to the Esslinger Maschinenfabrik where the engine could be erected and a steering gear installed under Daimler's directions.

The vertical engine was of 1½ h.p., air-cooled with tube

Under Prince Bismarck's patronage, Gottlieb Daimler's engines sold well for motor boats. (*The Edward Mayer Collection*)

ignition, which drove to the rear wheels through gears as can be seen from the illustration. There was a very crude form of differential gear which consisted of leather discs which slipped when one of the driven back wheels revolved at a different speed to the other.

It was given its first test run on a private road surrounding the Esslinger Maschinenfabrik, and then it was driven between Esslingen and Cannstatt; further journeys were undertaken at a very early hour between Cannstatt and Untertükheim, and in the archives of the Daimler-Benz A. G. there is a description of these journeys by Maybach, Paul Daimler and others. This famous vehicle is now carefully preserved in the Deutsches Museum in Munich.

In 1887, the Frankfurt Regatta Club wanted Maybach to demonstrate his motor-boat at one of their meetings. When he arrived the police refused him permission. Maybach, amid cheers from the spectators, defied them, carried out his demonstration, and was promptly arrested. Then the police discovered, rather late in the day, that no less a person than Prince Bismarck had not only been in the boat but was most favourably impressed, so with very red faces they hurriedly released Maybach.

But Daimler was turning his attention to other spheres in which his engine and ideas could be employed. He obtained permission from the local authorities in Cannstatt to construct a small public tramway from the Wilhelmplatz, through the Königestrasse to the Kursaal, to carry ten to twelve passengers. Owing to the marked success of this scheme, he was allowed to design a similar but larger public passenger-service tramway to run between Unterboihingen and Kirchheim. Everyone was immensely impressed with such a conveyance as a 'train without an engine', as it was termed locally, which made no smoke and only very little noise. Orders came in rapidly for Daimler engines.

The police were also impressed and they withdrew their veto on Daimler's machines using the public highways. By the autumn of 1888 a Daimler public taxi, the first in the world, was in service outside Stuttgart station.

This was followed by motor fire-engines. These had to be drawn to the scene of conflagration by horses, and then the engine pumped up water. One of these was purchased by the Hon. Evelyn Ellis at a very early date and it was demonstrated at the first exhibition-cum-demonstration of motor vehicles ever held in this country. This took place at Tunbridge Wells,

One of the very first Daimler horseless hackney carriages, plying for hire on Berlin's Grunewald, 1898/9. (*Mercedes-Benz*)

Kent, on October 14, 1895. Ellis kept this engine in the stables adjoining his house near Datchet, and it was used for a number of years for pumping water on a farm. These fire-engines were an even greater public success than the track-trolleys, and by July 1888 Daimler had been granted the necessary patents.

Inquiries were also numerous for adaptation of the Daimler engine for agricultural purposes. This would have entailed much experiment and neither Daimler nor Maybach could afford the time, as they were keenly desirous of developing the motor-car.

Daimler soon realized that the motor-car of the future would have to be a vehicle specially designed for the purpose and not merely a converted horse-drawn carriage, as he originally imagined. This fact is clearly apparent in every vehicle he designed after his first attempt.

Another factor that assisted the demand for Daimler's engines was the increasing use of electricity for lighting. His 'portable power plant' would drive a dynamo where no other source of energy was available. He also applied his motor to a far less prosaic purpose, dirigible balloons. He was interested in the balloons used by the French during the siege of Paris in the Franco-Prussian War of 1870. These sailed happily away from Paris well out of range of the German troops besieging the city, but to send balloons into Paris was a different matter, because there was no method of steering them. It seemed to Daimler that if he could attach an engine to a balloon, driving a propellor like a ship, it could be steered by a rudder. He would, in fact, have achieved a dirigible aircraft. He approached a bookseller called Wölffert, in Leipzig, whose hobby was building balloons, and between them they built the first lighter-than-air dirigible, propelled by a 4-h.p. single-cylinder engine.

The trial was set for a Sunday in August 1888, but the very corpulent Wölffert proved so heavy that the dirigible would not lift him in addition to the engine. A slim young spectator, as brave as he was light, volunteered to act as pilot. He flew for nearly three miles, but the engine was not powerful enough for complete control of the balloon. The German Ministry of War declared the idea to be quite worthless and refused to sponsor its development. In this, they were at complete variance with the German Admiralty, who subsequently gave Daimler much assistance and encouragement with his marine motor. Daimler was too busy to develop his dirigible aircraft any further, and Wölffert seems to have lost interest for a decade.

The year 1888 was a crowded one for Daimler, but he managed to witness the ceremonial launching of the first tugboat driven by one of his engines. His experience of heavy slow-turning engines at Otto & Langen was of the greatest use to him in building the first internal-combustion marine engine. The trials in the great harbour of Hamburg were an unqualified success, but the shipbuilding firms were not impressed and were not prepared to build lighters with these engines, so Daimler took an interest in a shipyard and started to build the complete thing, lighter, engine, and all. These sold rapidly, and in a very short time over a hundred lighters were in operation in Hamburg harbour alone, with orders coming in from different parts of the world. In 1890, Daimler's boats were operating in most of the harbours of the world, including New York.

Daimler must have had a quiet chuckle when, only three years after the arrest of Maybach for daring to demonstrate one in public, the police of Hamburg and other harbours placed orders for fast launches. Bismarck, remembering the Frankfurt meeting of the year before, ordered one for himself, and wrote complimentary remarks in the newspapers. No man's opinion in Germany of that time carried more weight

1886 Daimler. (*Mercedes-Benz*)

than that of the Iron Chancellor. It was an inestimable help. Kaiser Wilhelm II was also graciously pleased to approve, and the German Admiralty saw possibilities in the internal-combustion marine engines for use in naval craft, and many orders were placed by that authority for Daimler engines.

Daimler had some further difficulties with Otto and Langen, who endeavoured to stop him using his own patents on the grounds that they infringed the original ones. A law suit resulted which was decided in Daimler's favour.

While this was in progress, he constructed two motor-cars, and in 1889 he and Maybach designed and built a Vee-twin-cylinder engine similar in the essentials to those of today. One of these two cars somewhat resembled his first effort of 1886, but in his third car he and Maybach completely abandoned the motorized carriage idea and designed something entirely new. Although Daimler had not then seen the work Benz had carried out, this third production bore a certain superficial resemblance thereto.

It was a two-seater, four-wheeled machine with the engine mounted at the rear, and almost every part of the vehicle, including the wheels and tubular frame, was made of steel. The engine was cooled by a water-jacket round the cylinder, and power was transmitted to the rear wheels through an exposed train of gears which could be varied to suit the gradient. The cooling water was circulated through the tubular frame, and it is a remarkable fact that this method has been tried out during recent years on modern racing-cars with the object of saving weight. What saving is effected, however, seems to be counterbalanced by the fact that the slightest crack or porous weld means loss of water. This interesting vehicle caused some little sensation when it was exhibited and demonstrated at the Paris World's Fair of 1889.

Let us now examine the influence that Daimler and his inventions had on the French motor industry, which so soon was to outstrip that of Germany.

One of its foundation stones was a man named Edourd Sarazin, the son of a captain in the Belgian Artillery, who practised as a solicitor in Paris. When, in 1871, Otto & Langen became involved in disputes under French law with Etienne Lenoir over his various patents, Sarazin represented the Germans and soon became very friendly with Daimler who was then the technical director of this firm. In 1879, Sarazin had abandoned his legal practice and had become the French representative of Otto & Langen, but as Daimler's own production of petrol engines was increasing rapidly—Daimler having by then resigned his position with Otto &

1892 Daimler in the Black Forest. (*Mercedes-Benz*)

Langen—Sarazin inquired whether he could be appointed Daimler's agent in France and have control of the various Daimler patents in that country. A deal was quickly concluded between the two friends, and in 1886 Sarazin took out the first Daimler patents in France. He was also granted the manufacturing rights. It was necessary for him to have a few Daimler engines made in France in order to keep the patents alive, so he approached Emile Levassor, with whom he had worked as a young man at the Works of Cockerill in Seraing, and who had now joined René Panhard in a business devoted to the manufacture of band-saws and other wood-working machinery. Levassor agreed to make a few Daimler engines, and as a result, what had been little more than an acquaintanceship developed into a close and lasting friendship.

In 1887, Sarazin died very suddenly. His wife had always taken a practical interest in his commercial relations with Daimler, Levassor and others, and soon after his death she went to Cannstatt to negotiate with Daimler with regard to future arrangements. Daimler was greatly impressed with Madame Sarazin's commercial capabilities and her knowledge of her late husband's business. He felt that his interests in France would be in capable hands, so he agreed to appoint her his French representative, just as her husband had been; she returned to France with one of the latest Daimler engines forming part of her luggage; it is recorded that she had considerable difficulty in getting this past the Customs on the Belgian frontier.

Daimler and Maybach both came to Paris for the World's Fair in 1889, and they demonstrated a motor-boat, propelled by a Daimler engine, on the Seine, while Madame Sarazin and Emile Levassor demonstrated a second one. Before returning to Cannstatt, Daimler granted Madame Sarazin full manufacturing rights for France, an historic charter which is still in existence today, and which might almost be said to constitute the first brick in the edifice of the French motor industry.

During these proceedings, the association between Madame Sarazin and Emile Levassor had developed into something beyond mere friendship, and they were married in May 1890. Immediately after the wedding Madame Sarazin-Levassor placed the whole of the valuable Daimler patents for France in the hands of her new husband; henceforth, he was free to do with them as he wished.

Although Daimler and Levassor were close friends and keen admirers of each other's ability, Levassor was not taken with any vehicle Daimler had so far produced. He formed the

1893/4 Panhard Levassor with 4-h.p. two-cylinder engine, built under Daimler licence. (*Mercedes-Benz*)

impression that Daimler's talent lay more in the direction of engine than car design, so Levassor set himself the task of designing and building something better. In the course of his experiments, he placed the Daimler engine at the rear of the vehicle, amidships and finally, in front, and having decided that this was the correct place for the engine, he proceeded to design a car accordingly.

Just as Karl Benz made up his mind that his car should complete a certain course in Mannheim, unaided, so in 1890 did Levassor undertake to drive his car from the factory in the Avenue d'Ivry in Paris to the Point du Jour and back non-stop. It took him eighteen months to do it. Time after time he set out on his journey, only to be towed back by a horse or pushed home by a crowd of laughing people. A joke was made about his attempts; the firm of Panhard & Levassor were nicknamed 'Pannard & Levassor', the word 'Pannard' (*panne*) meaning, of course, 'breakdown'. These breakdowns occurred with maddening regularity, but gradually the distance covered increased, until, just as Benz had done five years earlier, Levassor had the supreme satisfaction of covering the whole nine or so kilometres non-stop. The firm celebrated the victory the same evening by flags and coloured lights. It was a great triumph for Daimler, the designer and inventor of the engine, and an even greater one for Emile Levassor, whose vehicle was immeasurably superior to anything hitherto produced by either Daimler or Maybach.

For the first few years, the automobile made slow progress in France, and those who owned and drove them were regarded as misguided cranks, but the Paris–Rouen trials—commonly and inaccurately termed a race—of 1894 opened the public eye to the new system of road-transport. Three Daimler-engined Peugeot cars came in second, third and fifth, while a Panhard car, also propelled by a Daimler engine, finished fourth. The car that finished first was a steam tractor, driven by Count de Dion. The prize-money, however, was distributed on a different system. This event, and more especially the triumph of the Daimler engine, attracted the attention of Emile Jellinek, about whom much will be recorded subsequently in this narrative.

In 1895, the famous Paris–Bordeaux–Paris race was held in which Emile Levassor put up that almost superhuman performance of driving a Panhard car, single-handed, 745 miles in 48 hours, 47 minutes, a feat that had never been approached in the history of automobilism. Here indeed was another triumph for the Daimler engine.

Let us now take a brief glance at the course automobilism

The author's mother used to drive one of these Daimler-engined Peugeots belonging to her brother in Ireland, circa 1895. (*Mercedes-Benz*)

was taking in England. From 1895, the Benz car was handled in this country by the late Henry Hewetson, a tea merchant, in association with Walter Arnold of East Peckham, both of whom took part in the 'Emancipation' run to Brighton in November 1895. Daimler himself had little or nothing to do with the development of the motor vehicle in England. The English Daimler Motor Co. Ltd., of Coventry, merely manufactured cars under the Daimler patents, full details of which are disclosed in St. John Nixon's book *Daimler—1896–1946*, which was compiled to celebrate the fiftieth jubilee of the Daimler Co., Ltd. A rough picture, however, can be gathered from the following facts.

In the 1880s, when Daimler was exhibiting his petrol-driven tramcar at the Bremen Exhibition, a young Englishman named Frederick Richard Simms was also showing an aerial cableway of his own design, for passenger transport. Simms and Daimler—a man many years older than Simms—formed a firm friendship which was to last the rest of Daimler's life. Simms went to Cannstatt to visit Daimler and the relations between them were very cordial. Simms was made a director of the Daimler Motoren Gesellschaft of Cannstatt, and an agreement was drawn up between the two, coming into effect in 1890, which gave Simms control over the disposal of the Daimler and Maybach patents in Great Britain and the British Empire, except Canada.

Simms swiftly became enthusiastic about the possibilities before the automobile, but was cool-headed enough to realize that nothing could be done until the antiquated Highways and Locomotives (Amendment) Act of 1878 was abolished. This restrictive legislation required that a person should walk in front of every self-propelled vehicle, but it rescinded the red flag proviso of a previous Act.

Simms concentrated, therefore, on boats and stationary engines. The first Daimler motor-boat arrived here in May 1891, but the prejudice against petrol as a motive power was as strong in this country as on the Continent, so he was refused permission to demonstrate it anywhere, except on the Thames.

Simms conducted the Daimler business in association with his practice as a consulting engineer, and in 1893 a small private company was formed by him to exploit the Daimler products in Great Britain.

A cousin of Simms, Mr. Robert Gray, a wine merchant, Mr. Theo Vasmer and one or two others formed the Daimler Motor Syndicate Ltd. with a capital of £6000. They brought over from Cannstatt a boat fitted with a Daimler engine for demonstration purposes, and a shed or two were hired from the District Railway Co. near Putney Bridge Station, in which boats could be fitted with Daimler engines. The foreman was a man named van Toll who had come over from Germany; afterwards, he went into partnership with H. G. Burford and marketed a small Belgian car known in this country as the New Orleans.

By 1895, the small firm was making some slight progress when it became rumoured that repeal of the repressive Locomotives and Highways (Amendment) Act was imminent. A Cannstatt-Daimler was brought into this country by Simms during 1895, following a Panhard car, propelled by a Daimler engine, which had been brought here by its owner, the Hon. Evelyn Ellis, and Simms in July 1895. The arrival of the Cannstatt–Daimler was reported in *The Autocar* of December 21, 1895, its eighth issue.

> On Wednesday last a party of pressmen to the number of about a score, representing most of the principal journals, assembled at the Crystal Palace on the invitation of Mr. F. R. Simms, of the Daimler Motor Co., for the purpose of inspecting the trials of the new improved autocar driven by the Daimler motor.
>
> The party were at first entertained to lunch in the garden restaurant, at the conclusion of which Mr. Simms informed those

present of the purpose for which they had been invited, and hoped that the journals which they generally represented would be unanimous in supporting the Act which would be brought forward at the next meeting of Parliament to remove the absurd restriction which at present prevented enterprise in autocar manufacture. . . .

After those present had drunk to the success of the Daimler motor carriage, the party adjourned to the grounds, where a handsome *Victoria* was placed at their disposal. Its mechanism was first explained. The Daimler engine by which it was driven was of three and a half brake h.p., and the carriage had been improved in several ways, notably by the substitution for the driving-chain of leather belts, and by the mounting of the motor upon springs, which materially reduced the vibration felt when the carriage was at rest and the motor running. This, although still present, was extremely slight, and when the carriage was running was not felt at all.

Another improvement, too, had been made in the construction of the engine, which removed the smell from it to the merest possible trace ['due' says Mr. Simms in a later article (1.2.96) 'to the perfect system of charging, reliable ignition by means of ignition tubes, as well as perfect combustion'].

By means of an ingenious cooling arrangement, it was now necessary to carry only four gallons of water, which would last for a run of sixty miles, whilst the stock of petroleum suffices for a journey of two hundred. The members of the party then in turn entered the carriage, and were taken on tours throughout the grounds. The carriage, despite the very soft state of the gravel paths, due to the recent rains, easily and steadily surmounted rises of about one in eleven.

On down grades and the level a speed equalling close on fifteen miles an hour was attained, and it was also demonstrated that the machine could be stopped when going at full speed in about twice its own length, and could be manœuvred and turned with quite as great facility as a horse-driven (*sic*) vehicle. The experiment was voted perfectly satisfactory, and we have no doubt those who will take themselves to the Palace this afternoon will be equally pleased with the running of the carriage.

A large number of inquiries resulted from the publicity obtained, and so it was decided to float a larger company with a capital of about £40,000 to handle Daimler cars in England.

When the proposed new company was on the point of being formed, that remarkable showman, H. J. Lawson, appeared dramatically. Lawson was a financier who had made almost a series of fortunes by promoting companies in connexion with the cycle trade. He claimed to have been the inventor of the safety bicycle; whether this was true or not is a highly arguable point, but it is undeniable that he had become an exceedingly wealthy man from his various financial deals, and in the coming of the motor-car he saw all his previous coups being as a curtain-raiser is to *Hamlet*; he laid plans to corner the, as then, unborn British motor industry.

Lawson, representing a syndicate of financiers consisting of himself, Martin Rucker and the notorious E. T. Hooley, offered Simms, on behalf of the Daimler Motor Syndicate, £25,000 for the Daimler patents they controlled. The directors demanded £35,000 and the deal was completed. Lawson and the others then floated off the British Motor Syndicate Ltd. to handle the Daimler patents just acquired, followed by another floatation in the form of the Daimler Motor Co. Ltd. of Coventry with a capital of £100,000 which, in spite of adverse criticism in the financial papers, was over-subscribed by some £10,000. Delay took place in finding a factory and equipping it with the necessary machinery, and while this was being done, cars were imported and sold.

Discord broke out very soon among the shareholders when the value of the £1 shares fell to only a shilling or so. The company underwent re-organization, and although the name of Gottlieb Daimler appeared on the official prospectus, he never took any part in the affairs of the company, and he never attended a meeting.

During the next few years, assisted by the fact that Daimler cars were used almost exclusively by the Royal family, the company forged ahead developing their own technical line, entirely independent of the Daimler Motoren Gesellschaft of Cannstatt; except for the fact that the first British-built Daimler cars were made under licence of the Daimler patents, there has never been any connexion between the two companies.

Such was the beginning of the British motor industry.

In Italy, where motor-racing is as much a national sport as football is in England, motoring itself first took concrete form rather later than elsewhere, but in 1895 there was a race from Turin to Asti which was won by a Daimler-engined Panhard, driven by Emile Levassor. Soon afterwards a company was formed in Turin to build cars under licence from Daimler.

The first motor races in America, of which there is any record, took place in 1895. They were the Chicago–Waukegan–Chicago and the Jackson Park–Evanston. Mannheim-built Benz cars, although even as early as this they had been renamed after their sponsors, won the Chicago race and were placed second and third in the Jackson Park event. A Daimler car had been exhibited at the World's Fair at Chicago in 1893. Daimler himself was there, for he was not slow to realize the vast potential market in the U.S.A. He spent three months of that year in Chicago, New York, and Philadelphia while he was on his second honeymoon, for he married again in July 1893 after the death of his first wife in July 1889. It is interesting to note that Henry Ford was building motor-cars in 1891–2, and that he had one running successfully in 1893.

Daimler's interests had been represented in the States by William Steinway—of pianoforte fame—since the summer of 1888. During that year Steinway founded the Daimler Motor Company with headquarters in Long Island City, New York; as early as April 30, 1889, this company had taken over Steinway's rights and had instituted a plan for furthering the sale of Daimler products when the correct moment arrived. It is of some interest to know that Maybach's elder brother had held an executive position with Steinway & Sons since the 'seventies.

As early as 1886, overtures had been made to Daimler to agree to form a company for exploiting his patents. The proposal did not appeal to him, although his first wife was strongly in favour of the idea, firstly, because he would probably be able to relax somewhat, and secondly because the suggestion came from an old schoolfellow named Max Duttenhofer, in whom Daimler had considerable trust.

In March 1890, after the death of his first wife, he signed an agreement of partnership with both Max Duttenhofer, who had become a rich gunpowder manufacturer in Rottweil, and William Lorenz, an engineer of Karlsruhe. Unhappily, disagreement soon arose, and it was in the hope that a board of directors controlling a public company with himself as the leading executive would smooth matters over that Daimler agreed to this more elaborate development of his business.

But matters went from bad to worse, and although every sympathy is due to Daimler for some questionable treatment he received, there is no denying the fact that he was an engineer first and a businessman a long way afterwards.

No ordinary man with normal commercial acumen would have allowed himself to be dominated in the way he did. When a number of experienced businessmen who have sunk considerable capital in a company see that the one from whom the concern takes its name does not possess that degree of diplomacy, tact and even personality essential to the holding of a high office, it is but human nature for them to overlook the courtesies and customs that would otherwise be exercised, and to take the initiative without consultation.

Nevertheless, Daimler's engineering ability and his attainments should have been respected by his fellow-directors, and the treatment he received at their hands does them little credit. It is neither practicable nor desirable to describe the cause and the effect of the quarrels in which Daimler was so often involved. He was a stubborn man and in certain respects he may well have been his own worst enemy.

Reports of these differences reached the ears of Madame Levassor, who journeyed to Cannstatt to beg Daimler to abandon further work in Germany and come to France to help build up the French motor industry, which was then in its cradle. Patriotism alone prohibited the acceptance of the proposal, but the unusually sincere atmosphere of trust which existed between Madame Levassor and Daimler will be gauged from the fact that she insisted, quite contrary to the will of Daimler, that she should pay him fifty per cent of all the profits that came to her from the Daimler patents.

The upshot of the dispute was that Daimler and Maybach cut themselves adrift from the company bearing Daimler's name, and retired to a private workshop they had installed in the then empty Hotel Hermann in Cannstatt, where they could continue research work.

There is a widespread belief that Emile Levassor designed the *Phoenix* engine, which consisted of two cylinders in line with exposed valve gear, governed on the exhaust tappets. This type of engine was designed by Daimler and was then adopted by Levassor on Panhard cars.

Unhappily, Levassor never saw the development of the motor industry of the world, in the formation of which he played such

The short-chassis 1899 *Phoenix* Daimler, a very successful car which was the parent of the 'Mercedes' model. (*Mercedes-Benz*)

a highly important role. He died in tragic circumstances. He took part in the Paris–Marseilles–Paris race of 1896 on a Panhard car fitted with one of the new *Phoenix* type of engines. Between Orange and Avignon, he struck a large dog and his car overturned. He and his passenger, although badly shaken, were apparently unhurt. They managed to right the car again and Levassor drove on to Avignon where he handed over the tiller to his passenger, an early pioneer racing-car driver named d'Hostingue. Over the course of 1080 miles, they finished fourth at an average speed of 14·18 m.p.h.

For a long time, he appeared to have recovered from the accident, but one day several months afterwards, Levassor complained of not feeling well, so he left his office and went home. By an unfortunate chance, Madame Levassor had gone out, so Levassor undressed and got into bed. He died quite suddenly without giving utterance to a single word. He died as he wished to die and as he had lived for so many years: with his hand still at work on the automobile.

Levassor and Daimler were close friends; on the day Levassor died (April 18, 1897), Daimler's daughter was born, and in his memory she was christened Emilie.

Precisely what influenced Daimler to return to his old associates at the Daimler Motoren Gesellschaft will probably never be fully established. No one reason was the cause of the reconciliation; a number of factors contributed thereto which were having a bad effect on all parties concerned. The continual disputes about who owned the Daimler patents, whether one infringed the other, whether Otto & Langen had any lien on them, and the uncertainty about the manufacturing policy of the company all contributed to the feeling among those in dispute that the hatchet should be buried and that all should pull together again for the common good of themselves and of automobilism generally.

In the forefront of those who made great efforts to bring about a peaceful solution to the troubles were F. R. Simms and Wilhelm Deurer. A provisional agreement of reconciliation was signed at the end of 1895, and in March 1897 the reorganization of the company was complete, with Daimler as chairman and Maybach as chief technical director; both of them enjoyed full administrative and executive powers.

It is generally admitted that Daimler's death was brought about largely by overwork. Disregarding medical advice and never taking a holiday put a severe strain on his heart, which began to trouble him as the end of the century approached. He was forced to delegate a great deal of detail work which he would normally have undertaken himself, but he con-

By 1896 Daimler already had a two-cylinder engine, mounted in front, with four speeds and reverse, and a honeycomb radiator. (*Mercedes-Benz*)

tinued to take an active part in the direction of the general policy to be followed. Law actions added to his worries, and it is an interesting fact that one such law suit was with the Benz Company!

Although Daimler was a tired and sick man, he lost but little of his genius, and with Maybach as chief technical director, the firm recorded record profits for the financial year of 1897–8. All the royalties received in respect of licences for the Daimler and Maybach patents were ploughed back into the business in order to extend the workshops to meet the increasing demands for Daimler products. Daimler was anxious to control a factory in which everything possible used in the cars bearing his name should be made; from April 1898 to March 1899 the number of employees increased from 191 to 333.

Two important productions of 1898 were a four-cylinder engine and a 6-h.p. 'racing-car'. At first Daimler was against such a car because, to use his own words in translation, 'it would render possible dangerously high speeds'. 'Why,' he added, 'use 6 h.p. when 4 are quite sufficient?' The racing-car took part in some Alpine trials and emerged with flying colours.

But primarily, Daimler was concerned with a car for every-day use, and for this purpose he built in 1897 a six-seater *Victoria* model with an arrangement, suggestive of present-day practice, whereby the back seats could be removed to allow for luggage. Daimler also wanted to go into the motor-cycle market, but was prevented by Duttenhofer, who had signed some agreement with a Berlin firm for their production. Daimler did, however, build some motor-buses, and the first petrol-driven bus service in the world was, by 1899, running between Kuenzelsau and Mergentheim in the Kingdom of Württemberg. This was followed by other regular bus services in South Germany, while from 1896 onwards, five-ton lorries were also being built.

In 1895, as has been said, the first complete Canstatt-Daimler car was brought to England by F. R. Simms. By this time there were twenty-nine branches of the firm in Germany alone and ten abroad.

The motor-boat side of the business, ever since its inception in Hamburg in 1890, was making progress, and within a few years Daimler motor-boats were winning races at a speed of about 12 knots. The Württemberg state railways placed orders for the Daimler railcar, with accommodation for ten sitting and eight standing passengers. There was also a contract for a petrol-driven goods locomotive. Owing to his father's poor health, this was completed by Paul Daimler in 1899–1900.

In 1897, after an interval of eleven years, both Daimler and Wölffert, the Liepzig bookseller, became interested once more in dirigible balloons, although Daimler always declared he felt that the real future of aerial conquest did not lie with lighter-than-air machines. Wölffert built a dirigible and powered it with a Daimler engine. He himself piloted it this time, but it crashed from an altitude of over 300 feet and this pioneer of flight was killed. Count Zeppelin, however, had followed the development and flight of Wölffert's machine with interest and began where Wölffert had left off. It was sad that Daimler did not live to see the first successful flight of the Daimler-engined Zeppelin, which took place a few weeks after his death.

During the closing years of Daimler's life it was abundantly clear that the factory at Cannstatt was insufficient for the expanding business, nor would it be possible to take in enough land for building. A much larger site was therefore acquired at Untertürkheim, where the main works and administrative offices still stand today. In his last report, as head of the company, to his directors, Daimler laid down his two principles of fine and lasting workmanship, coupled with constant research and development. It is fair to say that these, together with a long and expensive racing programme, have been the guiding policy of the firm ever since.

In September 1899, *The Automotor & Horseless Carriage*

*Journal* devoted much space to a new Cannstatt-Daimler ordered by the Duke of Westminster, fitted with a body built by Mulliner of Northampton. We quote from the technical description of the car and also from the trial it was given.

A DUCAL MOTOR CARRIAGE

. . . It is, it need hardly be said, not only a magnificent specimen of the best class of carriage building, but in its mechanism it represents the latest refinements and developments of the Daimler system of propulsion. The motor is known as the Cannstatt Daimler, and it has been fitted to the vehicle in compliance with a specification drawn up by the Motor Carriage Supply Company (Limited) of Donnington House, Norfolk Street, Strand. Many improvements have been made in the mechanism, the most important being perhaps the method of fixing the motor, which, together with the speed gear, is mounted upon a separate frame, so as to minimise the vibration imparted to the main frame and body of the car; next, the means employed for reducing the quantity of water required for cooling purposes, which is effected in a most efficient manner by Mr. Daimler's new water-cooling apparatus, consisting of a reservoir containing only 2½ gallons of water, placed in front of the car, and somewhat resembling in appearance the condenser of a marine engine, being closely packed with small tubes round which the cooling water circulates. A current of air is drawn through these tubes by means of a fan on the crankshaft of the motor, thus effectually preventing the circulating water becoming overheated, the temperature of the water never exceeding 125 deg. F. The evaporation is consequently extremely small, being only 1½ pints during eight hours working. Ignition is effected by the Simms-Bosch electro-magnetic apparatus, which is entirely independent of any battery and always ready for use. The arrangement of the speed gear is another important innovation. The four speeds are divided into pairs, each pair being placed into or out of gear by a separate lever, and is so arranged that while one speed is in gear it is impossible to move the other pair, the lever for that being locked. When one or the other speed lever is moved in order to change the speed, the friction cone on the main-shaft is also compulsorily out of gear. The plan of dividing the four speeds into pairs has many advantages, saving the wear and tear of the gear which, since only the pair of which one is driving is in gear at a time, the other pair being out of gear, and this method also renders the change from one speed to another both easy and silent. There is also only one lever for putting the speed gear into position, for going forward or backward, and for placing it out of gear. The foot-brake lever, as well as applying the brake, actuates the clutch on the main-shaft, thus throwing the friction cone out of gear and applying the brake with one movement only. Another special feature of the car is the rubber tyres, which are endless, being vulcanized to vulcanite, the latter being vulcanized to a special steel rim. It is, therefore, impossible for these tyres to come off, and, moreover, this tyre, with its broad tread, gives great comfort when running, and has a good adhesion even on muddy roads. Special attention should be given to the manner in which the frame is suspended, the arrangements of springs being similar to that employed in hansom cabs. . . . By this means great comfort and ease in travelling is obtained.

We have no doubt that His Grace the Duke of Westminster will find his new acquisition a decided improvement upon any horse-drawn vehicle and the example thus set will, we feel sure, be followed. . . .

TRIAL OF THE DUKE OF WESTMINSTER'S CANSTATT DAIMLER

. . . We were shown the new car in course of being photographed and looking as smart and spick-and-span as good coach-making and paint and varnish could make it. It is of the convertible wagonette type. . . . It is extremely roomy, and capable of carrying three persons on the driving seat and six behind. The motor and frame are of the Cannstatt Daimler construction supplied by the Motor Carriage Supply Co., of 4 h.p. nominal, and fitted with Simms-Bosch patent magneto electric ignition.

With a parting stirrup-cup at Mr. Mulliner's charming residence . . . we started in perfect weather with Mr. Lefébure, who, by the way, had only driven a Cannstatt car once or twice before, at the 'helm', leaving Mr. Mulliner's works at 10.30. Our 'sailing' orders were not to press the new car too much at first, and consequently, on reaching the romantic Queen Eleanor's Cross (outside Northampton—Ed.) we alighted to admire the monument and to examine our axle-boxes, one of which showed signs of heating. From there the car soon shook down into its paces, and we rattled along the perfect dustless roads with an invigorating breeze, reeling off mile after mile in four minutes and some in three minutes. . . .

[They went on through Woburn, Dunstable to St. Albans and then back.] One very amusing incident took place which shows that persons who have no right to be trusted with horses do not hesitate to risk their lives and the lives of others should anything untoward happen requiring skill and nerve. Three ladies, driving a very quiet animal in a low phaeton, when we approached within 100 yards, although the poor dumb animal showed no uneasiness, suddenly gave way to panic, and all jumped out of the trap, leaving our engineer to rush up and hold their certainly not fiery and untamed steed till we had passed. . . . We reached our destination without a single breakdown or adjustment beyond oiling the axle boxes . . . convinced that, in his new car, the Duke of Westminster will possess one of the most comfortable and reliable touring cars at present on the market, nor is a running time of averaging nearly 12 m.p.h. for 64 miles for a new car of this description to be despised.

Throughout 1898–9, Daimler and Maybach were building a Cannstatt-Daimler racing-car of 28 h.p. which was one of the most dangerous and unmanageable vehicles ever constructed. It was very heavy, it had an extremely short wheel-base and was far too high; due to the many shortcomings of this vehicle and the fact that Bauer, foreman of the Cannstatt works, was killed while racing on one of these cars, the design was cancelled and from its ashes arose the Mercedes, a car which was to revolutionize motor-car design.

Emile Jellinek was the Consul-General in Nice for the old Austro-Hungarian Empire. He was a wealthy man and a keen follower of motor racing. He had owned one of the heavy

The famous 'Mercedes' model Daimler, the first of a long line. (*Mercedes-Benz*)

and dangerous Cannstatt-Daimler racing-cars and had acted as a kind of unofficial agent for Daimler productions among his many wealthy friends.

Jellinek appreciated that these Cannstatt-Daimler cars were far too heavy and unwieldy, so he went to Cannstatt to discuss with either Daimler or Maybach the production of an entirely new type of car which could be used both for racing and normal purposes.

At the time of his visit, Paul Daimler had just designed a small car which seemed to Maybach to have the germ at least of what Jellinek had in mind. Jellinek was already responsible for the small 6-h.p. 'racing-car' which had performed so well in the Austrian Alps during 1897.

This 1899 car, designed by Paul Daimler, was interesting from several points of view. The gear-box and crankcase were cast in one piece, it had four speeds and reverse with the gear-shift lever on the steering column. The clutch consisted of an expanding spring and it had a foot accelerator, which was very unusual at the time. Paul Daimler had been unable to develop the design because he had been appointed manager of the recently formed Austrian Daimler Motor Company.

It is commonly said that Gottlieb Daimler was responsible for the design of the Mercedes car, but this is not supported by facts. When Jellinek's proposal was taken up, Daimler was suffering severely from heart trouble and he had to take things

Paul Daimler, Gottlieb's son, designed this small 4-h.p. car, circa 1900. (*The Edward Mayer Collection*)

with increasing ease. He could bear no excitement and his wife had to attend to most things for him.

The Mercedes owes its origin firstly to Paul Daimler for designing a car which gave Maybach the inspiration needed, and secondly to Wilhelm Maybach himself for producing this wonderful machine.

Before it appeared, rumours had been heard in France that something entirely new and revolutionary would soon be emerging from Cannstatt; at the beginning of July 1900, long before the new car had even been tested on the road, Paul Meyan of *La France Automobile* wrote:

> Every previous production is far surpassed by this new car. The chief advantage lies in its lightness. The metal used is an alloy of magnesium and aluminium termed magnalium. Further advantages are the long wheel-base, mechanically-operated inlet valves, low-tension electric ignition under Simms-Bosch patents, a new and improved type of carburettor and improvement in the cooling syetem in which only 6 litres of water are sufficient to cool an engine of 16 h.p.

Then he added:

> These 'pretty' rumours are not pretty rumours any longer but established facts. The French factories would do well to get busy

extremely quickly in order that Daimler shall not set the fashion in France.

It did not take long for the world to find out that this new engine was far more powerful than any engine used previously in a car. The cylinders and cylinder-head were cast in one piece; the mechanically-operated inlet and exhaust valves were on both sides of the engine and the crankcase was of aluminium. The bore and stroke of the engine was 116 × 140 mm. respectively, and the h.p. was 35 at 1000 r.p.m.

It was certainly a remarkable car, the like of which the world had never seen previously. Jellinek kept a careful eye on it as it approached completion, and he was so impressed that as early as April 18, 1900, he placed an order with the company for thirty-six Mercedes, which he wanted to be delivered to him not later than October 15 of the same year. Precisely how Maybach ever hoped to perform such a miracle has never been explained. The total sum involved was 550,000 marks. Jellinek was quite prepared to pay out this huge sum to gain a stranglehold on the production of the new car.

The first Mercedes 35-h.p. of 1901. (*The Edward Mayer Collection*)

For various reasons, some of which were of Jellinek's own making, it was not possible for the delivery of any of the cars to take place in time. Jellinek was particularly anxious to have the first Mercedes ready for the Grand Prix of Pau, a race of 206¼ miles on February 17, 1901. This was to be followed by the Nice–Salon–Nice and other races at Nice from March 25–29, 1901, and every possible effort was made at the Cannstatt works.

By this time, all kinds of reports were in circulation about this new wonder-car. When it did turn up, its performance was a great disappointment. It had been turned out hurriedly and in an untried state. It was sent by rail from Cannstatt to Paris and during its initial trials in France it stripped its gears, seized its bearings and generally misbehaved itself. It was sent on from Paris to Pau by rail, and did actually compete in the Grand Prix of Pau, driven by Loraine Barrow. At the start the clutch refused to hold, the change-speed lever jammed, and the car had to retire from the race within a few yards of the start.

This fiasco was a great disappointment to the sponsors of the Mercedes, and every effort was made to get it properly tuned up in time for the forthcoming Nice week during March.

The result far surpassed all expectations. The Mercedes ran right away from all the other competitors. Werner, the well-known Mercedes works driver, reached Nice half an hour in front of the next man, while Loraine Barrow was fifth, having averaged 32·9 m.p.h.

*The Autocar* has this to say of the Nice event.

The following particulars of the Cannstatt-built Mercedes car, which has swept the board in the south of France lately, will interest many of our readers. The car ran the full course—the course of Esterel, which is so hilly that high speeds thereon are regarded as impossible—of 279.45 miles at an average speed of 36.63 m.p.h., passing through no fewer than thirty villages in that distance, wherein speed must be reduced to 7½ m.p.h. The marine cooler with its 5800 tubes, through which the air is drawn by a rapidly revolving fan, and which offers about 120 square feet of cooling surface, requires, according to our contemporary, but 1·54 gallons of water to charge it. Roller bearings on the Lorenz system, which are fitted to this car, are held to have proved themselves by the above performance. The car without the racing body weighs 1 ton 15 lb., while the racing body weighs but 2 qr. 21 lb. The entire workmanship, design, and performances of this car have struck terror into the heart of a capable critic like Paul Meyan, who warns the French manufacturers that the pride of place in auto-car building is about to be wrested from them by the Germans. He quotes the remark made to him by M. Mercedes [this is Emile

Werner after winning the 1901 Nice–Salon–Nice 392-km. race in 6¾ hours. (*Mercedes-Benz*)

Jellinek] the day after his triumph, which ran as follows: 'That car will be as nothing beside what you will see next year,' and then asks if M. Mercedes could have been pulling his leg.

The Mercedes cars which swept the board in the Nice races were of 48 h.p.

This success was followed by Werner winning the La Turbie hill-climb in 18 minutes, 6 seconds, as well as being the fastest petrol-driven car in the flying kilometre speed trial, the time being 41·6 seconds.

To say that the Mercedes made a great impression both on the general public and on the French motor industry is no overstatement. Every car in existence became five years out of date; its new honeycomb radiator, its gate type of change-speed gear, its pressed-steel frame, steeply raked steering column, controls on the steering wheel, low-tension magneto ignition and, more than all else, its complete silence when the engine was running slowly, caused the Mercedes to be something totally different.

Immediately, it was copied by every manufacturer in the world, and if we examine a car today which has just come from the production line, we can see a number of features which were initiated by the first Mercedes in 1900.

The early history of the Mercedes car in France can be told

A 1905 120-h.p. Mercedes racing-car in Germany en route to the establishment of C. L. Charley in Paris. Charley, whose real name was Karl Lehmann, was a racing cyclist of Strasbourg and became sole concessionaire in France for Mercedes by arrangement with Emile Jellinek, who was a director of Credit Lyonnais and Austrian Consul in Nice. Charley opened beautiful showrooms in Paris and both he and Jellinek made a great deal of money from the sale of Mercedes cars. Jellinek's daughter, Mercedes, gave her name to the cars of Daimler Motoren Geseleschaft. (*The Edward Mayer Collection*)

in a very few words. Just before the first one was delivered to Jellinek, a Paris dealer named Charley Lehmann, an Alsatian and one-time racing cyclist, was at Cannstatt purchasing some of the old models. He noticed the new production and was told the circumstances in which it was built. He went to Nice and made arrangements with Jellinek to have the sole agency for France. At that time, Panhard and Levassor were badly in arrears with their orders on hand, and so almost any price could be asked by Lehmann for the Mercedes. He changed his name to 'Charley', omitting the rather German-sounding name of Lehmann, took beautiful showrooms in the Champs-Elysées, Paris, and after a very few years amassed a huge fortune that was said to run into millions of francs. Subsequently, the agency was converted into a public company, which meant a few more millions going into the pockets of Charley and Jellinek.

There is but little to add about the last days of Daimler's life. By the late autumn of 1899, it was obvious that he was in a very weak state. He was ordered complete rest by his doctor, which he spent comfortably at home, but even so, he could not cut himself entirely adrift from work. His sons had to report to him daily about the research work on which Maybach and they were engaged. In spite of the unsuitable weather for any invalid, he was driven on a new model to the top of the Fellbach to inspect a piece of land on which he intended to build a new factory. During the return journey he complained of feeling very unwell and suddenly collapsed, falling heavily on to the road. When he came to, one of his first thoughts was to forbid the driver to mention a word of the incident to anybody. After several days in bed he seemed to recover somewhat and he remained up until January 10. On this day he had another interview with Duttenhofer and this had the effect of a relapse. From the beginning of February it was clear that the end was approaching; his memory began to fail and at times he could not even recall the names of his own children.

From day to day his condition became worse, until dropsy developed and he died at 3 a.m. on March 6, 1900, in the presence of his family.

Daimler was a man who wrought mightily for the cause of automobilism and, more especially, of the internal combustion engine. He was very high-principled, and a great lover of the simple life; he was never happier than when he was with his own family, and had he studied his own domestic affairs more thoroughly and given less attention to engineering matters, it is generally admitted that his health would not have broken down when it did.

Daimler was twice married. His first wife, Emma Pauline, the daughter of a chemist, was born on April 29, 1843, and they were married on November 9, 1867 in Maulbronn. She died in July, 1889. Two sons, Paul Friedrich and Wilhelm Adolf were born on September 13, 1869 and on September 8, 1871 respectively, as well as Emma Friederike, Martha Emilie and Gottlieb Wilhelm, born respectively on April 11, 1873, October 22, 1878 and July 4, 1881.

His second marriage took place on July 8, 1893. Line Hartmann, the widow of an hotel proprietor, was born on May 16, 1855, and was therefore some twenty years younger than Daimler. They met while Daimler was in Florence during the winter of 1892–3 recuperating after an illness. She was a woman of outstanding attainments, and could converse quite fluently in three languages. By his second wife, Daimler had two children, Gottlieb Friedrich who was born on September 4, 1894, and was killed in 1916 at the battle of Ypres when leading the 119th Machine Gun Company, and Emilie, born on April 18, 1897.

So far in this book the reader has heard something of the early life and careers of two great pioneers in the development of the motor-car and of the cars which they evolved. From now on the accent is less on the touring-cars made by the two great firms to which Gottlieb Daimler and Karl Benz gave their names as on the racing-cars they made. Except for the five years 1909 to 1914 and a rather shorter period before 1934, Daimler Motoren Gessellschaft have never failed to send their teams of Mercedes cars to every important race in Europe, and even America, and it is not going too far to say that the white cars from Untertürkheim have dominated the sport over some half a century—in spite of the times when other makes have temporarily been world conquerors. Benz was one of those makes, and their great day was in those years between 1908 and the Mercedes triumph in the French Grand Prix on the eve of Armagheddon. Throughout these years both firms continued to build many fine touring-cars and after the fusion, in the 36/220 h.p. and 38/250 h.p., one of the greatest sports-cars. Nevertheless, the main interest lies in the wonderful line of racing-cars which have appeared, which have won so often and so kept the names of Mercedes and Benz ever in the public eye. It is impossible in the scope of this book to describe more than a tithe of the countless events to which Daimler and Benz sent their cars. The authors have tried to bring out the highlights, and to write of those events in which great cars and great drivers have achieved triumphs which deserve to be brought together in one volume.

# 2
# RISING STAR
# 1900~1922

The 1908 French Grand Prix: Lautenschlager's co-driver gives the tyre signal at the Mercedes tyre depot. There was only one tyre left in stock. (*Carlo Demand: The Big Race*)

# MERCEDES AND MAYBACH, 1900–1903

MAX DUTTENHOFER was, first and foremost, a financier. He was not specially interested in motor-cars, or in any form of engineering except as a vehicle for his financial transactions. Up to about 1900 it was possible that he held the opinion that if the Daimler Motoren Gesellschaft failed and the Daimler patents fell into his lap, the company would be worth more to him than if it continued. The developments of 1900–1901, however, changed the picture completely. The phenomenal success of the Mercedes model, the advent as director of Jellinek with virtually unlimited financial backing, and the new markets so rapidly opening up, made the firm a most desirable property. Further, they had under contract Wilhelm Maybach, the outstanding automobile engineer of his day. Potentially, it was the finest car manufacturing business of the many springing up everywhere. Daimler's death left Duttenhofer and his fellow-directors a free hand, for the two sons, Paul and Adolf Daimler, although being the most able executives, had no power or say whatever in conducting the business. Neither were to become directors for six years or more. Paul was a skilled engineer; Adolf was also an engineer and a specialist in business administration of a technical nature.

People who knew Jellinek describe him as a small, excitable man in pince-nez who, although a wizard at finance, was, in the matter of motor-cars, like Toad of Toad Hall—whatever he had he wanted something bigger and better. There is a report that on one occasion he was seriously annoyed because he was passed in his car by another Mercedes driven by Werner. He suspected it was a new model about which he had been kept in the dark.

During Daimler's lifetime, he had acted as an unofficial agent for Daimler by selling cars among his wealthy friends. As such, he had purchased no fewer than thirty-four cars (involving an expenditure of some 638,000 marks), the largest of which was the unwieldy 28-h.p. car mentioned in the last chapter. Immediately after Daimler's death, he undertook to purchase at once thirty-six Mercedes, to be delivered on October 15, 1900, provided that he was given the sole agency for them in respect of France, Belgium, America and Austro-

Hungary. In these countries the cars were to be known as Mercedes; in other countries as the New Daimler, if its makers so desired. Maybach, however, found this delivery date not possible of fulfilment, as has already been shown, and the first six were delivered to Jellinek at the end of January, 1901.

Jellinek himself had been racing for some years under the pseudonym 'Mercedes', his daughter's name. It is not entirely clear as to why so many people raced, in the early days, under assumed names. The two most obvious reasons are that they wished to avert ugly scenes with their families who would not care to have them participating in this new-fangled and dangerous sport, and to emphasize their amateur status. For, in the early nineteen hundreds, the gentleman and player snobbery was much stronger than it is today.

As we have said, six cars were delivered to Jellinek at Nice in January 1901. He entered these cars immediately for the Nice Week, starting on March 25, and then sold them, entries and all, to various rich friends such as Loraine Barrow and Baron Henri de Rothschild, who raced under the name of 'Dr. Pascal'. (This was not only de Rothschild's racing name, but one under which he practiced very efficiently as an oculist!) Some of the cars were driven by their owners, but others were driven for them by professionals, such as Wilhelm Werner, the works driver, and George Lemaître, of Panhard and Levassor. The result was a triumph for the new car and was a complete reversal of the form shown at Pau, on their first appearance, when the cars stripped their gears and ran their bearings. The 35-h.p. Mercedes swept the board, winning the new La Turbie fifteen kilometre hill-climb, the race over the Esterel Mountains, and the flying and standing mile on the Promenade des Anglais. Well might *Auto Velo* describe these events as an 'historic achievement'. After the racing was over, Werner's winning car was fitted with a comfortable body and was driven quietly about Nice—a masterstroke of salesmanship. Back at Cannstatt, Maybach said, 'This is a triumphant conclusion to four years' intensive work.' And so it was.

In May of that year, the Daimler Motoren Gesellschaft were far too busy getting their cars ready for the Paris–Berlin race to be able to enter for the Paris–Bordeaux, in conjunction with which was run the Gordon Bennett Trophy. This was awarded by James Gordon Bennett, the proprietor of the *New York Herald*, in 1899, to stimulate international motor racing. Teams of cars were to be chosen by the National Automobile Clubs and every component was to be made by the entrant nation. For an example, the mammoth Napier was disqualified because it had French tyres.

Although the works did not enter a team for the Paris–Bordeaux race, two wealthy amateurs, Thorn and Foxhall-Keene, friends of Jellinek, entered Mercedes which he had sold them. They were a complete failure, both cars breaking down *en route*.

As yet, no weight limit had been imposed, although for the year 1902 the limit of 1000 kilograms had been decreed. The 35-h.p. Mercedes were relatively light and handy, but Mors and Panhard were building racing-cars that, although fast were really freaks with engines of disproportionate size. The 35-h.p. Napier car was lighter, but not fast enough.

The Paris–Berlin race started on June 22, at Champigny, just outside Paris. In the early hours of the morning, the road through the Bois de Vincennes was crowded with cars, carriages, and cyclists, by the thousand, all on their way to see the start. The myriads of paper lanterns in the dark were like some lovely Japanese festival. And, like Le Mans today, thousands more camped out by the wayside.

The race was split into three stages: Paris–Aachen 285 miles, Aachen–Hanover 278, Hanover–Berlin 186. Even though thirty years or more had elapsed since the Franco–Prussian war, feelings between the peoples of both countries were not of the most cordial. Some of the French competitors, even though M. Serpollet had surveyed the course on his steam-car a few days before and reported perfect tranquillity, were in a twitter of xenophobia. However, their fears were quite groundless, for at the frontier each was presented with a charmingly engraved card, printed in French, bidding them welcome to Germany. And, at every stop, they were welcomed by high dignitaries. They were fêted and feasted and everything was done to make things pleasant for them.

In 1930, Charles Jarrott once said, 'The two things modern drivers can never realize about the early days are the incredible amount of tyre trouble we suffered, and the dust which was so thick that sometimes one had to steer by the tree-tops.' He added that he had witnessed the accident of Degrais, on a 35-h.p. Mercedes, who had been steering by this very means. While the road turned a sharp corner, the line of tree-tops which Degrais had been following went straight on. So did Degrais. It was a bad accident, but curiously enough, Degrais was practically unhurt, although his companion, Baron de Schwyter, was seriously injured.

The Mercedes were very disappointing in the race. Fournier won on a 60-h.p. Mors, after driving a magnificent race, followed by innumerable Panhards and Mors until Werner came in fourteenth in his 35-h.p. Mercedes, a very poor performance for the model that had shown so much promise at Nice.

In *The Autocar* of November 2, 1901 appeared an announcement of the Mercedes cars for 1902 as follows:

> The Mercedes car for 1902 will differ very materially from the vehicle we know at present under that name. With regard to the engine, the whole of the working parts of the motor will be enclosed, save for the four exhaust valve spindles and their springs, which will be visible. An entirely new form of ignition will be employed, in which an alternating current will be used, and into the details of which no springs, rods, or contact makers will enter. Naturally, coils and accumulators will be conspicuous by their absence. The engine will have no governor, its speed being entirely controlled by the action of the carburettor. The engine speed will be variable from 200 to 1,200 revolutions. The water-cooling apparatus will be as at present, employing one and a half gallons of water only, but the draught-inducing fan will be improved. The change speed gear and all bearings will run on Maybach ball bearings, with a coefficient of friction of 0·012. The gear will be changed without withdrawing the clutch. The weights of the different cars will be as follows: 40 h.p., 17·1 cwt.; 28 h.p., 15·67 cwt.; 20 h.p., 13·60 cwt. The weight of the *chassis* of the 10-h.p. car will be about 12·35 cwt.

Soon after, a new 6-h.p. two-cylinder car is mentioned. In this, the crankshaft was set transversely. The car was water-

The 1902 model 40-h.p. Mercedes. (*The Edward Mayer Collection*)

Consul Jellinek at Nice in 1902, under the *nom de guerre* 'Mr. Mercedes' and driving a Mercedes-engined Porsche Mixte. The car was powered by a Mercedes 40-h.p. engine which drove a dynamo which in turn energized the electric motors built onto the wheels. (*Mercedes-Benz*)

cooled, had four gears, and handlebar steering. It was said to be capable of 'working up to 8 h.p.' To the authors' knowledge and belief, however, no two-cylinder Mercedes was ever actually put on the market.

The new 40-h.p. car, a development of the all-conquering 35-h.p. of 1901, like its predecessor, carried all before it at the Nice Week of 1902. The impression the car made on the motoring public is well shown in the interesting article we quote from *The Autocar* of April 19, 1902, under the heading 'Automobile meeting at Nice'.

It is to the Cannstatt works that we have to look at the moment for the most remarkable advance in automobile engineering. During the past three years the Mercedes car has been improved to such an extent that nothing but admiration can be felt for the splendid new vehicles which made their first appearance in view of the Abbazzia race. [Nice–Abbazzia–Nice.] The first thing that strikes one is their wonderfully quiet running. When the vehicle is standing, a rapid rhythmical beat is only just audible, scarcely more than a low hum, and there is absolutely no vibration. It is generally supposed that the motor is then turning at not more than 150 revolutions a minute, but Herr Daimler assured us that it was still running at 500 revolutions, and our explanation of this quietness is the method of synchronizing, as it were, the exhaust with the admission, both of which are operated mechanically, and in this way, at whatever rate the motor may be running, the exhaust is always rapidly cleared at the precise moment the charge is being drawn in. The motor is regulated by the well-known Mercedes tubular regulator, with ports forming part of the carburettor, and the running of the engine can be varied instantly from 500 to 1200 revolutions by means of a small lever on the dashboard moving on a toothed sector. The four cylinders are in a line, and the motor develops 40 nominal h.p. On some of the cars magneto ignition is employed, and on others a small dynamo is fitted, similar to the well-known form of American 'self-sparker', and with both systems great facility has been obtained in retarding and advancing ignition. The petrol is carried in a cylindrical tank under the back of the car, and being at a lower level than the motor, it seems as if the spirit is brought to the carburettor under a certain pressure, but we were unable to understand from the German mechanics precisely in what way this is done. In some of the cars the ventilator behind the tubular water tank forming the front of the bonnet has been done away with, as it is found that the fly-wheel is quite sufficient to create a draught through the tubes, especially in cars which are propelled at a high rate of speed. The weight of the motor is said to be only 407 lb. Owing to the great elasticity of the engine, it is rarely necessary to use the change-speed gear, and the vehicle can be slowed down to a crawl with the highest gear in mesh, while speeds can be changed with perfect ease and silence without throwing out the motor. The underframe is built of channel section steel, tapering away in front with a long extension, so that the front axle is brought forward underneath the end of the frame. The wheelbase is exactly 8 ft. All the moving parts run on ball bearings in oil, and the vehicle can be pushed forward with only a slight effort. Every part is made of the best material, the steel for the underframe being supplied by Krupp of Essen, and the wheels and springs are made by leading French firms. It is difficult to imagine how elasticity of engine power and economy of effort can be brought to a higher stage of development in an autocar, but it is nevertheless certain that finality has not yet been reached, and we may now confidently look to the time when the petrol car will become as quiet and docile as the electric vehicle.

A full description of one of these 40-h.p. Mercedes, which had been sold to Alfred Harmsworth, appeared in *The Autocar*, and is reprinted in Appendix IV at the end of this book.

Mercedes cars did not take part in the first of the '*Grandes épreuves*' in 1902, the Circuit du Nord. This was staged by the French Government to stimulate the sale of alcohol as a fuel for motor-cars, but the Daimler Motoren Gesellschaft were much too occupied with the preparation of cars for the forthcoming Paris–Vienna race to take part in these alcohol trials.

Even twenty years after the Paris–Vienna race, feelings still ran very high indeed over the question of whether Count Eliot Zborowski (Zborowski *père*) really did or did not win in his Mercedes. Undoubtedly, Eliot Zborowski did make the fastest time between the two cities, but the Automobile Club de France penalized him, by slightly over half an hour, on some technical point about Customs formalities, thus giving a French car, a 70-h.p. Panhard driven by Frenchman Henri Farman, the first place. It seems probable that by the letter of the law the French Club was acting strictly within its rights, but the justice of its action has been long and keenly debated.

The three other Mercedes cars in the race did nothing at all. Werner arrived at Belfort twenty-fourth and retired. Bellamy lost control of his car going down a steep hill and crashed. It may—or may not—have been the same hill on which one of the many bizarre incidents of this race are said to have occurred. Captain Genty, driving a Clément, was going down, his brakes working well and everything under good control, when above the rattles and rumbles of his governed engine, he heard agonized shouts for help. A motor-cyclist, whose brakes had completely failed, came tearing down the hill screaming for help at the top of his voice. Captain Genty, a serving soldier and a man of action, reached out and grabbed the unfortunate man by his coat as he passed, and pulled him to safety on the running board of the Clément! One cannot help wondering

Charles Cordingley's 40-h.p. Mercedes, 1902. (*The Edward Mayer Collection*)

whether the passage of time has not coloured this picturesque story somewhat.

Baron de Forest on a Mercedes experienced very bad luck. Just outside Vienna his petrol tank, hammered beyond all endurance by the vile Austrian roads, burst irreparably and he had to be towed to the finish on the trotting ground at the Prater.

As in the case of Eliot Zborowski in the Paris–Vienna race, controls inevitably led to bad feelings, and the de Crawhez brothers, Baron Pierre and Baron Jean, both racing drivers, prevailed on the Automobile Club de Belgique to stage a race round a fifty-three mile course in the Ardennes, starting and finishing at Bastogne, without controls. Daimler as a firm did not enter a team, and some of the wealthy amateurs had temporarily forsaken these cars. The Mercedes cars, rated at 40 h.p. with a bore of 120 mm. and a stroke of 150 mm. were not nearly as powerful as the monsters turned out by Panhard and Mors. There was, however, one Mercedes, Eliot Zborowski's, which from all contemporary accounts he drove magnificently. Jarrott won the race on a 70-h.p. Panhard, and Zborowski was fourth. Jenatzy, later to become one of the most famous of all Mercedes drivers, driving a 40-h.p. Mercedes, had the most appalling crash. Eye-witnesses say that the car ended upside down in a ditch on one side of the road and all four wheels in the ditch on the other! Needless to say, Camille Jenatzy 'the indestructible' escaped with a few slight bruises.

Apart from these classic races in 1902, Mercedes did well in many sprints and hill-climbs.

In December 1902, Milnes, Daimler Ltd., announced that Mercedes Simplex cars for 1903 would be made in three powers, 18 h.p., 28 h.p., and 60 h.p. The 8-h.p., 20-h.p. and 40-h.p. models were all to be dropped. The 18 h.p., or *18/22* as it became known, was very popular and was on the market for several years, being known as the *18/28* in 1904. Its engine size was 110 × 140 mm., and its maximum r.p.m. 1000. The wheelbase was 7 ft. 6½ in. and the chassis weight, less petrol and water, 20 cwt. 48 lb. *The Autocar* described, in delightful terms, a run on this model in May 1903, and we cannot resist quoting this report in full.

A few days since Mr. J. E. Hutton of 23 Regent Street, S.W. was good enough to afford us a short, but none the less most enjoyable trip out from London to Cobham Street and back, via Richmond Park on the third 18-h.p. Mercedes which has come to him from the Continent. Except for twice in traffic and the Test Hill (i.e. Broomfield Hill in Richmond Park) Mr. Hutton did not come off his fourth speed, and though at times the carriage was slowed down almost to a crawl, the engine picked the car up on its top speed

1903 60-h.p. 9-litre chain-driven Mercedes limousine. (*Mercedes-Benz*)

with such smoothness that no thump or vibration was felt. Naturally, our watch was out for the trial bit on the Test Hill, and we made the time $27\frac{3}{8}$ sec. between the tree and the danger-board. Those who wish to arrive at the speed at which this beautiful-running carriage climbed this steep may work it out for themselves by means of the section referred to above. It is not meet that we give it in naked figures here. [The course covered 1062 ft., 650 of which being on a gradient of between 1 in 8 and 1 in 13. Mr. Hutton's time, therefore, represents an average speed of about $26\frac{1}{4}$ m.p.h.] Thence to Cobham the car ran on its fourth, the sole control from slow to fast and fast to slow being by the throttle lever set centrally in the steering wheel. The manner in which this car with three up took Esher, Horseshoe Clump, and the White Hills, with Tartar Hill coming back, and the reverse of the test hill from the Kingston Gate of the Park, was perfectly delightful. Our only possible comparison is to say that it was like riding on silk. We particularly remarked the extreme ease and quietude with which Mr. Hutton changed the gears when we requested to be shown the operation. The gear-striking lever does not appear to be drawn or thrust backward or forward in the sector; it is just flicked over, almost thrown from the hand from one position to another. It is unnecessary to dwell here upon the quiet running of the engine when the car is at rest; that commendable feature of the Mercedes motor has been frequently commented upon. We can compare it to nothing else but the ticking of a somewhat robust eight-day clock. After our short but pleasing experience of the dainty white eighteen, we are not surprised that many whose pockets are sufficiently well-lined go in for Mercedes.

Interest in new Mercedes racing-cars was now considerable and *The Autocar* managed to glean some details of the new 60-h.p. racing model from its contemporary *La France Automobile* which it published on November 15, 1902. We quote from this article, entitled 'The New Mercedes'.

Judging from the bare indications published in *La France Automobile*, we are likely to see some noteworthy improvements in the new type of Mercedes cars which will be making their first public appearance at the Nice meeting in March next. Having visited the Cannstatt works, Mr. Paul Meyan is greatly struck with what he has seen, and only regrets that he is not permitted to describe fully the many ingenious devices that are destined once more to make the Mercedes one of the most interesting vehicles of the year. The weight of the frame, springs, and axles, has been further reduced by 220 lb., and at the same time their solidity and rigidity have been increased. Armoured wood construction has given way to steel, and the frame members are stamped out of sheet-steel U-shape, the weight being only 77 lb. This is also the weight of the rear axle, which is forged with a double-T section. The cooling surface of the radiator has been doubled by a new method of arranging the tubes without increasing the volume. There are many new features about the motor, which will have a double system of ignition, if required, the one being the usual magneto and the other, apparently, a dynamo without accumulators. The magneto is situated in front of the motor where it is easily accessible. The French visitor was shown a 300-h.p. engine being constructed for the Russian navy, which is noteworthy for the method of starting it. A charge of gunpowder is inserted in one of the cylinders, and when the piston is brought to the compression the cartridge is exploded. This method is said to be infallible. For the cars to be sent to Nice, the motors will have a bore of 170 mm. and a stroke of 140 mm., and will run at from 1000 to 1200 revolutions. In view of the big demand for Mercedes cars, the company are making preparations for considerably increasing their productive capacity, and instead of building fifteen cars a month, as at present, they will soon be able to turn out forty. . . .

This new *60* racer made up for the lack of power in their racing-cars of the previous year. Within the weight limit required, it was much less cumbersome than the immense Mors and Panhard. Daimler Motoren Gesellschaft were also building a few racing-cars of 90 h.p., later to become world-famous. Six of these ran in the Paris-Madrid race of 1903, but all were destroyed later in the year, when being prepared for the Gordon Bennett race, in the great fire at the Cannstatt works.

The new 60-h.p. Mercedes cars made their début at the Nice week of 1903, and they put up a very impressive performance. Prince Lubecki won the event over the Esterel mountains. Two new works drivers made their appearance under the leadership of that old maestro, Wilhelm Werner:

1903 90-h.p. low-tension ignition engine. The car was chain-driven. (*Mercedes-Benz*)

Hermann Braun, and Otto Hieronymus of Vienna. The former established a new record for the standing mile, and the latter for the fifteen-and-a-half kilometre La Turbie climb. Other events were also won, but a gloomy shadow was cast over the whole meeting by the death of gay, debonair Count Eliot Zborowski. He was going very fast in his new 60-h.p. Mercedes, attempting the record. His car struck a rock and overturned, killing him instantaneously. His companion, Baron de Pollange, was badly injured, but eventually recovered. Zborowski was a great loss to motor racing, not only because of his dashing driving and charm, but because of his sportsmanship. He was about the only person at the time of the Paris–Vienna storm who had very little to say about the penalization that robbed him of first place. He was a very handsome man and always exquisitely dressed. He shared with Tim Birkin the extraordinary ability to remain spotless and immaculate throughout the dirtiest automobile operation.

Soon afterwards, Count Hugo Boos-Waldeck, gained second place in the Exelberg climb in a 1902 40-h.p. car, and expectation ran high in anticipation of the next classic race,

Foxhall-Keene in a 60-h.p. Mercedes. (*The Edward Mayer Collection*)

the Paris–Madrid. The entries included 112 heavy cars, 64 light cars and 59 cycles. Numerous Mercedes cars were entered; six were of the new 90-h.p. type, driven by Jenatzy, Baron de Caters, Kohler, Hieronymus, Degrais and Wilhelm Werner, and which were considered prospective winners, and five were 60-h.p. cars, driven by the American J. B. Warden, Gasteaux, Foxhall-Keene and Hermann Braun. There were also some old 40-h.p. cars, one of which, driven by a Mr. 'Max'—probably a pseudonym—finished well up at Bordeaux in fifteenth place.

All the manufacturers were competing against each other to obtain the maximum power within the weight limit of 1000 kg., and every part of a car was drilled drastically to reduce the weight.

It is beyond question that had the race been continued over the unspeakably bad Spanish roads, a very large number of the competitors' cars would have broken up, but it is doubtful whether the Mercedes cars would have suffered as badly as the others. Sacrificing strength for engine-power never appealed to Maybach, and it is questionable whether a Mercedes car ever failed in a race because of excessive weight reduction.

It is now history how, because of the appalling accidents,

mostly caused by the uncontrolled crowds, the French Government stopped the race at Bordeaux, not even allowing the engines of the racing-cars to be started again, but insisting that they should be towed to Bordeaux railway station by horses. A typical accident occurred at Châtellerault. The crowd was, as elsewhere, surging on to the course, leaving barely room for one car at a time to pass. A child dashed out, followed by a soldier who tried to pull it back. A car attempting to avoid them not only struck and killed both, but hurtled into the crowd, killing or maiming fully twenty people. All along the road there were accidents of this nature.

Werner, veteran ace of the Mercedes team, had every chance of winning. Louis Renault led most of the way to Bordeaux, with Charles Jarrott on the latest 45-h.p. de Dietrich second. Jarrott related that, soon after Tours, Werner on the new 90-h.p. Mercedes, passed him almost as if he were standing still. Werner who had started sixth, although he was number 14, was going well. Louis Renault, who was driving a 30-h.p. light car of his own build within the 650 kg. class, was going faster than anyone except Gabriel on a Mors, but Werner stood every chance of catching him.

Fate had, however, a nasty surprise for Wilhelm Werner, in the shape of a metallurgical fault in the back axle, which

De Caters, Jenatzy and Werner with a 90-h.p. Mercedes. (*The Edward Mayer Collection*)

Marius Barbarou driving a Benz in the ill-fated Paris–Madrid in 1903. (*Mercedes-Benz*)

broke, spinning the car upside down into a ditch. Afterwards, Werner and his mechanic, who had been thrown clear of the smash and were quite unhurt, were seen lighting cigarettes with complete sang-froid, as if nothing unusual had happened. This was only equalled by an English competitor who, when his voiturette overturned, at once rescued his camera from the wreckage and proceeded to photograph it from all possible angles! The best performance by a Mercedes, or any other German car, was put up by J. B. Warden in a 60-h.p. car, finishing sixth at Bordeaux in the general category.

Jenatzy was harrying Jarrott so badly that the Englishman, although told at Angoulême that his wooden-spoked front wheels were disintegrating, decided to take a chance that they would hold out, without repair, a further eighty miles to Bordeaux. By a miracle, they did. Jenatzy did not catch him and finished fourteenth in the general category. 'Max', on an old *40*, finished fifteenth, but Gasteaux on a *60* had done better than either, gaining eighth place. Hermann Braun, also on a *60*, came in twentieth and Baron de Caters on a *90* twenty-seventh. Kohler, also on a *90*, was just over three hours behind the winner and was thirty-sixth in the general category. Hieronymus was sixty-second and Degrais sixty-ninth, just beating two Serpollet steam-cars. These were all the Mercedes cars among the ninety-nine finishers at Bordeaux. Werner and two other cars had dropped out, and it cannot be said that the new 90-h.p. cars fulfilled expectations. Gabriel, on a 70-h.p. Mors, was the winner when the race was stopped at Bordeaux.

This was the end of an era, the last of the great and epic races from one capital city to another. The attitude of the motor clubs is that their biggest difficulty today, even for circuit racing, is crowd-control, and, even if Governments would consider it, they doubt very much whether it would be possible to keep spectators off the course in a city-to-city race.

At the same time as the suppression of such classics, the Gordon Bennett Trophy race had assumed great importance. Although S. F. Edge on his small Napier only finished eighteenth in the Paris–Vienna race, he had, in the face of heart-breaking obstacles which would have broken the spirit of any less determined man, won for England the Gordon Bennett race, having beaten the pick of Europe. His car was made and designed in a dingy little workshop in a Lambeth slum, and his victory is a classic which has few if any equals in the annals of motor racing.

Under the conditions governing the Gordon Bennett Trophy, the race had to be held in the country last winning it, and as the British Club well knew that the Government would not sanction any such proposal, a Bill was hurried through the House authorizing the race to be held in Ireland. Eliminating trials decided that Britain should be represented by three Napier cars. An American team was entered and the French chartered the liner *Ferdinand de Lesseps* to bring over two Panhards and a Mors.

There was a dispute between Jellinek and the Deutsche Automobil Club which throws an interesting light on the rigid class distinctions of those days. Jellinek had nominated his two best works drivers, Werner and Hieronymus. The DAC rejected their entry on the grounds that they were 'players not gentlemen', adding that equally good drivers could be found among the more blue-blooded members of the DAC. As the drivers had, under the rules laid down by Gordon Bennett, to be nominated by the DAC, the club was in a rather strong position.

It has always been rumoured that Jellinek then tried to mollify the DAC by offering the third wheel to C. S. Rolls, of

Rolls-Royce fame. A team of three was entered consisting of Baron de Caters, Foxhall-Keene and Jenatzy, to none of whom the DAC could object on social grounds. However, the dispute was brought to nothing by the disastrous fire which destroyed the complete Cannstatt factory and five of the six 90-h.p. cars prepared for the Gordon Bennett race. The firm were not unduly worried, as the 60-h.p. cars had proved themselves very reliable and nearly as fast as the still rather embryonic *90*s.

Clarence Gray Dinsmore, a wealthy American sportsman, and a Mercedes owner of long standing, promptly offered to lend his *60* to Jenatzy. This was immediately stripped down for the 1000 kg. limit and given as much preparation as possible. Curiously enough, although the Panhards, and Mooer's American 'Peerless' had considerable difficulty in getting past the weigh-in, Gray Dinsmore's *60* passed without difficulty. A protest was lodged against the Mercedes cars being fitted with Michelin tyres, on the grounds that this was not in keeping with the Gordon Bennett regulations. Luckily, the Germans had plenty of spare Continental (a German make) tyres and these were duly fitted.

The circuit measured 103 miles, and, in spite of the last-minute efforts of the local authorities, the roads were in none too good condition. Much credit, however, is due to the Government who drafted in police from all over Ireland. These typically good-humoured Irish constables, far larger in number than ever before at any motor race, succeeded in a very

The Daimler works at Cannstatt in 1903 after the fire that destroyed the racing-cars for the Gordon Bennett. (*The Edward Mayer Collection*)

Clarence Gray Dinsmore's 60-h.p. Mercedes. (*The Edward Mayer Collection*)

capable manner in keeping the course clear of spectators.

The big cars started in a cloud of dust, led by Edge, the last year's winner, on a Napier. The rest followed at seven-minute intervals, because the road was too narrow to start all cars at once. The German cars were white, as today, the French blue, and the British green. But the American cars were red, a colour that, when they ceased to race in first-class events, was given to Italy. Foxhall-Keene, in his 60-h.p. Mercedes, starting last, made the fastest first lap, but Jenatzy led from the second round onwards.

The Napier team consisted of J. W. Stocks and Charles Jarrott at the wheels of light but considerably under-powered cars. The Napier driven by Edge was more powerful, but the British tyres gave incessant trouble and were quite unsuitable. He lost much time through tyre trouble, and also because of an over-heated engine, while Stocks ran through a fence and Jarrott crashed when his steering gear failed.

A few of the Irish spectators who saw Jarrott's accident thought that he had been killed, and when he regained consciousness he found that a sheet had been thrown over him. For an instant, he thought he had been blinded.

Baron de Caters saw Jarrott examining the wreckage of his

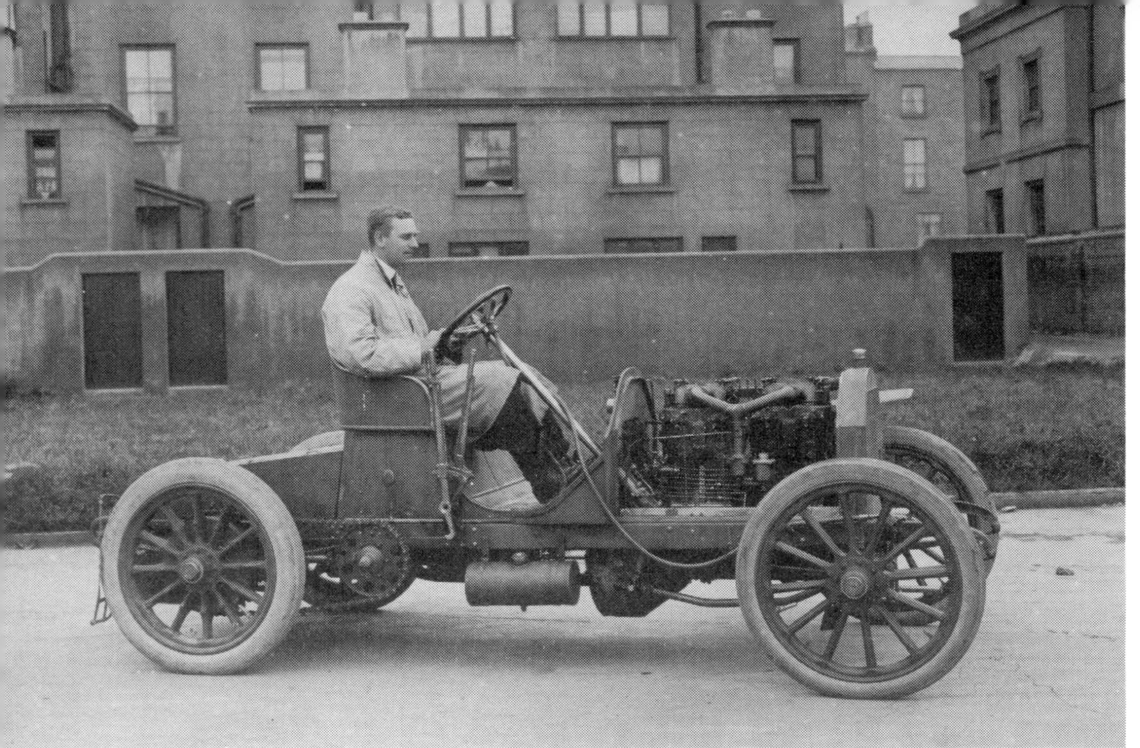

1903/4 60-h.p. four-cylinder Mercedes racing-car. Jenatzy won the 1903 Gordon Bennett in Ireland in a similar car. J. E. Hutton is at the wheel. (*The Edward Mayer Collection*)

car and stopped to inquire if he was hurt, and then stopped again at the grandstands to tell Jarrott's friends, who had heard the report that Jarrott had been killed, that he was relatively uninjured. Such chivalry, would not, of course, be possible in today's split-second Grand Prix racing, but even in those far off, more leisurely days, it was a rare and sportsmanlike action.

The race was won by Jenatzy on Gray Dinsmore's 60-h.p. Mercedes, but the other Mercedes cars driven by Baron de Caters and Foxhall-Keene broke down and failed to finish. The Chevalier René de Knyff, who was a hot favourite on his Panhard, was a very experienced driver. He had started racing in the 1896 Paris–Marseilles–Paris contest and had been at it ever since. He saw that the Mercedes of Foxhall-Keene and de Caters were out of the race, and he also saw the way Jenatzy was driving.

Jenatzy had a genius for taking great risks and surviving. De Knyff knew well that Jenatzy had been racing for years and rarely finished, and decided that he need not jeopardize his big Panhard by pressing it too hard. He miscalculated, for Jenatzy was for once driving a good car that probably handled better than anything else of its year, and it was also his lucky day. There were, of course, no pit signals in those days, and de Knyff discovered, far too late, that if he wanted to catch Jenatzy he would have to drive like a fiend, but he had left

Wilhelm Werner in Jenatzy's Gordon-Bennett-winning Mercedes. (*The Edward Mayer Collection*)

it too late and Jenatzy won the Gordon Bennett Trophy for Germany and Mercedes.

A number of wealthy Britons had already become Mercedes enthusiasts, and a few days later three of these, Campbell Muir on a *90*, Higginbotham driving a *60* and G. P. Burton in an older *40*, did very well in the Phoenix Park races in Dublin. J. E. Hutton also drove a Mercedes in these races, but he was in the motor trade, and was actually a sales agent for Mercedes in England. Campbell Muir was a friend of Alfred Harmsworth (Lord Northcliffe) and used to drive his cars in competitions. Gerald Higginbotham, of Macclesfield, had about the only Mercedes ever fitted with a quadrant instead of a gate change. Clarence Gray Dinsmore brought Werner over from Germany to drive one of his Mercedes in the Castlewellan hill-climb. The redoubtable Werner, however, only managed to achieve third place, the climb being won by Campbell Muir on Harmsworth's *60*.

This all happened at the beginning of July 1903, and at the end of the month the Ostend Motor Race Week was held. Here, a new name appeared: Willy Poege, wealthy proprietor of an electrical firm at Chemnitz. He had just bought a *60* and won almost everything that could be won at Ostend.

In September Gray Dinsmore sent his two *60*s to the Semmering hill-climb. Hermann Braun won his class with one, and Werner was second with the other. This double success must have greatly pleased the wealthy American.

In England, young Andrew Fletcher of Saltoun, a Scotsman, took his *60* out for the first time and won the flying kilometre on the sands at Southport, the seaside resort in Lancashire. A very tall young man in the 1st Life Guards, he was given the Mercedes as a present by his aunt, Miss Talbot of Port Talbot, one of the richest women in England. The competitions year was brought to a close by three Mercedes class wins at a race meeting on a trotting track in the West End of Berlin. Willy Poege and Müller, both in *60*s, won the races for amateur and professional drivers respectively and the touring class was won by Herr Auffmordt Jun., on a 35-h.p. Mercedes.

From the point of view of competitions, 1903 had been a successful year for the Daimler Motoren Gesellschaft. But they suffered two severe setbacks. There was the catastrophic fire of June 10 at the Cannstatt works which, in only two and a half hours, destroyed not only the five 90-h.p. racing-cars, but also a good deal of the plant and about seventy cars either finished or in course of construction. Also, during the same year, Max Duttenhofer died. While one cannot condone the manner in which Gottlieb Daimler was treated, it is undeniable that Duttenhofer was a man of great ability. Much of the sound administration that had already put the firm among the first rank of manufacturers was due to him.

For 1904, many models were available. There were four chain-driven cars, the *18/22* (price £1100), the *24/28* (price £1300), the *35/40* (price £1500) and the *60* (price £1800). In addition, there were four models with 'gear transmission' and with a new type clutch. These were the *18* at £1200, the *24/28*

Mercedes lorry works at Marienfeld, with one of their early models. (*The Edward Mayer Collection*)

at £1350, the *38/40* at £1550 and the *60* at £2500.

The *60*s, which had been so successful in 1903, were full of new features which were to become standardized for many years to come. The front axle, for example, was of I section, a feature which continued until the introduction of independent suspension.

## MERCEDES AND MAYBACH, 1904–1907

In the carefree days before 1914, when collars and incomes were high and taxation was low, the acme of smartness was to be seen with a girl from a George Edwardes show at the Gaiety, driving a 90-h.p. Mercedes with well-polished brass fittings and a well-raked steering column; but in 1904 there were as yet very few of these cars in England, and it was still essentially a racing-car.

Just as, nearly half a century later, after the huge Untertürkheim works had been bombed almost flat, the Daimler-Benz A. G. worked twenty-four hours a day, seven days a week, to get going again, so their predecessors, by colossal effort, recovered quickly from the disastrous fire of 1903. By the end of the year several *90*s had been shipped to America. W. K. Vanderbilt Jun., H. W. Fletcher of New York, and J. B. Warden who had done so well in the Paris–Madrid race, all had them. L. H. Bowden and Sam B. Stevens had *60*s while J. L. Breeze had an old *40* which performed outstandingly well. Practically every week in January 1904 there were motor races in America, and in the record book there are two pages of successes won by Vanderbilt, Howden, Stevens, and Breeze.

In March, the Nice Automobile Week was held. The 90-h.p. cars were well placed but recorded no outright wins. Although they were beaten by a Serpollet steam-car, this was no disgrace, because acceleration of steam-cars over a short distance is phenomenal. (Two or three years ago, a 1911 steam-car was entered in some short sprint speed trials in England and made second fastest time of the day, being beaten only by an E.R.A.) The drivers at Nice were Werner, Jenatzy, Hermann Braun on cars entered by the works, and Warden and Fletcher of New York on their own *90*s. Lionel de Cesti drove his *60* in which he had scored second place in the Cannes mountain

90-h.p. engine with low-tension ignition. (*The Edward Mayer Collection*)

kilometre the previous week. In May, that great sportsman Baron de Caters captured the World's Record for the flying kilometre at Ostend on his new *90*, of which he had just taken delivery.

Both the French and English Automobile Clubs had been endeavouring to find somewhere to hold their eliminating trials for the Gordon Bennett races to be run in June and organized by Germany, the victors of the previous year. The English solved the problem by staging their eliminating trials in the Isle of Man, which has its own Parliament, and there the House of Keys had no objection to passing the necessary legislation. But after Clifford Earp's accident on a Napier the eliminating trials were curtailed and a team of one Napier and two Wolseleys were chosen, with two Napiers in reserve.

The French had an even more difficult task, for there were twenty-nine entrants with ten makes of car between them from which to choose their team of three. In addition, the Chamber of Deputies, with the Paris–Madrid race fresh in their minds, were much averse to motor racing on public roads. Baron de Caters and the Belgian Automobile Club came to the rescue with the offer of a course in Belgium. The French club, although it struck a hard blow to their pride, would have accepted, but the Comte de Dion, who came from one of France's oldest and proudest families, would not accept this charity. He was a man of great wealth, influence, and was also (and this may have carried considerable weight with individual members) a deadly duellist. He managed to get a bill hurried through the Chamber legalizing the eliminating trials in a deserted part of the Argonne district. These trials turned out to be an exciting motor race in themselves, which it is not, unfortunately, within the compass of this book to describe. A Brasier, driven by Théry 'The Chronometer', Rougier's 100-h.p. Turcat-Méry, and Salleron's Mors were chosen. Italy sent three 75-h.p. Fiats driven by Lancia, Cagno, and Storero. There was no American entry; the Belgians sent three 60-h.p. models of the long defunct marque of Pipe. Monsieur Dufaux, driving a lone entry of his own make for Switzerland, crashed on the way to the weighing-in and did not start. Germany was represented by de Caters and Jenatzy with *90*s and Fritz von Opel, who later became an important motor manufacturer, on an Opel-Darracq. This 100-h.p. car, although of the same type as the cars which had competed unsuccessfully in the French trials, had been entirely built

1904 90-h.p. Mercedes Gordon-Bennett racer. Low-tension magneto, half-compression, double exhaust camshaft for starting. First owned by Andrew Fletcher, it was later acquired by Edward Mayer, who fitted the touring body. (*The Edward Mayer Collection*)

Hermann Braun and Lautenschlager's 90-h.p. Austrian-built Mercedes in Germany, 1904. (*The Edward Mayer Collection*)

under licence in Germany and was, therefore, eligible under the Gordon Bennett ruling. The records do not make it clear whether the Opel-Darracq failed to complete the first lap or did not start. At the time there was a rumour that, as Fritz von Opel was a wild and rash driver, his wealthy parents paid a mechanic to sabotage the car so that it broke down on or near the starting line. Rumour had it that the driving-shaft was almost cut in two.

Hermann Braun, the veteran driver Werner, and J. B. Warden also drove *90*s, officially for Austria. This gave Mercedes five entries instead of the statutory three. Although Jenatzy's *90* had been prepared by the works it was not strictly a works entry, for Clarence Gray Dinsmore had bought the car for Jenatzy to drive. There is an untrue supposition that this rich American was too cowardly, or at least too blasé, to race his own cars. To drive a racing-car of the heroic age one needed to be young and very fit. Gray Dinsmore was at this time fifty-seven years of age and far from strong, but he took real pleasure in financing drivers in the sport from which he was debarred but dearly loved. He was a tall, thin man with a grey beard and a pleasant manner, but looked what he was, a sick man. He suffered badly from asthma and his doctor had prescribed that he should, by way of a cure, be driven fast in an open car. He died in the early years of the century, and with his passing the sport was deprived of a true devotee and a more than generous patron.

Jenatzy, a very fine racing-car driver, had an exceptionally quiet and gentle manner. He was very keen to win the 1904 Gordon Bennett race for the second time and Gray Dinsmore had offered him a private reward of £4,000 if he did so. Every moment that practising was allowed, Jenatzy was out on the course, judging to the finest limits his cut-off points and cornering. He was a past master of the controlled four-wheel slide, forerunner of the power drift.

The Kaiser had given the contest his gracious approval. He was, in fact, present, and the Germans had been working for months, with their very real genius for organization, to make the event the success it was, from the perfect weather, for which they could not claim credit, to the perfect crowd control by five thousand troops, for which they could. The road was broad and good and ran through a particularly pleasant piece of country. Starting from Homburg, where many of the competitors had their headquarters, the course ran through Saalburg and on through the site of an old Roman Camp which the Germans had excavated and beautifully preserved. From there it wound through pine forests to Weilburg and on

Jenatzy's Mercedes weighing in. (*The Edward Mayer Collection*)

Weighing in the racing cars at Bad Homberg, 1904. (*The Edward Mayer Collection*)

through queer little villages, with black and white houses, to Limburg. Then followed a fast stretch to a hairpin turn at Neuhof, winding again through Idstein to Esch. After Esch there were pine forests almost all the way back to Homburg. It was an ideally laid-out course with just the right mixture of fast straights, hills, and turns. Throughout the district a general holiday was proclaimed, and the crowds, though immense, were under perfect control.

At the end of the first lap Théry was leading Jenatzy over the eighty-seven mile course by exactly one second. Edge, Girling, and Jarrott were third, fourth, and fifth respectively. It looked like a close finish, with the English team sure of a place. Jenatzy was driving with all his erratic brilliance, but

he was no match for Théry who drove with all the regularity that gave him the nickname 'The Chronometer', and steadily increased his lead. But, to be fair to Jenatzy, it was not only the difference in driving technique. The Richard Brasier car which Théry was driving had far better road adhesion than Jenatzy's car. It made the fastest lap of the day at 53·5 m.p.h. The reason for this was that, for the first time in history, the designers of the Richard Brasier had paid very careful attention to the question of shock absorbers. It was additional road holding that enabled Théry to increase his lead, until at the end of four laps he had won from Jenatzy by a full eleven minutes. This lead might not have been so great had not Jenatzy at one point run out of petrol.

Werner driving an Austrian-built 90-h.p. Mercedes in the 1904 Gordon Bennett run in Germany. (*The Edward Mayer Collection*)

As for the English team that had promised so well, Girling and Jarrott had trouble and finished ninth and twelfth respectively. Edge also had trouble and did not finish at all. There was a battle royal for third place between de Caters on his Mercedes and Rougier's 100-h.p. Turcat-Méry. They finished three-quarters of an hour after Jenatzy with only thirty-one seconds between them. The Mercedes was in third place, but Rougier was awarded one minute on a protest, which put him in third place and de Caters was fourth. He was followed a quarter of an hour later by Hermann Braun on a sister car. Werner's 'works' *90* did not do so well and only finished in eleventh place, while the American J. B. Warden went out on the third lap. So the Gordon Bennett trophy, which Jenatzy had tried so hard to hold for Germany, went back to France, whence S. F. Edge had wrested it two years earlier. This was one of the most important and sensational victories the French motor industry ever achieved. Pitted against five 90-h.p. Mercedes cars, two Fiats, a Mors and a number of others, the lone Brasier car beat them all. It was the only car of this make running, and it established the reputation of Brasier as a brilliant designer.

We now hear, for the first time, a very familiar name:

Cavaliere Florio, who founded the Sicilian race called after him, in his 90-h.p. Mercedes. (*The Edward Mayer Collection*)

Cavaliere Vincenzo Florio, founder of the most thrilling motor race in Europe. In 1904, he was a wealthy young man (he owned vast estates in Sicily) who had bought a *90* and was determined to enjoy it. The previous year he had given a cup for motor racing in the North of Italy. Now, in 1904, he drove his car in the Brescia–Cremona–Brescia race for his own cup. He must have been a fine driver, for he beat those three giants of the age, Duray (Darracq), Nazarro (Panhard), and Cagno (Fiat), gaining third place. The race was won on a protest. Teste on a 90-h.p. Panhard actually made the fastest time, but was penalized three minutes for filling his petrol tank in a control, letting Lancia on a 75-h.p. Fiat into first place. Two years later the Sicilian landowner was to organize that fabulous round-the-mountains race that takes its name from the shield he gave—Targa Florio.

In America W. K. Vanderbilt Jun., one of the earliest of Mercedes drivers, gave the Vanderbilt cup. This was intended to focus interest on motor racing in America and stimulate the American manufacturers, who for the past twelve months had given the sport less and less support. The European entry was formidable, including three 90-h.p. Panhards, a de Dietrich, an 80-h.p. Clément Bayard, and five Mercedes. The American opposition was, in the main, amateur prepared and driven. Their star turn, to everyone's surprise, as it was believed to be unsuitable for the course, was Schmidt's little old Packard *Grey Wolf.* Of only 30 h.p., *Grey Wolf* had been specially built for dirt-track racing some years previously. There were also two 75-h.p. Fiats which went out with clutch trouble on the first lap.

The Mercedes team consisted of four amateur-driven *60*s and Wilhelm Werner, on C. G. Dinsmore's *90*. Werner damaged his brakes by pulling up too sharply at a level crossing and had to retire on his second lap. Arents, driving a *60*, burst a tyre on his second lap and overturned. His mechanic, Mensel, was killed. Hawley on a Mercedes *60* was making splendid and consistent lap times. Had he been able to keep it up, instead of dropping out on the fifth lap, he might well have won the race, for his average speed was considerably higher than that of the winner Heath, on a big Panhard. Campbell's and Luttgen's *60*s were still running when the race finished, and gained fourth and sixth places respectively. Campbell's Mercedes was just beaten for third place by the astonishing little *Grey Wolf*, which like its namesake, loped quietly round with no signs of effort or fatigue.

## 1905

The year started for Mercedes with the usual blaze of success in America, and, for the French Automobile Club, with a very stormy dispute. Everyone in France connected with motoring felt strongly that the Gordon Bennett rules were unfair to France. They certainly had some grounds for complaint, for under the rules as they were laid down, France, as the leading car-producing nation, could only put three cars in the field.

The club and manufacturers together produced what appeared at first sight a quite reasonable scheme in which the Gordon Bennett race became merged in a French Grand Prix with very lavish prizes. But no one outside France had a good word to say for the scheme, and after a long and acrimonious wrangle, the idea was dropped. The French declared that after 1905 they would boycott and sabotage the Gordon Bennett race in all possible ways, although as holders of the Trophy they were obliged to organize it in 1905.

In America, the January meeting at Daytona was a field-day for Mercedes. A number of records, including the ten-mile world record were taken. The drivers were E. R. Thomas, Sam Stevens, and W. K. Vanderbilt Jun. on *90*s, James L. Breeze on his antique but effective *40* and H. L. Bowden on a new eight-cylinder 120-h.p. Mercedes-based special which he had produced himself. This astonishing car was powered by two more or less standard *60* engines. Just for good measure, one engine had been made at Untertürkheim and one at the Austrian works at Wiener Neustadt.

However, this was all in keeping with one school of thought

in 1904, which held that as big an engine as possible should be built within the permitted weight limit. Maybach and his team of technicians belonged to this group and they brought out, during the year, an even more powerful 120-h.p. four-cylinder racer. There was another school that, seeing the smaller, lighter cars of a mere four litres or so going nearly as fast as the monsters, felt that in the development of these the future lay.

In the issue of June 3, 1905, *The Autocar* illustrated the engine of one of the new Mercedes racing cars—of 123 h.p., according to contemporary information. One picture showed the inlet side of the engine . . .

> The most remarkable feature of which is the splendid arrangement of the throttle and carburettor. Both throttle and carburettor are mounted as close as possible to the inlet ports of the cylinders, and are almost combined in one piece and inserted direct into the connecting pipe to the two inlet ports. Such an arrangement, in the first place, saves a good deal of weight in piping, and, furthermore, will doubtless make it possible to control the speed of the engine in a most effective way, as scarcely any mixture whatever is stored between the inlet port of the engine and the throttle and the vaporizer, and therefore the slightest movement of the latter must immediately influence the speed of the motor—a point which should prove most valuable on this year's Gordon Bennett course in France.

In July, all was set for the last Gordon Bennett Trophy race. The competing nations had completed their eliminating trials and the local authorities of the Auvergne had spent over three thousand pounds, a very considerable sum of money in those days, in preparing the course. Germany was represented by Wilhelm Werner, Baron de Caters and Jenatzy, all on the new 120-h.p. Mercedes. Works drivers Braun and Hieronymus, and amateur Burton, similarly mounted, represented Austria. France was represented by two Brasiers and a de Dietrich, England by two Wolseleys and a Napier, and America by two Pope-Toledos and a Locomobile. The Italians had 110-h.p. Fiats.

In practising, matters did not run smoothly. The course was one which required careful learning, and the French, all of whose drivers knew it well, closed the circuit prematurely. The Germans, British and Italians naturally objected, ignored the closure, and went on practising. So, to save face, the French 'reopened' the circuit. The star of the practising was Jenatzy who, on his *120* Mercedes, started a firm favourite for the race. However, when it came to the day, persistent tyre trouble and oiling up of plugs put him right out of the running. An elaborate system of telephones was rigged up between the controls but as, during practice, the locals, living up to all the stories that are told about the peasants of the Auvergne, stole the wires, the system was of little practical use. One of the worst troubles that bedevilled the organizing committee was the lack of accommodation for spectators. People were sleeping on the billards tables in Royat and Clermont-Ferrand and, in this sparsely-populated area, there were, outside the towns, few other houses. Then, just prior to the race, one of those nightmare hurricanes that spring up from nowhere without warning in the Auvergne, demolished most of the grandstand and other temporary buildings, including the weighing tent where Cagno's Fiat was being weighed at the time.

However, in spite of all the difficulties, the first man was dispatched on time at 6 a.m. on the morning of July 5. The day started fine, but soon the sky was overcast and there was even a little rain. So it certainly was not excessive heat that caused the tyre troubles that virtually put the Mercedes cars out of the race. It must have come as a great surprise to both Maybach and the drivers to find that in the new *120* they had a motor-car that was too powerful and fast for its tyres. Burton and Hieronymus, on their *120*s were both out after the second lap, and Jenatzy did not last much longer than the third. Nor was Lancia on his Fiat much better. He put up wonderful lap speeds for the first two laps, which remained unbroken all day. He was leading the race by a comfortable thirteen minutes, when his good fortune deserted him, and his radiator fell to pieces. There was no answer to that. The speed of the three remaining Mercedes cars was more or less limited by the amount of tyre trouble suffered by each individual car, also by the sensitivity of the eyes of each individual driver. Just prior to the race, the authorities had sprinkled the roads with a chemical compound to lay the dust. This was blown up into the eyes of the drivers and some, who were more allergic to it than others, finished the race almost blind.

All three *120* drivers completed the course. Braun was tenth, Baron de Caters seventh, and Werner fifth. Théry 'The Chronometer' won again on a Richard Brasier, so the Gordon Bennett Trophy remained in France.

This was the second great victory for the French motor industry. A Richard Brasier car was the only one to win the Gordon Bennett Trophy two years running and it did so in the face of intense competition.

This was the last of the big international races in which that great early master Wilhelm Werner drove. For the previous two or three years he had been in the direct employ of the

American, Clarence Gray Dinsmore. He only drove in two more events that year, for Dinsmore died, and Werner proudly accepted the position as head chauffeur to Kaiser Wilhelm II. The Emperor also took over Gray Dinsmore's *70* with its beautiful six-seater body.

The fact that the French, who had so firmly renounced the Gordon Bennett race, had won the Trophy again created a rather Gilbertian situation. They were bound under the regulations to hold it themselves in their own country the following year. But they had also sworn, publicly, with considerable venom, to boycott the race. One could speculate on what would have happened had the other nations insisted on the Gordon Bennett being run again. Luckily, however, the Automobile Clubs of the other countries concerned agreed not to press their claims and allowed the French to replace it with a first-class Grand Prix race. The rules were very much the same as those of the Gordon Bennett, with the same 1000-kg weight limit. There were, however, two notable exceptions. Any country could enter all the cars it wanted, which was the main reason why the French rejected the Gordon Bennett, and in future all work on competing cars, during the race, had to be done by the driver and the mechanic carried on the car.

But to return to the season of 1905. At the speed trials at Brighton, held just after the Gordon Bennett race, J. E. Hutton, the Mercedes dealer, did very well on his *120*, an Austrian-built model that had been raced by Hermann Braun,

Sir Ralph Gore's 90-h.p. Mercedes at the Brighton Speed Trials, July 1905. (*The Edward Mayer Collection*)

as did Sir Ralph Gore, the famous yachtsman, on his *100*. Edward Mayer said that Hutton had been exhibiting the *100*, unbelievably glorious in its scarlet and brightly polished brass. Mayer had fallen in love with it at first sight, but went for a short walk to think over such very considerable expenditure. When he came back he had made the decision to buy it, but he found it had been sold to Sir Ralph Gore! Hutton and Sir Ralph divided the honours between them at Brighton, collecting among other awards the *Autocar* Cup and the *Daily Mail* Cup.

Three weeks later came the first Herkomer trials. Sir Hubert von Herkomer was a fashionable portrait painter of German extraction, living near London. He was a keen motorist and endowed handsomely a competition based on elegance of coachwork, comfort, speed, and reliability over a set course. It was won by Edgar Ladenburg, a cousin of Edward Mayer, who had consoled himself by buying Jenatzy's Homburg 'Gordon Bennett' car. Hermann Weigand of Dusseldorf was second on a *40* and Willy Poege third in a *60*. Mercedes as well as Benz won a number of lesser awards, too numerous to mention.

It is a pity no one could make a colour film of the 1905 Semmering hill-climb. All up the long hill were lines of spectators: officers in the brilliantly coloured uniforms of the

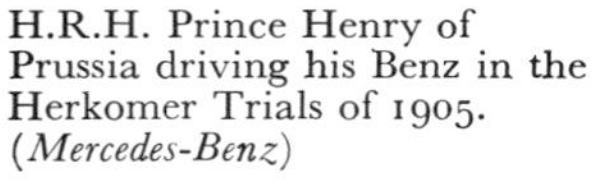

H.R.H. Prince Henry of Prussia driving his Benz in the Herkomer Trials of 1905. (*Mercedes-Benz*)

Twin acetylene searchlights on one of Edward Mayer's cars. Note drip-feed lubricators, pressure pumps, etc. (*The Edward Mayer Collection*)

Emperor Franz Josef's army, the ladies in their big gaily-feathered hats and lovely clothes, and the peasant girls in their brightly coloured dirndls. At the bottom, at a very discreet distance from the brightly polished cars, were beautifully coach-painted carriages with their well-matched horses. Little did the so gay young people, thrilled by the great bolides thundering up the 10-kilometre climb at an average speed of fifty miles an hour, realize that in a brief decade their world and way of life would have gone for ever.

A London bus on a Milnes-Daimler chassis. (*The Edward Mayer Collection*)

Experimental car with compressed air-transmission, designed by Maybach in 1905. (*Mercedes-Benz*)

At this meeting Mercedes did well, with several class wins. Star performer was Hermann Braun, driver for the Austrian works, at the wheels of a *100* and a *90* belonging to Theodor Dreher, the wealthy brewer from Trieste.

In matters of design, Wilhelm Maybach was very active about this time. In the previous year he had produced an 80-h.p. four-cylinder racing-car, and in 1905 a similar machine of 100 h.p., as well as a number of new touringc-ars. There was a choice of *10/20* and *21/35* four-cylinder shaft-driven cars. The little *10/20* had for the first time a cone clutch. The larger touring-cars, *26/45*, *31/35* and *36/65*, were all chain-driven, and all had four cylinders. On the English market, however, only the *28/32*, *40/45* and the new 70-h.p. cars were to be bought. The *28/32* cost £1050 and the *40/45* £1260 as touring-cars.

## 1906

With the end of the Gordon Bennett races, the most important event of the motor racing year in 1906 was the French Grand Prix. The same formula for racing-cars was in force, for the last time. As a result of this, few manufacturers brought out new racing models, but all were modified versions of the huge, dangerous, over-engined bolides of the previous year. Mercedes raced with 100-h.p. and 120-h.p. four-cylinder cars, but also made a 100-h.p. six-cylinder car. This was undoubtedly a fast car, but it is said by people who have owned them that they gave more mechanical trouble than any Mercedes car built before or since. They had a 'square' engine 140 mm. × 140 mm. with overhead valves. The chassis and transmission were standard Mercedes practice, four speeds, final chain drive, channel steel chassis, honeycomb radiator and wooden wheels.

Competitions started off, as usual, with the January meeting in Florida. Two old *40*s driven by Downey and Breeze both got second places. These were good performances, as they were 1903 models and high speeds were being achieved by the 1906 cars, Demogeot reaching over 100 m.p.h. on the 200-h.p. Darracq, and Marriot doing 127 m.p.h. on a Stanley steam-car!

The first prize in the Württemberg Automobile Club's Trials was won by a 28-h.p. Mercedes driven by 'Robert Bosch, Electrical Engineer'. Maybach had, in 1903, fitted the Bosch high tension magneto to the cars, replacing the old low tension ignition.

There were a number of trials, of various kinds, in Germany during the next few months. Nearly all the events were won by Benz cars, which were definitely rising in the competition world. Even in the Herkomer Trials, they won almost every award—although that very successful amateur driver Willy Poege won the hill-climb on his *70*, gaining third place in the general category. Meanwhile, the Automobile Club de France, which had so thoroughly sabotaged the Gordon Bennett races, felt honour bound to stage the best Grand Prix race ever. A circuit was chosen near Le Mans in the Sarthe district, running round a triangle from La Ferté Bernard to St. Calais and then St. Mars-le-Brière. The local authorities, knowing well the trade that a great race would bring to their little town, did everything they possibly could to help. They built wooden tracks to save the cars going through the narrow, dangerous villages at the corners of the triangle; they tarred the roads to lay the dust; they even dug a tunnel under the road for spectators to pass through without crossing the track. If they had known how, they might even have built something like the Mellaha circuit in Tripoli!

The race was run on two days. After the first day, the cars were driven into a fenced park where they were locked in and guarded. Mechanics were not allowed to touch them till they had been dragged to the starting line by horses the following morning! Then, only two mechanics and the driver were allowed to approach any car.

No official team was entered from Stuttgart, but Mariaux, Jenatzy and Cavaliere Florio drove as independents. They were in competition with all sorts of cars, ranging from formidable works teams of Fiat, Hotchkiss, Panhard, Darracq, and others, to such queer freaks as the Vulpès and the opposed piston Gobron-Brillié. The Vulpès was a very odd vehicle which looked like a monstrous marine engine with a wheel at each corner and the driver peering over the top of it. The Gobron-Brillié was built in 1903 and, usually driven by Rigolly, acquitted itself well against all the latest models. This strange old 1903 racing-car must have been quite fast, as it beat Mariaux's 100-h.p. Mercedes into eleventh place by several minutes. According to eye-witnesses, one of the sights of the first day was the duel between Duray's monster de Dietrich and Mariaux. The Mercedes beat the de Dietrich by several minutes and a couple of places. Both cars were severely handicapped by the pitiless sun which beat down on the course all day. The tyres were not up to the task demanded of them, and in the great heat they failed with sickening frequency, the race in consequence going to the manufacturers who had equipped their cars with the newly introduced detachable rims. Notable amongst these were Renault and Fiat, while Mercedes, de Dietrich and Panhard still changed their tyres by the old laborious method. An interesting illustration of the weakness of the tyres of the time is that Charles Rolls never went on any long-distance record attempt without carrying a professional tyre changer borrowed for the purpose. Jenatzy, no longer up to his usual form, was down to sixteenth place, and Cavaliere Florio, who was running twelfth in the fourth lap fell out on the fifth.

On the second day, the surface was so badly torn up, especially on corners, that tyres suffered worse than ever. A wonderful feat was that of Albert Clément (whose father built the original Clément manufactured in England under licence as Clément-Talbot) who, in spite of the fact that he did not have detachable rims and had lost ten minutes over every tyre change, finished second.

There was a rule that a driver might hand over to a substitute. The only one to avail himself of this was Jenatzy, who handed over his Mercedes to Burton, the American amateur. Burton drove an excellent race. He came home in tenth place driving against a large field comprising the flower of Europe's professional drivers. Mariaux, eleventh, followed him over the line some twenty minutes later. Szisz was the winner on a Renault.

Driving one of the new *70* Mercedes, which first appeared at the West German trials in July 1906, was another man whose name was to become a household word, Ernst Büssing, whose Büssing-NAG trucks are now world renowned.

At Ostend, Mercedes had great success, honours being divided between de Jochems and Sir Algernon Lee Guinness, later to win fame at the wheel of a Sunbeam, on his *90*.

The Circuit des Ardennes, started by the Belgians in 1902, was now becoming a race of first-class importance. Three 120-h.p. four-cylinder Mercedes started, driven by Burton, the American, Otto Salzer, a promising young works tester, and Camille Jenatzy, who did not seem deterred by his bad accident in the first Circuit des Ardennes.

First Wagner's Darracq and then Duray's de Dietrich led the race, with Salzer running a steady second from the beginning. But just as prospects began to look really good for him he dropped back. He finished in ninth place followed one minute later by Jenatzy who was tenth. Burton did not survive the second lap. Duray was the ultimate winner.

September came, and with it Semmering. Theodor Dreher, the brewer, had ordered a new six-cylinder Mercedes; Hermann Braun, as usual, drove for him. Braun thrilled the crowd by tearing up the hill and knocking three and a half seconds off the record. Willy Poege, who had bought a similar car, finished second, eleven seconds slower. At least one of these great six-cylinder racing-cars is still in existence. It is in Australia, and largely in original condition.

There were not many big races in 1906 and the last of them

135-h.p. Grand Prix Mercedes at Brooklands, 1906. (*The Edward Mayer Collection*)

was the Vanderbilt Cup. There had been some curious cars entered in the Grand Prix at Le Mans but there were some, even stranger, entered at Long Island. One, the Frayer-Miller, had a huge 110-h.p. engine with a fan on the front end of the crankcase, cooling the finned cylinders through ducts. The chassis looked rather light for a 40-h.p. engine and, if a contemporary photograph is to be believed, no attempt at shock absorbers had been made. Lytle's Pope-Toledo had only one spring between each pair of valves, and there were other oddities too numerous to mention. However, the eliminating trials produced five American cars, a Locomobile, a Thomas, a Christie, a Haynes, and one of the odd air-cooled Frayer-Millers, to face a very formidable challenge from the cream of the European racing world.

Only three Mercedes ran, all *120*s. Jenatzy drove one, Foxhall-Keene a second, the other being driven by Lüttgen, a German. It was a race full of incident. At one stage, Duray grabbed his mechanic and dragged him back into the car when he had almost fallen out. There is in existence a photograph of Duray doing this with one hand, and hauling his enormous de Dietrich round a corner, in a sort of four-wheel slide worthy of Nuvolari, with the other. But it was not a very

45-h.p. 1906 Touring Mercedes. (*The Edward Mayer Collection*)

Gearbox of a chain-driven Mercedes, circa 1907. (*The Edward Mayer Collection*)

eventful race for the Mercedes. Jenatzy was at one time running second, but fell back into fifth place at the finish. Lüttgen was still lapping when the race was declared over, Wagner on a Darracq being the winner at an average speed of 61·4 m.p.h.

We hear now for the first time a name with which we shall become very familiar—Théodore Pilette. He was a friend of Camille Jenatzy, and an agent for Mercedes in Antwerp, and he was placed in some kilometre speed trials at Origny St. Benoite, driving a 45-h.p. Mercedes.

The Mercedes cars on the British market during 1906, according to *The Autocar* of November 18, 1905, were as follows:

20 h.p. four-cylinder. 100 x 120 mm. bore and stroke. Chain drive. Four speeds. 1100 r.p.m. Weight 19 cwt. Wheelbase 10 ft. 4 in. Price £850.

30 h.p. four-cylinder. 110 x 140 mm. bore and stroke. Chain drive. Four speeds. 1100 r.p.m. Weight 20½ cwt. Wheelbase 10 ft. 4 in. Price £1010.

28 h.p. 1000 r.p.m. Otherwise as above. Price £1010.

45 h.p. four-cylinder. 120 x 150 mm. bore and stroke. 1000 r.p.m. Weight 21 cwt. Same wheelbase. Price £1200.

70 h.p. four-cylinder. 140 x 150 mm. bore and stroke. 1250 r.p.m. Weight 24 cwt. Wheelbase 11 ft. 1 in. Price £1800.

## 1907

The Grand Prix formula of 1907 was simple. The rules said that each competitor might have, in sealed cans, thirty litres of petrol for every 100 kilometres of racing distance; that is, an allowance of 9·4 miles per gallon; otherwise, within this limitation, he was given a free hand. At this early stage of motor racing there was no real universal formula, and any club running a race was at liberty to make its own rules. The two first big European races, the Targa Florio and the Kaiserpreis, both had differing formulæ. For the Targa Florio it was based on a limiting bore and stroke, varying with the number of cylinders, and for the Kaiserpreis, cubic capacity was simply limited to eight litres. In both races a minimum weight limit of 1000 kg. was imposed.

To go back to the beginning of the year, the first meeting of 1907 was held at Daytona, Florida, the scene of many Mercedes triumphs. E. P. Blakely, of New York, won no less than three races on a 70-h.p. 'American Mercedes'. These cars, marketed by Steinway, the piano manufacturer, are believed to have been bare chassis shipped from Untertürkheim and fitted with coachwork, tyres and accessories in America. The Americans did this job very thoroughly, and the finish was worthy of Untertürkheim.

As, most surprisingly, not a single Mercedes was entered for the Targa Florio, we need not concern ourselves with that race. For the Kaiserpreis, on the other hand, there were five Mercedes among the ninety-two entries: three from Stuttgart and two from Wiener Neustadt. Because of the large entry two eliminating races were held, and only three Mercedes survived for the final race on June 14. These were driven by Salzer, Willy Poege, and Jenatzy. The course was over part of the old Gordon Bennett circuit, with additions, so that it passed through Homburg, Oberursel, Königstein, Esch, Weilmünster, Weilburg, Usingen, and Wehrheim. The Kaiser rose early to see the first man, Schmidt on a Durkopp, sent away at 4 a.m., the rest following at two-minute intervals. The roads were dry and the times were good. Mercedes were unsuccessful; it was a three-cornered struggle between the Fiats, the Opels, and Hautvast on a Pipe. This last was a Belgian car with a very high turn of speed. After these came Minoia's Isotta-Fraschini and Fournier's Itala, followed by Salzer's Mercedes in eighth place. Jenatzy was fourteenth and Poege did not survive the first lap. Nazzaro on a Fiat was the winner, followed by Hautvast on his Pipe. An Opel was third.

In July 1907, Mr. H. F. Locke King opened the Brooklands

race track, near Weybridge. The thirty-mile race was won by Hutton, the British Mercedes agent, on a 120-h.p. car, with Dario Resta, an English-born Italian, in second place driving Fry's 120-h.p. Mercedes.

July was the month of the French Grand Prix, which manufacturers were beginning to take very seriously. They rented villas and houses near the course, set up workshops, and had their drivers on the spot for weeks to memorise every bend and irregularity of the circuit. The Mercedes team of three consisted of Jenatzy, Héméry, and Otto Salzer. At no time were any of them seriously in the running, although at the beginning Salzer kept fourth place for one lap. Héméry finished tenth and Salzer and Jenatzy were still going when the race was over but were flagged off the course. Nazzaro on the Fiat was once again the winner, followed by Szisz on the Renault.

In July, also, the Ardennes races were run in Belgium. These were divided into two classes, with admirable good sense, one class for cars conforming to Kaiserpreis formula, the other to Grand Prix formula. The first class was won by Lord Brabazon of Tara, whose name in those days was Moore-Brabazon. His Minerva was first, with two other Minervas second and third. Soon after this he gave up motor-racing to become one of our earliest aeronauts. There was only one Mercedes car in this race, Pilette's, which did not perform at all well. The Grand Prix formula was, however, an exciting race and a triumph for Mercedes, Baron de Caters on his *120* winning from Algernon Lee Guinness on a Darracq by a minute and a half. Jenatzy brought his *120* into third place.

Grand Prix Mercedes of 1907.
(*The Edward Mayer Collection*)

There was a car which was entered in many races and hill-climbs in the period around 1906–7. This was the Mercedes-Mixte, also known as the Lohner-Porsche. It was an interesting failure but is worth describing. A standard 45-h.p. Mercedes chassis, less clutch and all transmission, was the basis. A dynamo was coupled to the engine and a motor built into the back axle like the old Tilling Stevens buses that ran in London in about 1920. The infinitely variable transmission was clever and, as a piece of engineering, the car was sound, but the great weight and extreme complexity made it quite unsuitable for racing, and these factors coupled with the very high cost of manufacture made it a hopeless proposition to sell. *The Motor*, on December 8, 1906, says that the Mercedes-Mixte will be 'one of the most interesting cars for 1907.'

No new types of racing-cars were built by Mercedes in 1907, and only two new touring-cars, a 70-h.p. four-cylinder and a 75-h.p. six-cylinder. The latter had a crankshaft supported on ball bearings, and must be classed as one of Wilhelm Maybach's failures.

*The Motor*, in its issue of July 13, 1907, provides some details of the 75-h.p. six-cylinder car. Its bore and stroke were 110 × 140 mm., the cylinders being cast in pairs and fed through a

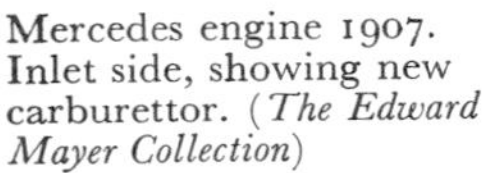

Mercedes engine 1907. Inlet side, showing new carburettor. (*The Edward Mayer Collection*)

1907 Mercedes, showing new lubricator and magneto switch. (*The Edward Mayer Collection*)

1907 type Mercedes carburettor, the special feature being a swinging, suction-influenced, and spring-controlled automatic mixture valve. The jet chamber was hot-water-jacketed. Petrol was delivered through an adjustable jet, controlled by means of a very accessible vertical tapered spigot. There was a 30-gallon rear petrol-tank, petrol being fed under pressure to the carburettor. A low tension magneto was fitted. The front springs had six 'blades', the rear springs ten 'blades'. The 'steering wheels' were 910 mm. × 90 mm., the 'drivers' 920 mm. × 120 mm. The wheelbase was twelve feet. The Duke of Westminster had the first model to arrive in England.

In general, 1907 was not a good year for the Daimler Motoren Gesellschaft, and their labour force dropped from over 3,000 in 1906 to 2,460 in 1907, and, a reflection on this bad year, to 1,650 in 1908. There were labour troubles and the management had to make concessions to the workers, a 9½-hour day, to include an hour for dinner, for the same weekly wage that they had earned for longer hours. Then, and this was a great loss to the company, in May, 1907 that dynamic sales booster, Emile Jellinek, retired from the board for reasons of health.

Their greatest loss, however, was Wilhelm Maybach. It has been recorded already that Count Zeppelin, pioneer of lighter-than-air dirigibles, was a close friend of Gottlieb Daimler. After Daimler's death, the Count and Maybach continued on excellent terms. The desire had been growing within Wilhelm Maybach to have a small place of his own. In 1907, he arranged to start a small factory at Schaffhausen on Lake Constance, primarily for the production of engines. As Count Zeppelin was prepared to give him all the work he needed to keep his small establishment going, he had few worries in that direction. The surprising fact is that Wilhelm Maybach, now sixty-one, an age when most men think of retiring, should have been ready to start a new business. Maybach, however, was made of sterner stuff and, like his lifelong friend Gottlieb Daimler, believed that there was no relaxation like work. It is gratifying to record that his small firm went from strength to strength and in later years, besides aircraft engines, built motor-cars, most of which were of elephantine size. They were superbly built, with a finish equal to Hispano-Suiza and Rolls-Royce at their very best, but they were very complex

King Edward VII and Kaiser Wilhelm II in a 70-h.p. Mercedes, circa 1907. (*The Edward Mayer Collection*)

mechanically, and one cannot withstand the thought that any Maybach car would need a specialist mechanic, trained at the factory, to maintain it.

Wilhelm Maybach left the Mercedes works early in 1907 with a proud record on which to look back. In the seven years of his technical direction, the *Phoenix* Daimler which was little more than a voiturette, even if of very advanced design, had blossomed into the most popular and important of high-powered racing- and touring-cars, the Mercedes.

# MORE BENZ

THE policy of Karl Benz was not dissimilar to that of the late Lord Austin. He maintained that he had built a good car, and he opposed any modification or development with jealous fervour. While he persisted in this static policy, the Daimler concern turned out two winners in succession. There was Daimler's V-twin engine, infinitely more up-to-date than the horizontal single-cylinder built by Karl Benz, followed by the first Mercedes of 1900. Small wonder therefore, that at the turn of the century, Benz sales began to sag.

## 1899–1907

There was at this time considerable dissension within the Benz Company. In 1899 a joint stock company was formed, with a board of five directors together with eight executives. This expansion, to cope with increased demands, had been planned by that wise and far-seeing director, von Fischer, on his death-bed. To say that they found Karl Benz difficult would be an understatement. By this time the vast economic possibilities of the automobile had been acknowleged, and it was quite clear that world markets were wide open. The firm began to lay plans for immensely increased production, building what was, for those days, a formidable number of vehicles. But Karl Benz had the greatest mistrust of any part that was not made by hand on the bench and strongly opposed all this. He detested anything savouring of mass production.

The company had a long way to go, for the 3½-h.p. Benz car of 1900 was little more than a refined and lightened edition of the Benz car of a decade earlier. Further, although many Benz cars appeared in the earliest motor races, Karl Benz himself was fundamentally opposed to motor racing. He always said that comfort, and not speed, should be the primary consideration in building a car. For the first five years of motor racing there were no works entries from Mannheim, although Thum, the works driver, often drove privately entered cars for their owners. But, in spite of the lack of works entries, there was hardly a race in which there were not a number of privately entered Benz cars competing.

Emile Roger, the Paris agent, was a consistent competitor. His car was called the Roger-Benz, for it was thought that its essentially German name might hamper the sales in France. It was, in fact, a Mannheim-built Benz car, or, at a later date, assembled in Paris with Benz parts to avoid paying import duty on the completed car. It is probable that a Roger-Benz, now in the Science Museum at South Kensington, was the first petrol-driven car ever brought into England. It was almost certainly imported in 1894 by a long-defunct firm in Birmingham. As however, the written records of the firm have disappeared, this cannot be definitely proved. Leon L'Hollier, of Birmingham, became, shortly after this, the English agent for Roger-Benz cars and sold a few. Roger was also responsible for the first Paris taxi, a Benz, in December 1896. It is claimed by wits that this taxi still emerges with other ancient relics, after the 'Metro' has stopped, to convey belated travellers home at a fee far in excess of the market value of the cab!

Fritz Held, the Benz retailer in Mannheim, also raced, and Richard Benz used to race with him and drive his cars. But it was not until 1901 that there were any 'works' entries, and in that year Richard, his brother Eugen, and Hans Thum drove.

The racing record of the privately entered Benz cars is good. They did not score many wins, but they nearly always finished, a difficult feat to accomplish in those days. In the Paris–Rouen race of 1894, Roger finished fourteenth and won fifth prize. With the exception of the de Dion steam tractor that won, all the cars leading the Benz were Panhards and Peugeots with Daimler engines. The following year, in the gruelling Paris–Bordeaux-Paris race, when Levassor put up the magnificent single-handed drive that has been described already, Hans Thum and Fritz Held driving one of Roger's cars finished fifth, while Roger himself was eighth. In 1896, Benz cars ran second, fourth and fifth in the Lyons–Lagnieu race, and in the Paris–Marseilles–Paris race two French-entered Benz cars, with German drivers, made seventh and eighth places.

In that year, also, the famous London–Brighton 'Emancipation' run took place. Benz entries were almost as numerous as today, arriving tortoise-like hours after the dashing Daimlers and Panhards.

In 1897, with Daimler-engined Panhards getting progressively faster, private entrants seem to have been rather discouraged. Only one is recorded, when the charmingly named Lara Bibal drove to fifth place in the Lyon–Uriage–Lyon race.

In 1899, Benz cars, although basically much the same, had increased their horse-power, and for the first time began to win races. The first to score was Lara Bibal who won the Lyon–Vals, and in the following month Fritz Held and Emil Graf were first and second in a 125-mile contest between Frankfurt and Cologne. They were awarded a large and a small gold medal respectively.

The run of victories continued, and in September, in the Berlin–Baumgartenbruck–Berlin race, Benz were first and second in the touring class. The Berlin–Leipzig race was won outright by Fritz Held and Richard Benz on one of the new 12-h.p. cars. This would appear to have been a 'works' entry rather than one by Held, the Benz concessionaire, for the prize for fastest time, a gold medal, bearing a portrait of the Kaiser, and several lesser trophies, were awarded to the Benz Company. Baron von Liebieg was sixth and Hans Thum completed the course, both on 8-h.p. Benz cars.

Nevertheless, in spite of a certain amount of success in competitions, the public were growing less and less interested in buying a car with belt transmission; front-engined cars had ousted ones with engines at the rear. In 1900, 603 cars were sold, but by 1903 this figure had sunk to 172; obviously the car was badly out of date.

All the same individual cars were highly prized by their owners and the following pseudo-humorous account of a run in a 4½-h.p. Benz appears in *The Motor* of October 25, 1910, and seems to the authors to be worth quoting in full, so redolent is it of the atmosphere of the period and showing also as it does that the vintage enthusiast has been in existence longer than might be supposed. A Mr. George Johnson is the author of the article.

Paton remarked that he supposed I was ashamed to be seen in his archaic machine. Maybe there was some truth in the statement, for the 4½-h.p. Benz was just about making her adieux at the time I fell a victim to motoritis—and that was years ago. Paton bought his Benz in 1901; he has never owned another car, and, therefore, from a modern motorist's point of view is somewhat behind the times. Dating from a later period, I have had five cars, and my friend points out the multitude of sorrow he has escaped by being true to his first love. Perhaps he is right. We two motorists are both members of a photographic club, whose first snapshotting expedition for the season was arranged at a beauty spot some 24 miles away; and at Paton's invitation, though not without misgivings, I decided to do the journey in his car.

I found my friend pouring petrol through a neat brass funnel that screwed in to the pipe leading to the tank.

'This is one of the little refinements that are somehow dispensed with on most modern cars,' he said. I acquiesced. The spoutless funnel permitted no dust to enter the tank, and adapted itself just as cheerfully to the radiator supply later on. Somewhere behind the works, what looked like a home-made thermometer turned out to be a petrol gauge, graduated with pints.

'Why pints?' I inquired. Paton smiled.

'I only use it by the pint,' he said. 'Wait and see.'

We had ambled merrily along for about six miles, careering at 16 m.p.h. or thereabouts, when the car suddenly slowed down. From my seat on the footboards, as being more comfortable than the left perch above, I gazed inquiringly at Paton.

'Petrol,' he said. 'Can you manage to turn the tap under the wing? It's on your side.'

At the risk of barked knuckles from the 36-inch wire wheel at the back, I did as requested.

'I thought it was about time for her to dry up,' continued my friend. 'You see the ball valve is a bit worn, so I let a few ounces of petrol in at a time, and there's no waste!'

After covering a few more miles, we succeeded in taking a wrong turning, resulting in the car having to be reversed in a narrow lane. The driver managed it single-handed, and inquired how I would get on under similar circumstances with my 9 ft. wheel-base.

'Break the law by driving backwards for half a mile, I suppose,' he said; and I had to agree.

At length we arrived at our destination, and my friend anxiously inspected the petrol gauge.

'Five pints exactly,' he said gleefully; 'that's not bad.' Truly it was not, after over 24 miles of Cornish hills.

We did a little photography on meeting our colleagues of the camera, but eventually worked back to the inevitable topic of motors.

'Your back wheels look in a healthier state than the front,' I remarked.

'Oh yes, they are comparatively new,' said Paton. 'You see, never having to repair punctures, one gets the idea that wheels will last for ever, but they come in for a lot of nasty jars. I advertised for wheels over and over again, and at last was offered a complete car in almost better order than mine for seven pounds ten.'

'And you bought it?'

'Not I; but I got the wheels for fifty shillings, and the owner scrapped the rest of his machine.'

After refreshing ourselves with the rest of our party, Paton climbed into the seat and whisked round what he called his self-starter. It consisted of a shaft, with a handle by the driver's seat, under his knees, the other extremity connecting with the flywheel by means of a bevel pinion. The engine panted comfortably.

'Self-starters are new ideas rather, aren't they?' queried my friend.

'Yes,' I replied; 'but they don't work quite on your principle.'

The motorist sighed. 'Ah, we are not very up-to-date,' he said; 'this fitting has been on six years!'

Our journey back was mostly down hills, and the car's owner just bounced them. Once I ventured to expostulate.

'Supposing you met anything; with your engine out of gear, you haven't sufficient brake power to pull up?'

Paton did not answer until we reached the bottom; then as the belt swung on with a chirrup and the 'self-starter' again came into action, via the driver's energetic right arm, he said: 'I've driven her nine years now, and nothing much has happened; only a spoke now and then comes out. I collect them and take them home. It's amusement for wet days—refixing.'

As dusk fell, we neared home, and it became necessary to light the tiny lamps.

'You don't mean to say that you drive with these, when it is really dark?' I queried.

Paton pointed to a small acetylene cycle lamp in front.

'Oh no,' he said, 'if it's very dark we light the headlight!'

Paton is of an economical turn of mind, but it struck me that there are many of us who get much less pleasure out of our cars at far greater cost.

In the summer of 1900, the firm brought out the two-cylinder 20-h.p. 'Contra-motor' racing-car. The steering was most daringly raked backwards, a fashion Karl Benz strongly opposed. Basically it was not far removed from the original Benz of nearly a decade earlier. The bogus 'bonnet' concealed a water tank.

In the famous 1000-Mile Trial held in April and May of that year, from London to Edinburgh and back, several awards were won by small Benz cars in their particular classes.

The year 1901 was a 'Mercedes' year, when every other car, in point of design, was overshadowed, but Benz cars managed to do reasonably well in touring-car classes. In spite of these modest successes, it was quite clear to Julius Ganss that cars of more up-to-date design were monopolizing the markets. This had been worrying him for some years, and tension between him and Karl Benz had grown. Ganss was forever pleading, from his position as sales director, for a more up-to-date product to sell, and Benz was digging his toes in and opposing every change. Admittedly the balance sheet of the Benz Company showed a satisfactory profit for the financial year ending in 1901, but Ganss saw, only too clearly, the writing on the wall.

Finally, in desperation, Ganss took the law into his own hands. His first step was to import a shaft-driven Renault from Paris. He then persuaded his co-directors, in face of vigorous opposition from Karl Benz, to build a shaft-driven Benz prototype. There is little doubt that Ganss acted rightly, but unfortunately, unforeseen difficulties were met. The shaft-driven Benz, built to the order of Julius Ganss, although most progressive in design, was not a satisfactory car. But Ganss was not easily turned from his purpose. He saw, quite rightly, that shaft-drive was the design of the future and he knew that, if Germans could not build it, Frenchmen could. The following year, 1902, therefore, he engaged Marius Barbarou, works manager for Adolphe Clément (who later was associated with Lord Shrewsbury in building Talbot cars in England), and a team of French technicians and fitters. So we see the curious spectacle of two construction lines in the Benz works: on one side, the antiquated type of Benz cars being built by Germans; on the other side, a new, virtually French car by Frenchmen.

The modernized Benz car was called the *Parsifal* Benz. It was not a success. The engine did not produce the horse-power expected of it and the car was a poor and sluggish hill-climber. Twenty-four only were built. They could in no way compete with the Mercedes, or other cars of established reputation, so the sales, and consequently finances of the Benz Company, suffered accordingly. Ganss demanded that all cars produced by the factory should be shaft-driven, a demand which had the support of the shareholders, but this did not help the waning sales. In the meantime, however, Karl Benz and his technical assistants had been working on something that, for them, was very new and revolutionary. In 1901 and 1902, the little team worked from 6 a.m. to midnight, day in and day out, developing a vertical four-cylinder engine. In April 1903, however, so serious were the disagreements between the directors that Karl Benz, and his son Eugen, resigned their seats in the board and left the firm.

Ganss had fallen between two stools. No one wanted to buy either the antiquated Benz cars, now almost a joke, or the new *Parsifal* Benz models, which were poor motor-cars. Matters went from bad to worse and the financial year 1903–4 showed a deficit of half a million marks.

In the ensuing dispute, Ganss resigned, and Marius Barbarou left for his native France, where he went to the old-established marine-engine builders, Delaunay-Belleville.

Karl Benz now returned to the board of directors. He put his four-cylinder engine in the shaft-driven cars and, in a very short space of time, eradicated the chassis faults. The result was quite a good car which caught the public fancy, and the company's books for the financial year 1904–5 showed a profit of well over one hundred thousand marks.

One of the motoring achievements of the summer of 1903 was the great drive by Mr. Hewetson on a Benz. This might be described as the swan song of the belt-driven car. But let us hear the verbatim account in *The Autocar* of August 23, 1903. It provides a vivid picture of motoring in England at that time.

As far back as May last we announced Mr. Henry Hewetson's intention of driving a 5-h.p. belt-gear driven Benz car a distance of five thousand miles, by daily instalments of one hundred miles, until the full tale was completed. This would make fifty consecutive days' driving—a test sufficient to prove all that is desired of latter-day automobiles. Mr. Hewetson turned out for his first century on June 9 last and covered his concluding 100 on July 29. Chatting the other day with Mr. Hewetson over this most satisfactory experience, we elicited from him that it was as far back as the summer of 1894, two years and more before it was legal to dribble a car along at 12 m.p.h. in this country, Mr. Hewetson, who was then interested in coffee, found himself in Mannheim on business and noticed several of the earliest Benz cars running merrily about the town, and was much taken by, and attracted to, the little self-propelled machines; so much, indeed that he sought out Messrs. Benz & Co. and discussed cars with them. Ultimately, by persuasion and the assurance of these far-sighted German gentlemen that legal or illegal England must come to it, he bought two and took them back to Catford.

Boldly he made local trips thereabout, and for quite six weeks his automobile career was interrupted by a visit from the inspector of police, who, while expressing regret at the duty Scotland Yard imposed upon him, informed Mr. Hewetson that if he ran 'the thing' upon the public streets again he (the inspector) would be obliged to take notice of it.

In that distant age, the only automobilist for many miles, this would have discouraged most, but not Mr. Hewetson. He retained two youths; one he caused to ride like a vedette on a bicycle some way in front of the car, the other occupied the seat with Mr. Hewetson until the moment for his action arrived. As soon as the point on the bicycle descried a gentleman in blue afar off, he wheeled and returned with the information, when Mr. Hewetson dismounted his passenger-boy and caused that youth to stroll in front of the car carrying two square inches of red linen mounted on an exaggerated match-stick, and so complying with the law beneath the eyes of the law, avoided trouble.

Other pioneer work was later performed by Mr. Hewetson, but of that we have not space to speak now. Our concern is with Mr. Hewetson's latest performance, and we asked him what had prompted him to undertake the long drive.

'Well, you see,' returned Mr. Hewetson, 'a large percentage of the outside public are still imbued with the opinion that motor-cars break down, and I thought if I could drive a hundred miles a day for fifty days, taking just such gentlemen as would offer themselves, and a fresh one every day, the effect of such a drive, if accomplished without any breakdown which deserved the name of a breakdown, might help in removing an impression which you know today is an absurd one.'

'None better, Mr. Hewetson,' we replied, 'and as a matter of fact you did drive this standard 5-h.p. geared Benz the stated 100 miles per day until the total of 5000 miles had been piled up, without anything in the shape of a serious breakdown.'

'Most assuredly. Let me tell you just exactly what was done to that car during those fifty days.' Here Mr. Hewetson consulted a diary in which the route, exact distance, the name of his companion, weather, and state of the road, etc., for every day's drive was scrupulously entered, and presently ejaculated 'Oh, yes, I see I took my chains up once, and renewed my sprocket wheels once. This replacement was due to the bad weather through which I drove, and the gritty nature of the mud on the Surrey, Sussex and Hampshire roads I generally drove over. The belt I *never* touched from start to finish, which is, I think, something for the anti-belt-driving people to ponder. The car, as one and all of the fifty passengers I carried will testify, ran most satisfactorily from start to finish, and I may add runs better now than when first she started on her long job.'

'What routes did you particularly favour, Mr. Hewetson?' we asked.

'I preferred the run to Odiham, via Richmond Park, Kingston, Staines, Egham, Sunningdale, Bagshot, Blackwater, and over Hartford Bridge Flats to Odiham, returning through Farnham, over the Hog's Back to Guildford, and along the Ripley Road. I made thirty runs over this route, chiefly because I found my guest and I were so well looked after by Mr. Heath, the proprietor of the George Hotel at Odiham, whose hotel may be said to be a model house of call for the automobilist. No charge is made for housing the car, the cooking is excellent, and the wines are beyond reproach. Then I ran to Brighton and back, and once or twice fifty miles down the Bath road for the balance of the journeys.'

'Did you keep any record of your petrol consumption?'

'Oh, yes. I could generally cover forty-four miles on a gallon of petrol if the weather was dry: but if humid thirty miles was about as far as that quantity would run me.'

'Any trouble with horses during so much driving?'

'Only once, and that at Camberley, where a horse, driven by a Captain Le Brett, twisted clean out of its harness and cut its back on the lamp. . . .'

'How was your car tyred?' was our next question.

'Oh, I had Clipper-Michelin pneumatics on my steering-wheels and Connolly solids on my drivers, and I may say that I regard this as a splendid combination.'

'Punctures?' we queried.

'But three,' was the reply, 'and those simple ones. I only blew up those tyres ten times during the 5000 miles. Good, wasn't it?'

And so on. Mr. Hewetson sold the car by public auction, the proceeds going to a Hospital Fund.

Marius Barbarou was replaced by that brilliant engineer, Hans Nibel. This versatile genius was responsible not only for the world-famous *Blitzen* Benz, but the peerless Mercedes independent four-wheel suspension much as we know it today. He was born of German parents at Olleschau in what is now Czechoslovakia, and which was then part of the Austro-Hungarian Empire. Having studied engineering at Munich and passed with highest honours, he went at the early age of twenty-four to the firm of Benz and rapidly rose to the position of chief engineer. A few years later, between 1908 and 1911, Nibel drove the huge Benz cars of those days in competitions with considerable success. He remained with Benz until their fusion with Mercedes in 1926, when he was at once made a director of the combine.

Great days were now beginning for the Benz Company. The heroic age of motor-racing had begun; huge slow-turning engines, getting bigger every year, in light, high chassis.

There is something which catches the imagination in these unwieldy giants, and the race of heroes that drove them. To those of us who handle modern high-speed cars it would be a strange experience to sit high up with the whistle of the wind drowning the slow unmuffled beat of the engine. Such cars demanded a technique of their own with their heavy steering and rear-braking system. This usually consisted of a brake pedal as we know it today that operated on either the propeller-shaft or on the countershaft (if chain-driven) and an immense brake-lever like a signalman's which operated a hand-brake on each rear wheel. There can be nothing but admiration for the drivers who would hurl these monsters along the very mediocre roads of Europe at average speeds that many sports-car drivers of today would find difficult to equal.

In the competition world, however, 1904 and 1905 were not good years for the Benz Company. The firm scored only a few small successes in competitions in which Mercedes were not entered. But in 1906 Benz made a come-back with a 40-h.p. car at the Königstuhl hill-climb near Heidelberg. Their chief driver, Fritz Erle, with already a long list of successes dating back to the Paris–Marseilles–Paris of 1896, broke the record for the hill, beating the 42-h.p. Mercedes of wealthy amateur Edgar Ladenburg. It is interesting to observe that the year following, 1907, Edgar Ladenburg bought a big Benz car, which he ran with his Mercedes, and Fritz Erle drove it for him.

The course was nearly five miles long and Erle took 6 minutes 46 seconds. He also won the touring class at the Semmering hill-climb that year. This was a feather in his cap, for, since Emile Jellinek, driving one of his Daimlers, won the first Semmering climb in 1899, Mercedes had been consistently successful.

Erle, who was born in 1875 and came as a time-served fitter to Benz in 1894, was by 1907 in charge of the racing department. He stayed with the firm until, as chief of the Berlin service depot, he retired in 1935. He was the most successful

40-h.p. 1905/6 'Prince Henry' model Benz. (*Mercedes-Benz*)

racing driver Benz ever had, and is still alive.

A Benz advertisement in the motor press in November 1905 states that during the past year, their cars were supplied to the following people: H.R.H. Prince Henry of Prussia; H.R.H. Grand-Duke of Sachsen-Weimar-Eisenach; H.R.H. Grand-Duke of Oldenburg; H.R.H. Prince Eitel Friedrich of Prussia; H.R.H. Prince Ludwig Ferdinand of Bavaria; H.I.H. Grand-Duke Alexis Alexandrowitsch of Russia; H.R.H. Duke Siegfried of Bavaria; H.R.H. Duke of Calabria; Prince of Bourbon; H.R.H. Prince Halim; H.H. Prince of Hatzfeldt-Trachenberg; H.E. Sir Arthur Herbert, British Legate; Count Forgach, Austrian-Hungarian Ambassador. How splendidly Edwardian this collection sounds! The models Benz were producing at this time on the British market were four in number—of 18, 28, 40 and 60 h.p., all four-cylinder cars.

Benz made a good start in 1907. Three 60-h.p. cars were entered for the Targa Florio race. Two were driven by works drivers Erle and Spamann. The third was driven by the Duke of Bojano. All three cars finished.

There is one story about the first Targa Florio race that is well worth recording although the authors have not checked its accuracy. During practice for the race, competitors were horrified to find that local bandits, who abounded at that time, thought it good sport to shoot at the fast-moving cars. Luckily none of the drivers were hit. So Cavaliere Florio sent for the three principal bandits of the island and made them Stewards of the Meeting. The sense of importance and responsibility with which they were endowed not only restrained them from further marksmanship practice, but they saw to it that a cease-fire was immediately enforced on the smaller fry!

This modest success was followed up by a considerable

victory in an outright win in the Herkomer trials. Benz had been trying for this for the previous two years, but had been beaten by Mercedes.

In 1907, too, the Benz Company acquired the services of one of the greatest drivers of the heroic age, a Frenchman, Victor Hémèry, whose home town was Le Mans. He had served his time as a mechanic from 1895 to 1900 with Léon Bollée. From 1900 to 1906 he was 'Chief of the Research Division' at Darracq. Considering the size of the Darracq works at this time, this probably means head tester. He was also their race driver. During his first year with Benz, 1907, he did well for them. He was second in the Coppa Florio, second at Semmering, and second at the Château-Thierry hill-climb. He was first at the Gaillon hill-climb and scored three firsts at the Coupe d'Evreux meeting.

Up to and including this year, 1907, the organizers of each separate event had more or less made their own rules, governing the specification of entrants' cars. But by this time, the quantity of meetings all over Europe and elsewhere had so far increased that complete chaos reigned. So the A.I.A.C.R. (Association Internationale des Automobile Clubs Reconnus) called a meeting of all clubs sponsoring race meetings and concocted a common formula, acceptable to all, which would come into force for all meetings, wherever they were, in the following year.

At the Olympia Show, the Cannstatt Automobile Association, whose showrooms were in Regent Street, exhibited two

Fritz Erle, the Benz works driver, won the Herkomer Trials in 1907. (*Mercedes-Benz*)

40-h.p. four-cylinder chain-driven Benz cars. One was a chassis priced at £1060, and the other a limousine priced at £1360. Of this car *The Motor* said, in its issue of November 14, 'The 40-h.p. chassis is a splendid piece of workmanship without any extra gloss or finish. The cylinders are in pairs and ignition is by low tension magneto.'

## 1908

June of 1908 was a great month for Benz in the motor-racing world. Not only did Fritz Erle win the Prince Henry trials outright with a 50-h.p. Benz, but the new 120-h.p. Benz, designed by Nibel within the new formula, appeared for the first time to win a resounding victory in the St. Petersburg–Moscow race. The distance was about 429 miles and Victor Hémćry won at an average speed of a fraction over 51 m.p.h.! He had never seen the road before.

Hémćry's effort, driving his cart-sprung monster on narrow beaded-edge tyres over the sort of road that people who have never been outside England would not believe, was indeed superb. Many competitors retired with broken springs. Demogeot on a Darracq came in second eleven minutes later and Pope on an Itala was third. The St. Petersburg-Moscow race was never run again, but it is unlikely that, for at least a quarter of a century, anybody bettered Hémćry's time of eight and a half hours. To average 50 m.p.h., including stops, one must drive around the 'eighty mark' as much as possible. As the absolute maximum of the *120* Benz over the flying half-mile was about 98 m.p.h. (it was presumably using its highest-geared sprockets), it appears that Hémćry must have driven his car almost flat out all the way from St. Petersburg to Moscow! It was a great triumph for Benz and, in particular, for Nibel's new *120*.

In July, the French Grand Prix was run at Dieppe. The previous year it had been a great financial success, so it was decided to apply to the President for permission to hold it there a second year. Monsieur Clemenceau granted this without demur. There were fifteen makes entered in teams of three, and one lone American Thomas, driven by Lewis Strang. A new grandstand had been built and pits were quite literally pits. A deep trench had been dug in front of the stands and this was divided off into pens by wire netting divisions! Fiat, Panhard, de Dietrich, Renault, Itala and Brasier—indeed, all the great names were engaged. Rigal, Gabriel, and Hautvast on Clément-Bayards started hot favourites. England was represented by the Austin team, Dario Resta, Wright, and Lord Brabazon.

Lautenschlager at the start of the 1908 Dieppe Grand Prix. Some eighteen years later the author owned this car. (*Mercedes-Benz*)

A man who witnessed this classic race tells of how it soon became apparent that the results would be governed by tyres. The speed of the 1908 Grand Prix cars had far outstripped the skill of the tyre makers. The surface of the circuit was in poor condition as it had been badly cut up by the previous race for voiturettes. Tyres gave much trouble. Cissac, a novice driver of one of the big Panhards, lost a tyre at something approaching 100 m.p.h. near Sept Meules and was killed. Rigal changed tyres nineteen times but still managed to average 63·6 m.p.h., which suggests that the Clément-Bayards cars were the fastest of all.

On the fourth lap, Héméry was leading with his big *120* Benz. Lautenschlager, a newcomer to racing, was second on a Mercedes, and Hanriot, also on a *120*, third. The following lap, Lautenschlager passed Héméry into first place. They continued in that order till the end of the race, both holding their cars in check because of almost certain tyre troubles. The Mercedes pit staff had a most anxious time during those last few laps; had Lautenschlager come in for a change of tyres, they had none to give him, as they had exhausted their inadequate supply!

It was at the end of 1908 that the Daimler Motoren Gesellschaft, for reasons given already, decided to abandon racing, although there was, of course, considerable competition from Mercedes cars entered by private owners, many of whom were wealthy. This decision meant that Mercedes would produce no more new types of racing-car to compete with the new models Benz brought out year by year. In 1908, due largely to the advent of Hans Nibel to the Board of Directors, Benz as a firm had gone over completely to a policy of racing and voted large sums of money to that end.

At the 1908 Olympia exhibition, two 28-h p. cars were shown, both with live axles. A 40-h.p. chassis with chain-drive was also exhibited. Quoting from *The Motor*, 'Considerably more interest is being evinced in Benz models this year than in previous years, owing to their smart performance this season. In design, these cars possess no feature of novelty, being modelled entirely on approved lines.'

## 1909

In 1909, Benz had many successes in America. At least one of the previous year's cars, its power increased from 120 h.p. to 150 h.p., had crossed the Atlantic. In March, David Bruce-Brown gained the Dewar Trophy by taking the world speed record for amateur drivers over a mile at Daytona Beach at a speed of about 109 m.p.h., later taking the ten-miles record at 115 m.p.h. In August, at Indianapolis, the great Barney Oldfield took the world's record for the standing start mile in 43·1 seconds on one of the 150-h.p. cars. Three days later, the 200-h.p. *Blitzen* Benz made its debut.

At the Brussels 'World Championship' meeting in October, the 200-h.p. *Blitzen* Benz made its appearance with Victor Héméry at the wheel, in the class with the exciting title of 'Great racing-cars with absolutely no restrictions'; he was nearly 10 m.p.h. faster than Pilette's 1908 Grand Prix Mercedes, and with a time of 31·2 seconds, established a world record.

Towards the end of the year Victor Héméry took a *Blitzen*-Benz to Brooklands. He broke five records. The flying half-mile in 14·1 seconds and the flying kilometre in 17·8 seconds were both world records. This car is probably the *Blitzen* Benz shipped to America by Benz Auto Import, and driven by Barney Oldfield at Daytona Beach in 1910, as related below. After passing through a number of hands and being often modified, it is believed to have been burnt out in a garage fire some years later.

18- and 40-h.p. four-cylinder cars, both with live axles, were at the Motor Show. *The Motor* credits them with '. . . some features, which, though not novel, are seldom to be found on other present-day cars. The two sturdy water-cooled brakes on the chain countershaft are probably unique at the present day. In few cars, also, does one find . . . that of two countershaft brakes each should be independently operated, though one is interconnected with the clutch.' High tension magneto ignition was fitted.

## 1910

During the winter of 1909–10, Barney Oldfield had a *Blitzen* Benz shipped to America, and in the spring, at Daytona Beach, Florida, he took three records—two American and one world record, the flying mile. This latter was now accomplished in 27·3 seconds, which was then about as fast as a car had ever travelled.

A 75-h.p. car won the unlimited class at the Ries hill-climb in May. This was a private entry driven by a works driver, Franz Heim. Few people remember Heim today as he was completely overshadowed by his two great contemporaries, Héméry and Hanriot, with whom he used to travel round as reserve or co-driver. He was an extremely competent engineer and driver and later left the firm of Benz to set up on his own account.

In May, the Russians held the Moscow–Orel race, which, for the most part, was run over very bad roads. The consistent success of Benz cars in Russian races suggests that they were the only vehicles rugged enough to be driven at top speed over these appalling roads. The race was won by Isajeff on a 60-h.p. Benz with George Gass on the old 50-h.p. car that he had sold to the Russian Ministry of War, in second place.

In October, Jenatzy came face to face with the *Blitzen* Benz at the Gaillon hill-climb in France. But even the 'Red Devil', on his elderly 180-h.p. Mercedes was no match for that hardened campaigner Fritz Erle on a much faster machine. Fritz Erle made fastest time of the day, and established a new record for the course, 23 seconds over the measured flying kilometre. Jenatzy was second in 26·4 seconds. Soon after, the red-bearded Belgian tyre manufacturer, perhaps the most picturesque of all the bizarre and heroic figures of the earliest days, retired from active participation in racing.

On the other side of the Atlantic, David Bruce-Brown won the American Grand Prize and Héméry was second. This must have been about the closest-fought finish in the history of motor racing. Over a course of just over four hundred miles Bruce-Brown was the winner *by one-tenth of a second*! Both men were driving 150-h.p. Benz cars. It had been quite a good year, and on the whole the policy of the Benz Company seemed to be justified. This was to race as much as possible to increase the sales of their beautifully made, but rather dull and uninspired touring-cars. The truth of this is only too well borne out by the fact that Benz sales were never better than during the years that Mercedes withdrew from racing.

## 1911

In 1911 Benz brought out a new 200-h.p. model of curiously retrograde appearance. It looked more like a Grand Prix racing-car of Jenatzy's heyday, five years earlier. However, at its first appearance it won the Ries six-kilometre hill-climb at an average speed of 50 m.p.h. with Franz Heim at the wheel. More will be heard of this model in Major Hornsted's account of the Benz racing-cars he drove on pp. 114–116.

On August Bank Holiday at Brooklands, a record crowd had assembled to see the private match for a wager of one hundred guineas between Gordon Watney's fast Mercedes driven by Lord Vernon, and the Maharaja of Tikari's Grand Prix Renault. But in addition to this match there was plenty of good racing. Hornsted's 60-h.p. Benz was given eight seconds start of Watney's elderly but swift *120* Mercedes at scratch. This did not prove enough and the Mercedes romped home an easy winner. Re-handicapping provided some very close finishes in the 100-m.p.h. long and the August sprint handicaps. Hornsted, driving Arkwright's Benz, won both.

## 1912

Benz cars scored a number of successes in minor races during the year. Worthy of mention among the more important events was the Gaillon hill-climb, held on the long slope between Vernon and Rouen on the *grande route* between Paris and Dieppe. Fritz Erle, on a two-seater *Blitzen* Benz rocketed up, making much the fastest time of the day, and establishing a record at over 101 m.p.h. average speed. Some idea of how fast he went can be gauged from the fact that an early Bugatti, its class winner, took over twice as long! It was obvious to the spectators that Erle only just had the huge Benz under control and a good many of them, when the huge projectile thundered towards them, scurried madly up the banks to positions of greater safety. This epic climb was Fritz Erle's last but one appearance on the famous *Blitzen* Benz. He was now nearly forty years old and had been racing with great success for sixteen years. He was entitled to rest on his laurels.

On the British market at this time and during the next few

years many Benz models were to be bought. In the autumn of 1911 a new 12/20-h.p. four-cylinder car was produced. Its bore and stroke were 72 × 120 mm. It had a three-bearing crankshaft, a chain-driven camshaft, magneto ignition, a hot spot to the induction and pressure lubrication to the bearings. The price of the four-seater tourer was £365. *The Autocar* tested one of these cars in the autumn of 1911; this is what they had to say of it.

The small Benz may best be described as a full-size touring-car in miniature. The graceful narrow radiator with the bonnet upswept to the inwardly-curved dash, and the long straight lines of the body, terminating in the one-man hood encased in a neat black covering, are more than pleasing to the eye, while the quiet running of the engine allowed one audibly to hear remarks made by people on the pavement. Starting on a trial of one of these cars recently, one pull up of the handle sufficed to start the engine; tappet noises and carburettor hiss were seemingly non-existent, and apparently without sacrifice of efficiency. The presence of the engine, even at high speeds, may be felt rather than heard. It is excellently balanced, save at about 32 m.p.h. in top gear; at this point the engine has a slight 'period', barely perceptible. It must, however, be mentioned that the car placed at our disposal had evidently done some hard running, so that the quietness of the engine is distinctly a feature on which its manufacturers deserve congratulation. At speeds less or more than 32 m.p.h. no vibration was perceptible. The first part of our journey lay from Shepherd's Bush to Acton, where the road surface is in a condition of which those responsible should be thoroughly ashamed. But those who rode in the back said that the potholes were barely noticeable, and riding in the Benz caused us to cease to wonder why certain German competitors in the Prince Henry Tour made such a splendid average from Osnabruck to Bremen and beyond. The gate on the little Benz is slightly out of the common, as the reverse is through first and then forward, but otherwise it presents no peculiarity. Speed changing up or down we found quite easy after a few minutes' practice, and the knack of a silent change was easily and quickly acquired. Traffic driving owing to the liveliness of the engine, the easy gear changing, and the excellence of the brakes (both of which were smooth in action and effective), was a real pleasure, and when the open country was reached it was hard to realize that the engine was only 72 mm. in the bore, and though it is rated as only 12 h.p., it pulled as well as many a 15·9. The carburettor works admirably. There is no hiss of the air intake, and the engine gets away swiftly and silently. The magneto is the self-advancing Eisemann. It appears to work splendidly, as the car will accelerate from slow speeds, even on an upgrade, without a trace of a knock or any sign of labouring. The steering is particularly good, being very light and quite irreversible. The steering position is good and the arrangement of the control pedals excellent, while the placing of the petrol tank behind the front seats, and parted by a plush-covered board allows plenty of locker space, and ample room for the feet of the driver's companion.

Leaving Ealing, we entered the lanes and reached Uxbridge by the back way, after which we took the main Oxford road to Beaconsfield, and did some more lane work among the Chilterns, where the roads are narrow and gradients abound. As this was a test run, steep hills were sought for. The first was Rectory Hill, Amersham, which has a gradient of 1 in 7 or worse. This with a load of four called for first speed, but clearly showed by the amount in hand that Gatten Bank alone would slow that Benz Baby in first. Gore Hill, Amersham was next tried. This is longer, but not so steep (1 in 8). Nearly half the hill was taken in third, it was just too steep for second on the crest, and the hill was finished in first with the throttle almost closed. The particular car we drove was very well equipped. Two speedometers were fitted—an A.T. and a Star—of which one was cardan-shaft and the other front wheel driven, and it was interesting to note that both agreed. The screen, which is peculiar to Benz cars, is entirely brass bound, and its angle can be controlled by a screw near the driver, so that he can alter it as he likes without assistance. If we may criticize, it is a trifle too narrow, and would be all the nicer if the brass binding went round the sides and bottom, and the top edge of the glass were left plain, as the brass binding is sometimes a little irritating to the vision.

Besides the new *12/20*, other Benz models available in 1912 were the *15/25* (80 × 130 mm.), the *28/35* (95 × 140 mm.), the *38/45* (120 × 140 mm.), the *45/65* (130 × 160 mm.), the *45/90* (130 × 190 mm.) later known as the 100 h.p., and finally the 100 h.p. (185 × 200 mm.) later known as the 200-h.p. Benz. In addition to this formidable array, there were three Benz-Sohne models of 16/20 (85 × 115 mm.), 17·9 and 20/30 h.p., and, like all the others, four-cylinder cars. The Benz-Sohne car was in one sense more truly a Benz than the products of Mannheim, in that it was actually made by Karl Benz and his sons at Ladenburg, Karl Benz having left the original company some time previously. *The Autocar*, incidentally, was 'very favourably impressed' with the new *16/20*.

Descriptive horse-power ratings were constantly being altered and it comes as no surprise therefore, that in the following amusing description of a run in a Benz it is said to be 'rated at 40 h.p. and described as 27/80 h.p.' We quote from an article entitled 'Touring in a Brooklands Benz', which appeared in *The Motor*, dated January 28, 1913.

In the moonlight stood revealed a Benz in Brooklands garb defiling the air with smoke and generally disturbing the peace which reigns in our little Stirlingshire village when the lights begin to twinkle on the hill-side. . . . With pointed stern and bonnet extensions, the length of the car seemed tremendous in the darkness, and the impression of speed was enhanced by the disc wheels and the powerful beat of the engine. The car's identity was, however, obvious, for it was the Benz which still holds the half-mile, mile and kilometre records at Brooklands in the 40-h.p. class. Rated at 40 h.p., described as 27–80 h.p., it carried a speedometer graduated to 100 m.p.h., and had done its half-mile in 17⅓ seconds, which worked out gives 103·759 m.p.h., so that here was a car of a new order for Scottish roads.

Once on the road we dropped down through the village [Strathblane] and out half a mile on the black road, it seemed, with one tap of the accelerator. In a moment a hill faced us, but with the accelerator left down there was a rush of cold air and we were swooping quietly down the other side. Over the rough and twisting road we went in a series of swoops which did not settle down to a steady pull till the long stretches of the Stirling road were reached. Here, where the road stretches wide, straight and quiet for mile after mile the car could be given its head, and the vision of that pointed bonnet burrowing its way through the night in the white lane of the lamps had a fascination which made one feel as if, with the engine, one must cry for more speed. In Stirling we stopped to clean a faulty burner . . . we were soon out on the North Road, only to be stopped again by lack of light.

For a while back we had put the road down as being particularly bumpy, but now not only did we find the generator empty but two of the coils of the lever spring suspension had given way. . . . From Dunkeld to Perth was over wet roads with a drizzling rain, which had perforce to be faced, as our car boasted no screen or hood. But on wet roads or dry the big car never skidded, thanks to the long wheelbase and our big-ribbed Palmers. . . . In Perth we stopped for a moment to make sure of the way and unwittingly gave the fright of his life to the constable who answered us. As he stepped back and the car moved away there was a thunderous explosion in the silencer and a three-fork tongue of flame shot out of the exhaust pipe, to the consternation of the onlookers, but no harm was done. . . .

Of the car one must write some words of praise. Such a car was obviously not intended for touring on Scottish roads, yet nobody could say that it was unsuitable for the high road. The steering was delightful, and the engine, considering its high compression, wonderfully flexible. Certainly, despite the power, one could not hang on to top gear on a twisty hill, but as even on first she could do very much in excess of the limit there was no objection to changing down, particularly as the change was as sweet as in a 'Baby' Benz.

Naturally the engine had a healthy appetite for oil and petrol but against this is the fact that the car never needed a moment's attention—barring, of course, the supplementary suspension—and was wonderfully comfortable over all kinds of surface. And so I look back with pleasure to that September week-end in the long grey Benz which threw the miles behind it in effortless speed up and down those Scottish hills.

## 1913

Other firms were producing new racing-cars, and Mercedes came back with a 75-h.p. six-cylinder aero-engine prototype in a short, compact, well-balanced chassis. Benz had produced nothing new since the 1908 Grand Prix cars and the wonderful 200-h.p. *Blitzen*. In the bigger events they were losing ground, although in the more outlying European countries they still won a number of races and speed trials. The Benz Company were in a difficult position, as they were much occupied with demands from the German military and naval authorities.

They were employing a staff of 5,500 at this time.

Early in the year, Fritz Erle made his last appearance at the Limonest hill-climb near Lyons. It is a long hill of three and three-quarter kilometres. He raced up it, at an average speed of about 70 m.p.h., winning his class and breaking all records for the hill. This was the last time this great driver was seen in a *Blitzen* Benz, although later he drove in a number of small events in lower-powered cars.

In two entertaining articles which he wrote for *The Autocar* (published on December 22 and 29, 1944) Major L. G. Hornsted, a very well-known racing-driver of bygone days, describes the three racing Benz cars which he had prior to the 1914 war. They were owned by H. A. Arkwright and 'Cupid' Hornsted drove them for him.

The first which came his way was the 'Little Benz' with a 5715 cc. engine, bore and stroke 105 × 165 mm., and an R.A.C. rating of 27·3 h.p. This car was, of course, the 'Brooklands' Benz in which the contributor to *The Motor* had so enjoyed a drive in Scotland as just described. The four cylinders had two inlet and two exhaust valves per cylinder and two magnetos supplied the eight sparking plugs. Splash lubrication was employed, assisted by a Friedeman oiler. After winning a 'Two Mile Sprint' at Brooklands at the end of 1910, Hornsted and his mechanics converted the lubrication system to direct forced feed at about 80 lb. pressure, assisted by centrifugal force. Many other modifications were made from time to time, and the car was a 'tiger for plugs and oil'. However, all troubles apart, Hornsted won many races with the car and in 1911 took the then 40-h.p. class records, the flying half-mile at 103·759 previously referred to, the flying kilometre at 102.990 and the flying mile at 96·264 m.p.h. He also took the 'Long Record', as it was known, which consisted of ten laps from a standing start, 26·8 miles, at 84·41 m.p.h. Major Hornsted summed up the Little Benz as 'a great little car and an education in the perversity of inanimate matter and how to do without sleep on Fridays. But we eventually got it civilized and quite reliable.'

In January, 1912, the 150-h.p. Benz arrived in London. This had a four-cylinder engine with a bore of 155 mm. and a stroke of 200 mm., giving a capacity of 15,095 cc. and an R.A.C. rating of 59·6 h.p. The single inlet and exhaust valve per cylinder were operated by push rods, and two magnetos supplied the two plugs for each cylinder. Final drive was by chains. When Major Hornsted got the car to Brooklands 'the first thing we did was to take down the road springs, remove the third leaf, turn it bottom upwards and pull it down as a damper spring on top of the main leaf in each case. Instead of being almost impossible to sit in, the car became quite reasonable at speed. In common with all the Benz cars the 150-h.p. steered like a dream. There never was, and I think there never will be, anything with better steering.' The car won a number of races at Brooklands and, after a visit to America, where the great car, with Hornsted at the wheel was successful in a race at Weymouth, New Jersey, made fastest time of the day on the sands at Saltburn. Prior to Saltburn, however, certain troubles developed.

Before taking it [i.e. the 150 h.p.] to Saltburn we decided to attend to the clutch, which had developed a ridge. When this was refitted and re-erected the clutch thrust withdrawal ball race was put up slightly too tightly. We were going up the hill near Esher at about 25 m.p.h. on our way to Brooklands for a final tune-up when the clutch and brake pedals suddenly disappeared through the floorboards, came up again on the other side, caught the steering column a mighty blow and disappeared again. Somehow I got my feet and legs out of the way and switched off. The ball race had seized solid and torn the cross-tube carrying the pedals out of its sockets, and the whole lot was whirling round with the clutch shaft.

This all happened on Thursday afternoon and the race at Saltburn was on the following Saturday at midday. I ran the car back to a little garage on the right-hand side of the road, where I dismantled things and more or less straightened the pedal tube, but the ball race was solid. With the help of a lathe whose chuck ran like a swash-plate, and a screwdriver as a tool, I turned up a phosphor-bronze (or brass) thrust block. On getting back to the workshop at about 11 p.m. I robbed a standard *38/60* Benz chassis of its clutch withdrawal assembly, and, with an unrivalled crew of mechanics working like fiends, we got everything done by about midnight on the Friday. We then went for a trial spin up the Cromwell Road, taking good care to come back a different way, the car being notorious at Brooklands for its thunderous exhaust!

They left for Saltburn at 5 a.m. on the Saturday, getting there at 10.30, won two races and averaged 90.93 m.p.h. over the flying kilometre. Then home to London in the dark with the aid of three 2s. 6d. cycle oil-lamps, a moon and no glass screen.

The third car was the famous Big Benz of 200 h.p. This was exactly the same as the 150 h.p. except for having forced feed lubrication (the 150 h.p. had splash) and for a bore increased to 185 mm., giving a capacity of 21,504 cc. and an R.A.C. rating of 84·9 h.p. The rear sprockets for the chain drive were 44 to 44, giving 140 m.p.h. at 1400 r.p.m. on top. The wheelbase was about 8 ft. 6 in.

This car arrived just before the 1913 Olympia show, and we were all wildly excited to see what it could do. . . . Off we started for

Brooklands, and I soon found that on wood paving the engine had so much power that the rear wheels just spun if you even looked at the accelerator too sharply. . . . We got the standing start records for the half-mile at 70·47 m.p.h. and the kilometre at 73·57 m.p.h. These two records had stood for five years, being set up by Hémery on a similar Benz in 1909. . . . I think that we beat world's records twenty-seven times altogether on this car, taking the half-mile standing start at 71·25, thus improving on our old figure, the standing kilometre at 73·57 m.p.h., the standing mile at 87·34 m.p.h., the flying half-mile at 123·88 m.p.h., the mile at 124·10 (doing 128·16 m.p.h. in one direction) and the 2, 5 and 10 miles from a flying start.

In July 1914 Hornsted won three races on the 21½-litre Benz at Ostend and that was the last time he drove it. He heard that the car was in Brussels as late as 1916.

## 1914

On January 14, Hornsted was out again at Brooklands, and, as related, amassed, with the great *Blitzen* Benz, no less than seven flying-start records from the half-mile to the ten-miles. Jack Toop, who was later killed in a Peugeot, drove with him. But the shape of things to come were beginning to show only too plainly. The Russian Ministry of War ordained a petrol consumption competition. This foreshadowing of wartime austerity was won by Fritz Erle on a 10/30-h.p. Benz with a Zenith carburettor. Apart from this, the pattern of 1914 was very similar to the previous year. Benz cars won most of the Russian events, including a 54-verst race on the ice at St. Petersburg. There were minor successes in small events and Hornsted did quite well at Brooklands, among other successes capturing the lap record at about 106 m.p.h. While he was attempting the hour record, a back tyre tread came adrift and hit his elbow. No bones were broken but Colonel Lindsay Lloyd, Clerk of the Course, persuaded him to postpone the attempt on the record in case the joint stiffened.

Back in 1908, about the time when Diesel was beginning to make the compression ignition engine work, a young French inventor, Prosper L'Orange, was doing much the same thing. Nibel and the directors of Benz A.G. were not slow to realize the tremendous potentialities in the heavy-fuel engine and although they knew that his engine, like Diesel's, was a very long way from perfection, persuaded Prosper L'Orange to join them at Mannheim. He must have taken German nationality, for he remained a director of the Benz Company throughout the 1914–18 war. His work did not bear fruit, as far as wheel vehicles were concerned, until 1923, when he had been with the firm for fifteen years. They exhibited their

Diesel tractor at the Königsberg Fair in 1923 and sold the first one to a farmer in East Prussia. Two months later, in August, the Benz Diesel lorry came on the market.

The directors of the Benz Company had long realized that some form of combination with the Mercedes Company would solve many difficulties for both parties. Dr. Jahr originally mooted the scheme in 1919, but, as neither of these firms would yield any of their jealously guarded sovereign rights, the merger made little headway. In 1923, however, inflation in Germany, together with other economic troubles, caused both sides to view the question in a much more realistic manner. Dr. Jahr opened the question again, and in May 1924 an 'Agreement of Mutual Interest' was signed between the two firms. It is pleasant to note that the first article on the Agenda was that the two firms should jointly guarantee Karl and Berta Benz complete freedom from all financial worries for the rest of their lives. This may seem a little superfluous at first, but at that time Germany was in the grip of galloping inflation when the life savings of old people could vanish practically overnight. Wilhelm Kissel, an able administrator and engineer was made, in 1924, a director for co-ordination of the combined interests of the firms of Daimler and Benz. One of the first outward and visible signs of this was that those three very brilliant engineers, Porsche, Nibel, and Nallinger, all went on the board of the Daimler-Benz Company.

An immediate blow was struck at production costs. Both firms pooled their entire coach-building work in a huge factory at Sindelfingen. But, in spite of all this, crippling taxation handicapped the markets both at home and abroad, while American competition was more than fierce. Matters were so serious that early in 1926 some of the board considered shutting down the plant. Dr. Jahr, who was firmly against such a step, rallied the opposition and they carried the day. On June 29, 1926, the two companies were finally and completely fused into one, under the name of Daimler-Benz Aktiengesellschaft.

In 1925, there was the great motor jubilee in Munich. Karl Benz, although he was in poor health, sat beside his son Eugen on one of his earliest cars, to the delight of the huge crowds; a large number of early Benz cars took part in the procession. Daimler's first car and the replica of his first motor-cycle were on view, and all the early cars that could be mustered throughout the length and breadth of Germany. Lautenschlager and Salzer, victors of the historic 1914 Grand Prix, and many other early racing-drivers attended. This was the last public appearance of Karl Benz.

When it became known that the end of the great pioneer was near, motorists from all over Germany assembled on April 2, 1929, on the road from Heidelberg to Handschusheim. From there, they drove in solemn cortège to Ladenburg where they left their cars in and around Karl Benz Platz. Then they and many thousands of people from neighbouring towns gathered under the windows of the modest Benz house and made laudatory and formal speeches in his honour. Frau Benz, his sons, grandsons, and relations came forward and acknowledged them, but it is feared that Karl Benz was too feeble to realize the honours that were being paid him. Two days later he died, aged eighty-five. Frau Berta Benz, heroine of the first long-distance drive so long ago, died in 1944 at the age of ninety-five.

In 1933, a memorial to Benz was unveiled in Ladenburg and a plaque placed upon his house. But, in truth, of Karl Benz it could be said, as with our own Sir Christopher Wren, '*Si monumentum requiris circumspice.*'

## PAUL DAIMLER

It will be remembered that Gottlieb Daimler had four sons, of whom Paul and Adolf were the eldest. Paul inherited in full the engineering talents of his father, while Adolf, who died at the early age of forty-two, demonstrated his gifts in technical management, rather than in designing.

In 1902, Paul carried out one of his father's last wishes and took over the direction of the Austrian Daimler works at Wiener Neustadt, the industrial town just outside Vienna. His particular fancy was a light car he had designed himself, known as the *P.D.Wagen*. This was ready to go into production in 1900, but in view of the tremendous demand for the successful bigger-engined Mercedes cars, only very few were made. While Paul was at the Wiener Neustadt works from 1902 to 1905, he showed his versatility by building a racing-car developing 120 h.p. In 1905, he went to Untertürkheim where he and his brother Adolf worked together. When Wilhelm Maybach retired, Paul Daimler became chief engineer and designer and in March 1913, on the death of his brother Adolf, he took over the technical directorship as well.

In July 1907, some months before Paul Daimler took over, the international commission, meeting at Ostend to decide on a formula for the year 1908, agreed to abandon the 'fuel allowance', and impose in its stead a limitation of bore of 155 mm. and a minimum weight of 1100 kg. There was no restriction on engine stroke, so most manufacturers began to build engines with abnormally long strokes, the Grand Prix Mercedes for 1908 having a stroke of 180 mm. Even allowing for a maximum engine speed of about 1600 r.p.m. the piston speed must have been rather alarming. However, as we shall see, the Grand Prix Mercedes cars of 1908 were very successful for several years.

## 1908

Early in April, Dario Resta took Fry's *120* to Brooklands for some records. People who remember motor racing before 1914 say that the Mercedes which Fry drove was always beautifully prepared and turned out. On this occasion, he gained the world's record for the flying half-mile and also a long-distance track record. Needless to say, after this, the handicappers at the Easter Brooklands meeting were rather hard on him and he only managed to achieve one second place.

We have already described the French Grand Prix, won by Lautenschlager on a Mercedes. After the race two of the team cars came to England. C. R. Fry bought one for Resta to drive and later sold it to A. W. Tate. This car is now in America, beautifully preserved and in absolutely original condition. Gordon Watney bought another for Lord Vernon.

At Semmering, two racing-car classes were run, one to the Prince Henry 8-litre formula, the other for Grand Prix formula.

120-h.p. Mercedes. (*The Edward Mayer Collection*)

1908/9 130-h.p. Mercedes 'Semmering' racer, fitted with Mercedes racing body. Note the removable rims on the rear wheels. (*The Edward Mayer Collection*)

Willy Poege won the former, on his Prince Henry *90* and was second in the latter on the car he had driven at Dieppe. Theodore Dreher had bought one of the Grand Prix cars and Salzer drove it for him to win its class. There was also a class for racing-cars with no bore limit. Both Poege and Dreher had, among other cars, big-bore Mercedes, giving 150 h.p. Salzer, driving for Dreher, won this class and established a new record for Semmering. Poege was second. Both Dreher and Poege were wealthy men and kept large stables of cars. Dreher had been a pioneer motorist, and although he occasionally drove himself in trials, he generally hired a professional driver for racing. After 1911, he dropped somewhat out of the competition world, but still maintained a magnificent stable of motor-cars. He was killed in a car crash in 1914.

After a reasonably successful year it must have been a great disappointment when the directors announced that next year they would build no fresh racing-cars and that the firm would withdraw from racing, temporarily at least. There were a number of reasons for this, including the fact that, now they had made the concessions to labour, motor-cars were costing them more to build and they had less money to spend on racing, which even for those days was beginning to be fantastically expensive. Also, it may be remembered, in 1908, a number of the principal manufacturers, appalled at the mounting costs of Grand Prix racing, signed a pact together agreeing virtually to abstain from it. As a result of this there was no French Grand Prix in 1909. Later on, it became clear that for the Mercedes Company to give up racing was false economy. They still had a very full programme of touring-cars; at that time they were building at least six different models, all shaft-driven with poppet valves.

In the early months of this year H.M. King Edward VII took delivery of a 45-h.p. four-cylinder Mercedes. In *The Autocar* of February 1 there appeared a detailed technical account of this chassis.

Callers at the handsome premises in Long Acre where Messrs. Du Cros–Mercedes Ltd. show the various current types of the world-famous Mercedes cars may now inspect there a chassis of the 1908 45-h.p. Mercedes. . . . The frame is, as usual, of pressed cambered channel section steel, inswept forward of the dashboard to afford ample locking, but otherwise straight. The cross members are seen to be of similar section, properly splayed and gusseted where they make junction with the side members. The frame is supported on four semi-elliptical springs of considerable length, all the frictional or wearing parts in which are provided with lubricators. The engine is of the well-recognized Mercedes pattern, cylinders with opposed valve chambers being cast in pairs, inductions on right and exhausts on the left. The induction pipe and carburettor are kept well up to the top of the cylinders, giving excellent access to the valve tappets and spindles . . . the induction pipe is dually branched and carries the carburettor centrally, so that it and the dual induction pipe can be at once dismounted by detaching the four bolts which secure the latter to the valve chamber openings, the petrol union, and the throttle connexions. Drain cocks are fitted to the lower portion of the crank chamber, and also to the lowest point of the water circulation, viz. in the bend of the suction pipe below the pump.

The carburettor, which is hot-water jacketed, is of the traversing piston type, this design having proved itself to the satisfaction of the makers in the Herkomer Trophy of last year. The mixture is fired by Bosch low-tension magneto, gear-driven off the exhaust camshaft, and supplying current to the new Bosch magneto plugs. The magneto, water pump and connexions, lubricator thereto, and lubricating tank with enclosed pump are regarded as very accessible. The flanged exhaust port, which is kept well up to the top of the valve chambers, is encased to form a jacket, whence the hot air feed to the carburettor can be taken. A radiator belt-driven fan is fitted, but the arms of the flywheel are vaned, and the engine space is enclosed entirely by bonnet and apron. A sheet steel apron runs rearward to the back of the gear-box. A new type of lubricating tank is provided. It has eight direct-acting plunger pumps, and oil is delivered by three separate leads to the crankshaft bearings, one to the steering gear case, one to the clutch striking fork, one to the magneto spindle and one to each pair of spindles. The usual well-known Mercedes coil clutch conveys the drive from the engine to the change speed gear, a flexible coupling being introduced between the two. Both gearshafts and the countershaft run on ball bearings. The primary shaft, which is feathered, carries two sliding sleeves. Two powerful band brakes are fitted on the countershaft, one on each side of the gear-box. These brakes are water cooled from the dashboard. The car is controlled from the steering wheel, the ignition and throttle levers being mounted in quadrants stationary in the centre of the steering wheel. The control can also

45-h.p. Mercedes chassis. (*The Edward Mayer Collection*)

be operated from the pedal upon the footboard. On the dashboard is found a pressure-feed greaser to clutchshaft, a hand oil-pump to the crank chamber, a water tell-tale to countershaft brake drums, a petrol tank pressure gauge, a sight water circulating gauge, and ignition cut-outs, five in number, by which any one cylinder can be cut out or the ignition switched off. In design, finish and detail the Mercedes people have never been surpassed, and we are of the opinion that the examination of this chassis at the showrooms of Messrs. Du Cros–Mercedes Ltd. will convince anyone that the Mercedes standard of excellence has been fully maintained.

At the 1908 Olympia Show, three cars were exhibited, a 35-h.p. landaulet on a new live-axle chassis, a 45-h.p. chassis, chain-driven as in 1908, and a 65-h.p. limousine.

Early in 1909 we learn from *The Motor* that

Two Mercedes landaulets, each with a motor of 55 h.p., have been added to the German Emperor's already large stock of cars. They are upholstered in the firm's red-glazed leather, with dull-gilt mountings and door-handles of tortoiseshell. Altogether there are now five cars of this type and make in the Imperial garage.

## 1909

But even if the firm itself abstained from racing, there were plenty of private individuals keen enough to carry on in the year 1909, and they had many successes.

In the autumn at Semmering we find an interesting entry.

Salzer was driving for Theodore Dreher a *16/40* Knight-engined Mercedes. This must have been the first time that one of the sleeve-valve Mercedes had been seen; they were not on the market till some time later. In the unlimited racing-car class the struggle between Poege and Dreher continued on the same cars as the previous year. Salzer, driving for Dreher, put up a

45-h.p. Mercedes with detachable hard top. (*The Edward Mayer Collection*)

Four-cylinder sleeve-valve Mercedes, 1910. (*Mercedes-Benz*)

1909 45-h.p. Mercedes. (*The Edward Mayer Collection*)

new record for the hill and Poege, driving himself this time, was a very close second. At the Tervueren races in Belgium Jenatzy won his class on a 55-h.p. Mercedes, but both he and Théodore Pilette on their 1908 Grand Prix cars were soundly beaten by Victor Héméry on one of the first of the famous *Blitzen* Benz. In fact, striking a balance, 1909 was a Benz year much more than a Mercedes year.

Mercedes cars were not shown at the Olympia Show in 1909, but were on view at the showrooms in Long Acre. Two new cars were on view, the *15/20* and the 25 h.p. The *15/20* had at four-cylinder overhead valve engine, the bore and stroke being 80 × 130 mm. The chassis price was £490. *The Motor* said 'The two smaller models will be very light and very fast and are intended to appeal specially to a sporting clientele'. Shown as well were 35- and 45-h.p. cars, these, as well as the *15/20* and *25* having live axles. Finally, there was the heavy brigade, 45-, 65-, and 75-h.p. cars, all chain-driven. The King had recently taken delivery of a 65-h.p. Mercedes. The *75* had a six-cylinder engine, all the others having four cylinders.

There was an interesting article in *The Motor* in February 1909, written by Henry Sturmey, entitled 'The Mercedes Patents'. Daimler Motoren Gesellschaft had decided to enforce their rights in thirty-seven patents. We quote Mr. Sturmey.

Quite apart from the legal aspect of the case, however, an examination of the seven-and-thirty patents owned by the Mercedes people, and covering the last ten years is exceedingly interesting, as showing the trend of thought of the experts in the Mercedes works, and also as showing the influence which Mercedes practice has had upon Continental construction generally and to

A 'flat radiator 90' circa 1909, with very advanced coachwork for its date. (*The Edward Mayer Collection*)

a large extent on our own. The principal patent around which, I believe, the fight is to be waged—if fight there must be—is the 'gate' change, or selective gear system, which is now so very largely adopted in one form or another throughout the trade.

Other devices quoted of Mercedes construction, for all of which patents had been taken out, affected the honeycomb radiator with the fan at the back, the water-cooled brake system, the splaying of the wheels, four-wheel drive, a governor for automatically advancing and retarding the spark, and a method of starting the engine without turning the handle by the use of compressed air in conjunction with a carburettor device. The Daimler Co. in England had a right to use all Mercedes patents, as had also Rolls-Royce and S. F. Edge under licence, presumably for Napiers.

One thing of considerable importance did happen during the year 1909. The three-pointed star was adopted as the emblem of the company. The managing director, Alfred von Kaulla, was looking for a trade-mark. Paul and Adolf Daimler told him the story of the star on their father's house and of his having said, 'A star shall arise from here, and I hope that it will bring blessings to us and to our children.' Von Kaulla thought that it would be a charming tribute to the founder of the firm, if a star were adopted as trade-mark. Inquiries at

45-h.p. Mercedes. (*The Edward Mayer Collection*)

the patent office produced the information that thirty-one other firms also used a star as their trade-mark. However, the board of Directors were so keen on the idea that after some pressure it was found possible to register a star together with the name 'Mercedes'. At first, both a three-pointed star and a four-pointed star were used, the latter but rarely, and the four-pointed star was soon dropped. From 1911 to 1916 there were variations to the surround of the star which bore the name of the factory of origin, either Untertürkheim or Marienfeld. It was in 1909, also, that the two accents were dropped from the name Mercedes. From 1916 to 1922 the large three-pointed star was surrounded by a band containing miniature three-pointed stars.

The Benz trade-mark was a laurel wreath, and during the amalgamation of the two companies there were some heated exchanges between their respective directors as to which trade-mark should be adopted. Finally, a compromise was reached by putting the laurel wreath round the star, which was quite attractive. This was used from August 1926 until

65-h.p. Mercedes. (*The Edward Mayer Collection*)

1937, when it was replaced by the plain star and ring which remains today. Here is a small note that may be of interest to 'star-gazers'. The *33/180* (high chassis) and *36/220* models had a plain star soldered on either side of the radiator. But the *38/250* and some later models have just one enamelled plaque with the star and laurel wreath in the centre of the radiator.

## 1910

The major victory of the year, also the swan song of that great sportsman Willy Poege, came in the Tsar Nicholas touring trials in Russia. The course of over two thousand miles started and finished at St. Petersburg and went via Moscow and Kiev. Three *16/50* Mercedes finished in that traditional line ahead, first, second and third. They were driven by Willy Poege, Consul Fritsch, and Arthur von Lüde. As far as is known this was the last time that the redoubtable Willy Poege drove in competition. He had every right to rest on his laurels for he had, in his decade of motoring, achieved a record as fine as that of any amateur. He gave up motor racing to take up flying and was one of Germany's pioneer pilots. He died of heart failure in 1914 when he was only forty-five years old.

At the Ostend Week, Camille Jenatzy had no less than six class wins with what is described as an aero-engined Mercedes with a capacity of nearly 15 litres. Later in the year, as related earlier, he came in a good second to Fritz Erle's meteoric climb in the *Blitzen* Benz at Gaillon. And that too was Jenatzy's swan song. Every follower of the sport was sorry to see him go; a very colourful character whose career runs like a scarlet thread through the strange patchwork of early motoring history. It is uncertain when he started motor-racing, but he always seems to have been there; first driving weird and fantastic forlorn hopes, then Dinsmore's cars, and finally Mercedes of his own. This red-bearded Belgian probably reached the zenith of his career in 1903, when he won the Gordon Bennett race. The following year, when driving in the 1904 Gordon Bennett race on the Homburg circuit, he had a horrible experience. He was coming downhill to an open railway crossing at Wehrheim at about ninety miles an hour, when he was aghast to see a railway shunting-engine stationary across the road. Somehow, he managed to get his great rocking bolide under sufficient control to avoid it, but it broke his nerve, and everyone said that his driving was never quite the same again. Like von Delius, a quarter of a

King Edward VII and the Prince of Wales (later George V), in a Mercedes circa 1910 which may well have belonged to the Duke of Westminster. (*The Edward Mayer Collection*)

century later, after he had been hit in the face by a bird, it did something to his self-confidence. Jenatzy always used to tell his friends that he would die in a Mercedes. As he continued to say this after he had given up racing, it is not surprising that no one took it very seriously. He was, however, correct; in 1913 he died in his Mercedes touring-car, as a result of a shooting accident.

## 1911

During 1911, with other firms building newer and more modern racing-cars, Mercedes, who had produced nothing since the 1908 Grand Prix winners, were not in a position to do any good in the more important races, especially as the firm still held back from racing. In spite of this, some magnificent results were achieved by independent drivers at the wheels of quite old cars.

The only distinguishing feature of 1911 was the frequency with which Mercedes cars raced at Brooklands. Gordon Watney had established a small workshop near the track in which he removed the usually ugly German bodies from his various Mercedes, and replaced them with attractive sporting coachwork of his own design. He also tuned the cars and prepared them for speed events. In January, one of his cars, with Laurent driving for him, took a couple of records at Brooklands.

Edward Mayer with his 135-h.p. Mercedes. (*The Edward Mayer Collection*)

His foreman, C. H. Crowe, who died in 1952, was about the best Mercedes mechanic in the whole country. Crowe must share a good deal of the credit for the design of the bodies. They were simple, but most attractively designed, doorless metal shells made by the Ewart Geyser people for Watney, with red leather upholstery. They were nearly always painted the colour of aluminium and were beautifully turned out. At that time, he had about a dozen men working for him.

The August meeting at Brooklands was one of the most glorious days of the year and was enlivened by one of those delightful institutions of Regency times, a private match for a wager. Even the wording in the time-yellowed programme has Regency flavour: 'A match for one hundred pounds between Mr. Gordon Watney, as challenger, and the Maharaja of Tikari as acceptor. Distance 5¾ miles.' The Maharaja had a number of cars, including a 60-h.p. de Dietrich and a 60-h.p. Renault. He ran the Renault against Watney's Mercedes. The Mercedes was, for its day, remarkably well streamlined with a cowl over its radiator, but for the Renault, a bare chassis, no attempt at streamlining had been made. This probably did not matter very much at speeds of up to 100 m.p.h., which was about the maximum of which these two cars were capable. Eric Loder drove the Renault for the Maharaja and Lord Vernon drove Watney's Mercedes. The latter made a splendid getaway, streaking up the banking in a manner that delighted the crowd. The big Renault thundered in its rear, the open four-inch exhausts of both cars beating out a regular 1800 r.p.m. that could be heard right across the track, But the Renault never managed to catch up, and Lord Vernon in the Mercedes won the match quite easily. He also won the short 100-m.p.h. handicap from Hornsted's Benz, with Lambert's veteran 30-h.p. Mercedes third.

The Grand Prize of America was again run on the Savannah course. There was a great race for second place between Ed Hearne on a Benz *150* and de Palma on a 1908 Grand Prix Mercedes. Hearne won, by almost exactly a minute, after five hours' racing.

In *The Autocar* published on November 4, 1911, appeared a test of the 12/15-h.p. Mercedes.

It will be remembered that the 12/15-h.p. Mercedes, although a substantially built chassis, has an engine of which the dimensions are only 70 mm. bore by 120 mm. stroke. One has become accustomed to the large amount of power obtainable from engines with a similar stroke and a 10 mm. larger bore, and we were, therefore, prepared to find that this little Mercedes was possessed of quite a considerable range of speed and good hill-climbing ability, nor were we in any way disappointed. Of course, not much power is developed at very slow engine speeds, but there is quite sufficient to allow the car to be driven comfortably in slow-moving traffic with the fourth speed in engagement. On opening the throttle there is a rapid acceleration, although we are tempted to believe that the acceleration from, say, 7 or 6 m.p.h. is enhanced by engaging the third speed for an instant, the change being very easy to make. On the top speed, which is the direct drive, the hill-climbing power is little short of extraordinary. By this it is not meant that very steep gradients can be attacked successfully without descent to one of the lower gears, but the car will carry its full load of four up ordinary gradients without any rushing or faltering. Those who know Richmond Hill will be aware that it rises fairly steeply from the bridge, and that the gradient then eases off, but continues as a gradient practically the whole way to the Star and Garter. The road is throughout inside a ten-mile limit, and is also quite narrow. As a test the car was brought to a dead standstill on the steep part of the slope leading up from the bridge to the hill. Here it was started off on first speed, the second was engaged immediately the car was moving, and within a few yards the third was in use, whilst within twenty yards of the start the fourth was requisitioned, the rest of the climb being accomplished with the throttle a little more than a quarter open at the requisite legal speed of 10 m.p.h. At a considerably higher rate of travel, the Guildford side of Hindhead was surmounted easily on the top speed, also with a full complement of passengers. A word of praise is due to the control in all its details. The steering is light, and the gear-change mechanism can be handled with the proverbial one finger, while the throttle pedal is poised so delicately that it is quite easy to maintain it in any desired position without noticeable strain on the ankle muscles. There is an automatic advancing and retarding mechanism in connexion with the magneto, and this also seems to have advantages. Certainly the engine feels very different from one with quite fixed ignition. Even when the engine is cold, starting up is an easy operation, a couple of turns after flooding the carburettor being quite sufficient. The carburettor seems to improve steadily during the first few minutes' running until the exhaust pipe is warmed up, and a good supply of hot air has been obtained. On the end of the intake pipe is a sleeve containing a large opening, and this is linked up with a dashboard trigger, the intention being presumably that the best position for the prevailing weather may be ascertained when starting, and the adjustment then left alone. When running slowly it would appear necessary to close the extra air door completely, but on the open road we found that quite 4 or 5 m.p.h. more was obtained by opening it up to the full extent. This suggests that it might be worth the while of the Mercedes Company to experiment with an air control within easy reach of the driver, for the present trigger can hardly be said to be readily accessible. We found the brakes very smooth and powerful in action, while the springing was decidedly easy—with a comparatively heavy body. The life and the actual power of the little engine are difficult to convey on paper, but it will perhaps suffice to say that the early 80 mm. engines would make but a poor showing beside this 70 mm., although, of course, the Mercedes Company would be the last to claim that a modern 80 mm. is not still more powerful.

*The Motor* was equally enthusiastic about the 15/20-h.p.

Mercedes, which that paper tried at about the same time.

## 1912

Because the Daimler Motoren Gesellschaft had withdrawn from racing and were building no more racing-cars, it does not signify that they were not keeping an eye on fresh developments in the motoring world. In 1912 a Swiss engineer, Monsieur Henry, had designed a Grand Prix car for the Peugeot brothers that was as far ahead of the 1908 Grand Prix Mercedes as the *W.125* model of that make was ahead of the type *59* Bugatti in 1934. In fact, the Henry-Peugeot design was to influence the shape of things to come for at least a decade. The Peugeots had actually been designed for the 1911 Grand Prix, but, as they had not been run, they had attracted very little attention. When, however, in 1912, one finished first in the hands of Boillot, the really remarkable results achieved by their new and unconventional design caused a great many people, including the Daimler Motoren Gesellschaft, to think hard. Mercedes cars were not being raced, and there is not a single win, or even a place, to record in 1912 until the April Brooklands meeting.

The Easter Brooklands meeting included a handicap for Mercedes cars only and no less than ten were entered. Quite a number of these managed to find that extra turn of speed to beat the handicappers in other races. In the 100-m.p.h. short handicap Mercedes finished line ahead, beating all-comers, with Cumming first, Gordon Watney second, and Leonard Geach on a *45* third.

There was another imposing string of victories at the Whitsun Brooklands meeting; also a little-known item of interest to American readers. That very fine American driver, David Bruce-Brown, paid a visit to England and Gordon Watney gave him one of his fleet of extremely fast Mercedes cars to drive. In the short 100-m.p.h. Allan Mander ran second to Hornsted's Benz. The long 100-m.p.h. handicap was won by David Bruce-Brown on the car Gordon Watney had lent him. Allan Mander won the Whitsun Sprint Handicap with Bruce-Brown in third place and the 6½-mile handicap resulted in a line-ahead victory for Mercedes. A. W. Tate, who had now bought his car from the British concessionaires, Du Cros-Mercedes, won it, with Cumming second and Bruce-Brown third.

A few days later Ralph de Palma took his 1908 Grand Prix Mercedes to the 500-mile race at Indianapolis. He did magnificiently, leading until his engine blew up a few miles from the finish.

In 1910 Mercedes adopted the Knight patent and built sleeve-valve engines alongside the normal types. (*Mercedes-Benz*)

As a very large number of sleeve-valve-engined Mercedes were built under the Knight patents at this time it is not without interest to record a case in patent law tried before Mr Justice Neville in the summer of 1912. Knights sued the Argyll Company, whom they claimed were infringing their patents in the sleeve-valve cars they built. The judge decided, however, that the Knight patents had been anticipated by the King sleeve-valve gas engine in 1884 and found therefore for the Argyll Motor Company. This decision by an English Judge would have placed the German Daimler Company in a very strong position had they been involved in any litigation with Knights in the German courts.

At this time, Gordon Watney's little Mercedes business at Weybridge was making good progress. Every time that a Mercedes limousine of high horse-power, not more than two or three years old, came into the hands of Du Cros-Mercedes, Tankerville ('Tanky') Chamberlain, their sales manager, would sell it cheaply to Gordon Watney. At once, the huge and cumbrous limousine body would be stripped off, sprockets changed for a higher gear, and a light doorless aluminium shell containing four bucket seats fitted. Skilled labour was cheap enough in those days, so Gordon Watney made considerable profits on each transaction. There is a large photograph in a contemporary copy of the *Autocar* of young Count Lou Zborowski (who can only have been about sixteen at the time), son of the Zborowski killed at La Turbie, taking delivery of one of these Gordon Watney Mercedes.

The September Brooklands meeting was a most interesting object-lesson in the way things were going. A dull biting wind was blowing, and it seemed that the icy wind had thinned the ranks of Mercedes owners who, earlier in that same year, on a fine spring day, had been able to put ten cars in the field. They all appeared to have abandoned their huge machines for light, fast-turning cars of about 3-litre capacity. Leonard Geach had bought a 15·9-h.p. Singer and H. M. Bowden a 13·9-h.p. F.A.B. H. C. Lambert had a 15·9-h.p. Crossley and wealthy S. J. B. Lacon a 15·9-h.p. Gregoire. Only Gordon Watney remained faithful to the big old cars, and in the ninth race he had a duel with Bird's Sunbeam, just losing the race by about three times the length of his Mercedes. But the writing on the wall had not passed unnoticed and, at Untertürkheim, quite a few heads were bent over drawing-boards, intent on designing something to meet the challenge thrown out by M. Henry.

At the 1912 Motor Show at Olympia in London, three cars and a chassis were exhibited, but no less than ten different models were offered, from the little four-cylinder *10/25* two-seater at £420 to the noble *80/90* with coachwork to choice, whose price no one seems to have troubled to mention. The other models were the *12/15* with bore and stroke of 70 × 120 mm., the *15/20* 80 × 130 mm., the *25/30* 90 × 140 mm., the *35/40* 100 × 130 mm., with sleeve valves, the *35/40* 110 × 150 mm. with

1910 Mercedes *90* with body built by their own coachworks at Sindelfingen. (*The Edward Mayer Collection*)

poppet valves, the *45/50* 120 × 160 mm. made with both chain and live-axle transmission, the *65/70* 140 × 160 mm. and finally the *80/90* 130 × 180 mm. Both the two biggest cars were chain-driven.

*The Autocar* tested the *45/50* live-axle car early in 1913. It 'cannot speak in in too high praise' of the 'sweetness, silkiness and softness' of the engine. On its top gear of 2·6 to 1, the car

Kaiser Wilhelm II's 90-h.p. Mercedes open-fronted limousine. (*The Edward Mayer Collection*)

An unusually elegant German body on a 90-h.p. Mercedes, circa 1911. (*The Edward Mayer Collection*)

60-h.p. Mercedes. (*The Edward Mayer Collection*)

did ten to fifty-one miles an hour.

The competition year ended in a blaze of glory for Mercedes in America. On a Mercedes owned by E. J. Schroeder, Ralph de Palma won the Vanderbilt Cup against the latest American cars which, even if they were now more conventional in design, were becoming formidable competition. Spencer Wishart drove his similar car into third place against fierce competition, while Clark came in fifth with a Bertrand-owned Mercedes. Whether or not Wishart's and de Palma's cars were 1908 Grand Prix models is still an open question. De Palma himself believed that they were entirely new, but it may be that the works rebuilt existing 1908 team cars or, more probably, constructed two or possibly three new cars, based on the existing designs.

## 1913

The year 1913 was by no means an outstanding one for Mercedes in the way of racing victories. But they could hardly expect anything else, after abstaining from all classical events for nearly five years. Three conclusions can be drawn from 1913. The new aero-engined racing-cars which appeared in the French Grand Prix (referred to later in this year's events), did not come up to expectations; the small Knight-engined cars were more successful, and the 1908 Grand Prix machines, now approaching the antique stage, showed that they could hold their own in a most surprising manner.

Reference has been made already to the improvement in American cars, so there is no need to emphasize this when applauding the efforts of Pilette and Mulford in the 1913 Indianapolis 500-mile race. Pilette drove his small sleeve-valve Mercedes (it had a smaller engine capacity than any other car in the race) into fifth place and Mulford drove the de Palma 1912 Vanderbilt Cup car into sixth place only a few minutes behind him. The race was won by Goux on a Peugeot. Wishart, who had been so successful on a Mercedes in the past, had now transferred to the immortal Mercer, one of America's finest cars of that era.

Pre-1914 Mercedes aero-engine. (*The Edward Mayer Collection*)

The highlight of the year 1913, and the return of the three-pointed star to racing, was the second Grand Prix race in France, held on the Le Mans circuit under the auspices of the Automobile Club de la Sarthe. Both Peugeot and Fiat withdrew from the race. The Mercedes entry consisted of Elskamp and Pilette on very much modified 1908 Dieppe Grand Prix cars, with Salzer and Lautenschlager on the new experimental-engined chain-driven cars. From the beginning, Bablot on a Delage and Christaens on an Excelsior were determined to beat each other. The Mercedes team, on the other hand, seemed to be driving under instructions to take it steady and drive to finish rather than to win.

Christaens stripped a timing gear and was out of the race; Hornsted driving a car of the same make 'blew up', as did all the Schneiders except one. The Brasier, driven by Soldatenkoff, the amateur who did so well with a Mercedes in the Targa Florio, caught fire. The field was thinning out but the Mercedes team kept going steadily. At the end of the fourth lap the three Delages driven by Bablot, Duray, and Guyot were leading the three Mercedes and one Schneider. By the sixth lap Bablot had lapped Elskamp on the oldest and slowest Mercedes and was trying to pass him. It certainly looked, from the grandstand, as though Elskamp was baulking the Delage, and this resulted in an uproar of screams, curses, and fist-waving, so typical of an excited Gallic crowd. The high feeling spread to the Mercedes and Delage pits, where the mechanics hurled curses at each other in their respective languages. By the end of the race Pilette and Salzer had passed Duray and took third and fourth places to Bablot and Guyot in the winning Delages. Lautenschlager and Elskamp came in sixth and seventh respectively. It is not known to what extent the engine designers at Untertürkheim had been influenced by Henry, but presumably very little, for the aero engines, which were raced experimentally in the Grand Prix cars, had two inclined valves in the head. They were operated by a single overhead camshaft, as opposed to Henry's two camshafts, and four valves per cylinder. On the other hand, the Mercedes cylinder blocks, instead of being cast iron like those of the Peugeot, were fabricated from steel, being lighter and stronger, and giving far more generous water passages. It was not perhaps the most resounding of victories, nor were the aero-engined six-cylinder cars notably successful, but they did give the Mercedes technicians the data they required after being so long absent from racing. A glance at the drawings of the victorious 1914 cars, side-by-side with those of the not very successful 1913 experimental cars, will show that a very large number of features on the one have been developed from their earlier form on the other. From this 1913 design also sprang the successful 28/95-h.p. Mercedes.

The Belgian Grand Prix in August was a curious affair. Twice it was postponed owing to the lack of entries, and was eventually run under a formula based on cylinder capacity. Cars with smaller engines did not need to go so fast to win. Two-seater bodies were obligatory and there was a minimum weight formula based on cylinder capacity. Léon Elskamp drove his 100-mm. × 130-mm. sleeve-valve Mercedes-Knight much faster than anyone else on both days; he made fastest time of the day, and established a lap record. The *16/45* Mercedes was not a large car in engine capacity (a fraction over four litres), or in any other sense. But in spite of all this, two smaller cars, a Springuel and a S.A.V.A., neither of which had even approached the performance of Elskamp, were placed ahead of him under this strange formula.

At the end of September, a race, the Coupe de L'Auto, was held on the Boulogne circuit and must have caused a great deal of serious thought among the engineers at Untertürkheim. It was a race for cars with a capacity of not more than 3 litres, and was won by Monsieur Henry's latest Peugeot, which was nearly as fast as the 7·6-litre Peugeot he had designed the previous year!

At the Brooklands autumn meeting, Mercedes had lost much of their popularity. Whereas a year or so previously, perhaps a dozen of the marque would enter, there were now only two: Captain Brocklebank, a great enthusiast, and Gordon Watney. The latter was still very busy with his attractive 'rebuilds'. Both cars were a failure, nor were they even noticed, for all eyes were on the new Peugeots, Vauxhalls, and the fabulous twelve-cylinder Sunbeam.

This finished the competition year. Mercedes did not exhibit any cars at the Paris Salon, but a firm of coachbuilders showed one. This year, boat bodies were very popular. Judging from photographs, the most attractive was on a long-forgotten make, the Abadal, while quite the ugliest was on the only Mercedes shown.

For Olympia in London, however, Mercedes listed twelve different models and showed four. These latter were the *15/25*, the *25/30* and the *40/45*, all fitted with Mercedes-Knight sleeve-valve engines and the new Mercedes patent double-cone leather-faced clutch. The fourth car was an *80/90* (always called the *90*) which had an attractive bronze-green torpedo body by Salmons of Newport Pagnell. With the new pointed radiator and 'Bleriot petrol oxygen headlamps' (which sound most dangerous), the car must have been quite a sight. 'Mighty'

90-h.p. Mercedes, circa 1913, later owned by Count Zborowski. (*The Edward Mayer Collection*)

is the adjective *The Motor* used with which to describe the car. It was chain-driven and the price was £1,150, or £5 more than was asked for a 40/50-h.p. Rolls-Royce. In December 1932, *Motor Sport* had a run on a 1913 *90*. The bore and stroke were 130 × 180 mm. (8850 cc.). The body fitted was not thought to be original and the front axle had been lowered, the front springs being flat. An S.U. carburettor from a Vauxhall *30/98* had been substituted for the original. Maximum r.p.m. were found to be 1350, giving speeds of about 85 m.p.h. on top and 75 m.p.h. on third. The brakes were considered surprisingly powerful, the gear change easy, and the acceleration quite brisk.

The *25/30* landaulette and *40/45* limousine were shaft-driven and fitted with electric light. The English coachwork was more remarkable for comfort and good workmanship than elegance.

*28/32* extra-long chassis Mercedes Town Carriage. (*The Edward Mayer Collection*)

## 1914

In the autumn of 1913 speculation had been rife about French Grand Prix of the following summer, which promised to be one of the greatest races of motor history. Not only were two of the greatest names in racing, Fiat and Mercedes, returning to the sport; Britain was now well represented by Vauxhall and Sunbeam, while France had the unbeatable Delages and Peugeots. No one knew, until a few weeks before the event, what Mercedes would bring to the line, but all agreed that it would be something quite formidable.

The presumption was fully justified. The French Grand Prix of 1914 was such a sweeping victory for the Mercedes cars and was so dramatic in its action, and it took place at such a critical moment in the world's history, that a detailed description of this classic encounter is well merited.

No fewer than 47 cars and the manufacturers of six countries were represented in the race, which was held on Saturday, July 4, 1914.

Many such events in the past have been won and lost by some unforeseen human or mechanical influence which has robbed a gallant effort of well-merited victory or brought triumph where it was not expected; such happenings have often occurred at the final moment, but in this event nothing

Mercedes Touring Landaulet, probably with French coachwork. (*The Edward Mayer Collection*)

of the kind took place. In complete secrecy, victory had been planned months in advance and every contingency anticipated and catered for with clocklike precision.

Sound generalship and staff-work were turned to account to an extent never previously attempted in motor racing.

The essential ingredients of that which is the complement to the staff-work are discipline and strict obedience to orders: a lack of liaison between driver and pit-manager will ruin prospects as surely as will a dry fuel tank. The mathematician in the pit, surrounded by his stop-watches and complex scoring charts, is of equal importance to the driver of a racing-car as is ammunition to a rifle. Each is useless without the other: all are interdependent: they are a team. On such principles Mercedes based their plans for victory.

Since 1908, France had been extraordinarily successful in the racing field, thanks largely to two drivers, Georges Boillot and Jules Goux, who had won race after race including the Grand Prix of 1912 and that of 1913. Boillot, at the wheel of a Peugeot, had acquired almost legendary fame. An overpowering, swollen-headed man who played to the gallery, he might, in his general attitude, have stepped right out from the pages of a Dumas novel. He was a virtuoso of the road, and he knew it; his long string of triumphs had brought sporting France to his feet. He was the idol of his countrymen, as were Lenglen and Carpentier when they were at their zenith.

When the Mercedes company sent in their entries, there was no undue apprehension in the ranks of the French Club. Five Mercedes cars were entered to be driven by Lautenschlager —the hero of the 1908 Grand Prix—Salzer, Sailer, Pilette and Wagner. While the Mercedes company had been out of touch with racing for several years, France had the Peugeot and the two drivers mentioned which had carried all before them. The German entry was accepted, and that was that.

The course selected, some ten miles from Lyons, was triangular in shape and measured approximately 23⅓ miles, which had to be covered twenty times, giving a total distance of 466 miles.

The grandstand seated some 4000 spectators and provided an almost perfect view of the cars for two and a half miles. Each car could be seen descending a hill with two hairpin bends. The point at the top of the hill, where the cars first appeared, was known as Semaphore Station, the descent immediately following leading to the valley, La Descente des Esses, and the final corner, Les Sept Chemins. Thus, each car could be seen in the distance approaching the first corner at high speed, slowing down, accelerating again, slowing down once more for the final corner and then, with a mighty burst of acceleration, tearing past the grandstand.

The entries consisted of the five Mercedes cars mentioned, three each of Sunbeam, Vauxhall, Peugeot, Delage, Opel, Fiat, and Nazzaro, and a few others.

Three months before the race was due to take place, strange things began to happen on the course. A party of Germans, consisting of seven drivers, a team of mechanics and a manager, took up residence at an hotel in one of the villages. They brought with them seven half-finished cars of obviously high power. At 5 a.m. to the second, each morning, a whistle was blown by the team manager. The drivers would leave their rooms and find their cars, attended by the mechanics, all ready for them. Then they would proceed to certain parts of the course, and for hours each corner would be made the subject of careful experiment. Each driver would try getting round it at high speed, first on one gear and then on another, changing the point at which the engine would be cut off and finally memorizing some minor object on the roadside such as a tree or a milestone to indicate where to change gear or to cut off. These proceedings would continue until 11 a.m., and punctually at that hour the party would return to their hotel, have a meal and discuss matters. At 2 p.m. out they would come again, for further experiments of the same nature, until 7 p.m., when work would finish for the day.

Day after day, these proceedings continued, and then, just as suddenly as the party had arrived, it departed. A month later, back came the party again for further experiments, and the careful observer might have noticed that the cars seemed rather different; they were shorter; the wheelbases had been reduced.

And so matters continued until every twist and turn along the whole 23⅓ miles was as well known to each driver as he knew the path leading to his own front door. Backwards and forwards the Mercedes cars had been going to Untertürkheim for alterations, until on the day of the race each car fitted the course as a piece of glass fits a picture frame.

The Automobile Club de France felt confident of victory; a day or two before the race, Louis Delage said that he considered his chances of success 48 per cent, and those of the Peugeot team 48 per cent, while the remaining 4 per cent belonged to the field. The Fiat, Peugeot and Delage cars certainly had one immense advantage over the German team in that they had four-wheel brakes, which Mercedes refused to fit because they had not had sufficient time for trial and experiments. On this particular course it was said that

Wheel-changing on a 1914 Grand Prix Mercedes. (*Mercedes-Benz*)

four-wheel brakes were worth a minute per lap.

The order of starting was arranged by ballot; two cars at a time were sent off at half-minute intervals so that the whole field was away within 10½ minutes. Within ten minutes of the last car starting, Boillot on the Peugeot, the idol of the French crowd, was signalled, and a moment later his exhaust note was heard, and he was seen to take the hairpin bend, straighten out and dash down the hill towards Les Sept Chemins; a few seconds later he tore by the grandstand while the crowd roared at him as one man. From a standing start, he had covered his first lap of 23⅓ miles in 21 minutes, 11 seconds.

Hardly had the cheers died away when Sailer on the Mercedes was also signalled. It was noticed at once that he cut off earlier than Boillot because of his rear brakes, but his acceleration was appreciably better than the Peugeot. The jaws of ten thousand French people dropped when it was announced that Sailer was 18 seconds faster than Boillot, in spite of the disadvantage of his brakes.

At the end of the second lap, he led by 46 seconds and by the end of the fifth lap the flying Sailer had increased his lead on Boillot to 2 minutes, 44 seconds, although the latter was going flat out to hold him.

Man and metal could not stand this kind of treatment for long, and sure enough, on his sixth lap, Sailer's engine 'blew up', and Boillot moved up into first place, to the unspeakable delight of the crowd.

Up to this point, Lautenschlager and Wagner had held back but no sooner had Sailer fallen out than the team manager began work. Mysterious signs were given to Lautenschlager and Wagner, and just as though they were wooden pieces on a chess board, the former displaced Duray (Delage) for second place, while Wagner immediately moved up to sixth position.

At the end of the seventh lap, Goux (Peugeot) had gone forward into third position, both to support Boillot and if possible to harass Lautenschlager, whose car was palpably faster than the Peugeot.

And so this hectic struggle continued until half-distance, when once again there was a reshuffle in the positions; Lautenschlager was 1 minute 8 seconds behind Boillot, but Wagner and Salzer had moved up into fourth and fifth places respectively. Goux was still lying third.

It was during the fourteenth lap that the wily Goux tried to make Lautenschlager take a hairpin corner too fast; he was approaching behind and just as the corner came into sight he accelerated and raced Lautenschlager in the hope that he would forget that he only had rear brakes. But Lautenschlager

One of the historic 1914 Grand-Prix-winning Mercedes. (*The Edward Mayer Collection*)

was an old warrior at the game; he allowed Goux to pass, took the corner at his usual pace and then accelerated to pass Goux on the straight.

As the end of this epic struggle approached, orders were given from the Mercedes pit to the drivers to close up. Lautenschlager gradually reduced the lead of Boillot; at the end of the seventeenth lap he was only 14 seconds behind Boillot, and when the scoreboard announced this fact the grandstand positively rocked with excitement; every eye was fixed on the distant semaphore station, and a sudden hush came over the spectators when it was announced that Lautenschlager had wrested the lead from Boillot and was actually leading him by 33 seconds. At the end of the nineteenth lap this lead had been increased to 1 minute 7 seconds with Wagner only 16 seconds behind Boillot and obviously awaiting orders from his pit to pass him on the last lap.

But the gallant Boillot, who had driven a truly magnificent race, was doomed never to finish. During the final lap he pressed his car too hard and he was forced to stop. Precisely what broke, if anything, is an arguable point; thus the end of this homeric struggle was a three-fold victory for Mercedes.

Lautenschlager, Wagner, and Salzer came home, first, second and third, in an atmosphere of stony silence. Not a cheer was given for the victors and not a hand was clapped.

One month later, France and Germany were at war.

On June 28, 1914, a politically-minded student called Princep decided, at Sarajevo, that the murder of an Austrian Archduke would benefit humanity. This was the spark that ignited the 1914–18 conflagration, and is well-known history, but few people know the name of the chauffeur who, though gravely wounded, kept on driving until the Archduke's car was out of range of the assassin. This was none other than Otto Merz, the legendary strong man and Mercedes racing driver of the twenties and thirties. Merz, who served his apprenticeship with Mercedes, was a racing mechanic for Willy Poege and later Theodor Dreher. Like the celebrated Wilhelm Werner he then entered the service of royalty as head driver and mechanic. It was in this capacity that he made his gallant but unsuccessful attempt to save his master's life by keeping the car moving. We shall hear much of him later.

There were only two more continental meetings in which Mercedes competed before the outbreak of war. At one, a trial and hill-climb, Count Ermes Berg on a sleeve-valve *16/45* won two classes. The other was a fitting epilogue to the heroic age, already ended. At the Ostend Week, the great Baron de Caters reappeared at the wheel of a *37/95* Mercedes; he won all the classes for which he entered, and made fastest time of the day for sports- and touring-cars.

Gordon Watney was still actively engaged in 1914 in selling his rebuilt Mercedes cars. Soon after the war started he took on Government contract work, and by 1918 his little shed, employing never more than two dozen craftsmen, had grown into a large factory with many hundreds of workers. At the end of the war he very wisely sold the business for a huge sum before the War Office cancelled his contracts. After this, instead of resuming Mercedes work, he embarked on theatrical ventures, and, it is understood, lost his entire fortune.

In America, which at that time was not embroiled in the European war, motor-racing went on. Ralph de Palma acquired one of the 1914 Grand Prix Mercedes, almost certainly Wagner's car. Between August 21 and November 3 he won the Chicago Cup, the Elgin National Trophy, no less than four races at Brighton Beach, two at Trenton, and then another race at Brighton Beach, in which John de Palma on a *37/95* was placed. And so, several thousand miles away from warring Europe, 1914 ended in a number of Mercedes victories.

At different times as the dreary war years went by, news filtered through of both Mercedes and Benz cars still being obtainable in Holland; also that Mercedes was still the most popular make in Germany. Even in Britain, the glamour of Mercedes was so little tarnished after four years of war that *The Motor* was constrained to suggest in August 1918 that 'a genuine British car built on Mercedes lines—and this ought not to be a difficult matter with our advanced knowledge in metallurgy—would make a prime favourite after the war'.

## 1915

In America, W. K. Vanderbilt put up a 1,000 guineas' cup, to be presented by his wife for a 300-mile race to be held at the Panama Pacific Exhibition. American sporting cars were making great headway, and in a field comprised largely of Mercer, Stutz, and Maxwell, there was Tom Alley on a very fast newcomer, the Duesenberg. Continental makes were represented by de Palma on the 1913 Sarthe Grand Prix 75-h.p. chain-driven Mercedes, and the Englishman Dario Resta, who had gone over to America on the off-chance of someone giving him a drive, and had acquired the old 1913 French Grand Prix Peugeot. The pace was so fierce that the field of thirty-one cars was soon reduced to nine or ten. At first it looked like a duel between the Duesenberg and the Mercedes, but the Duesenberg crashed badly, as did Burman's Case. Burman's mechanic was seriously injured. Then the Mercedes dropped back to fourth place and Resta, driving a beautiful race, brought his borrowed Peugeot to victory. The booby prize went to the pit mechanics of Harry Grant's Stutz, which was doing rather well; when he came in to refuel they were so excited that they filled his big bolster tank with water instead of petrol.

The Indianopolis 500-mile race, run on May 31, 1915, was more or less a straight fight between de Palma driving his Mercedes and Resta on his borrowed Peugeot. It was a ding-dong fight between the two cars until Resta came into the pit to change a tyre just a little too quickly, smote a wall and had to change a wheel. He now had little hope of catching Ralph de Palma who won at the fine average speed of 89·84 m.p.h. Resta was second; third and fourth were two Stutz—this time with petrol in their tanks.

## 1916

The Peugeot and the Mercedes cars seem to have been very evenly matched, for on June 11, 1916, they met again at the new Chicago track. It was again a neck-and-neck race but the Mercedes had to come in to change a plug, which gave the victory to Resta's Peugeot. Tracks were springing up all over America, and de Palma brought his Grand Prix Mercedes out again for the Omaha meeting. He won the 50-mile race from Rickenbacker by about 4 m.p.h. Prize money was good; de Palma collected £300 and Rickenbacker £150. De Palma went on to win the 100-mile race at Kansas City on July 25, but a fortnight later dropped out of the 300-mile race at Tacoma with engine trouble, after leading the field for 175 miles. There was a little more racing before the war closed it down, but as far as can be traced, towards the end of the season de Palma drove other cars instead of his Mercedes. The final score at the end of the season was Peugeot 14 victories, Mercedes 5, Maxwell 2, and Delage, Duesenberg, and Frontenac, one each.

Although the Mercedes factory at Untertürkheim and their branch establishments had not suffered bombing in the 1914–18 war, the dislocation due to getting back to peace-time products from war material was immense. And it took at least a year for both key men and ordinary artisans to trickle back from the army. Paul Daimler and that capable man Carl Schippert decided to market the *28/95*, which had been 'tooled up' and was in production just before the war; also

This magnificent *28/95* with Edward Mayer at the wheel must have been built circa 1919/20. (*The Edward Mayer Collection*)

a smaller car, a *16/45* sleeve valve. The pre-war *28/95* had open valve gear, and after the war this was boxed in with three aluminium covers. Germany was, at this time, in a serious economic situation and certain raw materials were virtually unobtainable. Among these were non-ferrous metals, so the Mercedes cars turned out immediately after the war were of an extremely austere nature, with none of the copper and brass fittings that made the earlier and later cars so attractive. Tyres were also virtually non-existent, except on the black market. So it was normal practice for all car manufacturers, including Mercedes, to sell their cars without tyres and let the purchaser make his own arrangements for obtaining these rare commodities.

In December 1919, *The Motor* published an article on a visit to various German motor manufacturing firms, Mercedes at Stuttgart and Benz at Mannheim among them, reporting that several thousand chassis of private cars were available, all without tyres. The 'black market' was then in full swing, as was inflation, but even so prices were competitive, e.g. a Mercedes chassis catalogued at 15,000 marks would be sold

The small Benz, a surprisingly sporting little car, produced in 1918. (*Mercedes-Benz*)

at 60,000 marks.

At this same time we hear that Benz had 300 chassis waiting on the docks at Hamburg for shipment to India.

For 1920 Benz turned out two cars, the pre-war 12 h.p. with various improvements to bring it up to date and a new 27/70-h.p. four-cylinder motor. *The Motor* said that this would 'undoubtedly be classed among the finest of Germany's cars'.

## 1920

The history of the two 1914 Grand Prix Mercedes that came to England is interesting. One of them turned up in the experimental department of Rolls-Royce just after the outbreak of war in 1914. There has been for many years a charming legend that our Intelligence Department stole it on its way back to Stuttgart after the race. Unfortunately, it is not true. What happened was this: The car was sent over for exhibition at the British Mercedes showrooms and on the outbreak of war it was requisitioned by Rolls-Royce to see whether they could learn anything from it. After the war it was bought by Lou Zborowski, and a little later was either destroyed by fire or, at any rate, very badly damaged, and not rebuilt. The other one, which was Ralph de Palma's car, was owned by an American named Patterson who brought it to England and left it here when he returned to the U.S.A. Edward Mayer bought it but did not like it, for he is a tall man and both the seating and the distance between pedals and steering wheel were unsuitable for him. In his view, the steering was about the best in any car he has ever had before or since. Its next owner stored it for many years, after which it was unearthed by Peter and Ariel Clark who ran it occasionally and eventually sold it to Cameron Peck. So it crossed the Atlantic once more.

During the year various items of news filtered through from Germany about the production of ordinary cars. In March, it was said that a fairly large batch of Mercedes chassis would shortly be reaching England and that the price would be £1250. Soon after, we are told, once more through *The Motor*, that some seventy chassis are on the point of being delivered to the Mercedes concessionaires in Huddersfield, and that bodies are to be built by the Bristol Carriage and Wagon Co. These chassis were all of the *16/45* or *16/36* four-cylinder sleeve-valve car, basically a pre-war production.

Benz were also very cautious about new designs. Their *16/40* car for 1920, the bore and stroke of the engine of which was 90 × 140 mm., was exactly the same as the 1914 model. *The Motor*, commenting on this car says: 'It will be seen that there is nothing startling about German productions so far, the manufacturers have evidently not been influenced by any war experiences to alter their design. The workmanship and

A competition model *28/95*, circa 1920. (*The Edward Mayer Collection*)

material appeared to be quite up to pre-war standard, so far as can be judged.' Labour troubles also presented serious problems to both Daimler and Benz. In the autumn of this year we hear of the Untertürkheim works being 'closed down', together with Bosch and one or two others, because the workers refused to agree to a Württemberg Government decree of a ten per cent wages reduction for income-tax. Presumably this stoppage was only of short duration.

## 1921

During May 1921 Max Sailer carried out a brave enterprise. The Germans, as a conquered nation, were hedged around with all manner of petty restrictions. They were not allowed fuel, foreign money for travel, or anything else, without the endless form-filling that made such things virtually impossible to acquire in any legal manner. The European roads were in a terrible condition. Tyres existed only on the black market, and even there were very scarce. Any fuel obtainable had been stolen from military dumps.

In face of all these difficulties, Max Sailer proceeded to drive his short chassis *28/95* Mercedes car from Stuttgart to Sicily. It is a matter of the greatest wonder that he ever arrived at

Max Sailer won the 1921 Coppa Florio with a short, light supercharged *28/95*. (*Mercedes-Benz*)

his destination, and even more remarkable that he won the Coppa Florio, now run in conjunction with the Targa in the same race. The Targa Florio was won by Count Masetti, driving a 1914 Fiat which had been modified during the war, having a built-up steel block like the 1914 Grand Prix Mercedes, instead of its original cast-iron block. The Targa was for genuine racing-cars and the Coppa for stock cars.

Mercedes were beginning to get back into their race-winning form remarkably quickly, for Minoia, one of the giants of the heroic age who used to throw a 100-h.p. Isotta about as if it were a Topolino Fiat, won his class in the St. Bernard Pass 30-kilometre hill-climb and Count Masetti, who now had one of the 1914 Grand Prix cars, won the kilometre speed trials in 22·3 seconds from a standing start, establishing an Italian record.

This kilometre speed event was by way of being an eliminating trial for the Italian Grand Prix run on a circuit near Brescia. Count Masetti won his class, made fastest time of the day, fastest lap, and won the Italian Amateur Driver's Championship for 1921.

It was a reward for the hard work and initiative of all concerned at Untertürkheim that Mercedes had made such a successful 'come-back' in the competition world so soon after the war.

At the Berlin Motor Show, the first held since 1911, Mercedes exhibits comprised a 45-h.p. Knight-engined (i.e. sleeve-valve) four-cylinder model, a 32/98-h.p. six-cylinder car, the engine of which was the same as that installed in the racing *28/95*, and a new 12-h.p. car (called in Germany a 6/20 h.p.) with a bore and stroke of 68 × 108 mm., 'a beautiful little monobloc engine' as *The Motor* described it. Mercedes cars were not shown at Olympia in October, but the 1922 range was announced as the *6/20*, a *10/35*, *16/45* and the *28/95*. Chassis prices varied from £150 to £1500.

Meanwhile, it was announced in October that a British company known as Benz Motors (England) Ltd., was to be formed to market 14- and 20-h.p. four-cylinder cars and 24- and 37-h.p. six-cylinder cars. At the end of November, however, the British vice-consul at Frankfurt reported that Benz had closed down the Mannheim works and discharged the entire staff of 3500 persons. The management stated that the constant and threatening demonstrations of the workmen and a recent case of maltreatment of one of the managing directors had made further orderly administration of the works impossible. These labour troubles were no doubt of but temporary duration, and by December we learn that Benz was to take

One of the dear little 2-litre, four-cylinder supercharged cars of 1921. (*The Edward Mayer Collection*).

over the manufacture of the rear-engined Rumpler car which had created something of a sensation at the Berlin Show in the autumn.

## 1922

The Mercedes Company began with a determined assault on the Targa Florio. Count Masetti drove the 1914 Grand Prix car which he had acquired the previous year; Lautenschlager and Salzer also drove two similar cars entered by the works. Max Sailer and Christian Werner drove short-chassis supercharged *28/95*s. Scheef drove the first of what was to be the schoolboy's dream for many years to come, a 1½-litre supercharged Mercedes.

The Italians were there in force, so were some of the French, and it was a keenly contested race. There were two bad crashes, and in one, Brilli-Peri was injured.

Masetti, after a terrific struggle with Goux and Forresti, both driving Ballot cars, won the race. Lautenschlager and Salzer were second and fourth in the racing class and tenth and thirteenth in the general category. Sailer, who was sixth in the general category, and Werner, who was eighth, were first and second in the big car class. Scheef was third in his class with the new little car. Masetti made fastest lap time and established a new record for the race, bringing home a list of awards too long to mention. He also joined that very select band of ten drivers who have twice won the Targa Florio. It is sad to record that he was killed in 1926, driving a Delage in this same race.

After the Targa Florio came the Königsaal-Jilowischt hill-climb, won by Salzer on a *28/95*, who in so doing made fastest time of the day, establishing a new record for the hill. The production-car class was won by Director J. Junek, of Prague, who was killed a decade later at Nürburgring driving a Bugatti. He was the husband of Madame Junek, who ranks with Gwenda Hawkes and Madame du Gast among the finest women drivers in motoring history. This astonishing woman drove Bugatti cars better than most men, and once it was only an unlucky breakdown near the end that prevented her from winning the Targa Florio!

At the Brooklands Whitsun meeting Count Lou Zborowski's 1914 Grand Prix Mercedes went well. He won the 100-m.p.h. long handicap and gained second place in another race. He also put in an appearance on that famous old car *Chitty-Bang-Bang I*. There were in all five *Chittys*, so, as they all are based on Mercedes, and are typical of the aero-engined monsters that raced in 1920–25, it might be as well to sort them out.

*Chitty I*. Benz aero-engined pre-1914 *75* Mercedes chain-driven chassis. This car went backwards through the timing-box at Brooklands, was sold to the Conan Doyle brothers and subsequently broken up.

*Chitty II*. A fast four-seater 120-m.p.h. touring-car in which Lou Zborowski tried to cross the Sahara. It was a much improved version of *Chitty I*. David Scott-Moncrieff bought it and later sold it to a man who drove it but once. It frightened him so much that he put it away for twenty years. It has now been beautifully restored by Mr. Harris Mayes of Dover, and is in use again.

*Chitty III*. This utilized an aero-engine in a *28/95* chassis, and was a great improvement on the other two. It was afterwards raced by Pole and Noel, and was then sold to Lord Carlow. It has since been broken up.

*Chitty IV* or the *Higham Special*, or *Babs*. A pre-1914 *75* Mercedes chassis fitted with a Liberty aero-engine. This was the incredibly fast car on which Parry Thomas was killed while attempting the world's speed record on Pendine Sands. The wreckage was buried at Pendine.

*Chitty V*. This was to have been an aero-engined saloon based on a Mercedes chassis. It had not progressed much further than the drawing-board stage when Count Lou Zborowski's death caused work on it to cease.

It can be seen that only one of the original *Chitty-Bang-Bangs* remains in existence, although there are here and there one or two cars which are believed, quite erroneously, to be one of them.

The year closed with *28/95* and *16/50* cars winning small races and hill-climbs all over Europe. It was a *fait accompli*; Mercedes cars had definitely made a 'come-back'. Now Paul Daimler, tired from carrying a heavy burden of responsibility all through the 1914–18 war, and the troubled period of re-organization that followed, could lay down his burden and go into retirement. He had certainly earned it.

# 3
# BLAZING STARLIGHT 1922–1934

The 1924 Targa Florio, Sicily. After a stiff battle with dust, stones and very fast rivals, Werner won in his 2-litre, four-cylinder Mercedes. (*Carlo Demand: The Big Race*)

# FERDINAND PORSCHE

## 1923

THE first year with Ferdinand Porsche as chief engineer opened with some good victories, but it was quite clear that the 1923 season was not going to be at all easy for Mercedes. They had made a good start after the war, but competition was becoming keener. Fiat were back with some cars which, after an unsuccessful beginning, looked very promising. It is interesting to note that during the war the Fiat engineers had adopted the Mercedes system of fabricating steel cylinders. They had pre-war cars ready to race, immediately after the cessation of hostilities, with cylinders so constructed.

In America, Miller was at about his peak as a builder with a car very reminiscent of Henry's 1913 Peugeot. Henry himself was not idle; he designed an eight-cylinder racing-car for the Ballot brothers and was promptly engaged by the Sunbeam Motor Company, in England. Here, for some unexplained reason he failed to do anything of note, and by 1923 had been replaced by Bertarione of the Fiat Company, who built a very formidable challenger. Vauxhall had lost their best man, Pomeroy, to the Aluminium Corporation, but under chief engineer King had evolved a fine racing-car, which, although not quite as potent as the Sunbeam in its 1924 form, was very fast. Finally, Ettore Bugatti, while designing yachts, chicken houses, shoes for himself and his horses, and roller skates for his children, built an eight-cylinder racing-car which in a slightly modified later form, was to win more races than any other car ever built before or since. Competition was indeed very fierce, and the *28/95* found itself, by 1923, hopelessly out of date. That did not stop the *28/95*s winning events for years to come, a peculiarity that Mercedes can share with Bugattis; however ancient they are, they usually manage to win a surprising number of events.

But the Daimler Motoren Gesellschaft were not going to be left behind in the race to produce newer and better cars, and in 1923 they came out with a very modern small supercharged four-cylinder car that existed in both 1½-litre and 2-litre form. Mercedes had been experimenting with supercharging for some time. They claim that Gottlieb Daimler made drawings of a device for forced induction. Renault took out some patents

*28/95* sports car, possibly supercharged. (*Mercedes-Benz*)

in 1902, but neither he nor Gottlieb Daimler seems to have developed the idea at all. The first practical supercharger ever constructed and used was on that beautifully engineered American car, the Chadwick, in 1907. In 1911, Marc Birkigt built a piston-type supercharger on his Hispano-Suiza, but it is doubtful whether it was ever raced.

This was the first type of supercharger built by Mercedes soon after the end of the 1914–18 war, but it was quickly discarded in favour of a Roots-type blower under Wittig's patents. The Roots blower was quite normal, in that it consisted of a pair of figure-of-eight shaped rotors, geared together and ground to fine clearance. It was driven at 2·2 times engine speed by a clutch that came into action when the throttle pedal was pressed down to its full extent. Unlike any other system, it blew *through* the carburettor, instead of sucking *from* it. Mercedes supercharging continued much on these lines up to 1937. The blowers were first tried on the sleeve-valve engine which had done so well, but the raised temperatures caused the sleeves to burn round the ports. Then the *28/95*s were supercharged, which was quite satisfactory, or would have been, had not the engine been so out of date. In 1922, two 1½-litre supercharged cars were built for the Targa Florio. These were not nearly so successful as the 1914 Grand Prix cars or the *28/95*s. The 1923 cars were rather better than those of the previous year, but, nevertheless, the acquisition from the Austro-Daimler works at Wiener Neustadt of Dr. Ferdinand

Porsche, who was first and foremost an engine man, was the year's great asset.

At the end of May came the Indianapolis 500-mile race on which Mercedes had staked so much. Just as in the Carrera Pan-American race of thirty years later, they were racing for the American market. Colonel Clive Gallop, who was at Indianapolis with Count Lou Zborowski (he was Zborowski's chief engineer) has recorded his impressions of the race. Not only had Porsche been with the firm too short a time to apply all his genius of designing, but it was generally felt that the Mercedes drivers, who had been used to the heavy cars with large engines, had not fully accustomed themselves to the light 2-litre cars, the driving of which required a different technique. Sailer was forty-one years old and the mighty Lautenschlager already forty-six. Lou Zborowski had deserted his beloved Mercedes for one of the new straight-eight 2-litre Bugattis. A second Bugatti was driven by de Viscaya.

During practice, Max Sailer, driving with all his magnificent dash, crashed badly into the wall at North Turn. His mechanic's spine was seriously injured, but Sailer sustained only minor contusions and a sprained wrist. It was clear that he would not be fit to drive in the race, so his nephew, Carl Sailer, took his place.

The race started at a very fierce speed, and on the fourteenth lap Lautenschlager, who was going well, spun round and crashed into the wall. The car was wrecked and his mechanic's leg broken. By the twentieth lap, Christian Werner had forced his Mercedes into third place, but it was becoming abundantly clear that the 1923 2-litre cars were, when driven really hard, extremely tiring. At half distance Werner had to be helped out of the car, and Max Sailer, who was always game for anything, took over in spite of his injured wrist. The car was still running third, but at 350 miles was overhauled by de Viscaya's Bugatti and started to drop back. About this time, Werner had recovered sufficiently to relieve Carl Sailer. But these gallant efforts were futile. The best Max Sailer could do was to bring his car home eighth while Werner followed in eleventh place. The first prize of 3500 dollars was won by Milton on an *H.C.S.*, a special built by Harry Stutz. Second and third were Hartz and Murphy on Durants. These were, in fact, nothing more nor less than Los Angeles-built Millers. The firm of Durant had paid a goodly sum for the privilege of painting their name on the bonnets!

At home, in Germany, the country was in the throes of galloping inflation. The workmen at Untertürkheim had to bring satchels in which to take home their week's pay, and when they received it they found that prices had spiralled up out of reach again. In fact, the whole financial situation was so out of hand that the Daimler Motoren Gesellschaft had to print their own banknotes for millions of marks and in its issue of February 23, *The Autocar* reported that a large Benz cost between twenty-five and twenty-eight million marks! Even this did not stop the firm going ahead with their new models and entering for competitions. Sales both at home and abroad were reported to be brisk.

At the endurance trials at Scheveningen, Mercedes had successes they enjoyed there nearly twenty years earlier. Theo Wiemann of the Hague drove his supercharged *28/95*. Edward Mayer has driven this car and was much impressed by its speed. Ernst Sauer drove one of the small 'blown' sports-cars. From 1904 to 1914 Sauer had been foreman at 'Atelier Mercedes-Daimler' at Puteaux near Paris. During the 1914–18 war he built aero engines at Untertürkheim and then went in 1919 as foreman to Theo Wiemann, the Mercedes agent at the Hague. He and Wiemann won most of the events at Scheveningen for which they had entered.

The Hessian Automobile Club's flat races were won by August Momberger, of whom we shall hear much more, at the wheel of a 1½-litre supercharged car. He won again, a few days later, at Bad Homburg.

In Holland, some speed trials were held to celebrate the Queen's Jubilee. Sauer's small car won its class, as did the *28/95*s, veteran-driver de Jochems reappearing at the wheel of one of them. Mercedes also gained a few awards at the Baden-Baden motor week and we hear—for the first time—a very familiar name. Second in the class for small touring-cars was Rudolf Caracciola, then a twenty-two-year-old motor salesman from Dresden. A few days later he drove a 1½-litre 'blown' Mercedes at the Muennerstadt hill-climb, entering in four events and winning them all.

In England, the smaller supercharged Mercedes, known as the *12/40*, made its appearance to supplement the existing *16/50*, and was heralded with considerable praise in the motoring Press. To say that the prices of such cars were fierce would be an understatement; the smaller car cost £1250 and the larger £1475, with German-built bodies. But the workmanship was so fine that British Mercedes (as Milnes, Daimler Ltd. and Du Cros-Mercedes had been called since 1919), sold a number of them. A Fulham man bought one new in 1924 and ran it for a quarter of a century with no mechanical trouble whatever.

In the summer of 1925, *The Brooklands Gazette* (later *Motor*

*Sport*) tested the *12/40*. The price for the two-seater was, by then, £775. The engine, which had overhead valves, was of just over 1½ litre capacity; the bore and stroke were 68 × 108 mm. Springing was semi-elleptic in front and full cantilever in the rear. Final drive of the transmission was of interest, a double bevel and pinion being used—to prevent wheelspin, it was claimed. The usual Mercedes 'blower' practice was followed. Gear ratios were not unduly low and the chassis weight, 13 cwt., not unduly high, but the tester was disappointed to find that he could not get the speedometer over 80 m.p.h. However, no distress was shown by the engine after an hour's hard driving at Brooklands and the car proved rock steady at high speed, though the absence of shock absorbers produced bounce on bad roads. The fly in the ointment, which applied to other supercharged Mercedes road cars, is well summed up by the *Gazette* tester: 'To get the best results from the engine, one must get up to a fairly high speed in third gear, then change into top and allow the car to pick up speed still further before the supercharger is brought into engagement. In these conditions the benefits are apparent at once, but otherwise the engine is handicapped by having to operate the blower, which is not working fast enough to exact any useful pressure on the carburettor.' In other words, the car, without the 'blower', was sluggish. The two-wheeled brakes were found inadequate at over 70 m.p.h., and it was suggested that 50 m.p.h. was the ideal cruising speed.

The year 1923 had not been a good one in competitions, but Mercedes had at least held their own against the nightmare of inflation which liquidated quite a number of other German firms, and already Porsche and his team were doing some useful work for the future on their drawing-boards, and in the experimental department.

The honours this year, as far as German racing-cars are concerned, go to Benz. The result of long preoccupation with rear-engined motor-cars bore fruit in a team of 2-litre six-cylinder racing-cars which ran in the Grand Prix of Europe, held at Monza in September. The engine, with a bore and stroke of 65 × 100 mm., had inclined valves operated by twin overhead camshafts, aluminium alloy pistons and roller bearings. A three-speed gear-box was provided behind the engine, the rear suspension was independent and inboard brake drums were fitted. The team of three cars were driven by Minoia, Hörner and Walb. Walb 'blew up' but Minoia and Hörner finished fourth and fifth respectively, creditable efforts at this first, and apparently last, showing of these cars in a race of the first importance. For the record, Salamano was the winner on the all-conquering Fiat, Nazzaro, also on a Fiat, was second, and Murphy on the American Miller was third.

## 1924

This year saw further progress and two major wins for Mercedes. The company's long-term policy was very shrewd. They must have seen that few manufacturers could survive the financially suicidal policy of building new and improved Grand Prix cars every year, especially with the post-war boom already on the wane. They carried on with the development of a new 2-litre eight-cylinder Grand Prix car, of which we shall hear much more, but they were also developing something that was going to dominate sports-car racing for almost a decade: the big 7½-litre, road-equipped, supercharged touring-car.

The Targa Florio and Coppa Florio, run jointly over the Madonie circuit in Sicily on April 27, was one of the highlights of the year. The small, plain, 2-litre four-cylinder cars had now reached perfection and the team entered had as drivers Christian Werner, now at his peak, Lautenschlager and Alfred Neubauer, now the famous *Rennleiter* of the Daimler-Benz A.G.

There was a great race against the cream of Italian cars. Werner drove brilliantly, and in one epic outright win gained the Targa Florio, the Coppa Florio, and a host of minor

One of the 1924 team of 2-litre Targa Florio cars. (*The Edward Mayer Collection*)

Neubauer and Hemminger in the 1924 Targa Florio car. (*Mercedes-Benz*)

awards. In the general category, Masetti, who had won for Mercedes in 1922, was second on an Alfa-Romeo, and Ascari was third on a similar car. These Alfas were tiring cars to handle and it was all that their drivers, tough, wiry Italians, could do to hold them. After the race, Ascari (father of Alberto Ascari*), collapsed and had to be lifted out of his car. On the other hand, the German drivers finished relatively fresh. An interesting entry in the 2-litre class was a Diatto, driven by its designer, whose fame is now world-wide—Signor Maserati. The Germans finished one, two, and three in this class—Werner, Lautenschlager and Neubauer. The last two were a good deal further down in the general category. Among other trophies they carried home was the Coppa Termini for the best works drivers as a team. Alfred Neubauer, in his very early thirties, must on this occasion have been a very proud young man. For an officer in the Horse Artillery of the Austro-Hungarian Emperor, life was bright indeed in August 1914. After the war, like so many others, he was suddenly unemployed, for the upper classes in Austria of 1918 were as hard hit as those in England today. However, it was not long before his engineering training and outstanding ability as an organizer got him work at the Austrian Daimler works at Wiener Neustadt. On July 1, 1923, he went to Mercedes to take charge of all driving tests, delivery, demonstration and so forth. Less than a year later, he was racing for the firm and

* Alberto Ascari was killed during a practice run at Monza in 1955.

keeping up with the top-line men like Christian Werner and Lautenschlager.

In May, the Solitude hill-climb from Stuttgart was a real field day for Mercedes. The works team of fast 2-litre 'blown' four-cylinder cars finished first, second, and third in their class, and two other small Mercedes won theirs. The same day, Caracciola won his class at the Hercules climb, with Kappler second.

On June 1, Caracciola won both the flat race at Hirschfeld and the 4-kilometre Lückendorfer Pass hill-climb in Saxony on his 1½-litre 'blown' car. At Brooklands, Count Lou Zborowski, who was also driving his Ballot, brought out the Mercedes-based *Higham Special* (*Chitty IV*), resplendent in a coat of fresh white paint. This he drove in two races. In the first his handicap was too severe, and in an encounter with his friend Howey's Leyland-Thomas, he was not placed. But he won that large trophy, the Brooklands Gold Vase, later on in the afternoon at an average speed of 98½ m.p.h. Cars had become too fast to be brought in the Finishing Straight to finish. This was the first meeting at which the finishing line was on the Railway Straight, which spoilt much of the fun for the spectators.

The results at Gottleuba hill-climb held later in the month were interesting. There were two classes, one for amateur drivers, one for professional. This was also a common practice in England at the time. Caracciola won the professional class, but Gerhard Kluge won the amateur, beating Caracciola by eight seconds, making fastest time of the day, and winning a Gold Medal.

July was another good month that began with Caracciola and Kappler winning their classes at the hill-climb with the delightful name of Kupferhammer—Copper Hammer! Willy Hof won his class in the 24-hour endurance test through the Taunus mountains on a *28/95*, and Gerhard Kluge made fastest time of the day at the Kodelberg races, on his 1½-litre supercharged car. These little cars were in good form, registering a great many wins for Mercedes, and Kluge, who came from Königswartha, drove them very well. This interesting figure only started racing in 1923, and in 1924 he consistently challenged Caracciola on equal terms and consistently beat him. He died early in 1925.

Another very interesting person also made an appearance: Frau Ernes Merck. This astonishing girl in her middle twenties used to drive supercharged Mercedes, and before that, quite big Mercedes and Benz cars, much better than most men. Later, driving a *36/220*, it was quite normal for her to finish a few seconds behind Caracciola. On July 6 she won her class and the Ladies' Cup at the Bickenbach hill-climb. Her death at the early age of twenty-nine, in December 1927, robbed the sport of a most colourful and attractive figure.

Mercedes did not win the Königstuhl hill-climb that year. It was won by that incredibly clever little car, so many years ahead of its time, the 'teardrop' Benz, driven by Willy Walb. The next three finishers were all Mercedes cars, Frau Ernes Merck among them.

Mercedes entered for the Spanish Grand Prix, won that year by Segrave on a Sunbeam, with Costantini's Bugatti in second place, followed by two Delages. Masetti crashed his Mercedes but was not seriously hurt. In another crash, however, Lee Guinness's mechanic was killed.

In England, in September, Dario Resta, who had been such a well-known figure at the wheel of the great chain-driven Mercedes bolides before the 1914–18 war, was killed driving a Sunbeam at Brooklands, his car charging through the corrugated iron fence on the Railway Straight.

On September 14, the marque achieved the other main triumph of the year. Christian Werner, on one of the small 2-litre four-cylinder cars, broke the record up Semmering, made fastest time of the day, and scored an outright win. Neubauer on a similar car was not very far behind. But the unsung hero of the day was Otto Salzer, whose time on a 1914 Grand Prix Mercedes was even better than Neubauer's on a 2-litre.

The works sent a team to San Sebastian for the meeting there. A Spaniard named Turbicio Bea had bought a 1½-litre supercharged car and brought Carl Sailer from Untertürkheim to drive it for him. This won its class, but works driver Walter Gärtner drove a *28/95* faster than Sailer, remaining at the wheel without relief for the whole of the 250-mile course. He also won his class.

Another outright victory followed. Otto Salzer, who had proved his mettle as a hill-climber at Semmering, made fastest time of the day and broke the class record for the Schwabenberg climb in Hungary. He was driving a 2-litre 'blown' car. Otto Merz on a 'blown' 1½-litre, von Zsolnay on his *28/95* and Imre Bardi, on what appears to have been one of the old 1914 Grand Prix Mercedes fitted with a supercharger all won their classes. The two last-named also annexed class records. In Italy, Anselmo Cesaroni won the Rocca di Papa Climb, breaking the record for the hill. To do this on a *28/95* was a fine performance.

Four Mercedes were entered for the Italian Grand Prix at Monza. Some of these were the new eight-cylinder 2-litre 'blown' Grand Prix cars, which were known to be extremely fast, but had not hitherto been seen in public. The race was held late in October, having been postponed from September 7. Ascari, on an Alfa-Romeo, started like a thunderbolt, with Masetti hot on his tail, followed by a pack of Alfas in the very capable hands of Campari, Wagner, and Minoia. Neubauer, Werner, and Zborowski on Mercedes were not forcing the new cars, which proved exhausting to drive, and were well behind. Masetti replaced his mechanic and the other Mercedes drivers took turns to relieve each other at the wheel. On the forty-seventh lap Zborowski ran off the course. The Mercedes hit a tree and Zborowski was flung out and killed. Martin, his mechanic, remained in the car and was not very seriously injured. It was found at the three-day inquiry at Monza that the accident was due to a patch of oil on the track let down by one of the dry-sump Alfa-Romeos, although many people believed bad chassis design to be the cause. The manufacturers have never made public the results of their own subsequent investigation, but facts speak for themselves. The other Mercedes were withdrawn from the race as a mark of respect to their dead team-mate.

A word about these Porsche-designed two-litre racing-cars will not be out of place. Bore and stroke were 61·7 × 82·8 mm. (1980 cc.), the very stiff crankshaft having nine roller bearings. The engine was stressed to run up to 8000 r.p.m., lubrication being by dry sump. Twin overhead camshafts were fitted with four valves per cylinder; the engine was supercharged by a Roots blower. The brakes were cable-operated. Five cars in all were built.

After the Monza inquiry was over, the cars were brought back to Stuttgart and were hardly seen again for nearly eighteen months.

S. C. H. (Sammy) Davis has brought two curious facts to light. The cause of Zborowski's father's death in the La Turbie hill-climb was, that while swinging his great motor round a corner, his cuff caught in the handle throttle (there were no foot accelerators in those days) pulling it wide open. After this, racing motorists started to wear shirts or overalls buttoned tightly at the wrists. But Lou Zborowski was wearing, when he was killed at Monza, the cuff-links his father had been wearing when he was killed at La Turbie twenty-one years before.

Certainly young Zborowski was very much missed among the motor-racing set in England, where he and his gang of young friends had enlivened things so very much with their parties, their funny hats, and their practical jokes. Some of his friends subscribed for a memorial to him by the French sculptor Diosi, which was erected at Le Mans in 1928.

The year 1924 had been a very full one in which the Mercedes Company had learned a number of lessons. The fact that the new eight-cylinder Grand Prix cars were not at concert pitch was partially balanced by the great number of successes gained by amateur drivers who paid their own expenses and received little unpaid works support. The following year, 1925, was to see the beginnings of the large supercharged Mercedes sports-cars, which would vie with the *30/98* Vauxhall, the 3-litre Sunbeam and the Bentley as the beau idéal of the sporting amateur in England.

## 1925

The first victory in 1925 was Gerhard Kluge's last race. He made fastest time of the day and won his class on a 1½-litre supercharged car, at the Oberau-Ettal hill-climb. A few months later he was dead and Germany had lost one of her two most promising cadet drivers.

In England, a trim white 2-litre 'Targa Florio' type Mercedes made its appearance at Shelsley Walsh hill-climb in the hands of E. Mayner. The shrill squeal of its blower excited the crowd, which included a teen-age Cambridge undergraduate named Scott-Moncrieff. Mayner, who was a salesman at British Mercedes, did extremely well, being less than one second behind the immortal Segrave on a Grand Prix Sunbeam, and beating Coe's *30/98* Vauxhall by nearly five seconds. This car, one of the Targa Florio team, is still in England, but the double-cam engine has now been removed and it is powered by an ordinary single-cam 'blown' Mercedes engine.

In May, the new, Porsche-designed, 6-litre supercharged sports-car made its début in the hands of that fine Italian amateur driver, Anselmo Cesaroni, who brought it into third place in the Coppa del Perugia. There is bound to be a certain amount of confusion here owing to the different system in Germany of rating horse-power to our own, although the developed horse-power is the same. Thus, what the Germans call the *24/100/140* is what we call the *33/140*. Mercedes also made a smaller and not very good version of this car, called in England the *24/100*. In the following pages the English designations will be used. In 1926, an improved and shorter model of the *33/140* was produced called, in England, the *33/180*, and in Germany the model *K*.

Although the war had been over for seven years, German cars were debarred from taking part in French or Belgian classic races. In any case, in this, the last year of the 2-litre formula, Mercedes had little to put forward. The wonderful 2-litre four-

Alfred Neubauer in the car which he drove in the 1925 Targa Florio. (*The Edward Mayer Collection*)

cylinder 'Targa Florio' type cars were not really a match for the 1925 type Bugatti, Alfa, and Delage, while the 2-litre eight-cylinder car which was, if it could be kept 'buttoned-down' to the road, a match for anything built for a decade, was not ready. By the following year, 1926, with the permitted capacity reduced to 1½ litres, they were already obsolete. In the German Grand Prix (of 1926), they were permitted a token victory, after which they were developed no further. One of them was brought to England by British Mercedes and bought by Miss Dorothy Paget. It had a reputed top speed in excess of 130 m.p.h., but Tim Birkin and everyone else who drove it said that its behaviour during the final 20 m.p.h. of its speed was so completely unpredictable that the car was a menace. So it languished under a dust-sheet in Thomson and Taylor's shed at Brooklands for most of the rest of its life. This unique car is now in possession of Mr. Peck of Ashford, who has refused some astronomical sums for it from collectors, and is still pondering on the rather curious geometry of its steering.

Some of the very few appearances made abroad by Mercedes during 1925 were entries by British Mercedes, one at Skegness, others at Herne Bay and Pendine. Mayner, driving for them, made fastest time of the day at Skegness, beating Howey's Leyland, Malcolm Campbell's Sunbeam, Joyce's very fast

A.C., and Thistlethwayte's *30/98* Vauxhall, among the faster cars. At Pendine, Campbell's monster twelve-cylinder Sunbeam just managed to beat Mayner to second place, but the following week, at Herne Bay, the Mercedes beat all-comers.

In July came the great Batschari Competition. This is a week of every kind of event, speed and otherwise, even to Concours D'Elegance. Mercedes were highly successful, taking the first four places. Caracciola was the winner, Fritz Nallinger second, Neubauer third and Max Sailer fourth. We do not hear much about the Batschari Prize in England, but at that time it was one of the most important car tests one could win in Germany.

In the middle of August, one of the 2-litre eight-cylinder 'Monza' cars appeared magically, from behind locked doors, for the combined flat racing and hill-climb at Freiburg. Driven by Werner, it went must faster than anything else and was whisked back to Untertürkheim before anyone could have a good look at it, the racing staff having presumably gathered some useful data.

If not exactly a disastrous year for Mercedes, 1925 had certainly not been a good one. They had 'showed the flag' by entering in a vast number of small competitions in a manner that would be an example, even today, to some British manufacturers. In these, they had been moderately successful. But there had been nothing in the International field like their resounding victory in the Targa Florio the previous year.

Mercedes never built any cars for the new 1½-litre formula. It is quite possible that the directors had a shrewd idea of what was going to happen. There is little doubt that they reasoned like this: 'We are a large and prosperous company, and the costs of Grand Prix racing are soaring so rapidly that we should find the expense almost prohibitive. It is therefore unlikely that smaller firms making only luxury cars, such as Delage, will be able to continue their support for long.' This is exactly what happened. By 1928 not only had Talbot and Delage abandoned racing, but even Fiat found the expenses too ruinous and also gave up. That left Bugatti and the new Maserati, the manufacture of which had only just begun, with sporadic works entries from Alfa-Romeo. The net result of this was just as Mercedes had foreseen: to attract sufficient entrants to make the races worth while, the organizers had to run the Grand Prix as *formule libre*. Thus we had the curious spectacle of Caracciola on a Mercedes sports-car of over 7-litre capacity finishing second to a full Grand Prix Bugatti in the 1929 Monaco Grand Prix.

Mercedes must also have known that they would be building

a sports-car that could be driven every day on the road and could also compete on equal terms with Grand Prix cars of the coming few years. For example, a 1928 *SSK* had a maximum speed of 126 m.p.h., although admittedly it was rather difficult to control anywhere within 10 m.p.h. of that. The *SSK* was a direct development of the cumbrous *33/140* and must have been envisaged, if not yet actually on the drawing-board, when the company came to decide their policy for the next few years. This was to leave the gadarene gallop into the financial abyss early in the proceedings, and concentrate on building such a fast sports-car that it could join in *formule libre* Grand Prix racing.

## 1926

In March of this year, *The Motor* tested the *24/100* Mercedes. This car, which was put on the market in 1924, is perhaps typical of Mercedes touring-car practice of the period. The supercharged engine was of four-litre capacity (3921 cc.), the bore and stroke being 80 × 130 mm. and the horse-power rating was 23·8. The Weyman saloon weighed no less than 47 cwt., so the chassis must have been a very massive affair indeed. The price was £1750. Performance was not remarkable. On the low top gear (4·7 to 1) the car was timed at 74·38 m.p.h. over a half-

Attractively bodied supercharged *24/100*, circa 1924. (*Mercedes-Benz*)

mile at Brooklands, with blower in action; without, the speed was 63·83 m.p.h. 58 m.p.h. was possible in third gear, with the help of the blower. From a standing start to 60 m.p.h. took $21\frac{1}{5}$ seconds. As is usual with Mercedes of the middle twenties, the brakes are described as 'poor'.

The year 1926 saw the introduction of the *33/180*, an improved version of the *33/140*. A very impressive and beautifully built car, it sold in England for £2200 upwards, according to the coachwork. The powerful, slow-turning engine reached its peak revs very quickly, giving it extremely useful acceleration and a maximum speed of a bare 100 m.p.h. This is borne out by a lap of Brooklands done by the Mercedes demonstration car, under R.A.C. observation, at just over 98 m.p.h.

To say that the road-holding and cornering when driven at high speeds left much to be desired would be a gross understatement. In fact, this *K* model was always known as the 'Death Trap', but its worst feature was its brakes, which were as bad as bad could be. Some early *Autocar* road tests give the stopping distance from 40 m.p.h. as 145 ft.! A Dewandre vacuum servo was sometimes fitted to them, which lessened the effort on the pedal, but did not much increase the stopping power. But in spite of these faults it was a very pleasant, fast, touring-car. Its great charm lay not only in the perfection of finish in every detail, but in the way it would cruise along at 60–70 m.p.h. with its engine turning over almost as slowly as a pre-1914 giant.

The *33/180* was tested by both *The Autocar* and *The Motor* in September 1926 and by *Motor Sport* in the summer of 1927. All show the vivid acceleration possible, 10 to 30 m.p.h. taking

H.R.H. The Crown Prince of Germany in his supercharged 6-litre model *K*. (*The Edward Mayer Collection*)

Castagna-bodied model *K 33/180*. (*Mercedes-Benz*)

but three seconds on a bottom gear of 12·6 to 1 and 0 to 60 m.p.h. twenty seconds dead, using the gears and the blower. Maximum speeds over the half-mile at Brooklands was quoted as 94·75 m.p.h. by *The Motor*. *Motor Sport* found that 90 m.p.h. was quite an ordinary speed and the enthusiastic tester managed to reach the magic 100 m.p.h. twice on a run from London to Coventry. Indeed, this gentleman could find no criticism to make at all, even the brakes being thought adequate. Two years later, however, when testing a *38/250*, he did admit that driving the *33/180* at 100 m.p.h. on the ordinary road was a 'full-time job for both hands'. The capacity of the engine of the *33/180* was 6246 cc. (bore and stroke 94 × 150 mm.) and the wheelbase was 11 ft. 2 in. The chassis price was £1800, though this was reduced to £1650 in 1927.

It is difficult to understand the great variation in brakes. Some manufacturers were building cars with first-class brakes by the middle twenties but others, such as Bugatti and Mercedes, appeared to be still experimenting five or six years later.

Mercedes began 1926 with a rather pleasing victory. Count Emilio Orti-Manara, driving a *28/95* built in 1921, made fastest time of the day at the Merluzza hill-climb and Giorgio Montefiore, driving another, was second in his class. Those old *28/95*s may have been out of date from the point of view of design, but they were certainly not dead. In the Esterel and

Mont Angel hill-climbs in the south of France, with Frau Monzies driving, they scored a couple of wins. And at La Turbie, Williams, later to become an ace driver for Bugattis, won his class on a *28/85*, followed by Ernst Carstens making fastest time of the day on his *28/95* at Rendsburg.

Early in April that great sportsman, Count Giulio Masetti, renowned Mercedes driver, Florentine nobleman, and amateur champion of Italy, was killed in the first lap of the Targa Florio, driving Delage number 13. Spectators, after his crash, picked little bunches of mountain flowers and placed them reverently by his body where it lay.

The Mercedes Company brought out two new models during this year, the 2-litre *Type 200 Stuttgart* and the 3-litre *Type Mannheim*. Both were six-cylinder, side-valve motors of very conventional design. Seven bearing crankshafts were used, which is typical of these two models in which everything was built to last for ever. The price in this country, in saloon form, was £710, which even in those days was not excessive for such a well-built car. The performance of the 2-litre was very disappointing. It was heavy, incredibly low-geared and the engine, in any case, lacked power: the maximum speed over the flying half-mile at Brooklands 'in the teeth of a stiff head wind', according to *The Motor*, was 47 m.p.h. As top gear was the remarkably low ratio of 6 to 1, *The Autocar*'s effort in attaining 55 m.p.h. on the speedometer must be regarded as creditable. 14 and 25 were the speeds on the two indirect gears. Both journals found the brakes poor; in fact, *The Autocar* found that it took 92 feet in which to pull up from 40 m.p.h. Two selling points were the very smooth engine that did everything one could desire within its limited range in top gear, and the ingenious robot lubricator for the various chassis points. It was marketed in England as the *16/50* model. The 3-litre was much the same sort of car and, although it performed a little better, it was by no means exciting. It had, like its bigger brothers, wet cylinder liners, a sure hall-mark of Porsche design.

As stated on p. 129, the firms of Daimler and Benz were officially amalgamated on June 29 of this year, and future products were known as Mercedes-Benz cars.

The first major race for the new firm of Mercedes-Benz was the long-awaited German Grand Prix, at the Avus track, on July 11. The policy of the German club in having classes for 1½-litre, 2-litre and 3-litre cars was outstandingly successful. While other European Grand Prix run to the 1½-litre formula were already having difficulty in obtaining support, the German Club attracted no less than forty starters. Rain had made the

Caracciola winning the German Grand Prix on the Avus, 1926. (*Mercedes-Benz*)

surface of the Avus extremely dangerous and there was one very bad crash, Rosenberger, driving one of the eight-cylinder Grand Prix cars, going very fast, skidded into the timing-box under the big scoreboard, killing one of the occupants and injuring three others. He and his mechanic were slightly injured. Rudolf Caracciola on one of the 2-litre eight-cylinder Mercedes beat all-comers in all classes, averaging 84·5 m.p.h. for 254 miles.

In England, on Southport sands, Mayner won a ten-mile race on a *33/140*, while in Spain an extraordinary 'David and Goliath' comedy was played. The Spanish Grand Prix for racing-cars was followed by a similar race for touring-cars. Daimler-Benz sent down a team consisting of three *33/140*s and the following pairs of drivers—Merz and Gärtner, Caracciola and Kuehnle, and Christian Werner and Willy Walb. The *33/140*s came to the starting line weighing nearly three tons, and their brakes can only be described as pathetic. The result was that not only did Minoia win on an O.M. touring-car of only 2-litre capacity, but the Mercedes were hopelessly outclassed by the little 1096-cc. 'dish-cover' Chenard Walckers, of the type that had won the Rudge-Whitworth cup the previous year at Le Mans. Mercedes also used up all the Continental tyres they had brought with them and had to search frantically for some others with which to finish the race. All that can be said for this fiasco is that they won their class and learned some valuable lessons.

The model *K* (or *33/180*), now made its first public appearance. Caracciola broke the record for sports-cars with it over the flying kilometre at Freiburg, which he covered at about 95 m.p.h. Werner on the eight-cylinder Grand Prix car went a good deal faster but only scored second place in the racing class. Count Oeynhausen-Sierstorpff's *33/140* won the touring class. When it came to the 7-mile hill-climb, run in conjunction with this, Christian Werner managed to get the eight-cylinder car going in no uncertain manner, making fastest time of the day and taking the record for the hill.

We now come to a rather interesting comparison in times. Mercedes-Benz sent three *K*-type cars to the International Klausen hill-climb, which is 21½ kilometres in length. Two were driven by Caracciola and Otto Merz, and the third by the dashing amateur, Ernst Günther von Wentzel-Mosau. They finished in that order, with Caracciola making best time of the day for touring-cars. He also took the touring-car record. Georg Zettritz of Berlin brought his *33/140* into fourth place. Now, let us compare for a moment, Caracciola's time with that of Rosenberger on the 2-litre eight-cylinder Grand Prix car, third in the racing-car class. In 21½ kilometres, Caracciola was only 13·2 seconds behind Rosenberger. Even allowing for the fact that Rosenberger did not go quite as fast as Werner on a similar car the previous year, it is quite clear that the *K* model was going to be an infinitely better car than its predecessor, the *33/140*. In the speed trials run the following day, in conjunction with the Klausen climb, Caracciola made best time of the day for a touring-car.

It will be observed that Alfred Neubauer's name has not been seen among competing drivers of this year. The reason for this was that in 1926, the directors of Daimler-Benz, realizing that although only a moderately successful racing driver, he was without equal for organization and attention to detail, had placed him in charge of the racing department. This position he continued to hold for over thirty years.

Now that Daimler and Benz had amalgamated, Willy Walb, the Benz driver, was driving Mercedes cars. He had gone to Benz in 1914 to build aero-engines. After the war he took over Fritz Erle's position in the research and development department. He has a long and formidable list of successes to his name. Among them, he won the sports-car class in the Solitude races that year. Curiously, the fastest lap was put up by another works driver called Hailer, also on a *K* model. The racing class was won by Otto Merz on one of the eight-cylinder Grand Prix cars.

For nearly a quarter of a century, both Mercedes and Benz had been sending cars to the Semmering hill-climb. This year, for the first time, the firm of Mercedes-Benz made its entry, and very successful it was. Caracciola made fastest time of the day for any touring-car and won the class for touring-cars up to 8 litres, driving a *K* model. Count von Berckheim was second, about two minutes slower. It was a very creditable performance on Caracciola's part to get that difficult car up the 10-kilometre climb in eight minutes, an *average* speed of nearly 50 m.p.h. The fastest time of the day was made by a most interesting car, also driven by Caracciola. This was one of the old 1914 Grand Prix cars, fitted, under the direction of Dr. Porsche, with a supercharger. The time taken for the 10 kilometres was 6 minutes 40·8 seconds which makes interesting comparison with Otto Salzer's climb in 1924 with the car in unsupercharged condition, in 7 minutes 5·4 seconds. No one else approached this performance till 1928 when Caracciola, driving an *SSK*, just managed to knock half a second off the time! Even von Brauchitsch driving an *SSK* in 1930 could get no nearer to it than 7 minutes 21·2 seconds. Caracciola has put up some epic performances, but this particular drive on the 1914 car is outstanding.

The year 1926 ended with a rather interesting indication of the shape of things to come. Hitherto, organizers of competitions had been rather indifferent about whether engines were supercharged or not, but now official cognizance began to be taken. At the Zirleberg climb, Count von Berckheim made fastest time of all touring-cars, but, because his *K* model was supercharged, he had 5 per cent added to his time, which brought him down to second place in his class.

## 1927

The following year the policy of the directors of Mercedes-Benz in turning their backs, temporarily, on Grand Prix racing and concentrating on very fast sports-cars began to bear fruit. Grand Prix racing was already on the wane, and in June 1927, at exactly the right moment, they brought out the *S* model or *36/220* supercharged sports-car. The *33/140* was rather a poor car, and the *K* model a very dangerous one, but the *36/220* developed from them was one of the finest sports-cars that has ever been built in the history of motoring. From the moment it appeared, the makers received orders for it from all over the world. In many ways it was preferable to its successor the *SS* model, or *38/250*.

*Motor Sport* tried the car early in 1928. Their first reaction was the extraordinary ease with which this large and very high-powered sports-car would trickle along in heavy traffic in top gear. Cornering was considered to be more certain than on the *33/180*, as was also the gear change, which they found to be more rapid. At Brooklands, they discovered the car would do 110 m.p.h. on the Railway Straight and comment was made on the extreme comfort at this speed of the front seats and the extreme discomfort of the rear seats. On the road, seventy was found to be a normal speed, ninety easily attained, whilst one hundred appeared twice on the speedometer. The steering was considered very light, but the Mercedes Achilles heel, the brakes, were not thought good enough. Criticism was made of the 'blower' control; it was considered that some more delicate method of operation should be provided. 'Full blast or nothing' was found disconcerting.

In this year, Mercedes-Benz entered for over ninety competitions. It is quite impossible, indeed would be tedious, to describe even the majority of them; if there has been a tendency to mention events on English soil to the exclusion of races elsewhere, this may be excused on the grounds that English readers of this book will predominate.

Von Wentzel-Mosau led off by winning his class in the Eibseestrasse hill-climb in February. In March, that very fine driver Ernst Carstens, who had exchanged his valiant *28/95* for a model *K*, christened it by making fastest time of all sports- and racing-cars at Rendsburg. But, even though Carstens had replaced his, the ancient *28/95*s were still going strong. In Italy, Giorgio Montefiore brought his into second place in both the Monte Mario and Merluzza races. In Switzerland, Hurlimann's *K* model made fastest time for sports-cars over the Genf kilometre, and in the Göttinger Hainberg races Carstens did the same. One of the old *28/95*s was the sole representative of Mercedes at the Königsaal-Jilowsicht climb where they usually did so well, and this veteran upheld the honour of the house by scoring second place in its class.

A run of small successes followed, until the Herkules 4½-kilometre hill-climb at the end of May, when another veteran gave an astonishing performance. Rosenberger, driving the Porsche 'blown' 1914 Grand Prix car, not only made fastest time of the day, but broke the record! It is not surprising that von Mosch on a *K* model, although he won his class and made best time for sports-cars, was nearly a minute slower.

Daimler-Benz did not enter any cars in the Targa Florio. It was won in May, for the third time in succession, by a Bugatti

The 1924 eight-cylinder 'blown' Grand Prix Mercedes was as fast or faster than the 2-litre single-cam Bugatti. Brakes were not the strongest point of either car, but the road holding of the Bugatti at high speeds was infinitely superior.

The most exciting event of the Wiesbaden Week was Rosenberger's remarkable performance at the Hohe Wurzel climb. With the 'blown' 1914 Grand Prix car he repeated his performance at the Herkules climb, not only making fastest time of the day but also breaking the record. Von Wentzel-Mosau on his *K* model won the circuit race and the Mercks, husband and wife, driving a *33/140* and a 1½-litre respectively, won their classes.

At Blackpool, in England, an exciting duel took place between Raymond Mays driving a 2-litre four-cylinder supercharged 'Targa-type' Mercedes and Basil Davenport's ancient, two-cylinder chain-driven G.N. This latter machine was incredibly swift, and although over forty years old still wins awards today. One novel feature of this event was that the tramway track ran alongside the course and trams were drawn up and used as grandstands. It was an exciting contest. The event was held over a half-mile from a standing start. In the first run Davenport had clutch slip and Mays scored a win by ⅜ of a second. Mays took 27 seconds. In the next run, Davenport took 27 seconds and Mays 27⅕ seconds. Excitement was at fever heat, and the judges decided to run both cars together to decide which one should win the Dunlop Trophy for fastest time of the day. Again Davenport clocked 27 seconds, but Mays broke something in his gear-box. So the judges decided that as neither car had done better than 27 seconds, they would declare it a dead heat and Mays and Davenport should share the Trophy.

There were some minor successes in Germany, and then Raymond Mays brought out the Targa car, its gear-box repaired, for the one-mile sprint run together with the 100-mile race on the sands at Southport. Mays was an easy winner of all classes, the car going beautifully and crossing the finishing line at over 100 m.p.h.

At Skegness, the Mercedes was going well, but apparently Basil Davenport's G.N. was not, because Mays beat it easily, winning the 2-litre racing class. Mays then had a close duel with Eyston driving d'Erlanger's 2-litre single-cam Grand Prix Bugatti. Mays clocked 32 seconds and Eyston 32⅛ over the distance of six hundred yards. They had one more run together, each going faster than ever, Eyston taking 31 seconds and Mays 31⅛. So Eyston made fastest time of the day. They were to have another match on the second day, but

Mays had more gear-box trouble in the form of a bent selector fork.

On June 19, the model *S—36/220*—made its first public appearance in competition. Daimler-Benz sent three cars to the opening meeting at the Nürburgring. Christian Werner drove one of the 2-litre eight-cylinder Grand Prix cars and Caracciola and Rosenberger *36/220*s. Caracciola made fastest time of the day and, what is most interesting, both *S* model cars were lapping a good deal faster than Werner's Grand Prix car. Third place in the big sports-car class went to von Mosch, of Hanover, who drove his *K* model very fast.

In July, the Baden-Baden week came round. This proved to be a walk-over for Mercedes. Caracciola and Willy Walb, driving *S*-type cars for Daimler-Benz, swept the board, with von Mosch, who had driven a *K* model with such gusto, now driving a *36/220*, very close behind them. Von Wentzel-Mosau, returned from Hungary, made fastest time of the day for touring-cars with his *K* model. Caracciola made fastest time of the day with his *36/220*, and for the second time, won the coveted Batschari prize.

A good entry, perfect weather, and a large crowd of spec-

The opening of the Nürburgring, 1927. In the front row Caracciola and Rosenberger are driving works entries, and Major von Mosch is in a privately entered *K*. (*Mercedes-Benz*)

tators made the Colwyn Bay speed trials a great success. The three-cornered struggle between Davenport's G.N., Dan Higgin's 3-litre T.T. Vauxhall, and Mays in the 2-litre four-cylinder car continued. Higgin won his class, but on this particular day was nowhere near the other two. As usual, Mays and Davenport were fighting it out on fairly equal terms. Mays was just leading with 26⅗ against Davenport's 26⅘ seconds. Then they had a second bout, both returning poorer times. On the final run, Davenport's engine quite literally burst, spraying fragments of metal all over the place like a bomb. This left the Mercedes holding fastest time of the day and the record for the track, winning the Mersey Cup, the Atlanta Trophy, and a few other awards.

On July 17 came the German Grand Prix. Once more it was divided into classes. The 1½-litre class was won by a French Talbot; Baader on a Bugatti won the 3-litre class, but was disqualified, letting that first-class woman driver, Madame Junek, also on a Bugatti, who had been running second, into first place. Of course, the *36/220* Mercedes had a 'walk-over' in the big-car class. Otto Merz, Christian Werner, and Willy Walb came home first, second and third, Werner putting in fastest lap.

The works sent a very interesting car to the two-day international meeting near Freiburg. This consisted of the old 1914 French Grand Prix engine, which Porsche had supercharged, installed in a 2-litre racing chassis! This fascinating hybrid proved to be very fast. It was not run in the flat race but in the 7-mile hill-climb. Rosenberger, who drove it, broke the record for the hill and made fastest time of the day. In the flat race, Kimpel, Walb, and Caracciola came in first, second, and third. Christian Werner made fastest time of the day on the flat and won the racing class on the 2-litre eight-cylinder 1924 Grand Prix car. Caracciola was the fastest up the hill in the sports-car class, and Kimpel and Walb were hard on his heels. Werner made very fast time up the hill on the 2-litre eight-cylinder racing-car.

The International hill-climb up the 21½-kilometre Klausen Pass was another triumph for Mercedes. Caracciola gained the class record for touring-cars with his *36/220*. He drove it again in the sports-car class and gained the record for that as well. A *36/220* was even entered in the unlimited class for racing-cars, with Otto Merz driving, and won. The *36/220*s took the first four places in both touring- and sports-car classes, with Georg Zettritz of Berlin driving an old 'flying death-trap' model *K* into fifth place. Christian Werner won the 2-litre racing class on an eight-cylinder 1924 Grand Prix car, and Rosenberger, at the wheel of the 'Porsche-blown' 1914 engine in the 2-litre chassis rocketed up in 17 minutes 17 seconds to take the Klausen record.

It was a triumphant field day for Mercedes-Benz, but the star of the meeting was Frau Ernes Merck. This was the first time she had driven a *36/220* in competition and she made second best time to Caracciola, and was not far behind him.

Frau Ernes Merck, the brilliant woman driver of Mercedes cars. (*Mercedes-Benz*)

On her second run, she clipped half a minute off her time to gain the Ladies' Prize.

Few people who were at the September meeting at Boulogne will forget it. The rain was torrential and soaked everyone to the very skin. Mud was everywhere and a great deal of it transferred itself to those portions of the faces of the competitors which were not covered by goggles. Von Wentzel-Mosau won his class in all the three sports-car contests, but in the general aggregate, the winner of the 5-litre class, Pollack on a sports Panhard-Levassor, was a fifth of a second quicker. Those big, heavily built sleeve-valve sporting Panhards were very fast, but it seems well nigh incredible that one should have beaten a *36/220* Mercedes in the aggregate of two sprints and a hill-climb.

Semmering, that hardy Mercedes annual, came round again. Rosenberger and Prince Max zu Schaumburg-Lippe were the victors. Rosenberger drove a *36/220* in the sports class and took the sports-car record for the hill. The Prince drove his *36/220* in the touring class and gained the touring-car record.

At Brooklands, a week later, Raymond Mays brought the 2-litre eight-cylinder 1924 Grand Prix Mercedes to the line, the first time that it had been run in this country. The crowd were on their toes to see this little car that, although three years old, had the reputation of being able to out-perform almost anything else on the track. It had been brought into the country, some months previously, by British Mercedes and great things were expected of it. Its first race, the Lightning Short Handicap, could not have been a greater fiasco. Most of the eight cylinders oiled their plugs, and the Mercedes was left on the starting line looking remarkably stupid. In the 100 m.p.h. long handicap (8½ miles) Mays was on scratch with George Eyston who was driving a type *39* Bugatti. The type *39* Bugatti is a temperamental machine, not noted for its reliability, but on this occasion it ran well, and although the Mercedes went splendidly, it had to take second place to Eyston's car. But few spectators noticed this; they were all too busy watching John Cobb, who had dropped the track rod of his monster Fiat at over a hundred miles an hour and was wrestling with the steering of the huge car on his one remaining wheel, while the other one flapped about like a mad thing.

Shelsley Walsh came round again. The early autumn day could not have been wetter. Mays was driving the four-cylinder Targa Florio Mercedes. It was soon abundantly clear that it was going to be a three-cornered struggle between Davenport's two-cylinder G.N., the Mercedes, and the immensely powerful twelve-cylinder Sunbeam which did not seem at all easy to manage on the narrow tricky hill. Mays beat the Sunbeam easily and the last year's record as well, but he could not equal Davenport's 47⅘ seconds, which was fastest time of the day and a new record for the hill.

At the London Motor Show in October crowds jostled each other for a glimpse of the wonderful new world-beating *36/220* Mercedes. Three other cars were shown, a *33/140*, a *Mannheim*, and a *Stuttgart.*

In December, Frau Ernes Merck died. She was only twenty-nine years old. Had she lived we might well have seen a woman in the first line of Mercedes drivers.

In December also, we heard a new name from South America. Carlos Zatuszek, who emigrated from the old Austro-Hungarian Empire to the Argentine, was fourth in one race and second in another on one of the old 'death-trap' model *K*s. We shall hear more of him.

During the year, the directors of Daimler-Benz found that they had now gained a firm grasp on building extremely fast sporting cars instead of Grand Prix cars, and 1928 was to see the support for Grand Prix racing sink to an even lower ebb. They were not resting on their laurels but were hard at work on the *SS* and *SSK* models which were to appear in the summer of 1928. The capacity of the engine was increased to 7·1 litres

*SSK* built specially for the Hon. Dorothy Paget, with body by Barker. She used it very little and sold it to David Scott-Moncrieff. Now in Briggs Cunningham's museum. (*The Edward Mayer Collection*)

for the *SS*, and a number of detail modifications were made. The *SSK* was a short chassis edition of the *SS*, some eight or ten miles an hour faster. During 1928, the *Mannheim* and the *Stuttgart* models were given engines of a bigger capacity, 3½ litres and 2·6 litres respectively. They were now known as the *Mannheim 350* and the *Stuttgart 260*. Porsche had also designed a 4½-litre straight-eight touring-car called the *Nürburg*, which appeared in 1928. It was shown in this country, but nobody liked it, and the general concensus of opinion was that, for this type of car, a good American car was better value for money.

At the Motor Show at Olympia, six models were exhibited. These were the *16/50*, chassis price £540, and the *21/60*, chassis price £700. These two were unsupercharged. The other four, all 'blown', were the *24/100*, the *33/140*, the *33/180* and the *36/220*. The chassis prices were, respectively, £1200, £1550, £1650 and £2000.

## 1928

The German Grand Prix at Nürburgring was the début of the *SS* model, or *38/250* as it was called in England. Caracciola, who was fast becoming a master on this track, won it, making fastest lap of the day. Otto Merz was second, winning the Ernes Merck Memorial prize. Another *SS* model was third, driven by the veteran Christian Werner, and Georg Kimpel brought another into fifth place. Considering that they were opposed by a large number of fast Grand Prix Bugattis, it was a very good performance by Mercedes to get first, second, and third places, even on their own ground. Ten days later, Caracciola showed, for the first time, an *SSK* at the Gabelbach hill-climb. He made best time of the day and broke the record.

In the paddock at Shelsley Walsh that summer an amusing comedy was witnessed. H. F. Clay, a wealthy Midlander no longer in his first youth, was driving his own *33/180*, and also a *36/220* which was being lent him for the occasion by British Mercedes. The opposition in the big sports-car class was very fierce, including as it did, E. R. Hall, one of the best *30/98* Vauxhall drivers in the country, Woolf Barnato on a Bentley, Hughes on another *30/98*, and so forth. Hans Gaedertz, who had just been sent over from Germany to manage the British Mercedes concern, was determined that Mercedes should win the class. Clay took his *33/180* up with considerable skill and caution, but not nearly fast enough to satisfy Gaedertz, who was now quite convinced that Clay would not get the *36/220* up fast enough to beat Hall, who had put up a very

good time on his *30/98*. So Gaedertz produced an enormous silver hip-glass, full of Kirschwasser, and persuaded Clay to take a liberal swig. Clay then proceeded to send the *36/220* rocketing up Shelsley Walsh in fine style, beating Hall's time and winning his class.

In Northern Ireland, an excellently organized long-distance road race, the Tourist Trophy, was run on Continental lines. There was no official Mercedes entry but an English amateur, T. H. Thistlethwayte, entered an attractive-looking white *36/220* that was the cynosure of all eyes. The car was prepared by British Mercedes and Fred Kindell, their tester, drove with him. Although they accomplished the fastest lap they were never very far up in the race, firstly because of plug trouble and secondly because a Riley just ahead of them dropped a gallon

*Above:*
1928 Mercedes-Benz *SS* 7·1-litre supercharged *38/250*. (*Mercedes-Benz*)

*Below:*
1928 *36/220* with outstandingly beautiful body by the Italian coachbuilder, Castagna. (*Mercedes-Benz*)

or so of oil out of its sump on to the road, so that the Mercedes spun round and was 'ditched'. They never knew by what superhuman efforts they managed to get the heavy car out again, but they did and were gradually picking up places. They had, however, lost too much time to do any good. Dick Watney, son of Gordon Watney of Mercedes fame, was driving a Stutz, which he also 'ditched' and somehow managed to 'unditch', just succeeding in beating the Mercedes.

In the Swiss hill-climb championship at Geneva, Blattler of Basle driving a *36/220* made best time of the day for sports-cars, and Caracciola, driving an *SSK* model was second in the Salzberg races. Then came Semmering, traditionally a red-letter day for Mercedes. This year was no exception. Caracciola on his *SSK* model broke the record for the hill, Baron von Wentzel-Mosau on his *SS* won his class, as did a Viennese, Wenzler, on a *36/220*.

The Motor Show at Olympia came round again. British Mercedes did not show an *SS*, but they showed the *K* model. It looked very high and old-fashioned beside the *S* model (selling at £2000 for the chassis) on the same stand. About this time, British Mercedes had given up their showrooms in Long Acre (now a fruit warehouse) and had taken an attractive modern showroom in Davies Street, almost opposite Claridge's Hotel. They also showed for the first time the *32/90* unsupercharged 4½-litre straight-eight. This was well enough built, but it was never popular in England. Probably no more than two or three, at the most, were sold. The type of buyer for whom it catered could get a Packard, which gave him everything he wanted, for about £300 less (the price of the

Caracciola's hat trick. He won the long Semmering hill-climb three times. This time in 1928 with an *SSK*. (*Mercedes-Benz*)

saloon, in 1929, was £1195). *The Autocar* tried this car on two occasions, in March 1929 and in March 1930. In 1929 they found that 33, 47 and 75 m.p.h. were possible on second, third and top gears. Acceleration, for a car weighing 42 cwt., was quite brisk. The brakes, operated by a Dewandre servo system, for once seemed to stop the vehicle. Petrol consumption was 16½ m.p.g. In 1930, the car tested gave a much poorer performance all round, which is curious as the specification, gear ratios and weight were all exactly the same as a year earlier. The very light and excellent steering is commented upon, as is also the excellent top gear performance. In truth, the *32/90* is most characteristic of Mercedes touring-cars of the twenties. Ultra-smooth engines and very refined controls spoilt by low axle ratios, necessitated by undue weight. A near parallel are Sunbeams of the period. Both firms had great racing records and produced one superb sports-car, whilst the remainder of their models were no better in performance than the products of less distinguished marques.

About this time, wealthy purchasers began to demand closed or drop-head bodies on the *36/220* chassis. Most of the resultant coachwork was ugly in the extreme. It was very unfortunate because the makers then raised the radiator on the *38/250*. Although this made for prettier closed bodies, not only were the open bodies far less pleasing, but the cars themselves never seemed to handle as well as the low radiator *S* model.

The year finished with a remarkable achievement by Carlos Zatuszek. He entered his *K* for the 12-hour Argentine stock-car race and won it at an average speed of nearly 70 m.p.h.! He won a silver trophy, but for driving a *33/180* at that speed for twelve hours, he deserved at least a gold one.

A week after Zatuszek's magnificent effort, Dr. Ferdinand Porsche retired, after five years as chief engineer of the company. He had come from the Austro-Daimler works at Wiener Neustadt just outside Vienna where, in 1906, he had replaced Paul Daimler as technical director. Anyone who remembers the *19/100* 3-litre sports Austro-Daimler of the late nineteen-twenties will have seen the imprint of Porsche plainly recognizable on the engine. In fact, looking at it and the *33/140* Mercedes engine together, it is not hard to realize that they were designed by one and the same man. Although Porsche had left Austro-Daimler for some years when the *19/100* Austro-Daimler began to race with considerable success, the engine was basically 'Porsche'.

When Porsche took over from Paul Daimler for the second time in his life, one of the first jobs was to develop the wonderful 2-litre straight-eight Grand Prix car, which had been started by Paul Daimler. He certainly developed the engine in no uncertain manner. It was a pity that the chassis did not equal it. Porsche should, however, be given the greatest credit for the development of supercharged engines, which he initiated and carried through during his time with Mercedes.

After the fusion of Daimler and Benz, the two 'construction bureaux' were amalgamated, with Dr. Porsche and Hans Nibel as joint chief engineers. Porsche left the firm on December 31, 1928, and Nibel was then in sole charge. But Porsche had already cut his niche in the hall of fame, for long after people have forgotten that he designed the *Tiger* tank and a great deal of the *Volkswagen*, not to mention the Auto-Union racing-car, and the 4-c.v. Renault, they will remember him as the creator of the *36/220* and *SSK*, both of which made history.

## 1929

Nothing very new or exciting in the way of touring-cars was produced during Hans Nibel's first year. The eight-cylinder engine was increased in capacity from 4·6 litres to 5 litres and was now known as the *Nürburg 500*. But even the small extra power failed to make it a very interesting car. The 3½-litre *Mannheim* was, however, becoming rather a nice car. It was increased to 3·7 litres and was known as the *Mannheim 370*. Some were made with a particularly attractive low-built coupé body, with a big trunk aft. Only a few were imported to England and the Secretary of the Mercedes-Benz Club has one, built about 1932, which is still in daily use. This car represented very good value in England for a vehicle of such fine quality; it cost rather less than £1000.

In 1929, it could be said metaphorically that Mercedes-Benz were just approaching 'top dead centre' in the competition world, reaching their highest point in 1930. In 1931 they were just beginning to decline, reaching the bottom of the 'stroke' in 1933, before coming up again in 1934.

The competition year started off with some successes at the Garmisch-Partenkirchen trials. A new name appears here, that of Hermann, Prince zu Leiningen, who was to race Mercedes cars with some success, and later drive on a number of occasions for E.R.As.

It was a sporting effort to run an *SSK* model in the Grand Prix of Monaco at Monte Carlo. There could be no car less suitable for the 'round-the-houses' course through the narrow twisting streets of the Principality of Monaco. However, Caracciola drove a magnificent race, and, although running sixth at one time, he worked his way up steadily to first place, with Williams and Bouriano on Bugattis hard on his heels. Petrol was poured in from cans, not pressure fed, so filling his tank lost him precious seconds. Also, the Bugattis managed to go through on one set of tyres, and Caracciola was forced to change his back wheels. These two items cost him the 133 seconds that he needed to win the race and he finished third to Williams on a Bugatti and Bouriano's bright yellow car of identical make and type.

In the Wiesbaden rally, Mercedes filled the first five places. They had started from all sorts of far-away spots like Tarifa, Valencia, and Varna in Bulgaria. In the race, run in conjunction with this rally, three *SSK*s driven by Willy Rosenstein, Wenzler of Vienna, and Wilhelm Merck finished in that order in their class.

Thistlethwayte won the 100-mile race on the sands at Southport. His *36/220* was hotly opposed by Dan Higgin on the old but swift French Talbot and Raymond Mays on his Vauxhall-Villiers. Thistlethwayte carried off, among other awards, a large Gold Vase given by the *Daily Dispatch*.

Nevertheless, although Mercedes-Benz were quite successful on the Continent, they were not doing so well in England. Two Mercedes were entered for the six-hour race at Brooklands and neither finished. In the case of Howey's *SSK* it was not really the car's fault. The special coachwork could not stand up to the appalling hammering it got and bits flew off in all directions. Thistlethwayte's car, unfortunately, lost its oil pressure with accompanying 'expensive noises'. Barnato and Jack Dunfee in a *Speed Six* Bentley met with no trouble at all and won the race easily.

Thistlethwayte entered his Mercedes for the Irish Grand Prix, run over the Phoenix Park circuit in July. His car was a good deal faster than the Bentleys in practice and led the race for a couple of hours with Tim Birkin's 4½-litre supercharged Bentley immediately behind him. However, a blown cylinder-head gasket robbed him of any chance of victory.

There were thirty-five starters in the Grand Prix des Nations at Nürburgring on the same day. Caracciola drove brilliantly and led for four laps, until his engine gave trouble and he had to retire. After that it was an 'all-Bugatti' race, but two *SSK*s driven by Momberger and Count Arco, and Rosenstein and Rosenberger, respectively, were first and second in the class for sports-cars over 3 litres.

W. F. Bradley, reporting the 1929 Alpine trials, said that they were particularly gruelling that year. Certainly a number of competitors crashed trying to keep up. Willy Walb was one of them and put the Mercedes team out of the running, but his two team-mates, Georg Kimpel on an *SSK* and Christian Werner on a *Stuttgart 260*, gained first-class awards. Seven other Mercedes drivers won medals of various kinds.

Caracciola flew straight over to Belfast for the T.T. races after the Alpine trials. Air travel was still sufficiently novel in 1929 for everyone to say it was rather enterprising. Four Mercedes cars were entered. There were two official works cars, *38/250*s, driven by Caracciola, still under thirty, and the veteran Otto Merz.

Merz was a man of terrific strength and an iron constitution; he was one of the very few who could lift a Mercedes on to the jack without any mechanical aid. There were, in addition, two private English entries, both *36/220*s, driven by Miss Maconachie and Thistlethwayte.

The drivers sprinted to their cars, there was a whir of starters and they were away, with Kidston's big Bentley leading Caracciola. The German drove magnificently and passed Kidston on the first lap. Tim Birkin driving one of the first of the supercharged Bentleys was lying third. The race

The Mercedes team for the 1929 Irish T.T.: Caracciola, 'Scrap' Thistlethwayte and Otto Merz. (*The Edward Mayer Collection*)

Otto Merz in the 1929 T.T., tearing off a crumpled mudguard with his bare hands. (*The Edward Mayer Collection*)

was being run at great speed and was, even in the first few laps, beginning to take its toll. Rubin crashed, which put one of the Bentleys out of the race. The Maconachie Mercedes lost a lot of time by overshooting the Newtownards turn. Beris Wood on a supercharged Bentley was dogged with plug trouble. That left only Kidston, on the *Speed Six*, and Birkin to oppose the Mercedes.

The rain began, and how it rained! Everyone, including Otto Merz, seemed bothered by it, if only for the reason that the surface of the course became very unpredictable. The rain had, however, its usual effect on Caracciola. When everyone else started to slow up he went rather faster. Merz skidded and damaged one of his front wings, so that it rubbed on the wheel. Then something happened about which people talk more than thirty years afterwards. Merz got out, and exerting all his legendary strength, tore the offending wing off with his bare hands. To run with only three wings was, strictly speaking, against the rules, but whether the officials were so amazed at the feat of strength or whether none of them spoke enough German to explain the rules to Merz, they took a lenient view of the incident.

At the end of the fourth hour, Caracciola had worked his way up against handicap to sixth place, the Maconachie car had run out of fuel on the course, and Merz and Thistlethwayte

*38/250* in the 1929 Irish T.T. Nobody worried about crash helmets in those days. (*The Edward Mayer Collection*)

were well behind. After five hours, the suspense was terrific. Campari's Alfa, followed by two Austin Sevens, were leading the Mercedes on handicap. Inexorably as fate, the big white car crept up on them and before the end of the race had passed them to receive the chequered flag first, having averaged 72·82 m.p.h. over the whole course. In the final placing, Otto Merz was thirteenth and Thistlethwayte, who had been bedevilled with small troubles the whole way, finished fifteenth.

Almost immediately after the race, Lord Howe bought the winning Mercedes and fitted it with a special metal-framed Birmabright body by Hoopers, the Royal coachbuilders. This wonderful car is now in America.

*The Autocar* tried the T.T. winner soon after the race and found that at 3000 r.p.m. it would do respectively 35, 72, 91·25 and 109·6 m.p.h. on the gears, the ratios of which were 7·88, 4·52, 3·04 and 2·5 to 1. Scott-Moncrieff owned the car at a later date and found it as fast as any of the three *SSK* types he owned and infinitely steadier right up to its maximum speed; it also had a far better gear-box. *Motor Sport* tested an ordinary *38/250* in November 1929 which had the standard axle ratio of 2·75 to 1. Rather surprisingly they claimed a speed of 114 m.p.h. They found the car very comfortable at 70 and running on half-throttle at 90. 8 m.p.h. was possible on top gear.

Eighteen months later, *The Motor* tried a *38/250* and with the lower axle ratio obtained 65, 85 and 103·2 m.p.h. on the gears. 0 to 90 m.p.h. took forty-five seconds. As this car was not fully run-in and the weight was 47 cwt., these figures are very good. Petrol consumption was 12/13 m.p.g.

The International Automobile Week at St. Moritz, for which Caracciola had flown back from Ireland, was quite a gala for Mercedes-Benz. In the touring class of the rally an eight-cylinder and six-cylinder were first and second, having been driven an astronomical number of miles by Georg Zettritz and Wessels respectively. The flat races were mostly Mercedes

The author's *38/250* having a complete rebuild. (*Staffordshire Sentinel*)

Engine of the *38/250*, in production from 1928 to 1932. (*Mercedes-Benz*)

victories. Momberger made fastest time for sports-cars with Prince zu Leiningen second, both on *SSK*s. In the touring class Georg Zettritz just managed to make best time on a *36/220*. He only beat, by one-tenth of a second, Frau Paula Merz, a Swiss lady, driving a *38/250* who won the Ladies' Prize. Alfred Hirte, junior, was third on an old *K*. Best time of the day was made by Rosenberger on the supercharged 1914 car in achieving 115 m.p.h. Caracciola and Rolf von Dojmi on *SSK*s were first and second in the class for racing-cars up to 8 litres. But even Caracciola did not go quite as fast as Rosenberger.

Mercedes-Benz achieved further victories at the Gaisberg races in Austria. Von Brauchitsch driving a *38/250*, made fastest time for a touring-car and Count Arco made best time of the day on an *SSK*. Prince zu Leiningen and Werner Billwiller, both on *SSK*s, were second and third to him. In the Italian Grand Prix at Monza, Mercedes were opposed by a veritable swarm of Bugattis and Alfa-Romeos. However, Momberger on his *SSK* and Caflisch on his *36/220* finished third and fifth, respectively, Varzi being the winner on an Alfa-Romeo.

In England, a delighted crowd watched Lord Howe tearing up Shelsley Walsh on his newly-acquired T.T.-winning *38/250*. He won his class by a handsome margin. Thistlethwayte on his *36/220* ran second to him. The *36/220* was being replaced by a *38/250* with a very attractive Le Mans-type 4-seater by Martin Walter of Folkestone, but it was not ready in time for Shelsley Walsh.

On the Mercedes-Benz stand at the Motor Show a *38/250* model was exhibited, as was a 2·6-litre coupé. A straight-eight of the *Nürburg* type was also shown, with 5-seater cabriolet coachwork. The general impression of the latter was that it was rather overpriced at £1125.

The year was brought to a triumphant conclusion by Carlos Zatuszek winning the Grand Prix of Audax Cordoba, in the Argentine, over a course of about 330 miles, with his *SSK*.

## 1930

The first important race of this year was the Mille Miglia in Italy, held in April. A flag, held aloft and dropped by a picturesquely bearded Fascist official, started the race from Brescia. It was Caracciola's first attempt in this heroic event and he realized only too well that he did not know the roads nearly as well as the native Italian drivers. The one hope for him, and his co-driver Christian Werner, was to make the most of their superior speed on the long straights over the dusty plains of Lombardy. The nippy little Alfas, driven by Italians who knew every bump and every corner, would be a good deal faster on the twisty portions of the course.

This was indeed the case, and Caracciola and Werner drove a magnificent race to finish sixth out of thirty-seven competitors. Nuvolari, Varzi, and Campari, all driving Alfa-Romeos, were the first three home. Then came Cortese's Alfa, Bassi's O.M., and the *SSK* very close together with only three or four minutes between the three of them. It was a good performance on the part of the two Germans and laid well the groundwork for the victory the following year.

The 1930 Twenty-four Hour race at Le Mans was one of the most thrilling ever run. Caracciola and that wily old veteran, Christian Werner, were pitted on an *SS* (*not* an *SSK*), against all the might of the Bentley team, in the heyday of their glory, and the 'blown' Stutzes, which were quite fast and reliable enough to present a very real menace.

The saga of the Birkin-Caracciola duel, with the Bentley, minus one tyre tread, nipping past on the grass, is history, and there is not, alas, space to tell the epic story in detail. Very briefly, what happened was this: Kensington-Moir's orders to the Bentley team were that Sammy Davis should sit on the tail of the Mercedes and never leave him, and that Birkin should do all in his power to 'drive him to death', just as Sailer had tried to break up Boillot's Peugeot in the 1914 Grand Prix. The Mercedes led the race for a long time. Although the Bentleys and Mercedes were both running on the same tyres, the former had constant tyre trouble and the latter did not. One Stutz caught fire and was destroyed, the other went out with transmission trouble. The ding-dong battle between the lone Mercedes and the Bentleys went on and on. First one Bentley then another harried and hustled the great white car which constantly lost and regained the lead. Then, at 1 a.m., the Mercedes, which came into the pits with flickering yellow headlamps, was withdrawn; the dynamo had broken down. Woolf Barnato won the race on that wonderful old *Speed Six* Bentley, the winner the previous year, with Clement on another Bentley in second place. A fine touch of sportsmanship, appreciated by everybody, was Caracciola and Werner waiting at the finish to congratulate the drivers of the winning Bentley.

This year, both the Cuneo della Maddalena in Italy and Shelsley Walsh in England were included in the climbs for the European hill-climb championship. Caracciola won his class on an *SSK* at the former and then came over to drive in the latter. Shelsley Walsh was extremely interesting in 1930, as not only Caracciola's *SSK* but Stuck's almost legendary Austro-Daimler were opposed by Basil Davenport on his V-twin-cylinder G.N. special. There were three very fast climbs. Stuck made a fresh record for the hill (42·8 seconds) that was to remain unbroken for three years. Davenport roared up in magnificent style in 44·6 seconds and Caracciola, seeing the hill for the first time, put his *SSK* up in 46·8 seconds, to make a new sports-car record.

The third round of the Mercedes-Bentley duel was fought out in the Irish Grand Prix at Phoenix Park. On handicap, owing to their bigger capacity, Mercedes had to do two more laps than the Bentleys. On the other hand, on form they should have been faster, for not only were the Mercedes engines a good deal more powerful, but the cars were somewhat lighter, 3822 pounds, as opposed to the Bentleys' 4047 pounds. It was, however, doubtful whether the extra power and speed would be of much use, for with intermittent rain, the track became very slippery. One corner, known as the 'Hole in the Wall' was particularly bad, and even Caracciola, who was at his

Caracciola after winning the 1930 Irish G.P. in a *38/250 SSK*. (*The Edward Mayer Collection*)

Lord Howe driving the ex-Caracciola *38/250* in the 1930 Irish T.T. He sold this marvellous car in 1936 to the author. (*The Edward Mayer Collection*)

best under these circumstances, had some very nasty skids there. The other two Mercedes, driven by Howe and Campbell, were also off and on the road again several times. Campbell had clutch trouble which was cured by the rough surgery of squirting a Pyrene fire extinguisher into it.

All the supercharged Bentleys were in trouble. Birkin, after a tremendous duel with Caracciola, managed to nurse a very sick car into fifth place. None of the others finished. Caracciola's *SSK* came in first, a very popular win. Lord Howe was fourth, and Campbell, a minute later, sixth.

Caracciola could learn a circuit as quickly as anyone in the world, and at the T.T. race round the Newtownards circuit at Belfast, no bookmaker would lay better than even money against him winning the race a second time. Three Mercedes-Benz cars were entered by Malcolm Campbell, Lord Howe, and Caracciola. For the *38/250* engine, three different sizes of supercharger were made. There was the standard size fitted to all *SS* and *SSK* models, and the large size, of which three later came to England. There was also an extra-large size which was used only on works-entered cars driven by Mercedes-nominated drivers. Malcolm Campbell, who only had the middle size, asked the factory to sell him one of these but they refused. So, when Caracciola appeared in Belfast with an extra-large blower, Campbell entered a protest.

The committee were very embarrassed, but all they could do was to wire to the German Automobile Club to ask if the extra-large superchargers were in series production. The situation was made even more delicate because the scrutineers at Le Mans had completely failed to notice that Caracciola was running with an oversize blower!

The German Club was unable to confirm series production, so Caracciola's Mercedes was barred from the race on Malcolm Campbell's protest. In spite of this rather unattractive incident, throughout which Caracciola behaved with admirable dignity, it was a good race. Alfa-Romeo gained the first three places, Campbell's *38/250* was tenth and Lord Howe's eighteenth.

Quite a few interesting cars were pitted against Caracciola's *SSK* and Caflisch's *36/220* in the Italian Grand Prix in the old Royal Park at Monza. Ernesto Maserati was driving the sixteen-cylinder Maserati which was probably potentially the fastest road car built at that time, but it was only too obvious that the engine had far more power than the chassis could accommodate. 'Babe' Stapp had brought over his Indianapolis Duesenberg, which was very fast and reliable, but had not the 'urge' of Caracciola's Mercedes. Lehoux's Bugatti led the race until, near the end, his gear-box broke. This left the Alfas the first three places, with Caracciola seventh and Caflisch ninth.

For 1931, Daimler-Benz produced the following cars: the *21/60* (chassis price £595), the *33/140* (chassis price £1350), the *33/180* (chassis price £1425; long chassis £1450), the *38/250* (chassis price £1950; long chassis £1985), the *32/90* (chassis price £795) and the new *42/280* (chassis price £2185). The last two models had eight cylinders; the rest six cylinders. The *21/60* and the *42/280* were fitted with the new Mercedes-Maybach six-speed gear-box. Quoting from *The Autocar*, this was 'a normal 3-speed gear-box to the front end of which is added an auxiliary 2-speed gear, the second pair of gears of the auxiliary gear being, however, utilized as the constant-mesh pinions of the normal gear-box to enable the transmission ratio to be adapted to the road conditions and to allow engine speed to be reduced.' This box had been exhibited for the first time at the Berlin Show of 1928.

The *42/280* eight-cylinder car was unsupercharged. The engine capacity was 7655 cc. and the bore and stroke 95 × 135 mm. R.A.C. horse-power rating was 44·75. The car had the enormous wheelbase of 12 ft. 4 in. and the chassis weight was 36 cwt. 280 b.h.p. was developed at 2700 r.p.m.

At the Olympia Motor Show, the Mercedes stand was not very interesting. A *38/250* drophead foursome coupé was shown which was unattractive with the hood erected, and positively

1930 7·7-litre 'Grosser' Mercedes. Probably with Italian coachwork. (*Mercedes-Benz*)

ugly when it was lowered. In addition, a *Stuttgart 21/60* cabriolet was on exhibition and a *42/280* fitted with a limousine body. This looked very vulgar and carried no price ticket. It was the prototype of the fabulous *Grosser Mercedes*, supplied to the heads of State in Germany under the Hitler régime.

At the end of December, Zatuszek, by winning a race in the Argentine and being placed in another in Chile, rounded off nicely one of the most successful competition years Mercedes or Benz have ever had.

## 1931

One may say, with considerable truth, that by 1931 the Porsche-designed sports-cars, even though the legendary *SSKL* model was still to come, were already a little out-of-date. They were being pressed hard on all sides. There was the 4·9-litre Bugatti, which, if it had not been such an extremely dangerous car in its higher ranges of speed, would have been a most serious rival. And, of course, for Grand Prix racing as opposed to sports-car racing, there was the new, almost unbeatable type *51* Bugatti. In 1931, the 2·3-litre Alfa-Romeo appeared, which as it was developed, became a more-and-more formidable competitor. All sorts of cars came out of the factory of the Maserati brothers, some of which constituted a potential threat to Mercedes-Benz. And there was the 8-litre Bentley.

When Scott-Moncrieff was once a member of a 'Brains Trust', he was asked what would be his ideal touring-car. He replied that it would be an 8-litre Bentley developed by the experimental department of Mercedes-Benz. Mackenzie, who was responsible for the development of Forrest Lycett's wonderful 8-litre car, happened to be in the audience and burst out laughing. But Rudolf Uhlenhaut, who is responsible for the building and preparation of Mercedes-Benz racing-cars, and who has been in Lycett's car, the only 8-litre that was properly developed, would be the first to admit that a works-prepared team of these cars would have constituted a very grave menace to the *SSK*s. However, as we know, Bentleys went into liquidation and were bought up by Rolls-Royce, and the 8-litre Bentley never grew to maturity.

Mercedes-Benz thus began racing in 1931 against stiffening opposition. The organizers of Grand Prix races had failed completely to reach any form of agreement with the manufacturers and so races were run under a *formule libre*, and no mechanics could be carried.

The first race of importance was the Mille Miglia in Italy, and with it we come to one of the most epic single-handed drives in the history of motor-racing, which ranks with Levassor's fantastic feat of 1895 and one or two more. The *SSKL*, a faster, lighter model of the *SSK*, made its début in the Mille Miglia driven by Rudolf Caracciola. Although he carried a reserve driver, Wilhelm Sebastian, he himself drove the whole way.

Nearly all who witnessed this race say that the big white

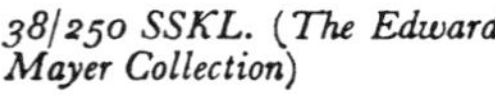

*38/250 SSKL. (The Edward Mayer Collection)*

car did not appear to be going fast. Caracciola gave the impression of taking it very easily. All round him was a swarm of Alfas with orders to catch him up and lure him on. But he took no notice and continued to run to schedule. And what a schedule! Over the 129 miles from Brescia to Bologna he averaged 95·8 m.p.h. Besides refuelling, even allowing for a stop because of a puncture, and another to fix his silencer, which was coming adrift, Caracciola completed the course nearly nine minutes quicker than the record of the previous year. Over a distance of a thousand miles he averaged 62·84 m.p.h., including all stops. Campari came in second on an Alfa, then Morandi and Rosa on an O.M. Ten Alfas followed in a row. The 4·9-litre Bugatti, in the hands of the great Italian ace, Achille Varzi, had been very much fancied as a winner. But Varzi retired, his car making very 'agricultural' noises.

Caracciola had played a lone hand (his was the only Mercedes in the race) and won. He did not know that he had won, and when he was told he was too numbed by his terrific ordeal to be surprised, or even to take it in properly. It was an epic victory.

On the same day Carlos Zatuszek won the 400-mile Easter race in the Argentine, making best time of the day and breaking the record. Ten days later Caracciola took his *SSKL* down to the blue skies of Monte Carlo, where there was a strong mistral blowing which kept on all through practice and persisted on the day of the Monaco Grand Prix. Originally, two *SSKL* cars should have run. But Boris Ivanowsky, a burly ex-officer of the Russian Imperial Guards, went to Untertürkheim to take delivery of his car, was snowed up on the way, and did not arrive at Monte Carlo in time to qualify. Caracciola's *SSKL* was probably a good deal faster and more powerful than anything else running, but its size and weight made it highly unsuitable for the corkscrew Monaco course. However, he was going very well, usually up in the first half-dozen, and his private duel with veteran Delage driver Divo, on a type *51* Bugatti, was well worth seeing and a great delight to the crowd. In the event, although Caracciola's chances of victory were of a moderate nature, he had to come in half-way through the race in trouble with his clutch, which on the *SSK* had always been rather a weak point. Chiron won the race on a Bugatti, and the veteran Andre Boillot brought a Peugeot, that looked old enough to be one of the 1913 cars, into sixth place.

In June, the third Irish Grand Prix was run over the Phoenix Park course in Dublin, in extremely bad weather. Two Mercedes cars were entered: Lord Howe's ex-Caracciola *SS* and the ex-Campbell *SS* now owned and driven by Bernard

Davis, sales manager to Jack Barclay. The handicapping was based on engine capacity, with further penalties for supercharging, so it was quite clear, long before the start, that the Mercedes cars were handicapped out of the race. This, however, did not worry Lord Howe at all. He simply rang down 'full ahead', Navy fashion, to his engine-room and charged through the spray and rain like a destroyer. In spite of his crippling handicap and the weather he was making up time in no uncertain manner. During the first half-hour he had already twice beaten the record set up by Caracciola the previous year. Bernard Davis, who had very little racing experience, was driving a magnificent race and keeping close to Lord Howe the whole time. He was outstandingly fast at Gough corner, but on one occasion executed the most petrifying skid, turning round right in front of Birkin's Alfa.

Then Davis had trouble with his supercharger not engaging properly, and came in for a brief pit stop, which only partially restored its efficiency. At this time he had been running fifth, but his blower trouble cost him fifth place to Lord Howe and he finished sixth, fifty-two seconds behind Lord Howe after three and a half hours' driving. The race was won by Birkin on the Alfa-Romeo, with Campari second on a Maserati.

The 1931 Le Mans race was unusually exciting, partly because of the dramatic behaviour of the 4·9-litre Bugattis and partly because of the extraordinary business about the Mercedes tyres, which enabled Stoffel and Ivanovsky to come in second to the 2·3-litre Alfa which had won the Targa Florio, run in the Mille Miglia, and was now driven by Lord Howe and Tim Birkin.

Glancing down the entry list, it seemed that the Bugattis could hardly fail to win. To begin with, they were at least 25 m.p.h. faster than the Alfa-Romeos, and in addition they were a beautifully prepared works entry of four cars. Moreover, they were handled by such famous drivers as Chiron, Divo and Varzi. There was also the usual gaggle of Bugattis of all shapes, sizes, and ages which a Le Mans of the nineteen-thirties always produced. Against this array of might was one solitary *SSK* Mercedes. Stoffel on the Mercedes led off and soon passed Chiron into the lead, which he held for eight laps when he slowed down, as his tyres were not enjoying the brisk pace. But much worse was happening to the Bugattis. There seems little doubt that Le Patron had gone somewhat adrift in his design of the cast-aluminium wheels-cum-brake drums, and at anything over 120 m.p.h. they shed tyres with the greatest abandon. Rost had a bad crash, due to this, but fortunately was not very seriously hurt. As for the car, Pierre Marco said years afterwards that it was the most completely demolished wreck he had ever seen. Chiron narrowly escaped the same fate when he lost a tyre for the third time and frightened himself badly. So the drivers held a quick conference with Jean Bugatti, who was managing the team, and the cars were withdrawn.

Nearly as bad a time was in store for the Mercedes, which, although it was not being driven as hard as it would go, was running through tyres voraciously. Finally, in desperation, Ivanovsky said that he would withdraw the car. There was no point in going on losing more and more time on tyre changes. Then a most remarkable and sporting gesture occurred, reminiscent of the early days of motor racing. Stoffel and Ivanovsky were under contract to Englebert tyres, and the Englebert representative suddenly suggested, on his own initiative, that before finally throwing in the sponge, they might like to give Dunlops a trial. Dunlops were fitted, first to the back and later to the front, and they had no more tyre trouble! The Mercedes went better and faster than ever, and would undoubtedly have covered a record number of miles in the twenty-four hours, had it not been for the early tyre troubles. As it was, it covered 1805 miles against the winner's 1875. Immediately after it, in third place, came the white Talbot *105*, driven by Rose-Richards and Saunders-Davis which, although appreciably slower than the Mercedes, had run throughout the race with watch-like precision.

It was a lovely June day for the French Grand Prix and record crowds streamed out from Paris to watch the race, held at Monthlery. This did not help the organizers much, because the coach carrying the gate-keepers and cashiers broke down and the record crowd swarmed in without paying.

It was a three-cornered race between Bugatti, Alfa-Romeo, and Maserati. But two Mercedes were entered, the Le Mans *SSK* and an *SSKL* driven by Caracciola and Merz. This was an occasion when there was every excuse for Ivanovsky to use unparliamentary language in his mother tongue. He and Stoffel had fitted the Le Mans *SSK* with a higher axle ratio for the Monthlery circuit. This let them down and they were out of the race at an early stage. Caracciola and Merz also had bad luck. They seem to have decided to play a waiting game and so they toured round without joining in the duel going on between the first half-dozen cars. After about two hours, however, the continuous rise and fall of the squeal from the Mercedes blower told spectators that it was not disengaging.

A prolonged pit stop, with mechanics working feverishly, failed to cure the trouble and soon afterwards the one hope that Mercedes-Benz had left in the French Grand Prix was withdrawn. Chiron and Varzi were the winners on a Bugatti, Campari and Borzacchini being second on an Alfa-Romeo.

In the Belgian twenty-four-hour race, on the Spa circuit, a magnificent duel took place between Stoffel's *SSK* and an Alfa driven by Birkin and Eyston. Another Mercedes was driven by Prince Djordjadze and Geoffrey Zehender. Both cars suffered from tyre trouble until, as at Le Mans, they changed over to Dunlop. Then bad luck overtook Stoffel and Ivanowsky. Something went wrong in the gear-box and, in spite of a brisk cross-country sprint by Stoffel to the pits, it could not be mended in time. The other Mercedes, however, forged ahead, covering the greatest number of miles in the twenty-four hours and winning its class.

Lord Howe had a small fleet of cars at the International Shelsley Walsh climb in July. He took his Alfa, his Grand Prix Delage, and his Mercedes, and drove them all very fast. He completed the climb on his *38/250* Mercedes in the excellent time of 46⅘ seconds, equalling Caracciola's sports-car record of the previous year.

The German Grand Prix of 1931 is reputed to have been one of the best ever held. There was plenty of competition for Mercedes from England, France, and Italy. There was a works entry of Bugattis. Tim Birkin was driving his Alfa; Lord Howe, and sundry other private entrants, Bugattis; Dudley Froy a Riley; Sir Francis Samuelson and Fred Kindell an M.G.; and many others. Finally, to make it really international, Shafer had brought over his Indianapolis Special from America. Shafer, incidentally, goes down to history as the first racing driver to start his car by plugging it in to an external power source instead of swinging or pushing it. This method has now become common practice.

Caracciola got his *SSKL* in front and stayed there. The weather was bad, which was in his favour, for nobody except perhaps Chiron has ever taken quite as much advantage of it as he. It was also quite clear that the racing department was getting the road-holding of the *SSKL* noticeably better than it had been. It must, however, have been a terribly tiring race, for after the winner's honours had been showered on him, Caracciola said that all he wanted was a bath and bed. The fight for second place was very keen. The following times will serve to show how close the race was: Caracciola, 4 hours, 38 minutes, 10 seconds; Otto Merz, fifth, 4 hours, 43 minutes, 54 seconds; only about five minutes between the first five competitors. Chiron and Varzi were second and third on Bugattis;

Nuvolari fourth on an Alfa. Stuck was sixth on an *SSKL* and Spandel, with Prince Hohenlohe-Bartenstein, ninth on an *SSKL*. Dudley Froy, on a Riley, won the 1100-cc. class with Count Arco, brother of the Mercedes driver, second on an Amilcar.

*The Autocar* tested the *21/60* this summer and gave an account of it in its issue of August 7. The *21/60*, it will be remembered, was one of the two models fitted with the Maybach six-speed gear-box. The engine had six cylinders, the bore and stroke being 74 × 100 mm. (2650 cc.). Normal gear ratios were 18 to 1, 9·4 to 1 and 5·3 to 1. High ratios were 11·3 to 1, 5·9 to 1 and 3·3 to 1. The saloon weighed 30 cwt. so acceleration figures of 6⅕ and 7 seconds respectively on the normal and high second gears from 10 to 30 m.p.h. were quite brisk. Maximum speed was 62·5 m.p.h. Cruising speed was given as 55 m.p.h. or rather more. Petrol consumption was 25 to 30 m.p.g. *The Autocar* regarded the *21/60* as very much of a touring-car and criticized the springing as being too soft.

Two Mercedes appeared at the Brookland August Bank Holiday meeting. Captain J. C. Davis, R.N., lost a race with his little Targa Florio car by overshooting a bend, and a 1903 *60* appeared in the parade of early cars. This latter, mounted with a Roi de Belges touring body, electrified the crowds by travelling at over 70 m.p.h., a speed of which many of the production cars of the time were quite incapable.

Every boat and aircraft going to Ireland was crammed with people going over to see the T.T. races at Belfast, which, in three years, had become an established favourite. Mercedes-Benz were content to rest on their laurels and had not entered a team. The only Mercedes running was Bernard Davis's ex-Malcolm Campbell car. It was never well up in the race and, at one moment, with co-driver Clifford Taylor at the wheel, was involved in a crash with Colonel Goldie Gardner's M.G. The Mercedes continued but later was withdrawn owing to the disappearance of the oil pressure. The race was won by an M.G. entered by Lord March, now the Duke of Richmond and Gordon, and driven by Norman Black.

It must have been about this time that Daimler-Benz made public the first of their *170* models. It was shown at the 1931 Paris Salon and made a very determined bid for the medium-priced car market. The chassis itself was one of Nibel's masterpieces of design. It only weighed about a ton with a four-door saloon body, but the small 1700-cc. side-valve six-cylinder engine did not endow it with a particularly brilliant performance. However, even if it was rather sluggish, the road-holding and springing was so good that a high average speed could be

*Above:*
The little 1931 type *170* pioneered the swing-axle behind and transverse front springing. (*Mercedes-Benz*)

*Below:*
Swing axle on the type *170*. (*Mercedes-Benz*)

maintained, especially over indifferent roads. Another innovation was a synchromesh 4-speed gear-box built under Maybach patents. This little car was the father of the thousands of mass-produced small Mercedes to be seen on the roads in years to come.

Caracciola won the 4-kilometre Drei-Hotter hill-climb, thus securing for himself the title of 'European hill-climb champion'.

In 1932 Mercedes came out with independent front springing as can be seen on this type *200*. (*Mercedes-Benz*)

Mercedes-Benz entered a works team for the Czechoslovak Grand Prix at the Masaryk ring, the distance being 310 miles. Caracciola was going well when he made one of his rare misjudgements; he hit a post which damaged his *SSKL* just badly enough to put it out of the race. The third *SSKL* also broke down, leaving Stuck, the remaining Mercedes driver, to finish second to Chiron's Bugatti, and just ahead of von Morgen, the German Bugatti ace.

At the Olympia show in London that autumn, it was quite clear that Mercedes-Benz were trying to capture the cheaper markets. The small *170* saloon was priced at only £385, which even for 1931 was quite good value. It had a six-cylinder engine, bore and stroke being 65 × 85 mm. (1692 cc.) The crankshaft had four bearings and the valves were at the side. 32 brake horse power was developed at 3200 r.p.m. 24/25 m.p.g. was to be expected. The car was independently sprung all round, coil springs at the rear and two inverted half elliptics at the front, above and below a cross member. A $2\frac{1}{2}$-litre 'six', priced at £720 for a saloon, and a *Mannheim 370* with a two-door sportsman's saloon at £795 did not attract quite so much attention. And, whether they could afford it or not, everyone came to

1931 $3\frac{1}{2}$-litre, six-cylinder *Mannheim*. (*The Edward Mayer Collection*)

see the famous *38/250* with an open 4-seater body. Freestone and Webb, the coachbuilders, exhibited an attractive little 2-door coupé on the low-chassis *Mannheim 370*.

The change of policy by the directors to enter the cheap car market was a very wise one, for in the coming years many great names, Lorraine and Sunbeam to give only two, once as famous as Mercedes, were to find that they could no longer support themselves by building expensive luxury cars. Lorraine has vanished altogether and Sunbeam is a name amalgamated with a large group and which has no direct relation with the traditional Sunbeams.

## 1932

The year 1932 cannot have been an easy one for Mercedes-Benz. Though they had entered the market for mass-produced, fairly inexpensive cars, they had to fight a world recession. In the racing world it was a hard fight too. The *SSKL* was, perhaps, the finest flowering of the vintage type of car, the lineal descendant of the great machines of the heroic age, but it had become no match for the *P3* Alfa, one of the best racing-cars ever built, and one of the easiest to drive. The type *51* Bugatti was getting somewhat less temperamental and the sixteen-cylinder Maserati, even if temperamental, was incredibly fast. The writing was already on the wall. Although the *S*, the *SSK* and *SSKL* would continue to win races for another couple of decades, they were already beginning to be outclassed in the major international events. However, all this did not stop 1932 being a successful competition year for Mercedes-Benz.

Once more a Mercedes won its class at La Turbie, this time an *SSKL* driven by Manfred von Brauchitsch. Second, and only some twenty seconds behind, came the Italian Count Trossi, on an *SSK*. Trossi was one of the greatest of sportsmen. Although he drove for nearly twenty years in first-class motor-racing, the whole time he was fighting a losing battle against the worst enemy of all, ill-health.

At the end of May, the Avus races were held. This year the meeting was remarkable for a number of happenings, including the wonderful time that the Germans gave the English drivers, the streamline body of the winning Mercedes-Benz, and the curious business surrounding the death of Prince Lobkowicz from Czechoslovakia, who was killed driving a 2·3-litre Bugatti. A fortune-teller had foretold the circumstances of his death exactly as it happened, and everybody seemed to know about it before the race, although they did not take it seriously. The *SSKL* which von Brauchitsch drove had fully aerodynamic coachwork designed by Baron Koenig-Fachsenfeld, one of the leading German aircraft designers. As usual, two races were run, in front of an immense crowd. Lord Howe won the small car race (up to 1500 cc.) on one of the five-year-old 'flat-iron' Delages, and von Brauchitsch won the race for big cars on the aerodynamic *SSKL*. The crowd of nearly a quarter of a million had the thrill of their lives over the Caracciola–von Brauchitsch duel, especially as their beloved Caracciola was

The 1932 Avus Track *SSKL*. Von Brauchitsch won the world record for 200 km. in this car. (*Mercedes-Benz*)

driving not a Mercedes, but an Alfa-Romeo! In spite of the fact that his Alfa was not nearly as fast as the aerodynamic *SSKL*, Caracciola finished the 183-mile race only 4·1 seconds behind the winner, whose average speed was over 120 m.p.h. Stuber, the Swiss champion, was third on a type *51* Bugatti, and Stuck, who had been in trouble and stopped for some time at the pits, still managed to gain fourth place on an *SSKL.*

In England, Sir Malcolm Campbell entered his lone *38/250* in the 1000-mile race at Brooklands. It could not have behaved worse; it broke a piston in practice, tore its rear tyres off, and finally, after 900 miles, dropped out of the race with some sort of transmission trouble.

The 1932 Monza Grand Prix was enlivened by the fact that no less than five lovely ladies presented themselves at different entrances to the sacred enclosure where only racing-car drivers, mechanics, and a few privileged ones are allowed, all claiming to be Mrs. Nuvolari. All five managed to get the coveted badges before a gateman who had already let in a bogus Mrs. Nuvolari refused admission to the real one, and the deception was discovered! It was a long time before the little maestro, a most respectable and happily married man with a family, lived down the chaff occasioned by his becoming, entirely without his knowledge, so extremely polygamous. Broscheck's *SSK* was the only Mercedes running and did not finish among the first ten.

The competition year for Mercedes ended with six hill-climb successes for Hans Stuck's *SSKL*. These were the 5-kilometre Kesselberg, the 12-kilometre Gaisberg, the 21½-kilometre Klausen, the 12-kilometre Freiburg, the 14-kilometre Stilfserjoch and the 21½-kilometre Mont Ventoux. At all these events, Stuck made fastest time of the day for sports-cars and on the Klausen and Stilfserjoch he broke the record as well, ending up third in the Alpine Championship for the year.

For 1933, Mercedes-Benz announced the following models: the *38/250*, the *Stuttgart 21/60* (2560 cc.), the *Mannheim 26/80* (4592 cc.) and the type *170* or *16/45* (1692 cc.). At the Olympia Motor Show, they exhibited an attractive *38/250* open 4-seater, painted black and scarlet, with red leather upholstery. The *Grosser* was not shown again, which was probably just as well, as the limelight for that particular type of car was completely stolen by the first appearance of the Bugatti *Royale* at Olympia. A *21/60* was shown with a very smart coupé body, finished in white and priced reasonably at £795. A *Nürburg* 5 litre eight cylinder (a 1928 production of Porsche's, first made with an engine of 4·6 litres and enlarged the following year to 5 litres by Nibel) was also shown with the Maybach six-

A one-off casting for the radiator cap of the ex-Kaiser Mercedes, 1932. (*Mercedes-Benz*)

speed gear-box, vacuum-servo braking, and one-shot lubrication. This car, with a drophead coupé body of very fine quality, cost £995.

## 1933

Mercedes were not, like so many other firms, allowing the aftermath of the depression to stamp out enterprise. Behind locked doors the all-conquering cars for the 1934 formula were being built and the production models improved and augmented. At the Berlin Show in February a very much improved edition of the 1·7 litre with a longer wheelbase appeared. The 2·9 litre, later to be developed under the technical directorship of Max Sailer into 3·2- and 3·4-litre cars, made its bow. In its initial stage as it first appeared at the Berlin Show, the 2·9-litre engine only developed 60 b.h.p. As it was a fairly heavy car, the performance was by no means brilliant. More will be said about the 2·9 litre (type *290*) later on. Also, the father of the *500* and *540* models was shown for the first time to the public. This consisted of a chassis, very similar to the type *500*, with an engine similar in design but small and supercharged. This produced 90 b.h.p. 'unblown' and 120 b.h.p. 'blown', which together with an 'overtop' gear that could be engaged at will, gave it a maximum speed in excess of 80 m.p.h. There are only one or two examples of this interesting car in England. The owner of one speaks very highly of it and claims petrol consumption better than 16 m.p.g. if the car is not driven too hard. Daimler-Benz were also making great progress in the field of Diesel heavy oil engines and as early as 1933 had built a twelve-cylinder unit.

This was an ill-starred year for Daimler-Benz. In April, Caracciola was practising for the Grand Prix of Monaco when his attention was momentarily distracted. He left his braking too late and rammed a wall. He felt no ill effects, and it was only when he tried to get out of the car that he realized that his thigh was broken in several places. But worse was to follow. A special streamlined *SSKL* had been prepared for Caracciola to drive at the Eifel Races round Nürburgring. As he was now in hospital, this car was given to that most reliable works driver, Otto Merz. Rain had been falling heavily during practice and the surface was slippery in an unpredictable sort of way. Merz skidded at high speed, crashed, and was killed.

It was in 1933, too, that the realm of motor racing suffered a sad loss when Tim Birkin died of blood poisoning as a result of a burn on the arm from his Maserati in Tripoli. There was all the chivalry and panache of the Middle Ages in the Caracciola–Birkin duels. It seems to those of us, now verging on middle-age, that there will never again be anything with quite the same glamour as the blue scarf with white polka dots, fluttering from the green Bentley, forever duelling with Caracciola's Mercedes. His competitors on the race-tracks of Europe grieved for him as deeply as his many friends.

Daimler-Benz did not exhibit at Olympia in 1933, but at the Paris Salon they showed a drophead foursome coupé on the new 3·8-litre chassis that stood out, even among the beautiful French coachwork, as being very attractive. The 3·8 litre, called the type *380*, had a supercharged eight-cylinder engine, the bore and stroke of which was 75 × 100 mm. (3796 cc.). The overhead valves were operated by pushrods and the crankshaft had five main bearings. Compression ratio was 6 to 1. 120 b.h.p. was developed at 3400 r.p.m. with the use of the blower, 90 b.h.p. without. The car was independently sprung all round and was fitted with hydraulic brakes. The wheelbase was 10 ft. 3½ in. The chassis price was £1140 and the saloon cost £1534.

Early in 1934, the little rear-engined type *130* appeared on the British market. This excellent little car was beautifully made but never became popular here. Perhaps its price was against it. £425 was the price of the saloon. The 1318 cc. four-cylinder engine (70 × 85 mm.) developed 26 b.h.p. at 3400 r.p.m. Its top speed was about 55 m.p.h. and it took 37⅕ seconds to get from standstill to 50 m.p.h. Petrol consumption was 30 m.p.g. The brakes were good; only thirty-one feet were needed to pull up from 30 m.p.h. The type *130* was independently sprung all round, with two transverse springs in front and coil springs in the rear.

# 4
# STAR TRIUMPHANT 1934~1939

The 1937 Avus race: Lang (Mercedes) No. 37 and Rosemeyer (Auto-Union) No. 31 in the northern curve. (*Carlo Demand: The Big Race*)

# MERCEDES BENZ *v.* AUTO-UNION

IN 1932, the prospects of Mercedes in first-class racing were none too good. The old *SSK* had been replaced by that very fast and very frightening car, the *SSKL*. This was still, basically, an infinitely refined version of the sort of car that Henry had designed for Peugeot twenty years earlier. It was also an incredibly fast sports-car, that could be used daily on the roads, rather than an out-and-out racing-car. The *SSKL* could, therefore, hardly be expected to compete with the up-to-date racing-cars built by Bugatti, Maserati, and Alfa-Romeo. This triumvirate divided most of the spoils between them in the classic races; it is remarkable that Mercedes won as much as they did.

In 1932, the A.I.A.C.R. had come to one of those periods in their history, which had occurred before, when the speed of the racing-cars was outstripping their road-holding capacity and a fresh formula would have to be devised. A classic contemporary example of this was the 4·9 supercharged Bugatti. A formula of 750 kilograms, or just over 14½ cwt., was therefore laid down for the car, without driver, oil, petrol, water, or tyres. There was also a frontal area specified, with a minimum body width of 33½ inches. It is doubtful if anyone on the committee of the A.I.A.C.R. had any idea how very fast a motor-car weighing only this amount would go, otherwise they might have had some second thoughts. This formula was to take effect in the 1934 season.

It is extraordinary to think that Dr. Nibel, who was responsible for the *Blitzen* Benz, was also responsible for the first of the ultra-modern, world-beating Mercedes racing-cars. It seems more than a fortunate coincidence that he should have been appointed to this job for he was, first and foremost, an expert on suspension and chassis design.

The directors decided to apply the grant of £20,000 a year, offered by Hitler for the year 1932, to the development of a racing-car to be ready for the 1934 season. Nibel, who was in charge of this, assisted by Max Wagner, also late of Benz, lived just long enough to see the partial success of his work, for he died in November 1934 at the age of fifty-four. A good deal of research was carried out to decide the question of whether or not to mount the engine aft. Wagner, at least, was no novice on this subject, for he had worked on the 'teardrop' Benz a decade earlier. This question was considered so important that it was eventually referred to the directors. The 'cons' very slightly outweighed the 'pros' and they decided on a conventionally-placed engine. As we know, Auto-Union did not.

In May 1933, Nibel's team started to design and build the racing car, known as *Model W25*. By the following January, the car was shown privately to Hitler, who had supported its development. By March, a team of cars, which ten months before had not even existed on paper, were undergoing tests at Monza. This, it must be agreed, was remarkably smart work. The reason why Mercedes do their testing at Monza is that early in the year, before the racing season starts, their own track, the Eifel circuit, is usually under snow.

The designers were taking a grave risk with a 4-litre engine developing 400 h.p. The all-conquering *P3* Alfa-Romeo of 2·6-litres was developing 190 h.p., which was about all the power that any chassis then designed had been able to bear. The 4·9-litre Bugatti has already been cited as an example of this. Another was the fantastic *Bimotore* Alfa-Romeo, one engine in front of the driver, one behind, which Enzo Ferrari himself said was of very little practical use. Maserati had done the same sort of thing with two eight-cylinder blocks and common crankcase, but it was not a success. However, Nibel and Wagner had decided to build something fully thirty miles an hour faster than anything yet produced so they had to have the power, and, if they had the power, they had to have chassis that could cope with it.

One acknowledged axiom is that one can go on feeding power to the road wheels till a point is reached when the wheels go round but the ground refuses to disappear. A way to bring this point much further up the scale is to keep the powered road wheels always parallel to each other and continuously in contact with the ground. This was attempted in the *W25* by fitting swing axles aft. In effect, this was two enclosed driving shafts, rigidly mounted to the wheels, but swinging on universal joints from either side of the differential casing. Movement in a vertical plane was controlled by short quarter-elliptic leaf springs, attached to the chassis underneath one end of the driving shafts, and shackled to the wheel-bearing housing at the other.

Having thus achieved independent suspension at the back, the designer proceeded to do the same in front with a wishbone and coil action. Both front and rear suspension were damped by friction disc shock absorbers.

Not content with a completely unorthodox racing chassis, Lockheed brakes were fitted, which at that time were almost unknown on European racing-cars, all of which, except the Maseratis, were using various forms of mechanical systems. Safety precautions consisted of a device which ensured that if one tube fractured, the front or rear part with the defective tube could be sealed off and the unaffected pair remain in action. A further precaution was a hand brake, coupled mechanically to the rear brake shoes.

The designers were not entirely without experience of four-wheel independent suspension, for the firm had for some years previously been building small touring-cars so equipped, but as these were considerably underpowered, such a design was evidently meant to realize a comfortable ride over rough roads rather than provide high-speed road-holding. Nevertheless, they had experience from which to work, just as they had with the engine. For this they went back to the cylinder-block arrangements of the victorious 1914 Grand Prix cars. Two blocks were built up separately from steel forgings, barrels and jackets all welded together with special metal valve seats welded into the heads. This form of construction has all the advantages over conventional castings—lightness, strength, and bigger water passages where they are most needed, i.e. round the valve seats. But the expense prohibits its use except for racing.

The engine itself was an eight-cylinder double-cam 78 × 88 mm. with a capacity of 3·36 litres, delivering 354 h.p. This was modified twice during the 1934 season, first to 3·71 litres and then to 3·99 litres, producing 430 h.p. and only weighing 15 lb. more than the original engine. Ignition was by Bosch. Naturally, the extreme lightness necessary to get an engine of this power down to the required weight was achieved by the use, wherever possible, of light alloy castings. Weight was also saved by abandoning the clutch which engaged the supercharger, blowing, as it had done in the *SSK*, through the carburettor and not sucking through it as on most other cars. This now ran at twice the engine speed and its clutch was replaced by relief valves operated by the carburettor throttles. But all this was not sufficient in itself to bring the weight down to the required 750 kg. The chassis itself had to be drastically drilled for lightness. Very thorough tests to destruction were carried out before the prototype was put on the road, which accounts for the fact that although Mercedes racing chassis looked like pieces of Gruyère cheese they never fractured. This entirely new and unconventional vehicle, built from scratch in ten months, had its full share of teething troubles. The only wonder is that it did not have more.

The new *W25* Mercedes racing-car was not the only new design to appear in Germany at this time, and to appreciate to the full the intense interest which arose and continued to exist right up to the advent of the Second World War, due to the close rivalry which developed between the two German teams of Mercedes-Benz and Auto-Union, it is necessary to say something about the history and design of the one racing-car which in these years ran Mercedes so close and indeed so often beat them.

In 1933 four of the biggest car manufacturers in Germany, Audi, D.K.W., Wanderer and Horch, forming the Auto-Union combine, decided to enter motor racing. Dr. Porsche, financed by the wealthy amateur driver Adolf Rosenberger, had already started a project. The combine, rather than start from scratch, took this over lock, stock and barrel, retaining the existing personnel.

Rosenberger had, in the middle-twenties, gained many successes with the 'teardrop' Benz, so many years ahead of its time, and accordingly decreed that the Porsche-Rosenberger car should be rear-engined. So a Porsche designed V16 engine was mounted behind the driver and ahead of the rear axle, with the gear-box outboard of the axle.

This car made its début under the name *P-Wagen* at Avus, in March 1934, when Hans Stuck, already famous as an Austro-Daimler driver, broke three World's Class records. In its original form it had a bore and stroke of 68 × 75 (4·36 litres) giving 295 b.h.p. at 4500 r.p.m. with a 9 lb. boost.

The basic engine design was successful and remained much the same throughout the years, although it was naturally modified to meet the increased demands made on it. Porsche had, initially, a first-class design bureau, under chief draughtsman Rauber, which was responsible for the A-type chassis. Soon after Auto-Union took over they were joined by Eberan von Eberhorst. In 1935 the original A-type was superseded by the B-type with torsion bar suspension at the rear and an engine of increased bore giving 357 b.h.p. at 4700 revs. with 11 lb. boost.

The C-type had an even greater engine capacity, getting 520 b.h.p. at 5000 r.p.m. This extremely fast car was actually timed to cover five kilometres at nearly two hundred miles an hour.

The frame itself was a simple rectangle made of approximately four-inch molybdenum tube of 13 gauge. There were two tubular cross-members. The suspension was constantly modified through the years, but it remained an extremely difficult car to handle. To quote Laurence Pomeroy, 'With nearly sixty per cent. of the weight carried on the rear wheels, and the exceptionally high roll centre at the rear brought about by the use of swing axles, and owing to the extremely forward mounting of the driver, the tail could move through a considerable angle before the pilot realized the breakaway point had been reached.'

It is in fact only fair to say that Bernd Rosemeyer, and possibly Nuvolari and Varzi, are the only drivers who succeeded in extracting from these extremely tricky cars the fullest performance of which they were capable.

## 1934

In June, the new *W25* made its appearance in the Eifel Races of about 214 miles. Von Brauchitsch won, breaking all previous records. A month later, the new type *W25* was confidently tipped as winner of the German Grand Prix for racing-cars at Nürburgring. Teething troubles, however, robbed them of victory, although Fagioli was second and works driver Geier finished fifth, the victory going to Stuck on an Auto-Union.

Disappointment over this turned to joy when Caracciola took a *W25* up a hill as only he knew how. The Klausen climb is both tricky and very long, 21·5 kilometres, and the maestro made fastest time of the day, establishing a new record for the hill. Ten days later, Neubauer had his whole circus assembled in the grilling August heat of dusty Pescara. This time, everything went well and Fagioli, who knew the circuit, won the Coppa Acerbo on a *W25* for Mercedes. In the German hill-climbing Grand Prix at Freiburg, Caracciola did not do as well as he had done at Klausen and only gained second place with his *W25*, Stuck being the winner on his Auto-Union. In the Swiss Grand Prix, in which Auto-Union took the first three places, the team did badly, as they had done in the French Grand Prix, when Alfa-Romeos had finished first, second and third, but two Mercedes cars managed to finish. September, however, was a good month, for the engineers were beginning to exorcise the gremlins, and Fagioli and Caracciola, driving together, won the Italian Grand Prix. The Spanish Grand Prix at San Sebastian was the next triumph with Fagioli, a new lap record to his credit, first, and Caracciola second. Fagioli was second also in the Czechoslovak Grand Prix to Stuck on an Auto-Union.

So 1934 was reasonably successful. Of the classic races in which it had figured, the *W25* had won four victories. Caracciola rounded off the year by taking three international class

Caracciola leading Fagioli's Alfa in the Italian Grand Prix at Monza, 1934. (*Mercedes-Benz*)

records and the world record for the standing mile on the road in Hungary and also at Avus. A car, with an all-enclosed aerodynamic body, was specially built for this attempt.

## 1935

It was sad that Dr. Nibel did not live to see the success of his cars in 1935. The type *W25* now had the bigger engine and had overcome its early troubles. Of the ten races in which they entered, they won nine. The year began with Fagioli winning that most gruelling of races to the driver, the Grand Prix of Monaco, followed by Caracciola winning the Grand Prix of Tripoli with Fagioli third. The following month Fagioli and Caracciola won the Avus and Eifel races respectively, with other *W25*s well placed.

Then came the greatest triumph of all, the French Grand Prix. The previous year had been a fiasco, but not so this. Mercedes finished line ahead, running strictly to team orders in the traditional manner. Caracciola was first, von Brauchitsch second, and Fagioli, who had encountered some trouble, was fourth. A week later they did the same thing in the Grand Prix at Barcelona, but this time it was Fagioli first, Caracciola second, breaking all records for the course. Success came again in the Belgian Grand Prix. Caracciola won it and a *W25* driven jointly by Fagioli and von Brauchitsch was second.

The German Grand Prix of 1935 yielded more than its usual quota of excitement—it was dramatic in the extreme. There were twenty-five entries, and it was anybody's money whether the red of Italy or the silver of Germany would be first past the chequered flag.

First away from the 'traffic-light' starter was Caracciola's Mercedes, with Fagioli similarly mounted and Nuvolari close on his heels. Stuck and Pietsch on Auto-Unions made bad starts. The field soon began to sort itself out. Caracciola, first time round, built up a twelve-second lead on Nuvolari's Alfa. Mays, driving a 2-litre E.R.A., was having a great fight with 'Fifi' Etancelin, his check cap on back to front, driving a Maserati, and managed to pass him. Suddenly the loud-speakers galvanized the crowd with the surprise announcement that young Bernd Rosemeyer in an Auto-Union had worked his way out of the pack and was in second place, pressing Caracciola hard. Nuvolari had dropped back, yielding third and fourth places to the Mercedes of von Brauchitsch and Fagioli. Soon he dropped even further back, leaving Chiron hard on the heels of the German cars. Brivio's Alfa had retired with differential trouble, and Rosemeyer had lost time changing a wheel which was running out of true.

By the ninth lap the struggle for the first places had become almost unbearably exciting. Rosemeyer and Caracciola were passing and repassing each other into the lead, with Nuvolari and von Brauchitsch close behind them. The German pit work was considerably better than the Italian and gave the former several seconds 'bonus'.

Gradually von Brauchitsch built up a lead of over a minute on the rest of the field, establishing, in the process, a lap record of 80·73 m.p.h. Rosemeyer dropped back with engine trouble and Hans Stuck, whose Auto-Union had been steadily recovering from a bad start, came up and joined in the dog-fight.

Von Brauchitsch was still leading with Nuvolari, Stuck and Caracciola fighting mercilessly for second place. Then, by one of those fantastic pieces of ill-luck that make motor-racing so exciting, just as von Brauchitsch looked like being a certain winner, he burst a tyre on the last lap, letting Nuvolari win the Grosser Preis von Deutschland for Alfa-Romeo. Stuck's Auto-Union was second, Caracciola's Mercedes third and Rosemeyer fourth. Von Brauchitsch, in tears, toured in on the rim to finish.

At Berne, for the Swiss Grand Prix at the end of August, the team was back on form, with Caracciola first and Fagioli second. There was also a *W25* in sixth place driven by a promising youngster, Hermann Lang, who had been picked out of the works, and given his chance like Wilhelm Werner forty years earlier. Lang, until recently one of the leading drivers for Mercedes-Benz, is eloquent proof that this policy, pursued by the firm for over half a century, pays good dividends. In practice for this race, Hans Geier, now stand-in for Neubauer, had a bad crash. Had it not been for the prompt arrival of Dr. Glaser, the Mercedes team doctor, always on duty during practice, he would certainly have died of injuries received.

In September, in the Spanish Grand Prix, the three musketeers, Caracciola, Fagioli, and von Brauchitsch finished first, second, and third. Over a course of about 340 miles, von Brauchitsch finished less than three minutes behind Caracciola, a striking example of Alfred Neubauer's team-control when not disturbed by external circumstances.

Max Sailer never won many races, but when the Mercedes company needed a driver who would drive 'flat out', to goad his opponents to burst their engines, this was usually his task. It was Max Sailer who, in 1921, won the Coppa Florio which seemed at the time as forlorn a hope as Baron von Ungern Sternberg's conquest of Mongolia, but unlike the Baron, he won. So, it was only to be expected that under his directorship, after Nibel's death, the racing department of Mercedes-Benz should turn out the most exciting racing-cars that have ever been built.

It is quite certain that when the 1934 formula of 750 kg. was laid down, no one on the Committee of the A.I.A.C.R. had any idea that Sailer, Wagner, and Hess would produce a 5·6-litre car developing over 600 h.p. with an unladen weight of little more than the 2-litre Grand Prix Bugatti of a decade earlier! The 1936 formula for 1937 turned out to be one of the major muddles in the history of motor racing, for the A.I.A.C.R. laid one down in February 1936, rescinded it in September of that year, and extended the 750 kg. formula to cover the year 1937.

## 1936

During 1936 Mercedes-Benz were racing the *W25* car with its engine in its most highly developed form, the *ME25*. But behind locked doors at Untertürkheim the most exciting of all racing-cars, the *W125*, was being developed. This car was originally envisaged with a 3-litre engine to comply with the formula of February 1936. But when, in September of that year, the 750 kg. formula was extended, Mercedes were not slow to take advantage of this by quickly slipping in, in time for the 1937 season, the fabulous 5·6-litre 600-h.p. engine

Chiron driving the 1936 type Mercedes-Benz in the Eifelrennen. The engine of this car represented the *W25* in its final form and was known as the *ME25*. It developed nearly 500 b.h.p., but the new chassis in which it was installed was not a success. (*George Monkhouse*)

that weighed only 45 lb. more than its 3-litre counterpart! The *W25* of 1936 was by no means an easy car to handle. It could not compare with its successor, the *W125*, for steering, road-holding, or power transmission to the road. The highly developed *ME25* engine was producing well over 400 h.p. and, as Dick Seaman said after one of his preliminary tests, 'It was rather a job to know what to do with so many horses.'

The 1936 team consisted of Caracciola, Luigi Fagioli, Chiron, von Brauchitsch, and Lang. It will be observed that for many years it has been the policy of Neubauer and the directors to include at least one foreign driver in the team. By this time, the personnel employed in all capacities in the racing department had reached something of the order of four hundred. And, of course, the annual subsidy had increased far beyond the original £20,000.

The racing year started off with the Finn, Karl Ebb, gaining second place in the Swedish winter Grand Prix with his grand old *SSK*. Then, for the second year running, Mercedes won the Grand Prix of Monaco with Caracciola driving a *W25*. Everyone who has driven this 'round-the-houses' race in Monte Carlo agrees on one point: that there is not a single

Caracciola practising for the 1936 Eifelrennen in a 1935 *W25*. (*George Monkhouse*)

place on the entire course where one can make a mistake and not suffer in consequence.

At Tripoli, Mercedes did not do so well, but a week later Caracciola won the Grand Prix of Tunis. While he was doing this, Zatuszek with his seven-year-old *SSK* was winning all manner of local events in the Argentine.

June was not a successful month. Caracciola and Chiron only achieved second and sixth in the Barcelona Grand Prix. In the Eifel races, Mercedes were well beaten on their own ground, Rosemeyer being the winner on an Auto-Union, followed by the three Alfa-Romeos. July was a bad month too; they only gained fifth and seventh places in the German Grand Prix, Auto-Union taking first, second, and fourth positions, with Rosemeyer the winner. In this race, Chiron developed a terrifying spin at 140 m.p.h. and went off the road tail first. Next month, Mercedes only achieved fourth place in the Swiss Grand Prix. Altogether, a disastrous season for Mercedes, but a wonderful one for Auto-Union, whose cars, led by the inspired Bernd Rosemeyer, swept the board, the Alfa-Romeos no longer being a match for the all-conquering German cars. But while all this was going on, the model which had every prospect of being a world-beater was under construction at Untertürkheim—the *W125*.

Mercedes also built a special twelve-cylinder 5·6-litre car especially to attack records on the Frankfurt–Darmstadt Autobahn. This record car, which bore certain superficial resemblances to Reid Railton's aerodynamic designs and had an open cockpit, did what was asked of it. In October, it took five International Class B records and a world record for the 10-mile flying start. This shed a little lustre on an otherwise dim year.

The star turn of 1936 was Zatuszek. Between the end of September and December 13 he entered his *SSK* for eleven races. Of these he won seven outright, was second twice, and third in the remaining two!

Among the production cars of this era, the most noteworthy perhaps were the type *500* and later type *540K*. Both models had an eight-cylinder engine, the valves being operated by pushrods. The bore and stroke of the *500* were 86 × 108 mm. and the h.p. rating was 36·9. The engine was supercharged on the usual Mercedes principle. The car was very heavy, a drophead cabriolet of 1936 weighing 48½ cwt. unladen and the performance, taking into account a blown engine of 5 litres, was somewhat disappointing. *The Motor* tested a car in July 1936. On the overdrive top of 3·03 to 1, maximum speed with the supercharger over the timed quarter-mile was 102 m.p.h.

*Above:*
Type *540K*, long-tailed roadster with Sindelfingen coachwork. (*Mercedes-Benz*)

*Below:*
*500K* Cabriolet A, built 1934/6. (*Mercedes-Benz*)

Unblown, the car could manage no more than 85 m.p.h. Valve clatter set in at 3400 r.p.m., equivalent to some 60 m.p.h. in third. 0 to 50 m.p.h., using the blower, took $11\frac{3}{5}$ seconds. Petrol consumption was 11 m.p.g. *The Motor* found the steering heavy. The price of the drophead cabriolet was £1890. A year, later, the same paper tested the *540K*. The bore and stroke were now 88 × 111 mm., but other details were the same, including the wheelbase of 10 ft. $9\frac{1}{2}$ in. But the weight had arisen to $49\frac{1}{4}$ cwt. 106 m.p.h. proved possible with the aid of the supercharger, over the flying half-mile, 75 on third and 45 on second. 0 to 50 m.p.h. took 10·8 seconds. Maximum r.p.m. were 3500, equal to 75 m.p.h. on third. The servo-assisted brakes were considered good. *The Motor* also found the blower quieter, the springing more comfortable, and that the

This pretty roadster is on a 1936 six-cylinder, 3·9-litre chassis. (*Mercedes-Benz*)

steering and handling required less effort than with the type *500*. Incidentally, springing was independent all round on both models. The *540K* developed 180 b.h.p. with the blower, 115 without.

## 1937

In 1937, everyone at Untertürkheim, from the directors downwards, was quite determined that even if it were not going to be quite such an *annus mirabilis* as 1935, they would, at least, do a great deal better than they had in 1936. The *W125* (described at the beginning of our account of the racing in 1936) was ready and tested in good time before the season, and Neubauer was re-organizing his team. Chiron and Fagioli, both of whom had been at the top of the tree for a long time, stepped down to make room for younger blood. Caracciola, then thirty-six years old and at the top of his form, stayed on, as did Lang, a youngster of twenty-seven, and von Brauchitsch, the Prussian aristocrat, who was thirty-two. Neubauer reinforced them by two very promising young men. Dick Seaman, although only twenty-three years old, had already made a great name for himself by his cool, masterly handling of M.G., E.R.A., and Delage cars. In addition, there was Christian Kautz, a wealthy young Swiss, who not only had enough money to buy really fast cars, but who possessed the ability to drive them thoroughly well; that is the one attribute that gets one a place in the Mercedes-Benz team. On one occasion a wealthy parent attempted to buy his offspring, only a very moderate driver, a place in the team, and Neubauer's reply was similar to that of a very famous character in German drama, Goetz von Berlichingen.

That, then, was the team for 1937, and in February, Caracciola, Lang, and Seaman were all practising on *W125*s at Monza. Seaman had a crash, on one of the 1936 cars, simply due to giving it too much acceleration coming out of a corner. The car was 'written off' and Seaman, while Doctor Glaser was patching him up, was steeling himself for an awful wigging from Neubauer for ruining a car that had cost many thousands of pounds to build. He found to his surprise that his chief considered racing-cars quite expendable in moderation, and was much more interested in the fact that the driver was but little hurt; in addition, Neubauer explained to him exactly where he went wrong in coming out of the corner.

Now, before we embark on the 1937 season, let us take a look at the fabulous *W125*. The straight-eight, 5·6-litre engine, was broadly a development of the *M25* engine with more main bearings, just as the 3½-litre Bentley engine was a development of the old 21·6-h.p. *Goshawk* Rolls engine of the early nineteen-twenties. But the chassis of the *W125* was brand new

Engine of the 1937 *W125* eight-cylinder Mercedes-Benz. This was developed from the earlier *M25* but was increased in size to 5·6 litres. In its ultimate form towards the end of 1937 it developed nearly 650 b.h.p. (*George Morkhouse*)

and very interesting. Already, as Seaman had found to his cost, the engines of the 1936 *W25* cars were producing far more power than could be translated into forward motion. So, quite clearly, with a further 250 h.p. coming down the propeller shaft, something drastic had to be done. Starting at the front end, the 1934–6 arrangement of wishbones, connected to coil springs resident inside the tubular front axle, was scrapped.

As will be apparent from the details given, the type *500* and *540K* Mercedes were not production cars of outstanding attraction. They had neither the performance nor the tautness of control of the old *SSK*, but their springing was very good. Sailer, Wagner, and Hess adapted this same system of springing, long wishbones connecting the chassis to the wheels, and exposed vertical coil springs, to the new Grand Prix type *W125*. The chassis was tubular and incredibly light, made from nickel chrome molybdenum steel. The back axle, of de Dion type, had been so long out of use that any patents covering it must have expired long ago. This form of axle has all the advantages except one—it is relatively expensive to build. Needless to say, this latter factor was of no importance in a programme of this magnitude when building Grand Prix cars to beat the world. There had been considerable teething troubles when Mercedes resurrected the de Dion axle,* unused for nearly forty years, but the engineers had overcome them all before the beginning of the 1937 season. The cumulative effect of these two new systems, fore and aft, was far softer springing than on previous models, but infinitely better road-holding and power transmission. A 4-speed gear-box was mounted in one light alloy unit with the Z.F. self-locking differential, which allowed one wheel to slip a small amount before the axle became solid. Brakes had, of necessity, been improved even more. The Lockheed double master cylinders were now considered so reliable that a pound or two could be saved by jettisoning the emergency mechanical hand brake. The two leading-shoe system was now used and brake lining area increased. Herr Sheerer's new '*Schieber*' carburettor was a most successful addition. The word *Schieber* means, in German, the type of man who will bargain up to the last farthing with the persistence and mental agility of a Pathan horse-dealer. It resulted in increased brake-horse-power, on the test bed, of 14 per cent. at peak revs. A paramount point borne in mind, when designing Mercedes

* For a detailed description of how the de Dion axle was applied to the *W125*, readers are referred to the *Grand Prix Car*, Vol. I, by Laurence Pomeroy (Motor Racing Publications Ltd., 1954). The de Dion axle 'consisted of open shafts driving the wheels through two universal joints from a bevel box mounted on the frame, the wheels being located by a dead tube attached to the hubs'. (Pomeroy, *op. cit.*)

G.P. cars, was that gear ratios in the box, the bevel wheels, and the final spur wheels should all be easy of access. By ringing the changes on these and also on different sizes of wheels and tyres, it was possible during practice to arrive at exactly the right set of ratios for any given course.

When practice was going on, Dr. Ing. Rudolf Uhlenhaut was usually in attendance, acting as liaison between the team on the spot and his own research and development division. Uhlenhaut, who is half English and speaks the language perfectly, is definitely a man of parts. He is not only an engineer of great distinction but a driver of Grand Prix standard. He is, therefore, able to carry out the testing at racing speeds himself. The story goes that while testing a *W125* he put up a lap speed better than any drivers practising that day. The result of this was a severe 'dressing down' from the directors, who told him that while racing-cars and their drivers were comparatively easily replaced, an engineer of his calibre and specialized experience was not, and he had strict orders in future not to regard himself as expendable!

Neubauer had entered for twelve races in that year and brought his équipe to the first one, the Grand Prix of Tripoli, on May 9. The Tripoli circuit is eight miles round and is what Germans call *kurvenreich*, or 'rich in curves'. None of these cause much difficulty below about 150 m.p.h., but at speeds above this they demand considerable nicety of judgement. With the extremely fast cars brought to the line this year by Auto-Union and Mercedes, it was quite clear that the race would be won, like the French Grand Prix at Dieppe so long ago, on tyre survival. Auto-Union decided to go 'flat out' and change their tyres. Neubauer may have had Lautenschlager's victory in 1908 in mind when he ordered his team to go steady and save their tyres. As a result, Mercedes had about one-third of the tyre-changing of Auto-Union, and won the race.

Young Seaman, handling a *W125* for the first time in a big race, drove magnificently, but some sand found its way into his supercharger and he dropped to sixth place. The hero of the day was Hermann Lang, who scored his first win for Mercedes at an average speed, over 327½ miles, of 134 m.p.h., including two tyre changes!

The Avus race had not been run in 1936 as the course, which is normally a public road, was under repair. In 1937 it was virtually a straight fight between Mercedes and Auto-Union. Both had entered enclosed cockpit streamlined models which were faster on this course than the normal open cars. Caracciola, Brauchitsch, and Zehender, a Parisian motor dealer, had open cars. Zehender's car had a twelve-cylinder engine fitted for experimental purposes and he became very unpopular when he 'over-revved' it and broke something in practice.

There were two eliminating heats and a final. Caracciola won the first and Lang the second on a protest, which was allowed, that Hasse on an Auto-Union, who actually came in first, had baulked him. In the final, Caracciola and von Brauchitsch fell out with transmission trouble; Lang, who drove beautifully, had no difficulty at all in winning the race for Mercedes. Seaman had been going very well, but he shed the treads of two back tyres and was forced back to fifth place. The fact that Lang won this 96-mile race round a circuit containing two U-turns at an average speed of 162·6 m.p.h. shows that on the straights he cannot have been going far short of 200 m.p.h.

A fortnight later, the Eifel races were held at the Nürburgring. During practice, von Delius was driving his Auto-Union very fast when a bird flew out of a hedge and struck him in the face, causing him to crash. This incident is mentioned because it is germane to what happened in the German Grand Prix the following month. Rosemeyer had won the race for the Auto-Union the last two years in succession. Mercedes made a determined effort but were beaten by fuel pump trouble, and so Rosemeyer on an Auto-Union achieved a hat-trick, with Caracciola fifty seconds behind, and von Brauchitsch in third place.

In 1936, the Vanderbilt Cup race in U.S.A., which lapsed in 1914, was revived, and was won by Nuvolari on an Alfa. Not only was the donor of the cup an old Mercedes driver, but the American export market was considered by the Mercedes Company to be of paramount importance. So, the directors decided to try their luck in 1937, with an eye to American sales, and made the highly expensive trip to woo the American market. Caracciola and Seaman went as drivers, with Neubauer and Uhlenhaut in charge of personnel. The cars for the Vanderbilt Cup, and subsequently, had the carburettors inboard of the superchargers, instead of outboard, which meant that the terrific noise of the Mercedes blower, famous for so many years, disappeared.

Auto-Union, not to be outdone, sent a team from Europe, and a number of Americans were driving imported Alfa-Romeos, but most of the native entries were hopelessly outclassed.

Before China was 'sovietized', when two armies were having a battle and it came on to rain, both sides put up their umbrellas and went home. They have much the same arrangement over motor races in America, and the Vanderbilt Cup was postponed for twenty-four hours. The race itself produced a most engaging tussle between Caracciola and Rosemeyer for first place. But, on the twenty-second lap, Caracciola's Mercedes retired with a fractured supercharger drive. Seaman drove the race of his life and finished second to Rosemeyer by only 51 seconds. But the star turn of the meeting was an American, Rex Mays, driving an elderly Alfa-Romeo. In spite of appallingly bad pit-work, he finished third.

While Caracciola and Seaman were in America, Mercedes also entered a team for the Belgian Grand Prix, which they had won in 1935, but which had not been run in 1936. Von Brauchitsch turned his car over in practice but was not much hurt and took part in the race. The other two were Lang and the Swiss, Kautz. This was really an Auto-Union race although at one point it did look as if Lang, driving with desperate courage, might get into the lead as he was lapping even faster than the leading Auto-Union. But this prodigious pace brought him in for a tyre change which, even allowing for the astonishing speed of this operation in the Mercedes pit, pulled him back to third place, where he finished. Kautz, in spite of two near-crashes, was fourth. The race was won by R. Hasse, followed by Hans Stuck, both on Auto-Unions.

In Germany, the most important race of the year is the German Grand Prix at the Nürburgring. The crowds are fantastic and by this race, prestige on the home market is measured. It was, once more, almost a straight fight between Mercedes and Auto-Union. True, there were Ferrari-Alfas running, but they were so much slower than the German cars that, on a course like the Nürburgring, it would need all Nuvolari's wonderful driving, plus much bad luck for his opponents, before he could hope to do any good. The field was made up of private entries, notably our own tall, thin Kenneth Evans driving, at his own expense, a relatively elderly *P2* Alfa-Romeo. The Mercedes team consisted of von Brauchitsch, Lang, Caracciola, Seaman, and Kautz. The weather was poor and overcast for a day in late July.

The starting grid was arranged according to times in practice and starting was by red-amber-green, as in a traffic light. Lang was leading after the first lap with Rosemeyer's Auto-Union a close second. On the next lap Rosemeyer went ahead in his own inimitable fashion, broke the lap record and came round nine seconds ahead of Lang. On the third lap, Caracciola had passed Lang into second place and was obviously chasing Rosemeyer. Then Rosemeyer suffered from a double stroke of bad luck. Not only did a hub cap disintegrate, but the tyre of the same wheel collapsed, thus necessitating its removal. It took two and a half minutes to cut off the remains of the hub cap and change the wheel, a loss of time which dropped him to tenth place. So Mercedes, driven by Caracciola, Lang, and von Brauchitsch were leading the race in that order.

Von Delius was not driving well. The reader will remember how he was struck in the face by a bird during the Eifel races. It appears that a first-class driver can crash for normal reasons without his nerve being seriously affected, but an unscheduled hazard appears to destroy his confidence. Jenatzy's railway engine, the pig that lay down in the road in a long-ago Targa Florio—both were examples of this. Just as Jenatzy never drove quite as well again, and indeed retired soon after his scare, so von Delius was put right off his stroke and talked, half seriously, of retiring. Already, earlier in the race, he had been inadvertently responsible for his team mate, Müller's, crash. Von Delius was running fifth to the four Mercedes, the only Auto-Union that had any possibility of doing any good, so the team manager hoisted the 'flat-out' signal over his number. Von Delius tried rather too hard, and misjudged matters at 170 m.p.h., by swerving in front of Seaman's Mercedes. He was flung out on his head and died later in hospital. Seaman crashed his Mercedes trying to avoid him and was badly but not seriously knocked about, although he was out of the team for several races. In the meantime Rosemeyer, who was driving in a manner that can only be described as inspired, gradually crept up from tenth place, while tyre trouble thrust Lang down to seventh. The finishing order was Caracciola first, von Brauchitsch second, Rosemeyer's Auto-Union third, and Nuvolari on his Alfa, after a superb drive, fourth. Kautz and Lang came in sixth and seventh respectively.

From a spectacular point of view the Freiburg 12-kilometre climb is quite remarkable. But it is so long as well as tricky and dangerous that only the old hands who have been at it year after year have any chance of winning. It is also the only one to count for points in the German road-racing championship. Caracciola, who was leading Rosemeyer by one point, was driving a Mercedes that was somewhat off-colour and only made third best time. Rosemeyer drove a brilliant climb and beat the Mercedes by 5 seconds, but was a second slower than Stuck on an Auto-Union, who made fastest time of the day. This was really not surprising, for Stuck was, first and foremost, a hill-climb man, whose brilliance in this branch of the sport led him into Grand Prix racing. So Caracciola and Rosemeyer were now equal with ten points each for the championship. Lang, deputizing for von Brauchitsch who was not well, made fourth fastest time, considerably slower than Caracciola.

The team for Monte Carlo in August consisted of Caracciola, von Brauchitsch and Kautz. Also, presumably because Seaman was still in hospital, Zehender was forgiven his 'crime' at Avus and was given a wheel. The Grand Prix of Monaco was really a Mercedes affair because the rear-engined Auto-Unions were not so suitable for this twisting, turning, relatively slow course with so many hairpin corners. This particular race resolved itself into a glorious scrap between von Brauchitsch and Caracciola. At one period, Neubauer became alarmed and flagged von Brauchitsch down. The mercurial Prussian, who was about the only member of the team who has ever disobeyed Neubauer and survived, ignored the signal and went on to win. Both Caracciola and von Brauchitsch had their troubles. The former lost a screw in his induction which cost him three minutes fifteen seconds and the latter had a brake stick on, after filling up, which cost him a minute and a half. So, although Caracciola actually drove faster, breaking the lap record several times, he could not make up his handicap of nearly two minutes and had to be content with second place, just over a minute behind the winner, von Brauchitsch. Kautz who had to come in several times with plug trouble, was third, two laps behind the winner, and Freddie Zehender gained fifth place, three laps behind. It was a triumph for young Kautz, for it was the first time he had been placed in a Grand Prix.

People who have been to Pescara say two things about it: 'There are quite a lot of other places in Italy which are vastly preferable to Pescara,' and 'They have jolly good motor-racing there.' Doubtless Neubauer arrived there with his team fully prepared for any local emergencies which might arise. There is a good story told that when he took his circus out for the Carrera Pan-Americana, the equipment included inflatable rubber life-boats for the use of key personnel in the event of shipwreck.

Only three Mercedes cars went to Pescara, to be driven by Caracciola, von Brauchitsch and Seaman, who had been summoned hastily from his convalescence to replace the sick Lang. No spare car was taken. Seaman, during practice, braked in order to pass through a village. One of the front brakes locked on and did not release. The Mercedes, which was still doing about 100 m.p.h., performed the most unmannerly gyrations and ended up as a sort of metallic omelette, after trying to get inside a house through the wall. Seaman was absolutely unscratched. Stuck, driving a rival Auto-Union, stopped for a moment like de Caters long ago, and brought the news back to the Mercedes pits that Seaman was unhurt.

Unfortunately, even with the 75-m.p.h. supercharged lorry for racing-car transport, it was not possible to get another car in time for the start. So only two cars, with Caracciola and von Brauchitsch driving, started. There are three races at Pescara: the Abruzzo shield for sports-cars, which is raced for after practising, and a 1500-cc. event for racing-cars as a 'curtain-raiser' for the Acerbo Cup for Grand Prix formula cars, with which we are concerned. Crowd control was, as is usual in Italy, not taken very seriously, and there was a very bad accident involving spectators in the 1500-cc. race.

As for the Acerbo Cup, the new Alfa-Romeos (prepared by the works, not Ferrari) of which so much was expected, proved a complete fiasco. Once more it was a straight fight between Mercedes and Auto-Union, and in particular, between Rosemeyer and Caracciola. There is no doubt that Rosemeyer was by far the outstanding driver of the late nineteen-thirties and, had he lived, would probably have reached to the same heights as Caracciola and Nuvolari. Rosemeyer built up quite a good lead, but lost some of it on a slow pit stop. Hurrying to make up for lost time he braked too late for a corner and wrecked a wheel on a kilometre stone. While this was being dealt with, Caracciola sailed into first place, and it looked like an easy win for Mercedes. But, just as the reporters in the Press box were mentally making notes as to what they would say about Caracciola's victory, his engine started to run badly. Caracciola handed the car over to Seaman to tour in to finish, which he did, in fifth place. Von Brauchitsch, who drove a steady, trouble-free race, finished second to Rosemeyer.

A week later, on August 22, came the Swiss Grand Prix at Berne. This was a particularly favourite event with the whole Mercedes team, both drivers and mechanics. Berne is one of the nicest places in Europe and everything to do with the race is extremely well done and superbly organized. The Bremgarten circuit too, like everything else in and around Berne, is always in apple-pie order. The fast downhill bends on the back leg of the course are rather frightening to most of the less experienced drivers, but they give no trouble to the real virtuosi. It very frequently rains for the Swiss G.P. and the year 1937 was no exception. The course was also wet and slippery for practice. Kautz hit some sandbags and bent both back wheels of his Mercedes while both Caracciola and von Brauchitsch 'played safe' in practice and turned in slower times than the Auto-Unions. But Lang went very fast, returning a practice time only three seconds slower than Rosemeyer.

Von Brauchitsch during a pit stop for refuelling and tyre changing in the Swiss Grand Prix at Berne in 1937. Dr. Max Sailer, head of Mercedes' racing department, is standing on the left and Uhlenhaut, responsible for the preparation of all the racing cars, in front of the car. (*George Monkhouse*)

The big sensation of the practice days was the moment when the small frail figure of Tazio Nuvolari quite suddenly materialized without any warning and took over one of the Auto-Unions.

The race started off with a duel between Stuck and Rosemeyer against the Mercedes team. Nuvolari did not take part in this but drove his unfamiliar mount fast, albeit with great caution. Rosemeyer ran off the road into boggy ground whence he was unable to extract his car. He walked back to the pits and took over from Nuvolari, who in turn took over from Fagioli, who had been taken ill during the race. Stuck was unable to keep up with Caracciola, Lang and von Brauchitsch, who were going like demons on the wet and slippery course. They finished in that order, pursued by Rosemeyer, who drove with great dash and brilliance. Stuck finished fifth, with Kautz on his Mercedes sixth. Particular credit must go to the Mercedes mechanics, for although only three were allowed on the course, they accomplished the refuelling and tyre changes in little more than thirty seconds.

It is the privilege of the organizing club to choose the circuit where their national Grand Prix shall be held. So it is not surprising that the Royal Automobile Club of Italy broke with precedent and, instead of holding the Italian Grand Prix at Monza, where it had always been held before, transferred it to Livorno, which favoured the slower but more easily handled Italian cars. It will be seen from the practice times how the chances of victory stood. Von Brauchitsch lapped the Livorno circuit in 3 minutes 19 seconds; Varzi, driving an Auto-Union, in 3 minutes 20 seconds. Nuvolari, on an Alfa, took 3 minutes 23 seconds (the same as Caracciola) while Lang and Seaman needed 3 minutes 31 seconds. In the race, although each corner was taken in one long glorious slide, with the power turned on again at exactly the right moment, Nuvolari's effort was of no avail. His Alfa was so hopelessly outclassed by the Mercedes and Auto-Unions that eventually, in boredom and disgust, he handed over to Farina to bring the car into seventh place. Caracciola won by four-fifths second from Lang, who, in three years, had come up from apprenticeship to championship form. Rosemeyer's Auto-Union was third and Seaman's Mercedes fourth. The winning of the Italian Grand Prix and the Coppa Ciano by Caracciola gave him the requisite points to win the European drivers' championship.

But even while the team was rejoicing over this, a telegram came from the Argentine bearing sad news. Carlos Zatuszek had crashed in practice for the Grand Prix of Cavilia and had been killed. He was only just forty years old. A few days earlier he had won the Argentine 500-mile race, driving an *SSK* Mercedes, averaging over 99 m.p.h. Anyone who has driven these heavy, tricky, iron-hard old 125-m.p.h. cars will realize what a difficult feat this must have been.

Brno, in Czechoslovakia, in certain respects rather resembles Birmingham. It is a town of many varied industries surrounded by an attractive countryside. The Masaryk circuit near by, which was first used in 1930, included considerable sections of public road. It was about twenty miles long and, because of this, one of the most difficult to 'learn'. Nuvolari and Brivio put in more or less 'token' appearances on Alfa-Romeos but the race was really the usual Mercedes–Auto-Union struggle. It is a generalization, but more or less true, to say, that when Germans and English make a team, they pull well together, but the reverse is the case with Germans and Italians. There were differences of opinion in the mixed Auto-Union outfit, and they were rather short of drivers, only two coming to the starting line. These were Rosemeyer and Müller, one-time champion motor-cyclist.

Rosemeyer drove with unsurpassed brilliance, and in attempting to catch him, Lang crashed, killing two spectators. England and Germany are, probably, the only two countries where the course is so very carefully arranged that it is virtually impossible for the spectators and the racing-cars to become involved. In Italy, in particular, there is always the possibility of a disaster of Paris–Madrid magnitude. Before

Czechoslovakia became a Communist country, it was said that there were not enough police to guard the course; now there are enough police and no motor-racing. In England, of course, the problem is made easier by the fact that all road circuits are on private ground and not on closed public roads. For this reason police are never needed to guard the circuits, so the famous clashes between police and highly-strung Grand Prix team members only occur abroad.

Caracciola was given the signal to go after Rosemeyer, which he proceeded to do in no uncertain manner. Rosemeyer, pursued by Caracciola, hit the kerb with a wheel, which put the car out of the race. Neubauer heaved a sigh of relief that the very real menace to victory in the form of Rosemeyer was out of the way, and signalled the team to slow down. Müller was running fourth and far enough behind von Brauchitsch and Seaman to constitute no threat to a Mercedes procession past the chequered flag. But Rosemeyer then proceeded to behave in the purest Jenatzy tradition. He walked a mile and a half across country to the Auto-Union pits and took over Müller's car which he proceeded to drive, attempting and achieving the impossible. Even Seaman, driving admirably, was no match for such virtuosity, and he had to yield third place to him. So the final order was Caracciola, von Brauchitsch, Rosemeyer's Auto-Union, and Seaman.

It was a personal triumph for Fred Craner, the Clerk of the Course, to have persuaded both Mercedes and Auto-Union to come over for the British Grand Prix at Donington, and he was rewarded by the enthusiasm of the English crowd, which was immense. In practice, the German cars all lapped at between 2 minutes 10 seconds and 2 minutes 17 seconds. Lord Howe and Raymond Mays, the best of the English contingent, could do no better than 2 minutes 26 seconds, which was good for 1½-litre E.R.As against the 5½-litre German cars.

The mass start was very impressive; thousands had seen mass starts before, but nothing quite like this. First time round, Lang was leading, with Rosemeyer playing a waiting game. On the second lap Seaman had bad luck; Müller, who had left his braking too late, bumped Seaman's Mercedes at Coppice Corner and butted him up the escape road. Müller's Auto-Union was more or less undamaged, but Seaman, although he got going again, dropped further and further back and eventually had to retire from the race owing to damaged shock absorbers and petrol tank. Later, Lang, who had been leading, fell out with shock absorber trouble and the race resolved itself into a straight fight between Rosemeyer and von Brauchitsch, both of them, to the delight of the crowd, driving as hard as they knew how. The English crowd saw, for the first time, continental pit work at its very finest. Ever since Kensington-Moir, in the twenties, took the pit work of the Bentley team seriously, we have in England made sporadic attempts to improve our technique in this respect; but a glance at the stop-watch during pit stops at Donington showed how far we lagged behind. The Germans refuelled and changed tyres in under thirty seconds, while Raymond Mays' pit took fifty seconds to put in petrol and oil only.

Rosemeyer was leading and by the sixtieth lap had built up his lead over von Brauchitsch to twenty seconds. Then the Mercedes came into the pits with a rapidly disintegrating front tyre. The pit stop cost him so many seconds that there was now no hope of catching Rosemeyer, and he had to be content with second place, thirty-eight seconds after the winning Auto-Union. Caracciola came in third, quite a long way behind. His car had been off-colour all through the race and, like de Knyff who used to go steadily, trusting that Jenatzy would not finish, he spared his car in the hope that something might happen to Rosemeyer. It did very often, but not so on this occasion. Rosemeyer's win was very popular, for this gay young man, so full of fun, had in less than no time endeared himself to the English public. None of the English drivers were able to finish within the stipulated fifteen minutes after the winner and so they were flagged off. Two rather unfortunate notes were struck after the meeting. The German National Anthem was not played, which was perhaps discourteous, and most of

A characteristic action study of the great Bernd Rosemeyer at the wheel of the 6-litre sixteen-cylinder rear-engined Auto-Union in the Donington Grand Prix of 1937, which he won. (*George Monkhouse*)

the bookies welshed. The Auto-Union team and mechanics had all backed the winner quite heavily at rather good odds, but the Derby & District Motor Club very sportingly had a whip-round and paid them all out in full.

The authors take this opportunity to scotch a quite untrue story that was in circulation at the time. This was to the effect that when the well-known English driver Charles Brackenbury slid a thunderflash-cum-smoke-bomb, under the bonnet of Neubauer's car, which was electrically ignited when the starter was pressed, that Neubauer saw some political significance in it and took it amiss. There is not a word of truth in this; Neubauer laughed just as much as anybody else. After all, it was quite a mild joke compared to some of Rosemeyer's!

Donington brought Neubauer's original twelve entries for 1937 up to thirteen, out of which they had seven wins, nine second places, and, twice, team wins line ahead, first, second, third. The racing department had certainly won back the stripes they lost in 1936.

But, while the team in the field in 1937 was covering itself with glory, the design staff at Stuttgart had a major problem to solve in getting a car ready to conform with the new A.I.A.C.R. formula, to come into force in 1938. This was a complicated matter. Engines could be kept up to 3 litres 'blown' and 4½ litres 'unblown' and, instead of a maximum weight, a minimum weight was now imposed. This was, for the 'blown' 3-litre cars 850 kg. with tyres, which amounted to almost exactly the same as the old maximum limit 750 kg. dry. With Wagner, Hess, and Sailer in charge of the specialist designers, Mercedes produced an adequate answer to this in the type *154*, which grew up with very few modifications into the type *163*.

The object in view was quite simple. The drop from 5·6 litres to 3 litres could be partially offset by an increase of piston area in an engine with more cylinders. Such an engine could, and did, develop 400/500 b.h.p. The intention was, therefore, to build a motor-car that could go as fast or faster than the *W125*, even while dropping a couple of hundred horse power. Very surprisingly they accomplished this. The chassis was broadly the same as that of the *W125*, but advantage was taken of the much lower over-all height of the new twelve-cylinder 3-litre engine to build a very much lower and better streamlined car, particularly on the later models, in which the driver's head was only 42½ inches above ground level. The suspension was modified and made softer, and hydraulic shock absorbers were now universally used.

G. K. Burness driving a modified *33/180* at Shelsley Walsh, 1937.

The type *163* had vastly improved brakes and both *154* and *163* were fitted with 5-speed gear-boxes. Dual superchargers boosted the engine 26·95 lb. as opposed to the 12-lb. boost of the single supercharged *W125* models.

This ultra-efficient 3-litre engine had an enormous thirst, its fuel-consumption being about three miles to the gallon. Tank capacity of 70 to 80 gallons was required, and was obtained by a 48-gallon tank in the tail and a further, larger saddle tank in the dash over the driver's legs. It would perhaps be incorrect to say that if tankage of this type has not been built into Seaman's car he would not have been burned to death, but there is no doubt that the risk of fire was immeasurably increased and nobody, least of all the drivers, liked the arrangement. There does not, however, seem to have been any satisfactory alternative.

## 1938

The new cars did not have the same terrific power of their 5·6-litre predecessors. The 3-litre developed 405 b.h.p. as opposed to the 595 of the 5-litre car. But, in spite of this, the 1938 Grand Prix Mercedes were appreciably easier to handle and turned in comparable lap speeds. Neubauer started the year with the same team that had been so successful the previous year except that Kautz had been replaced as reserve by Walter Baumer who had been driving, among other things, English Austin Sevens.

But one thing was not the same. Bernd Rosemeyer was dead. He had been killed attempting records on the Frankfurt–Darmstadt autobahn. A sudden gust of side wind of gale force had driven under the aerodynamic body of his Auto-Union, lifting it so that its wheels ceased to adhere properly and he crashed, fatally. Although Rosemeyer was their deadliest rival on the track, off it he was the greatest friend of the Mercedes team, and it is the truth to say that the Mercedes équipe missed him quite as much as his own team-mates. Auto-Union started the season with Müller, Hasse, and Kautz; not what might be called a very strong team. Nuvolari had signed up for 1938 with Alfa-Corse, but was so disappointed with what they gave him to drive that he soon threw his hand in and joined Auto-Union.

Both Mercedes and Auto-Union went to Monza for tests during March 1938. Uhlenhaut and Neubauer were very pleased with the way the *154* performed, and, like Jellinek and Maybach nearly forty years earlier, decided to give the cars a curtain raiser at Pau. They probably knew, from Mercedes records, which are very complete, that there is a Germanophobe gremlin resident in the Basses Pyrénées who is guaranteed to produce all possible teething troubles in any Mercedes car past, present, or future. The gremlin who had so bedevilled the very first Mercedes ever built was on the top of his form, making Lang's car behave so badly that it had to be scratched, and caused so many minor troubles in the *154*, which Caracciola and Lang drove in the race, that it had to yield first place to the Delahaye, driven by Dreyfus, a car barely capable of 130 m.p.h.

The Grand Prix of Tripoli was held on the Mellaha circuit, one of the best laid out and certainly the best maintained long-distance race-course at that time. The reason for this was that Marshall Balbo, a keen motor-racing enthusiast, initiated a huge lottery on which the whole Italian nation gambled as keenly as we do on football pools. The first prize was £60,000. There were big prizes for drivers, entrants, and spectators; there was plenty of money for building grandstands and maintaining the circuit, and there was always a very handsome surplus for the Libyan Government.

Neubauer wanted to run four cars at Tripoli, but the R.A.C.I. produced a kind of 'Gordon Bennett' rule about three cars only from each entrant. Neubauer countered with the suggestion that Seaman should run his car painted British racing green as a British independent entry. The Italians refused, which flatly contradicted their own act when they ran a fourth Alfa-Corse car driven by Sommer as an independent French entry!

During practice, Lang, von Brauchitsch, and Caracciola put up fastest laps and Alfa-Corse brought out five exciting and beautifully finished cars. They had eight, twelve and sixteen cylinders, but none of them went as fast as the German cars. There were no Auto-Union starters. It is supposed to be essential, for the lottery, to have a big field and therefore to run all classes together. Certainly at Tripoli this led to two fatal accidents and a lot of drivers being frightened out of their wits. The Mercedes somehow disentangled themselves from the mass of small cars swarming all over the course and got into their stride, Farina on an Alfa and Trossi on a Maserati keeping up with them. Soon afterwards Farina was involved in a crash with the Magyar ace, Lazlo Hartmann, driving a Maserati. Both cars overturned and went skidding about the road with their wheels in the air. Caracciola took a deep breath and drove between them. It was the only thing he could do. Farina sustained only slight abrasions but poor Hartmann was terribly injured and died next day. Trossi and Varzi, both very fine drivers, managed to hang doggedly on to the Mercedes for a time, but the pace was far too hot for their Maseratis, both of which went out with back axle trouble. Lang's car ran like clockwork the whole way through and he won the Grand Prix of Tripoli for the second time; von Brauchitsch was second and Caracciola third.

The Eifel races were not held in 1938, through lack of entries, and the next major event was the French Grand Prix. Here, Auto-Unions managed to get two cars up to the starting line, driven by Hasse and Kautz. Müller had crashed in practice at Nürburgring and hurt himself so badly that he was unable to drive at Rheims. France was gallantly represented by a number of 'lost causes'. Philippe ('Fifi') Etancelin and Carriere drove 4½-litre 'unblown' Talbots. Jean Bugatti had designed, in his father's tradition, a beautiful car for Wimille, but, for all its beauty of design and construction, it was 40 m.p.h. slower than the German cars. Finally, there was a curious French car called Sefac about which nobody could say anything except 'that it goes quite fast for not very long'. There were no Italian entries. On the first lap, both Auto-Unions crashed and the Bugatti broke down, while next time round the Sefac retired. So the only remaining opposition consisted of the two Talbots running steadily but slowly, being constantly lapped by the Mercedes. Even when Lang's engine refused to restart for four minutes after refuelling, the foregone result of a line ahead victory was unaffected, the finishing order being von Brauchitsch, Caracciola, Lang.

The Auto-Union people were quite determined that the German Grand Prix at Nürburgring was not going to be another walk-over for Mercedes, and once again brought no less a driver than Nuvolari to the line. The little maestro had grown grey on Alfa-Romeos and could take liberties with them as nobody in the world. He also handled Auto-Unions better than almost anyone else, but he did not fling them around with the same gay abandon as he did Alfas. He had not quite acquired that Rosemeyer touch with them. Yet he was almost the only serious opposition to Mercedes in the German Grand Prix. There were admittedly some Alfa-Corse cars and a few Delahayes, but these were hopelessly outclassed. But, quite soon, even Nuvolari was out of it. He slid through the Brunchen rather too hard and ran off the road tail first. All was set for another Mercedes line ahead, one, two, three victory.

Von Brauchitsch's fire, however, altered the order of the drivers. The big tank in the tail was filled by three-inch pipes from the saddle tank. In spite of little inspection windows, it

The German Grand Prix 1938: Von Brauchitsch, Neubauer, Dick Seaman, Hermann Lang and Caracciola. (*Mercedes-Benz*)

was very difficult to judge exactly the right moment to cut off the pressure-fed fuel coming down at five gallons a second. Some fuel usually spilt. When von Brauschitsch's car was started up again after refuelling the loose petrol caught fire. Von Brauchitsch snatched off the steering wheel—which must be done before one can get out—and abandoned ship. Neubauer simultaneously put into action his fire-fighting drill, practised over and over again against the stop-watch. Within an incredibly short time the fire was out and von Brauchitsch was back in the cockpit and away. Very soon afterwards he crashed. He had not pushed the steering wheel down far enough to make it lock properly when he got back into the car. When he hit a bump at 130 m.p.h. it came away in his hands. Von Brauchitsch was quite unhurt, which is more than can be said for the car, and he walked back to the pits still carrying the wheel. George Monkhouse was an eye-witness of the conflagration and tells of the following incident. Seaman's Mercedes came in behind the burning car for fuelling. The pre-assigned job of Lindemaier, one of the Mercedes mechanics, was to restart it with a portable electric motor, from the front. In the course of this operation the back of his overalls caught well and truly alight. Lindemaier, however, carried on with his drill, as if nothing was happening, till the operation was complete and the car started. He had not the slightest intention of losing the driver one precious split second. This story has been recorded, not only because it is rather funny, but because it does shed a highlight on the devotion to duty of the Mercedes racing mechanics and, indeed, the *esprit de corps* of the whole équipe.

Dick Seaman, who was driving magnificently, was left by von Brauchitsch's crash in the lead, which he maintained, and came home to win the German Grand Prix. Neubauer's joy at seeing his favourite pupil winning such an important race was really touching. It was a popular win too, for just as Rosemeyer had caught the imagination of the English crowd, so the young Englishman had done as much and more in Germany. Caracciola, who was running second, did not feel well and brought his car into the pits to hand it over to Lang, whose own car had been withdrawn with incurable misfiring. This let Stuck, on an Auto-Union into third place whilst Nuvolari took over Hasse's car and worked that up into fourth place.

Alfa-Corse had decided that they were unable to compete with the German cars and had started to build 1½-litre cars for that class. These wonderful little vehicles from which the *Alfettes*, that thrilled us so much in post-war years, were developed, made their first appearance in the voiturette race held before the Coppa Ciano on the Livorno circuit. But in the big-car class, although Auto-Union were not running, there was hot competition, while it lasted, for Mercedes. Farina had managed to get one of the twelve-cylinder Alfas going really fast and Trossi who, in spite of constant ill-health, was a wonderful driver, had a Maserati that was not only capable of passing the Mercedes but of maintaining its lead. But it was not long before Trossi found the pace too hot for his car, which cracked up.

Caracciola, who was driving what was virtually an experimental prototype of the type *163*, retired. Von Brauchitsch finished first, and Lang, who had tyre trouble, second. Von Brauchitsch, however, was disqualified for obtaining help from spectators to free his car from straw bales where he had embedded it earlier in the race. Farina finished second.

Pescara is well down the Italian coast, so that when a heat wave strikes, it is to some purpose. Neubauer had prepared for just such an eventuality with solar topees, lemons and whatnot, but no one was prepared for the plague of troubles which the heat wave brought to the cars, and which spread like an epidemic of measles. At the end of the race the only German car left running was the winning one, Caracciola's. All the Auto-Unions went out, but not before Nuvolari had put up a lap record on one. This was twice broken later by Luigi Villoresi on Trossi's Maserati. Apart from Caracciola's victory it was an all-Italian race.

The Mercedes team for the 1938 Swiss Grand Prix, over the Bremgarten circuit at Berne, consisted of Caracciola, von Brauchitsch, Lang, and Seaman. The weather was beautiful on the practice days, but on the day of the race, as in 1937, it rained like a tropical monsoon. Seaman, driving the car with which he won the German Grand Prix, led the race till Caracciola went past him in a flurry of spray like a speedboat. Stuck did well with his Auto-Union until he retired with persistent plug trouble, and so did Müller who was lying third till he crashed, luckily without hurting himself. So that meant another triple victory, Caracciola, Seaman and von Brauchitsch finishing in first, second, and third places.

The Italian Grand Prix of this year was run at Monza, a very fast circuit. Sooner or later an end had to come to the long unbroken run of victories, and this was the occasion. Nuvolari had, at last, found his form with the Auto-Union and drove it as he used to drive Alfas. Von Brauchitsch's, Lang's, and Seaman's cars all went out with serious troubles. This left only Caracciola's Mercedes in the race, and the engine of this was running so hot that the pedals were burning the soles of his shoes and the skin off his feet. Caracciola and Manfred von Brauchitsch took it in turns to drive this instrument of torture, because the former had to finish the race in order to win the European drivers' championship. He finished, but his feet were so badly burned that he was unable to drive at Donington three weeks later. Auto-Unions had vile luck towards the end of the race. They had been running in first, second, and third positions, and showed every prospect of finishing in that order. Just before the end, both Stuck and Müller's engines 'blew up', leaving Farina to bring his Alfa into second place behind Nuvolari's Auto-Union, and Caracciola to finish third.

Between the Italian Grand Prix and the British Grand Prix at Donington news came in from the Argentine that Brosutti had upheld the Zatuszek tradition by winning the Argentine 500-mile race on an old *SSK* at an *average* speed of over 100 m.p.h. for the whole distance!

Neubauer brought his team across the Channel and with it the drivers, von Brauchitsch, Seaman, Lang, and Baumer. Ballet enthusiasts are already boring their grandchildren by their repetitive accounts of having seen Nijinsky dance. 'I expect', says Scott-Moncrieff, 'I shall be just as big a bore when the time comes, for I have seen Tazio Nuvolari at the top of his form. Sometimes he had his "off" days like other drivers, but given the right mood and the right car there was nobody in the world quite like him. Caracciola was a joy to watch, but you always felt that somewhere under all the dash and panache there was an underlying stratum of prudence. But with Tazio it was different; he appeared to throw all caution out of the window. We all knew something was going to happen at Donington for he donned his bright yellow pullover, which with him was an infallible sign, saying that he was going to try really hard.'

The little Mantuan was no idle boaster. Throughout the race it was Nuvolari's day, yet victory did not come easily to him. Right from the start he was in front and began to increase his lead. At twenty laps he was twenty seconds ahead of all four Mercedes. Müller and Hasse, also on Auto-Unions, were fighting it out between themselves. Müller was running second, and Seaman was sitting on his tail, but was not quite fast enough to pass him.

Then, on the twenty-sixth lap, a wuffle, rather than a crisp clear-cut note, from Nuvolari's exhaust told us that all was not well with his engine. He went into his pit but almost a minute later he was away again, the crisp, rising crescendo of his exhaust telling of a happy and contented engine giving of its best. This fifty-three second stop, however, had cost

Tazio his lead, and he was back in fourth place.

Then occurred a sensational incident. Robin Hanson was driving an Alfa, and was going well. Suddenly, the engine burst, depositing oil all over the track on the twisting downhill section after Holly Wood. Nuvolari was the first to hit it, and though he had to drive on the grass for some way he dealt with the whole incident in his masterly fashion and only lost a few seconds. Von Brauchitsch met the oil next and span round, just managing to regain control before the acute bend at the bottom of the hill. Hasse's Auto-Union did much the same thing, but ran off the road, knocked down some fencing and was out of the race. Seaman also ended up off the course but managed to get started again. This manœuvre cost him over two minutes, or one whole lap, and dropped him from second place to sixth.

As a result of all this, Müller's Auto-Union was leading, 5 seconds ahead of Lang. Nuvolari was third, with von Brauchitsch's and Baumer's Mercedes fourth and fifth. Lang, Müller, and Nuvolari made pit stops, all in very good time. Then the fun really began. At fifty laps Nuvolari was in third place, 58 seconds behind the leader, Lang, who was going extremely fast. Then Nuvolari proceeded to drive as only he knew how, passing Müller into second place, and knocking seconds off Lang's time on every lap. The Mercedes pit signals, of course, told Lang exactly what was happening, but as he had his windscreen shattered by a flying stone, he found it physically impossible to go much faster. Eventually, Nuvolari caught Lang and passed him to romp home an easy winner. It was an unforgettable thrill to see the little Italian creeping closer each lap to the Mercedes and the frenzied stop-watch calculations as to how soon Nuvolari could catch up and pass him. Lang, as we know, was second and Seaman by some magnificent driving managed to creep up to third place. Von Brauchitsch, whose car was not going well, was fifth.

The year had been a successful one for Mercedes-Benz, even if towards the end of the season, opposition, both from the Auto-Unions and the Italians, had begun to stiffen. Out of ten events entered, they had six firsts, seven seconds, and three line ahead victories. Also Rudolf Caracciola won, for the third time running, the European drivers' championship, for which he gained from the A.I.A.C.R. a large Gold Medal.

We must now say something of the ordinary cars being produced in 1938 and 1939. Five models were available in 1938. First comes the type *170V*, four-cylinder 13·9 h.p., with bore and stroke of 73·5 × 100 mm. (1697 cc.). This engine developed 38 b.h.p. at 3200 r.p.m. It had a three-bearing crankshaft and was capable of 75 to 80 m.p.h. The engine, unlike the *170H,* was in front. The chassis had an X-form oval tubular frame. The graceful roadster cost £525, but the saloon cost, in 1938, as little as £395. *The Motor* tested one in November of that year. The impression was very favourable. On top (ratio 4 to 1) the saloon, which weighed 23 cwt., would do 68 m.p.h., and on third (5·8 to 1) 45. 0 to 30 took 7·7 seconds, and 0 to 50 23·5 seconds. The car cruised at 55 to 60 very easily and the engine was sufficiently smooth as to be indistinguishable from a six. The riding was thought extremely good (the car was independently sprung all round) and the steering was found very light. The brakes also came in for praise. It was reported that over sixty thousand of this model had been sold by early 1939.

The type *230* was first announced in 1936. The engine was a six-cylinder side-valve unit, 72·5 × 90 mm. (2300 cc.). The h.p. rating was 19.5 and 55 b.h.p. was developed at 3200 r.p.m. *The Motor* test gave a maximum of 73 m.p.h. on top, with 50 on third (ratios of 4 to 1 and 5·96 to 1). 0 to 30 took 6·3 seconds and 0 to 50 18·4 seconds. Petrol consumption was 19 m.p.g. The saloon, unladen, weighed 29 cwt. and the price was £575. *The Motor* summed up as follows: 'We are not exaggerating when we say that the general comfort of this car is superior to practically any other vehicle in which we have had the pleasure of riding.'

The type *320* had first appeared as a 2·9 litre in 1932/3. It was then known as the type *290* (short). By 1936 the engine, a six-cylinder, had grown larger and was of 3218 cc. (82·5 ×

1938 type *230* with X-braced chassis and independent springing all round. (*Mercedes-Benz*)

1937 type *320*, 3-litre cabriolet. (*Mercedes-Benz*)

100). Horse-power rating was 23·5, and 78 b.h.p. was developed at 3200. The crankshaft had seven main bearings.

In June 1935 *The Autocar* tested the type *290* and in February 1938 the type *320*. It is interesting to compare the two tests as, clearly, much development had taken place over the three years. The type *290* had a 22·6 h.p. six-cylinder side-valve engine, of 78 × 100 mm. bore and stroke (2867 cc.). The four-door cabriolet tested weighed 36 cwt. and it cost £930. The car was independently sprung by two coil springs in front, together with a transverse leaf, and at the rear by two main coil springs at each side, together with two subsidiary coil springs mounted beneath the rear-axle casing. *The Autocar* found this system 'amazingly comfortable for all occupants, and remarkably stable on corners', though it found it difficult to gauge the speed at which a corner could be taken at first. The type *290* had a direct third gear and overdrive top with ratios of 4·327 to 1 and 5·77 to 1 (third). Top was not quite so silent as third. In performance the car did a best run over the timed quarter mile of 72·58, with a mean speed of 70·87. 0 to 50 took 25⅗ seconds and no less than 44⅖ seconds to 60. Though it would cruise at 65 all day, obviously it took a remarkably long time to get there. The type *320* has, as we have seen, a slightly larger engine, but the weight for the saloon had gone up to 39 cwt. It was the first model to be fitted with synchromesh on top, third and second. Top gear ratio was the same as on the type *290*, but third was slightly lower—

1938 eight-cylinder *Grosser*, its capacity now increased to 7·7 litres. (*Mercedes-Benz*)

6·45 to 1. Performance was vastly improved. Maximum speed over the timed quarter-mile was, at best, now 77·59 m.p.h., with a mean of 74·69. Acceleration from 0 to 50 took only 19·5 seconds and from 0 to 60 32 seconds. The price too was lower, £840 for the saloon. Incidentally, both models were supplied with hydraulic brakes which appeared well up to their work, and petrol consumption was in each case about 16 m.p.g.

Finally, there were the *540K*s of which we have written at some length and in which no apparent change was made, and the type *500N*, an unsupercharged 5-litre car (4918 cc., 82·5 × 115 mm.) the chassis price of which was £1040 and the tourer £1525.

## 1939

Caracciola started off the year 1939 by taking two separate 3-litre Mercedes cars to the autobahn near Dessau, one for flying-start, the other for standing-start records. This is just an example of how thoroughly Mercedes did everything. Both cars, exquisite examples of the panel-beater's art, were of totally different aerodynamic shapes. A third car, hidden somewhere at the back of Uhlenhaut's 'holy-of-holies', was built to attack the world's speed record in 1939. The attempt was to be made on an autobahn, but at the last minute the road was closed because a deposit of much needed brown coal was found underneath it. Then the war came and the project was dropped.

Caracciola was successful with his two cars, and between February 8 and 14, 1939, took no less than five Class D (2000–3000 cc.) records.

The type *154* was now superseded by the type *163* which was more or less a *154* with a host of detail improvements. Four cars were entered for the Pau Grand Prix on April 2. The competition was not formidable. Auto-Union were not ready and did not run. The French contingent was the best yet, a number of Darracqs, good cars, extremely well driven, but no match for the type *163* Mercedes. One, in fact, driven by 'Fifi' Etancelin achieved the same time in practice as Lang and was only 3 seconds slower than Caracciola. The Sefac made one of its momentary token appearances.

Caracciola made a splendid start and led, until brought into the pits through a highly inaccessible nut slacking off an oil pipe underneath the almost red-hot exhaust manifold. However, Lindemaier, whose middle name must be asbestos, had an answer even for this, but the delay put Caracciola well out of the running. Then von Brauchitsch's car showed every sign of running low on petrol, so he came in and lost time filling up, which definitely gave the race to Lang. Von Brauchitsch was to find after the race that he had not been short of petrol at all.

Hermann Lang winning the Pau Grand Prix in 1939. Von Brauchitsch had won the previous year. (*Mercedes-Benz*)

The next event was the Grand Prix of Tripoli. The Italians restricted the race to 1½-litre supercharged cars, keeping this dark right to the last minute. And here we may quote an amusing story, possibly apocryphal, about an Italian paper. They heard rumours that a 1½-litre Mercedes racing-car had been seen on test. So, to disarm all suspicion, they sent a reporter who knew nothing whatever about motor-cars, but was an excellent free-hand draughtsman. He presented himself, as he had been instructed, at the Mercedes-Benz works and asked to see the 1½-litre supercharged racing Mercedes that had been built for Caracciola. To his surprise, instead of being thrown out, the car was, after a very short delay, produced. He was not only allowed to examine it and make sketches but he was given a short but electrifying drive in it by Hermann Lang himself. The reporter hurried back to his paper delighted with his success and the editor, a non-technical man, had blocks made of all the lovely sketches and was about to rush into print before any other paper got the scoop. Only the arrival of the motoring correspondent spoiled what might have been one of the best jokes of all time. The reporter had been shown exactly what he had asked for, 'The 1½-litre supercharged racing Mercedes built for Rudolf Caracciola'. It had been built in 1924! This little incident reputedly took place at the end of 1938.

The Italians probably had an inkling that something was going on at Stuttgart, but it is unlikely that they had any idea that the car had advanced beyond the drawing-board stage. Certainly no one could have been more surprised than they were when two 1½-litre cars arrived, running perfectly, at Tripoli!

In practice, Luigi Villoresi drove his Maserati round nearly two seconds faster than the small Mercedes. But, on the day, Lang and Caracciola led from the start, with the Alfas hard on their tails. The pace was too hot for the Maseratis, all of which retired early. Lang was going in great style, lapping at 128 m.p.h. Farina, on one of the attractive little 1½-litre Alfas, passed Caracciola's Mercedes. But the effort of trying to catch Lang was altogether too much for Farina's car, which 'blew up'. The two 1½-litre Mercedes ran faultlessly throughout and finished line ahead with Lang leading Caracciola by about 3½ minutes. Four minutes behind him came Villoresi, who had driven a Maserati in practice, at the wheel of a 1½-litre Alfa, in third place. After this satisfying performance, the two cars vanished into the Mercedes racing department and Uhlenhaut's iron curtain clanged down behind them.

A fortnight after the Tripoli victory came the Eifel races

held on the Nürburgring. This proved a first-class tussle between Mercedes and Auto-Union. Certainly practising showed all the signs of a very close race, for there was only about ·01 of a second between the best times of the rival aces, Caracciola and Nuvolari. Both von Brauchitsch and Seaman made a good start and, getting well ahead of the field, showed every intention of staying there. But the strain of this brisk start seems to have been too much for the clutches of both cars, for Seaman's collapsed completely and von Brauchitsch's slipped sporadically and kept his speed down so that he could only finish fourth.

This was a race where tyres came very much into the picture. Lang, in the lead, was going at a terrific pace; he covered a lap in 9 minutes 52 seconds, the fastest ever recorded at the Nürburgring, but he had to change tyres before half time. The pace was even beginning to tell on Caracciola's tyres. It always had been a fact that the tyre wear on Caracciola's car was anything up to 20 per cent less than on other people's cars. When Caracciola came in for a tyre change in the sixth lap, and Nuvolari on his Auto Union did not, it soon became clear that the Italian maestro was going to try to drive straight through. After the race it was disclosed that Continental Tyres had advised him not to make the attempt. It was certainly a gamble trying to get through without a tyre change, when even Caracciola had to change his. However, the gamble succeeded and brought him into second place. So the final order was Lang, Nuvolari, Caracciola, with von Brauchitsch fourth, and a cadet driver, Hans Hugo Hartmann, also on a type *163*, in eighth place.

As we shall see, 1939 was Hermann Lang's year. So far Mercedes had entered in three events, and he had won them all. Lang was generally considered to be a better man than Stuck on circuits, but there were very few drivers who could compare with Stuck for hill-climbing, especially long climbs. Lang was very keen to challenge him, at least on the Vienna climb, and the directors of Mercedes-Benz were equally keen to assert their supremacy uphill as well as on the flat. So special cars were built just for the 5-mile Hohenstrassen climb near Vienna. Much attention was paid to the reduction of weight, and two 'specials' were prepared, one with a 5·6-litre engine, the other with a highly supercharged 3-litre. Auto-Union brought along one 'special', a 3-litre Grand Prix car, and one of the 750 kg. 6-litre type.

The organization of the event was an almost perfect example of *Osterreichische Schlamperei*. It is difficult to translate this; roughly it means 'Light-hearted but complete disregard of detail in which Austrians specialize'. The result was chaos, especially during practice. Both Lang and von Brauchitsch 'blew up' their engines by taking them well over permitted revs, but, being very senior boys, they did not get quite as severe a reprimand as Freddie Zehender had done for his similar misdemeanour.

The following day, both Mercedes cars were on the line in perfect tune. Each driver was to make two climbs and the winner was to be decided by the addition of both times. On the first climb Müller clocked 2 minutes 18·6 seconds, Lang 2 minutes 19·6 seconds, von Brauchitsch 2 minutes 20·6 seconds and Stuck, most surprisingly, 2 minutes 22 seconds. On the second climb Müller made a poor time, so Lang beat him by half a second on the aggregate. Müller just managed to beat von Brauchitsch into second place by 0·2 seconds. Either Stuck or his car must have been badly off form as neither of the times he returned could compare with the other three drivers.

After this fourth consecutive victory for Hermann Lang people were beginning to ask jokingly whether he was going to maintain the run in the Belgian Grand Prix at Spa, a fortnight later. The surface of the course was treacherous and slippery and visibility bad. At the end of the first lap Müller was leading, with Lang, Nuvolari, Caracciola, Farina on an Alfa, Seaman, Hasse, von Brauchitsch, and the rest in that order. Then, in spite of the weather, Seaman thought he had the feel of the circuit, and started to go very fast. Müller and Nuvolari had dropped back and after the third lap, the order was Lang, Caracciola, and Seaman.

Just as Caracciola used less tyre-tread than other people he also 'left the course' much less frequently. On the eighth lap, however, he ran off the road at La Source bend and 'ditched' his car too badly to get back into the race, thus letting Seaman into second place. Nuvolari also went off the course. On the eleventh lap Seaman, going very fast, passed Lang into first place. He was now lapping at over 94 m.p.h. On the seventeenth lap, he took 30 seconds to fill up with petrol, was passed by Lang, repassed him and, on the twenty-first lap, was leading by 30 seconds. Then he came into the La Source bend, was badly placed for it, and crashed into the trees. Seaman was knocked unconscious and the impact severed the three-inch pipes connecting saddle tank with rear tank, fifty gallons of petrol immediately flooding into the cockpit and catching fire. It was almost a minute before the heroic efforts of a Belgian gendarme, Meier (the Auto-Union driver who was out of the race), and some others managed to get

Seaman clear. By this time he was so terribly burned that he died a few hours later. Lang was dreadfully upset and wanted to retire but he was given orders to go on, which he did, to win his fifth consecutive victory. The final order was Lang, Hasse on an Auto-Union, and von Brauchitsch.

Five races in a row was about as much as anyone could expect, and, in the French Grand Prix, Mercedes had a short sharp run of bad luck. The Rheims circuit was now very fast, Auto-Unions had at last got going very well and the French Darracqs, if not as fast as the German cars, were fast enough to ensure that a delay of a few seconds could rob either the Mercedes or Auto-Union of victory. The pace was very fierce from the start. Nuvolari sent his Auto-Union streaking away from the line with Caracciola, Lang, and von Brauchitsch on his heels like a pack of hounds in full cry. Then Caracciola made one of his rare misjudgements, slid into a wall, and damaged his car too badly to go on. Lang sat on Nuvolari's tail and just squeezed past him, but at seven laps he had only managed to scrape a bare lead of five seconds. Müller, on an Auto-Union, was not far behind Nuvolari. The pace was terrific, so much so that the engine of Nuvolari's Auto-Union 'blew up', luckily not putting enough oil on the track to cause anyone else anxious moments. Meier's Auto-Union caught fire while being refuelled but it was put out and he went on. Just before this, von Brauchitsch's car had broken down and was wheeled away by mechanics with very long faces. However, now that Nuvolari was out, Lang, who was going well, was building up a very useful lead over Müller. It began to look like another win for Mercedes but it was not to be Lang's day. His car broke down and he was out of the race. So, with all Mercedes *hors de combat*, an Auto-Union driven by Müller won its first big race for a long time.

Admittedly the hitherto reliable type *163* had not been so hard pressed before, but now it was quite likely to occur again, especially with Nuvolari really 'getting the hang' of Auto-Union and Müller's driving improving enormously. So Uhlenhaut and his assistants responsible for preparing the cars worked hard with a view to ensuring that the Rheims fiasco should not repeat itself again in the German Grand Prix on July 23 at Nürburgring. The cars showed up well in practice, Lang beating Rosemeyer's record lap speed by three seconds. This showed conclusively that, even if the type *163* did not have quite the power or the maximum speed of the fabulous type *125*, it was faster over a given course; in spite of this, right up to the end of the 1939 season, *125*s or, rather, 'specials' based on the *125* were still used for hill-climbing.

Caracciola driving the 3-litre Mercedes-Benz in the 1939 German Grand Prix which he won. (*George Monkhouse*)

Lang made one of his terrific starts, leading von Brauchitsch, Stuck, and Müller. Caracciola, as usual, was saving his car and playing a waiting game. Pietsch's 3-litre Maserati was going extraordinarily well, and on the second lap, to everyone's surprise, he moved into second place behind Lang! Lang came in to the pits to change plugs, and thus let Pietsch into the lead. But Lang's trouble was something much more deep-seated than plug bother and soon his car was out of the race. Von Brauchitsch's car was also in trouble and he too was forced to retire.

This left only two Mercedes, driven by Caracciola and cadet driver Brendel. Neubauer signalled Brendel to come in so that the car could be handed over to Lang. Brendel appeared not to see the signal and went on. Most unfortunately in the next lap he got into a muddle trying to pass Pietsch and there was an accident. Eye-witnesses say that Neubauer has rarely been more furious, especially as there was still much of the race left to run, and only one Mercedes, Caracciola's car, remained. However, the old master saved the situation, for it began to rain and Caracciola immediately accelerated. Hasse, trying to go as fast as Caracciola, ran off the road. Nuvolari had retired, so only Müller's Auto-Union was left. Towards the end, the race became a procession led by Caracciola, who thus won the German Grand Prix for the sixth time. Müller and Pietsch were second and third.

Next on the calendar came the Grossglockner climb, carrying, for the winner, the title of 'German Hill-Climbing Champion'. Mercedes sent two 'specials' based on the *W125*, and, as at Hohenstrassen, the winner was decided by the aggregate time of two climbs. Lang made the climb of his life, scoring fastest time of the day, and, breaking Stuck's record of the previous year, he gained for himself the coveted title of 'Bergmeister'. Von Brauchitsch on a similar car put up fourth best time.

The Swiss Grand Prix of 1939 was run in two heats, one for 1½-litre cars and one for formula cars. The winners of each heat ran together in the final. The 1½-litre heat was won by two Alfas and a Maserati. In the formula heat Mercedes came in first, second and third, the drivers being Lang, Carracciola, and von Brauchitsch. The final was very exciting. Not only were Nuvolari and Müller on Auto-Unions in excellent form, but the 1½-litre Alfas were quite fast enough to keep up with the German cars. Indeed, for five or six laps Farina, on one of the 'baby' Alfas, was running second to Lang, ahead of everybody else. But it ended in the same way as a good many other events in 1939, with Mercedes filling the first three places, Lang being the winner, followed by Caracciola and von Brauchitsch, Müller and Nuvolari on Auto-Unions, finishing fourth and fifth respectively.

The Yugoslavs desired to have a Grand Prix. The A.I.A.C.R. agreed, but the stumbling block was the roads. Except for one short stretch near the Hungarian frontier they had no suitable course for racing, so they decided to have one round Belgrade itself. They could hardly have chosen anywhere less suitable. However, it was a sporting gesture in the right direction and the race was held on September 3, 1939. Mercedes and Auto-Union sent teams and these were augmented by a few privately-entered Italian cars not in their first youth. It was said that a local enthusiast unearthed a 1914 Prince Henry Austro-Daimler with a surprising turn of speed and was bitterly disappointed to find that the race was for formula cars only!

Mercedes were represented by von Brauchitsch, Lang, and Baumer. Lang led the race for a time but his engine 'blew up', which was unfortunate because, of the ten events in which he was entered in 1939, he had already won seven. The race itself was, due to the nature of the course, full of hair-raising incidents which must have given the spectators many thrills and Neubauer many anxious moments. In one of these Baumer left the road, and the race, but was unhurt. Von Brauchitsch, who had lost valuable seconds spinning his car like a top, and also in avoiding Baumer when he was sliding about, could not quite catch Nuvolari's Auto-Union, who won, with von Brauchitsch in second place.

The Mercedes racing-cars only made one more appearance before being swallowed up in the maelstrom of war. They put in a token appearance in the Brasov hill-climb in Rumania, at that time a neutral country, late in the year.

# 5
# STAR PHOENIX
# 1945~

The 1952 German Grand Prix for sports-cars. The *300SLs* lead the field, with Lang in front of Kling. (*Carlo Demand: The Big Race*)

# RENNLEITER NEUBAUER

During the war, the Mercedes-Benz works at Untertürkheim was a target of major military importance, and by 1945 the devastation was appalling. A tremendous task of reconstruction faced the staff, and everybody, directors included, worked 'round the clock' and continued to do so, year after year, with characteristic German thoroughness.

The form of direction of Mercedes-Benz should perhaps be explained. An executive board of directors (the *Vorstand*) controls the technical, financial, export and general sales policy. Its chairman is the head of the Company. A supervisory board (the *Aufsichtsrat*) checks the business activities of the Company and supervises its financial dealings. To this board are nominated the main shareholders of the Company, and personalities in the financial and business field, not of necessity connected with the manufacture of motor-cars.

In 1953, Prince von Urach was in charge of research, and Rudolf Uhlenhaut was responsible for the research, development, and construction of the racing-cars. As soon as a racing-car goes into 'active service', it is handled by the organization controlled by Alfred Neubauer. Naturally, building up this relatively small, but vitally important department was, after the war, a most difficult matter. But by the beginning of 1951, Neubauer felt that he had progressed far enough to stage a 'dress rehearsal'. Three of the pre-war 3-litre twelve-cylinder racing-cars were entered for the Argentine Grand Prix and the Eva Peron race. In spite of bad carburettor trouble they managed in both races to finish second and third to the Ferrari of Gonzalez. These events could in no wise be termed successes for Mercedes, but they provided a lot of information for the racing reorganization. While the racing department was hard at it, the rest of the huge works was being rebuilt and restored to peace-time production. The V8 that was to have superseded the *540K* was shelved and work was concentrated on ordinary five-seater saloons for which, during the immediate post-war years, there was a strong demand. First a start was made with the pre-war type *170* with both petrol and Diesel engines. Later a 3-litre car was produced with beautifully finished coachwork and quite a reasonable performance. 1952 saw the *300SL* which has proved itself one of the finest sports-cars in the world.

Quite a number of 3-litre Mercedes-Benz were entered for the 1952 Monte Carlo Rally, including a works team consisting of Kling and Geier, Caracciola and Kurle, Lang and Grupp. This team won the Charles Faroux award for the best team entered by the manufacturers. They also won a special prize for the excellence and suitability of their coachwork. Freiherr von Jungenfeld won the cup of the Automobile Club von Deutschland, and the Beckers, also driving a Mercedes-Benz, won one for the best radio installation.

What the designers were doing at Untertürkheim had been a closely guarded secret, but nobody thought very seriously that they would bother to build a car for the expiring formula. It did not therefore come as a great surprise when they produced, as they had done in 1926, a much faster sports-car than anybody else. This low-built coupé is a superb piece of aerodynamic design with the 3-litre engine canted over at an angle to reduce height. The first appearance of these remarkable cars was in the Mille Miglia race at the beginning of May. The drivers were Caracciola with Kurle, and Kling with Klenk. The preparations were of Teutonic thoroughness. The drivers and a very large specialist personnel were in residence on the course for two months before the race and practised for long hours daily until they could 'go round in their sleep'.

The Italians knew the course equally well, and it was a terrific race. Bracco was driving his 3-litre Ferrari at such a pace at the beginning of the race that he ran through his tyres in the first four hundred miles and dropped to fifth place. An Homeric duel was going on between Kling and Taruffi's Ferrari for the lead. The weather was, as usual, atrocious, and the road surface more than treacherous, but in spite of this Kling averaged 85 m.p.h. and was leading at Rome. The old axiom that the leader at Rome never wins the race proved itself again. For, although Taruffi's car retired with transmission trouble, Bracco, driving an inspired race, beat Kling back to second place by less than five minutes in twelve hours. Caracciola came in, a little over half an hour later, in fourth place.

In May also, the type *300SL* Mercedes coupés appeared on the Bremgarten circuit in the international sports-car race for the Prix de Berne. In practice, it became apparent that these new squat, businesslike-looking cars were much faster than anything else except the Swiss, Willy Daetwyler's, 4·1-litre Ferrari. They were, however, not to encounter even this opposition, for Daetwyler's car broke a half-shaft on the starting line. The three Mercedes type *300SLs* driven by Kling, Lang, and Caracciola had it all their own way, until Caracciola's crash put him out of the race. The other two finished first and second. Caracciola had to remain in hospital, which kept him out of the running for Le Mans.

After this successful curtain-raiser, three type *300SL* coupés came to the line in front of the biggest crowd ever assembled round the Sarthe circuit, to watch the toughtest and fastest 24-hour race ever held there. In practice, the Mercedes team were a little worried by the effortless speed of the closed American Cunningham and everybody else was worried by the air-brake on top of one of the Mercedes coupés. This 'secret weapon', however, was only on test and was not actually used in the race.

In practice, Ascari's 2·9-litre Ferrari recorded a lap speed nearly as fast as the German cars, but nobody felt very confident that this new and relatively untried twelve-cylinder car would last under the extremely fast pace that would be set. Their forebodings were justified, for after leading for a while it retired with clutch trouble.

The three *300SLs* were driven by Lang and new driver, Riess, Helfrich and Niedermayer, also relatively newcomers, Kling, who had a good record on B.M.W., and Klenk. Neubauer had no intention of allowing his team to be drawn into a cut-throat duel with the Ferraris, or even with Manzon's and Behra's astonishing six-cylinder Gordini which, after four hours, was leading the race. His orders kept them driving fast, but steadily, with a little in reserve, taking no notice of what anybody else did. During the fifth hour, the one car that was causing them anxiety, the coupé Cunningham, ran into a sandbank and could not be dug out. After night-fall the jinx that had once before put Mercedes out at Le Mans struck again. Kling and Klenk's car, which had been going very well, retired with a defective dynamo.

At four o'clock in the morning, after twelve hours driving, Manzon's Gordini was failing. Pierre Levegh's wonderful Talbot, which he drove alone throughout the whole race, had pushed its way up to first place and was leading Helfrich and Niedermayer by four laps, and Lang and Riess were lying a close third.

At 8 a.m., Helfrich and Niedermayer had decreased Levegh's lead to three laps; but the other Mercedes, although still running in third place, had dropped back a little. At noon, after twenty hours, Levegh had very slightly increased his lead again and the order was still the same. It looked very much as if Neubauer were 'playing safe' and would be prepared to be content with second and third places and winning the 3-litre class, rather than go all out to catch Levegh. However, by extreme bad luck, Levegh, right at the end of his magnificent 24-hour drive, with victory almost in his grasp, ran a big-end, letting the two Mercedes cars into first and second places.

At the Nürburgring races in 1952, the perfect timing of events and organization of the meeting was apparently even better than pre-war. The organizers seemed even to have organized the weather, for that was magnificent too. The German Grand Prix, for which, of course, no Mercedes were entered, was an 'all-Ferrari affair', in which they gained the first four places. But the 3-litre class of the sports-car races was a procession of *300SL* Mercedes, with open bodies this time, lapping at about 2 m.p.h. slower than the winning Ferrari in the Grand Prix! The only disappointment was that the supercharged *300SLs* which were to have run in the 8-litre class (a 'blown' engine being deemed to have double the capacity of an unblown one) were withdrawn in practice. The engine of this car looked most interesting with three carburettors, mounted outboard of a Roots-type 'blower', feeding straight into the inlet ports.

In December came the Carrera Pan-Americana, and Mercedes-Benz were very anxious to win this race, for victory would boost their American sports-car sales. It was this prize for which both Mercedes and Ferrari were struggling. Some time before the race, Uhlenhaut was asked how his firm were managing about carburation for this fantastic course, which ranges from sea level to mountain passes higher than anything in Europe, during the race of nearly two thousand miles. He said that they had achieved the desired results by dashing up and down the Stelvio which, if not quite as high, was as near as they could get to it. It was really a race between Mercedes-Benz and Ferrari, for the Gordinis, although very fast, were unlikely to be able to stand the pace. The Lancias, although reliable, were not fast enough, and the one Jaguar *XK120*, in spite of the long string of victories this famous British production had achieved, was not very suitable. The race was run in eight stages with overnight stops. Crowd control seems to have been quite good, but there were a great many moveable hazards in the way of dogs, cattle, and large low-flying birds, all imbued with a fanatical *Todeswunsch* or longing for death, which caused the competitors some very anxious moments. One of the birds, a sort of buzzard, did succeed in flying through Kling's windscreen, but luckily did little harm to anyone except itself.

Neubauer's organization was very complete. He even had tyre depots along the route to change to suitable types of tyre for the next section, whether it was twisty mountain roads, or long straights. At one time it looked as if the result of the Mille Miglia would repeat itself, for Bracco on a 2·7-litre Ferrari built up a quite appreciable lead over the first Mercedes. However, as has been so often the case with Ferraris, the transmission let them down and Bracco retired between Parral and Chihuahua with clutch trouble. Ascari and Manzon had been in trouble and retired, Bonetto and Behra had crashed, and later on Villoresi's gear-box broke up. The American driver, Fitch, had been in trouble too, but was now catching up.

So, towards the end of the race it looked like first and second places for Mercedes-Benz, with a battle royal for third place between the Ferrari driven by Chinetti and Lucas and Fitch's *300SL* Mercedes. And so it turned out at the finish, Kling and Klenk winning at the incredible average speed of 102·8 m.p.h., with Lang and Riess in second place. Fitch had lost so much time that he could not catch Chinetti, although the latter was forced by gear-box trouble to run almost entirely in top gear. But, in any case, this American-driven Mercedes which came in a close fourth was disqualified because Fitch had allowed a mechanic, other than the one riding with him, to work on the car.

It is a curious sensation driving one of these fabulous *300SLs*, and quite unlike anything hitherto experienced.* It is, indeed, owing to the insulation from road shocks provided by the springing and damped steering, more like flying an aircraft. The sense of unfamiliarity is heightened by the fact that the occupants have to step in through the roof (the over-all height is only four feet one inch) but once inside, the seats and driving position, as one would expect, leave nothing to be desired for comfort, and the controls all fall conveniently to hand. Probably the most striking feature of the car is the manner in which it reaches 120 m.p.h. as easily and quickly as most cars reach 50 m.p.h., and there is virtually nothing, apart from the way the road comes at you, to give you an indication that you have reached that speed. The red mark on the rev-counter is reached at 6300 r.p.m., which is in excess of 160 m.p.h. The *300SL* is a worthy successor to the great cars of forty years ago, the *SSK*s and pre-war Grand Prix cars, and will go down to history as a really great motor-car.

* This was written in 1955.

## Return to Grand Prix 1954

The eagerly awaited comeback of Mercedes to full Grand Prix racing must have been an anxious time for the whole équipe. This was the moment for which they had all worked for six long years. Preparations had, of course, been as meticulous and the secrecy as great as ever. Neubauer wore his best poker face and displayed no emotion whatever. But Rudolf Uhlenhaut's cheerful puckish grin did imply that there was something special up the Mercedes sleeve. The cars had been seen doing tests at Monza, but no one had succeeded in getting near them. All that was known was that the cars, even from a distance, were so very low and squat that it was impossible for the engines to be mounted vertically under the bonnet.

At the French Grand Prix, in July, 1954, details were released with a flourish of trumpets.

The engine, a 2496 cc. (76 × 68·8 mm.), unsupercharged straight eight, 'revving' up to nearly nine thousand r.p.m., had both fuel injection and ignition by Bosch. A five-speed gear-box, differential and inboard brakes with bimetallic drums were in one unit driving the back wheels by swing axles. As is usual Mercedes practice, the steering-wheel was detachable for easy entry to the cockpit. The streamlining, evolved after much wind tunnel testing, was of a very advanced nature and incorporated ducted air scoops for brake cooling.

The 1954 formula eight-cylinder racing Mercedes-Benz type *196*. Bore and stroke 76 × 68·8 mm. (2496 cc.). This is the fully streamlined version and is seen on the Nürburgring. (*George Monkhouse*)

Cockpit of the streamlined Grand Prix car. (*George Monkhouse*)

The team consisted of the Argentine, Juan Manuel Fangio, Karl Kling and that very promising youngster, Hans Herrmann. In practice, Fangio and Kling made the best times, with Ascari on a Maserati only a fraction of a second slower. At the beginning, Fangio and Kling led away from Gonzalez and Hawthorn, Herrmann apparently being held in reserve. This order was held for a dozen laps with Gonzalez dropping

The engine of the 2½-litre Grand Prix car. As readers will see, this lies on its side in the frame. The classic beauty, with this untidy array of oil and fuel pipes, is lost, but the reason is a sound one. Grand Prix racing today allows no time for repair work in the pits for a potential winner. If something goes wrong under the Mercedes bonnet, the car is just wheeled away to the 'dead-car' park! (*George Monkhouse*)

further behind. The only other serious challenger, Mike Hawthorn's Ferrari, retired with brake failure. On the twelfth lap Gonzalez' Ferrari, throwing oil all over the place, withdrew from the race, leaving Fangio and Kling to finish easily in first and second places. Herrmann had trouble with his car, possibly as a result of his scrap with Villoresi, and was out of the race on his nineteenth lap.

At the British Grand Prix at Silverstone, three weeks later, things did not go nearly so well for Mercedes. This debacle cannot be attributed to one particular cause, but the following reasons were all contributory. Although Neubauer has visited Silverstone, and Uhlenhaut has probably motored round it unofficially very fast indeed, the team, except for Fangio, had no experience whatever of this course. The cars were somewhat unsuitable for the event. Further, the weather became about as bad as anything Britain can produce, and it did not appear that the present Mercedes team could cope with this half as well as the old *Regenmeister* Caracciola of former days. Fangio made fastest time in practice (100·35 m.p.h.), Gonzalez and Hawthorn being one second behind on Ferraris, and these three shared the front line of the starting grid. Only one other Mercedes, driven by Kling, started. The cars were generally similar to the French Grand Prix winners, the wheels being enclosed by the streamlining.

Fangio did not have at all an easy time. From his seating position it was impossible to see the marker drums, and, indeed, on two occasions he struck them. Also, certainly to observers round the course, his Mercedes did not seem to be negotiating the corners with its usual ease. But in spite of all this, at half time he was running second to Gonzalez. Then, simultaneously with the tropical downpour, Fangio's Mercedes started to sound a trifle woolly and gradually he dropped back to finish in fourth place. Kling had never been in the picture at all and finished seventh.

The return match, the German Grand Prix, was played out on the home ground, the fourteen-mile-long, fascinating Nürburgring. For the Mercedes-Benz club this was a memorable occasion, for they drove from Ostend in great strength on their cars, which dated from 1898 onwards. The 1898 Benz had to be given lifts along the way by a lorry, not because of any doubts of reliability, but because it was so much slower than the other cars. Peter Hampton's 1903 (reputedly ex-Jenatzy) 60-h.p. Mercedes, and cars built later, all made the journey under their own steam. On practice day, the President of the Meeting kindly allowed all the old Mercedes cars from Great Britain to do a lap of the circuit. This proved a spectacle very much to the taste of the huge crowd, who cheered them to the echo. Of course, what was described as a 'demonstration round' soon developed into an unofficial race, some of the old *S*, *SS* and *SSK* cars going at a very respectable speed indeed. After the Grand Prix, the club cars drove on to Stuttgart, where the participants in the Rally were royally entertained for three days.

On the day of the race, at 1.15 p.m., four Mercedes cars started. Three, driven by Fangio, Kling and Lang had new, rather squat single-seater bodies, while the one driven by Hans Herrmann had the earlier type of streamline coachwork. Fangio shared the first line of the starting grid with Hawthorn and Moss (Ferrari and Maserati). Kling had not practised officially and so was on the back mark.

The start was a really magnificent dogfight, with Gonzalez (Ferrari) who had rather naughtily crept at the start (but not badly enough to be penalized) coming out in front. After the first lap, the order was Gonzalez, Fangio, Moss, going very well on his Maserati (later, however, he 'blew up' very thoroughly indeed), and Lang.

Hawthorn and Herrmann had a fine scrap which was won by the former. Then Kling came up, challenged Hawthorn and passed him. Soon afterwards the back axle of the Ferrari broke. Fangio had now passed Gonzalez and was increasing his lead over him. Of the two Argentinians, Gonzalez seemed to be feeling the death of their compatriot Marimon, killed on a Maserati in practice, far more keenly, and it was obvious that he was upset and off his usual brilliant form. On the fifth

Two 2½-litre Mercedes-Benz Grand Prix cars in unstreamlined form on the Nürburgring during the German Grand Prix, 1954. (*George Monkhouse*)

lap Hermann Lang passed him into second place and on the seventh Kling also passed the Argentinian.

Then things really started to happen. A rumour swept like wildfire through the crowd that Kling was getting 'pit signals' from his wife. Certainly, wherever the signal came from, and judging from the icy fury of Neubauer's face the signal may well have not come from him, Kling was going all out to win the race for himself from Fangio. He put up several extremely fast laps, breaking the lap record more than once. Then he fought a brilliant duel with Lang and started to build up such a lead on him as to cause Lang, experienced veteran that he is, to spin and stall his engine, putting him out of the race. At half-time, Fangio was leading with Kling a dangerous challenger. Kling was going much faster than Fangio and passed him on the fourteenth lap. On the sixteenth lap Kling made the fastest lap of the day, but the terrible punishment he was giving his car began to take effect, and next time he passed the pits he was pointing at his back wheel and, the following lap, he came in. An excited crowd pressed round Kling's car and Neubauer, in a fine rage, whacked them really hard with a marshal's flag till they drew back. A temporary repair was swiftly made, but the time it took dropped Kling to fourth place. This left Mercedes in first and fourth places, for Hans Herrmann had dropped out, with a burst fuel pipe, on the seventh lap. It had been a brilliant drive by Kling, whether authorized or not, but the sheer pace of it, putting out first Lang, then himself, had robbed the team of a chance of gaining the first three places.

As usual, the weather was bad at the end of August, when the Swiss Grand Prix was due to be run. It rained all through practice and the curtain-raising races, but cleared up in time for the Grand Prix and the course was dry. This is very relevant, as Moss on his own Maserati was materially faster than Fangio in the wet. Experienced racegoers were saying on the eve of the race that Stirling Moss who, like Carraciola and Chiron, shows real form in blinding rain, had a very good chance of beating the Mercedes team, if his Maserati held together.

Fangio, Kling and Hans Herrmann came to the line. As usual, the team tactics were for Fangio to get out ahead and stay there with the other two in reserve. Early on, Kling spun his car on the tricky Wohlenrampe, dented its tail and was passed by everybody else in the race. However, driving at the top of his form, he worked his way up to third place by two-thirds of the way through the race. Fangio was steadily increasing his lead on Gonzalez, and Kling was catching him. It looked like a triple victory for Mercedes, for Trintignant's retirement let Hans Herrmann in behind Kling. Then at the foot of the hill approaching Ematt, Kling's car cut out completely and he retired with what was believed to be ignition failure. So, the finishing order was Fangio, Gonzalez, Herrmann.

A fortnight later, in lovely Italian autumn weather the Italian Grand Prix took place at Monza. The Mercedes team did not disclose in practice just how fast they could go. They did not have to, for it will be remembered, the team always practice there when Nürburgring is under snow, and know it as well as the Italians. Gonzalez with Ascari and Villoresi, on loan from Lancia, were only fractionally slower in practice on Ferraris. And to the delight of the British contingent, Stirling Moss driving a Maserati was barely half a second slower than the ageing but still supremely efficient Villoresi. It is probable that it was at this meeting that Alfred Neubauer decided finally to incorporate Moss in the 1955 Mercedes team. For, on this day, Moss really showed that, even if British manufacturers at that time had not got around to building successful Grand Prix cars, Britain still had the drivers. Before practice had ended Moss put up a better time than anyone except Fangio, and he was less than one-third of a second behind him.

On the day, out of twenty starters, Fangio shared the front line of the grid with Ascari and Moss. Kling was on the second line and Herrmann, who had replaced Lang, was in the third. The pace was very hot from the start, for the Italians were more than keen to win on their home ground. By the fifth lap the race had resolved itself into two separate races, Ascari, Gonzalez, Fangio and Moss fighting, almost wheel to wheel, for leadership, and a little way behind Kling and Hawthorn having a battle royal on their own. Herrmann's car was not going well and was making pit stops for mechanical adjustments. After twenty laps (quarter distance) Ascari was leading Fangio by nine seconds, with Kling in fifth place nearly a minute behind. Then Kling's car broke a radius rod and ran off the road. Apart from a small injury to one arm, the driver was unhurt. By half time, things did not look too good for Daimler-Benz. Ascari had increased his lead on Fangio, Kling was out of the race, and Herrmann's rather unhappy car, though keeping going, appeared definitely to be an 'also ran'. Breakdowns and crashes had now reduced the field to twelve. Then, in the second half of the race, Stirling Moss really proved himself one of the great drivers of our time. He came up, passing everybody including Ascari and Fangio, and led the race for forty-five laps till his car broke down just before the finish. Ascari retired on his fiftieth lap with a broken valve.

So Fangio won once more, a whole lap ahead of the second car, Hawthorn's Ferrari. Herrmann's Mercedes, which had been going slowly, finished three laps behind the winner and, as so many cars had dropped out as a result of the sizzling pace, he achieved fourth place.

Fangio thus won his fourth *Grande Epreuve* in this year, a wonderful achievement, not only because of quite fabulous driving, but as a result of the fine showing by a brand-new and hitherto unproven model of Mercedes-Benz.

The last Grand Prix of the year is traditionally held in a warm country. And, indeed, Barcelona is a very pleasant place in late October. The Spanish Grand Prix is run on the Pedralbes circuit, just on four miles long, between eleven in the morning and three o'clock in the afternoon. This enables the Spaniards to get home in time for lunch, which they eat at what we call 'tea-time'.

The new Grand Prix Lancias, making their first appearance, extremely fast and workmanlike, absolutely stole the show from Mercedes-Benz, usually the focal point of all attention. Perhaps among the crowd were a few old-timers who had seen young Lancia, the tinned-soup manufacturer's son, pitting his sixteen-litre Fiat against the great Mercedes drivers of the heroic age, Jenatzy, Lautenschlager, and Poege.

Three Mercedes came to the line, all with the 'unstreamlined' bodies, driven by Fangio, Kling and Herrmann. Fangio alone was on the front of the starting grid, the others having done none too well in practice.

The Lancias set the pace at the start, but before twenty laps were run, both of them were out with mechanical trouble. Fangio's and Herrmann's cars were running fourth and fifth, with Kling somewhere in the background. Then, a new and most objectionable hazard appeared. A brisk wind blew up, bringing with it masses of leaves, waste-paper and other garbage. A lot of this was sucked into the cooling scoops of all the cars and, possibly because of their finer mesh wire gauze, this seemed to trouble Mercedes most. Kling's car was certainly boiling merrily. Before half-way, Herrmann, who had also suffered from the blown garbage, retired with a slipping clutch.

For the whole of the second half of the race Hawthorn, driving a Ferrari, led. Neubauer hung out signals to Fangio, telling him to go all out and catch Hawthorn. Great driver though he is, Fangio seemed to be making very little impression on the distance between him and Hawthorn. Then his car started to squirt oil all over itself and its driver. Soon the engine began to make noises indicative that the oil, now plastered all over Fangio's face, would be doing more good in its usual channels. He had to slow down and Musso, a young and relatively new driver on a Maserati, passed him into second place. The race was won by Hawthorn, the first time an Englishman had won two Grand Prix races since de Hane Segrave did so over a quarter of a century earlier on Sunbeams. Fangio finished third, a lap behind Hawthorn, and Kling steamed his way into fifth place.

This was not a particularly glorious finish to the season—but what a season's racing it had been! Very soon after the war Neubauer said to Scott-Moncrieff: 'I don't know when we shall come back to Grand Prix racing. And if I did, I should not tell you. But there is one thing of which you can be absolutely certain. There will be no half measures. We shall not race again until we have cars that can and will win.'

Neubauer's predictions were being carried out to the letter.

## The Last Year of Grand Prix 1955

The big news at the beginning of the 1955 season was that Stirling Moss, like Dick Seaman before him, had been invited to join the Mercedes team and had agreed to drive as number two to Fangio in Grand Prix and sports car races.

His first race for his new employers was the Argentine Grand Prix in January on a short, twisty autodrome circuit of under 2¼ miles at Buenos Aires, where a team of *W196* 2½-litre Grand Prix Mercedes was entered to be driven by Fangio, Moss, Kling and Herrmann. Altogether Mercedes took seven racing-cars over to the Argentine.

The race was run in searing heat which caused many drivers to collapse, only Fangio, the winner, managing to survive the three-hour race without a relief. Ascari (Lancia) had held the lead for twelve laps in the early stages until he crashed. Moss, who stopped on the circuit with a vapour lock, was thrust into an ambulance before he could protest, so convinced were the first-aid people that he had stopped because of sunstroke. Kling crashed and Herrmann needed a relief, so only two Mercedes finished. Second to Fangio was a Ferrari driven in turn by Gonzales, Farina and Trintignant, third another Ferrari in which Farina, Maglioli and Trintignant shared the driving, and the other Mercedes finished fourth through the combined efforts of Herrmann, Moss and Kling.

The circuit was altered to make it even more twisty for the Buenos Aires Grand Prix held a fortnight later in the form of two heats with the final result decided on aggregate times. In the first heat the three Mercedes of Fangio, Moss and Kling were beaten by Farina's Ferrari. In the second heat the Mercedes were fitted with different tyres which improved the handling, and Farina made a bad start and spun round on the first lap. Fangio and Moss were then happily in first and second places, but when they were threatened by Trintignant's Ferrari Moss pressed Fangio and won from him by three seconds. With his two second places and Moss's first and third, Fangio was declared the overall winner having been 30 seconds faster than Moss, who was placed second. This event did not count towards World Championship points as did the Argentine Grand Prix. It, too, was held in blistering heat so that in the second race even the chewing-gum melted in Moss's pocket, despite some holes hastily carved in the Mercedes bodywork for extra cooling by the pit staff between the two races.

On May 1 the Mille Miglia was held, and this saw the debut of the 3-litre *SLR* Mercedes sport-racing cars, with fuel-injection 8-cylinder engines. These cars had much more in common with the Grand Prix *W196* than the sports *300SL* and the drivers were Fangio, Moss, Kling and Herrmann. Mercedes,

Moss and 'Jenks' winning the 1955 Mille Miglia. (*Mercedes-Benz*)

with their usual thoroughness, were practising over the course in *300SL* sports cars and a 'hack' *300SLR* months before the race was due to be run. In England the 1955 Mille Miglia is probably the best remembered of the whole series for it resulted in a magnificent win by Stirling Moss at a speed of 97·99 m.p.h., ten miles an hour higher than the previous best average. Moss was considerably aided by the expert guidance of his passenger Denis Jenkinson, the famous motoring journalist, who had the whole route plotted on a roller-map, enabling him to predict the worst bumps and corners as they were approached. Although headed at times by Taruffi's 3·7-litre and Castellotti's 4·4-litre six-cylinder Ferraris, Moss got in front over the mountains to Rome and finished with a 30-minute lead over Fangio, who came second after being delayed by a fuel injection fault. Maglioli managed third place for Ferrari.

For the European Grand Prix at Monaco on May 22, two new *W196* cars were entered for Fangio and Moss with short 7 ft. ½ in.-wheelbase chassis and outboard front brakes. A third *W196* of the older type was entered for Hans Herrmann, but he crashed it in practice and his place in the race was taken at short notice by the Frenchman André Simon in the team's spare *W196*.

In this first Grand Prix at Monaco since 1950, Caracciola's 1937 lap record of 1 min. 46·5 secs. in the *W125* was shattered by no less than eleven drivers in practice and in the race Fangio set a new record of 1 min. 42·24 secs. (68·73 m.p.h.).

Nevertheless the race was a Mercedes disaster despite Fangio and Moss having a half-lap lead over the Lancias and Ferraris just before half distance. On the fiftieth lap Fangio retired with transmission trouble and then, on the eightieth lap, when he was about to lap second man Ascari (Lancia), Moss retired in a cloud of smoke with engine trouble. At about the same time Ascari drove into the harbour by mistake, leaving Maurice Trintignant to win for Ferrari. Simon had retired on his twenty-fifth lap with engine trouble.

The Eifelrennen meeting at the Nürburgring on May 29 was for sports cars and a *300SLR* duel between Fangio and Moss resulted in a hair's breadth win for the former by a tenth of a second with Masten Gregory's 3-litre Ferrari third and Karl Kling's *300SLR* fourth.

At Francorchamps for the Belgian Grand Prix on June 5 Fangio had a 7 ft. 2 in. medium-length wheelbase *W196* with outboard front brakes. Moss had a similar car with inboard brakes and Kling had an 8 ft. 1½ in. long-chassis car which was used for training. Castellotti, who made fastest practice lap in his Lancia, retired at half distance with a split axle whilst lying third to Fangio and Moss. Fangio finally won from Moss by 8 seconds with Farina's Ferrari third a minute and a half behind. Kling retired.

For Le Mans on June 11 and 12 three *300SLRs* were entered for Fangio/Moss, Kling/Simon and Levegh/Fitch. These cars were fitted with novel flip-up air brakes on the tail to assist their hot and bothered drum brakes at the ends of the long straights.

The race commenced with a great duel between Fangio and Mike Hawthorn on a D-type Jaguar. Then, after two and a half hours, Pierre Levegh struck a slow-moving Austin-Healey *100S* in front of the pits and his *300SLR* disintegrated against an earth bank. The engine and front assembly went amongst the closely-packed crowd, causing the greatest disaster in motor-racing history when over eighty people, including poor Levegh himself, were killed. At 2 a.m. the other Mercedes were withdrawn from the race on orders from Stuttgart when the Fangio/Moss car had a two-lap lead over the Hawthorn/Bueb Jaguar which, in turn, was two laps ahead of the Kling/Simon *300SLR*.

As a result of the Le Mans tragedy the French and German Grands Prix were cancelled, but the Dutch Grand Prix took place on June 19 at Zandvoort. This was another race won by Fangio and dominated by Fangio and Moss driving nose to tail, although Roberto Mieres (Maserati) put up fastest lap. His team mate Musso finished third behind the Mercedes.

3-litre *300SLR* in 1955, in the Le Mans Twenty-four Hour Race. (*Mercedes-Benz*)

If the 1955 Mille Miglia will always be remembered by British enthusiasts, so will the 1955 British Grand Prix at Aintree when they witnessed the sight of Stirling Moss and Fangio crossing the line almost together, but with Moss's car just in front. Third was Karl Kling and fourth yet another *W196* Mercedes driven by Piero Taruffi after a tussle with the Maseratis of Mieres and Musso. All the Mercedes had outboard front brakes, but Fangio and Moss had 7 ft. ½ in.-chassis cars and Kling and Taruffi 7 ft. 2 in. chassis.

The Swedish Grand Prix on the Babelov circuit at Kristianstad was for sports cars and the Le Mans type air-braked *300SLR* cars of Fangio and Moss finished first and second with Fangio leading by one-tenth of a second. Moss was in some pain at the finish as a stone had shattered his goggles. Eugenio Castellotti, after a fine drive, was third in his Ferrari.

The Italian Grand Prix at Monza on September 11 took in part of the high-speed banked track, so Mercedes reintroduced two of the aerodynamic *W196* cars for Fangio and Moss whilst Kling and Taruffi had 'open-wheel' cars. Stirling Moss had bad luck in this race for first his windscreen broke and had to be replaced during a pit stop and later he retired with mechanical trouble. Kling also retired, so it was Taruffi who finished in second place just a few yards behind Fangio with Castellotti third, a minute behind, in his Ferrari.

This was Taruffi's last race with Mercedes. Moss, on his first trial on a *W196* at the Hockenheim motor-cycle circuit, had found the five-speed gearchange awkward to handle as the gate was the opposite way round to normal. Taruffi had had the same trouble on his first run on a *W196* in practice at Aintree before the British Grand Prix. Fortunately when the revs went sky high after a missed change the desmodromic valve gear prevented a valve touching a piston.

With his win at Monza Fangio once again became World Champion on Mercedes cars as he had done in 1954, and this turned out to be the final Grand Prix for Mercedes.

A week later there came the 623-mile seven-hour sports-car Tourist Trophy race at Dundrod on September 17, now a scratch event counting towards the sports-car championship. The three *300SLR* cars entered were harassed by both the Hawthorn/Titterington D-type Jaguar and the Collins/Brooks DB3 Aston-Martin until both the British cars retired. The result was that the works Mercedes finished in the first three places, the drivers being Stirling Moss with the American John Fitch in first place followed by Juan Fangio with Karl Kling and Taffy von Trips with André Simon. Behind them came the Poore/Walker Aston-Martin and the Musso/Bordoni Maserati.

At this time Ferrari still led on points for the sports-car constructors' championship, and Neubauer persuaded Mercedes to send two *300SLR*s to Sicily to take part in the Targa Florio in an attempt to wrest the championship from the Italians. The drivers were Stirling Moss with Peter Collins and Juan Fangio with Karl Kling. Moss held the lead from Castellotti's Ferrari from the start, but on the fourth lap he was late when he was due to hand over his car to Collins. Anxiously Neubauer and Collins waited until, nine minutes to the bad, Moss finally appeared at the wheel of a thoroughly battered *300SLR*, having gone off the road.

After the car had been refuelled and bits of loose bodywork snipped away, the almost empty radiator was filled with water and Collins went off. In his badly damaged car he then proceeded to break the lap record, and by the end of the eighth lap when he handed over to Moss he had not only made up the nine minutes but had regained the lead. Moss, in his turn, broke the lap record yet again and when he won the race he was nearly five minutes ahead of Fangio and Kling in second place and nearly ten minutes ahead of Castellotti, who was third.

Thus with the Grand Prix drivers' championship and the sports-car constructors' championship safely won, Mercedes participation in big-time racing came to an end, the directors having decided that the firm's resources should be concentrated on the development of the production cars described in the next chapter.

## MERCEDES-BENZ 1945–1966

After their retirement from Grand Prix racing at the end of 1955 Mercedes-Benz continued to take part in international competitions with production cars in saloon-car races and rallies. To appreciate their many achievements in these fields it is necessary to take a close look at the models turned out by the firm since its resuscitation after the war.

In the spring of 1945 it was estimated that war damage to the private-car production plant at Untertürkheim amounted to 70%, whilst the coachbuilding plant at nearby Sindelfingen suffered 85% damage and the motor-truck works at Mannheim and Gaggenau 20% and 80% respectively. All that remained of the cross-country-vehicle and aero-engine plant at Berlin-

Marienfelde had to be entirely pulled down. In fact, according to a brief statement by the board of directors: 'Daimler-Benz had ceased to exist in 1945.'

The splitting up of Germany into the various zones after the war did not help the reconstruction, for whilst good progress was made at Untertürkheim, Sindelfingen and Mannheim, which were in the American zone, it was impossible for a long time to tie in the Gaggenau plant near Baden-Baden in the French zone, on whose management Daimler-Benz had only a very limited influence in the early post-war period.

As many of the old staff as were available were recalled, and as soon as the debris on the sites of the various factories had been cleared away a provisional programme was embarked upon consisting chiefly of vehicle repair work. I remember going to see Prince von Urach, at that time a chief engineer, and he told me 'I am in my office at 7 a.m. at the latest every morning.'

The currency reform in Germany during June 1948 had a highly beneficial effect on the economy of the firm and it was in that year that private-car production started up once more.

No new model was designed, but a successful pre-war model was reborn, the *170V*. It will be recalled (see p. 221) that the original *170* saloon had been introduced in 1931 with a six-cylinder side-valve 1·7-litre engine (hence the *170* designation). The most remarkable feature of this first venture by Mercedes-Benz into the cheap car market was the very advanced design of the car's chassis with a pressed box-section tube frame and independent suspension at the front by two transverse leaf springs and at the rear by coil springs and swinging half-axles. The consulting engineer to Mercedes-Benz in this design was Hungarian-born Dr. Josef Ganz, a man of remarkable foresight who had advocated swing-axles as long ago as 1923. Nearly 14,000 *170* models were sold in the five years following the commencement of large-scale production in 1932.

It was in 1935 that a development of the *170* called the *170V* was first introduced and it was so popular that it ousted the *130H* and *170H* rear-engined models. I had a *170H* rear-engined car for a time. The road holding and handling were lovely, but the performance was very pedestrian. The *170V* had a flexibly mounted 1·7-litre four-cylinder side-valve engine developing a few more b.h.p. than the six-cylinder engine it replaced. Front and rear independent suspension was similar to that on the *170*, but the chassis used an X-type cruciform frame of oval-shaped tubular members. This type of chassis was retained on all Mercedes cars until 1953, as was the basic swing-axle design of the 1931 *170*. Up until 1942

90,000 of the *170V* models had been sold.

During 1949 the *170S* and *170D* made their appearance. The *S* had a more powerful 1767-cc. side-valve engine than the *V* with a 6·5 to 1 compression ratio, developing 52 b.h.p. as against 45 b.h.p. The cylinder-head was of light alloy and the maximum speed was 75 m.p.h. On the *170S* the transverse leaf i.f.s. was abandoned, and open coil springs and double wish-bones were substituted, an almost identical system to that used on the 1937–9 Grand Prix cars. It was said the car was particularly suited for special requirements such as police patrol work. Its road holding was highly praised, but its heavy construction restricted top-gear acceleration and the brakes demanded high pedal pressures. In appearance it was somewhat old-fashioned looking.

The sensation of the Berlin Motor Show in February 1936 had been the showing of a private car powered by a 2·6-litre Diesel engine, the Mercedes *260D*. This was the first mass-produced Diesel-engined car, but it was rather heavily built and was intended more as a taxi cab or a hire car, or as a light delivery-van when fitted with suitable bodywork. Nevertheless many *260D*s performed successfully in the hands of private owners.

The *170D* was the first post-war venture into the compression-ignition-engined private-car market, and the accent was on fuel economy which was a much prized virtue at that time. In 1936 I wrote a road test on one of the first for some long defunct motoring journal, and was very impressed with it.

The first production diesel car, 2·6-litre, four-cylinder model *260D*, 1935. (*Mercedes-Benz*)

Mercedes diesel cars have been a huge success worldwide, particularly as taxis. In Germany today they are popular with commercial travellers who have to cover big mileages on small budgets. Over 40 m.p.g. was achievable under all conditions compared with the 23–25 m.p.g. of the petrol-engined *170S*. The *170D* engine had an output of 38 b.h.p. at 3200 r.p.m. and satisfied many people who were willing to put up with slow acceleration and a 62 m.p.h. maximum and the well known Diesel knock when the engine was idling. Push-rod-operated overhead valves and pre-combustion chambers were a feature of the engine, and the weight penalty of the Diesel and its necessarily robust starting gear with a compression ratio of 19 to 1 was an extra hundredweight, the car weighing 23¾ cwt. to the *170S*'s 22¾ cwt. Whereas the 0–60 m.p.h. acceleration figure for the *170S* was 29 secs., on the *170D* it took all of 47 secs. The *170D* retained the old transverse leaf i.f.s.

The *170S* and *170D* were the first post-war Mercedes models to be offered for sale in the U.K., where they were not particularly cheap to buy, the *170S* costing £1382 and the *170D* £1595; yet in Germany the basic price of the *170S* was £692. They continued in production until 1955, the *170D* being fitted with *170S* bodywork at the beginning of 1952, when it was known as the *170SD*. This, of course, must not be confused with the *170DS* of 1952, *DS* in this case standing for Special Model Diesel, improvements to the engine producing an extra 2 b.h.p. At the risk of alarming the reader still further regarding the profusion of Mercedes-Benz model classifications it might be mentioned here that the small letters (*a*, *b*, *c*) after a type designation refer to further developments of that particular model, hence *170Da*, *170Sb*, etcetera.

The Frankfurt Motor Show in the spring of 1951 saw the return of Mercedes-Benz to their traditional place in the high-quality market with the introduction of two new models, the *220* and the *300*. Like their modern descendants of today, these cars had six-cylinder single overhead camshaft engines with the valves set across the head instead of being in line, operated by rockers. On the *220* the engine had a bore and stroke of 80 × 72·8 mm., 2195 cc. With a 6·5 to 1 compression ratio and one Solex carburettor its output was 80 b.h.p. at 4600 r.p.m.

The performance was in a different class to that of the *170S* with a maximum speed of 90 m.p.h. and excellent third-gear acceleration, on which ratio the engine would sweep unobtrusively up to 5000 r.p.m. Fuel consumption was around 20 m.p.g. The roadworthiness was described by *The Motor* as astonishing, as the all-independent suspension gave a remarkably level ride over second-class roads together with good high-speed cornering and precise steering. The steering demanded three and one-third turns of the wheel from lock to lock, one-third more than on the *170S*. A 0–60 m.p.h. acceleration figure of 19½ seconds was nearly ten seconds better than the equivalent figure on the *170S*, but the criticisms that applied to the *170S* were also applied to the *220*. These were poor top-gear performance and brakes that required high pedal pressures. The high top gear of the *220* was doubtless ideal at speed on the *Autobahnen* but at low speed and r.p.m the 67-degree valve-overlap and large valves had a detrimental effect on torque. In order to prevent brake fade a very low servo effect was given to the brake shoes inside the rather small-diameter drums, and brake linings with a low coefficient of friction were employed. Stopping distances were quite adequate provided *220* Mercedes drivers did not suffer from leg-muscle fade. Although the basic price of the *220* in Germany was equivalent to £1098, in the U.K. the selling price was inflated to £2123.

By the autumn of 1951 Mercedes were producing 3000 cars a month, 800 of which were *220* models.

The *300* was a prestige six-seater limousine weighing 35 cwt. and costing £1690 in Germany and £3301 in the U.K. The 85 × 88 mm. 2996-cc. six-cylinder single o.h.c. engine had two Solex Type 40 PBJC carburettors and a 6·4 to 1 compression

This 1957 model is the classic shape of the type *300*, now very much a collector's piece. (*Mercedes-Benz*)

1952 type *300S* with extremely attractive cabriolet 'A' bodywork. (*Mercedes-Benz*)

ratio. Originally the engine produced 115 b.h.p., later increased after attention had been paid to combustion chamber design and valve gear on the *300a*, *b* and *c* models. On these *300* models the 9 ft. 4 in. wheelbase of the *170S* and the *220* was increased to 10 ft.

A novel feature of the *300* model was the manner in which the driver could control the rear suspension electrically to correspond with the weight being carried. By pressing a button connected to a servo motor controlling the auxiliary torsion-bar springs he could maintain the proper camber angle and stiffen the suspension by approximately one-third.

0–60 m.p.h. was achieved in under 15 secs. by the *300* and the maximum speed was a genuine 100 m.p.h. Overall fuel consumption was around the 17 m.p.g. mark. The makers claimed the engine was good for 70,000 to 100,000 miles without a major overhaul. The preciseness of the steering was remarked upon although it was slightly lower-geared than on the *170S* and *220*, 3·7 turns of the wheel from lock to lock. Instrumentation was particularly good and clear. This prestige car, however, suffered the same criticisms as its predecessors—a top-gear acceleration that was too modest and brakes that did not match the car's other outstanding qualities. It seems that even the sybarites who fell for the luxury of a *300* were expected to have strong legs for emergency braking.

During 1952 a more powerful short-chassis (9 ft. $4\frac{1}{8}$ in.) convertible version of the *300* came out, known as the *300S* (Sport). This had a 7·8 to 1 compression ratio and, with its three downdraught Solex carburettors, produced 150 b.h.p. It was a hundredweight lighter than the *300* and was capable of 110 m.p.h. Cost in the U.K. was £5530. Early in 1956 there came the *300Sc* which had fuel injection and an 8·5 to 1 compression ratio producing 200 b.h.p. This was a very expensive car; in drophead coupé form its price in the U.K. was £6166.

In 1955 the *300* in standard form progressed to the *300b* stage with a 7·4 to 1 compression ratio and 136 b.h.p., whilst the *300c* came soon after with automatic transmission and the same engine.

The famous *300SL* (Sport-Light) has already been mentioned in this book. In its original form in 1952 it had three carburettors like the *300S* but produced 200 b.h.p. When it was given Bosch fuel injection and went into production in 1954 it became the first car in the world to have a four-stroke petrol engine with fuel injection and the output went up to 240 b.h.p. The chassis was very short compared with the other models with a wheelbase of 7 ft. 10½ in. and its weight of 25½ cwt. compared with the 33 cwt. of the *300Sc*. The engine, of course, lay over at an angle of 45 degrees, necessitating left-hand steering that could not be altered to right-hand.

The first *300SL* to come to the U.K. was delivered to Rob Walker at the end of December 1954 and the second one went to David Brown a week later. With a low axle-ratio acceleration was in the order of 0–60 m.p.h. in 7·2 seconds, 0–100 in 16·2 secs. and 0–120 in 25·8 secs. Maximum speed on this ratio was about 145 m.p.h., but 160 m.p.h. was attainable on a higher ratio. In view of this it is a surprise to find the *300SL* had that unnecessary adjunct, a fast speedometer, which read as much as 150 m.p.h. when the car was doing 135 m.p.h. Drum brakes were fitted, cooled by turbo air fins and these were prone to fading, juddering and wheel locking if used really hard, although the first application gave magnificent results. The brakes were servo-assisted so that there was no footbrake without the engine. Personally, I found the *300SL* an unforgiving, difficult car at high speeds. Neubauer told me that one needs at least a month to learn it. As I have never managed to borrow one for more than a day, I still find it an unforgiving, difficult car at high speeds. But, my goodness, I would love to own one.

The *300SLR* (Super-Light-Racing) sports-racing car, introduced in 1954, had a fuel-injected eight-cylinder 78 × 78 mm. engine of 2982 cc. capacity with positively closed valves giving 300 b.h.p. at 7500 r.p.m. on normal fuel and was based on the *W196* 2·5-litre formula Grand Prix car and not the *300SL*. There was no flywheel, the drive being taken from the centre of the engine and transmitted through a five-speed gearbox with Porsche-designed synchromesh. Maximum speed was around 180 m.p.h. with the 0–125 m.p.h. acceleration figure of 22 seconds. An airbrake on the tail introduced for slowing down from high speeds at Le Mans was an unusual feature.

To return, now, to less heady wine; in 1953 a radically new type of chassis was introduced for the latest model known as the *180*. This consisted of a one-piece construction in the shape of a frame floor unit. To the front part of this a sub-frame was anchored on rubber blocks on the three-point system. This sub-frame carried the complete power unit and transmission as well as the steering and front wheel assembly, the arrangement offering advantages both in manufacture and maintenance.

The *180* had the same side-valve engine as the *170S* but its restyled saloon bodywork was more modern looking with a 40% larger window area. It was roomy, comfortable and refined but unfortunately received the same old criticisms of sluggish top-gear performance and brakes which needed high pedal pressure and also squealed. The U.K. price in 1954 was £1694.

The low-pivot axle was also fitted to the *180* and the cruciform-framed *300b*, but not to the *300SL*. Later, however, it was to be featured on all Mercedes models.

During the winter of 1953–4 the model *180D* was introduced with practically the same compression ignition engine as was fitted to the *170D*, but revving up to 3800 r.p.m. instead of 3200 r.p.m.

An interesting and striking sports car was introduced in 1955 called the *190SL*. In appearance it was rather like a smaller two-door, two-seater version of the *300SL*, but its chassis construction was on similar lines to that of the *180* and *220a* with a sub-frame assembly carrying the engine. This 1897 cc. 110 b.h.p. engine was a single overhead camshaft four-cylinder and with its 85 × 83·6 bore and stroke it was really a smaller version of the six-cylinder *300* engine. Unlike the *300SL* the *190SL* had its engine mounted upright. The maximum speed of the *190SL*, which had two carburettors, was claimed to be 118 m.p.h. and the U.K. price was £2734.

The increased power of the *220a* saloon (92 b.h.p. to the 80 b.h.p. of the *220*) paid a big dividend, for when *The Motor* road-tested one in June 1955 it proved to be the first post-war Mercedes-Benz which was not adversely criticized for its top-gear performance; in fact the top-gear acceleration was remarked upon as being 'notably rapid'. The brakes were still a bone of contention, for whilst their stopping-power was satisfactory their operation was criticized as inducing dipping of the nose, snatch, pull and squeak, and during the test pedal-travel increased quite rapidly. Yet the brakes had a positive feel which concealed the use of a vacuum servo.

In October 1955 production began of a convertible version of the *220a* on a shorter 8 ft. 10 in. wheelbase in place of the 9 ft. 3 in. wheelbase of the saloon.

In 1956 the *220a* was developed into the *220S* with a twin-carburettor 112 b.h.p. engine, the single-carburettor model now being called the *219*.

Also in 1956 the *190* saloon came along, consisting of a detuned version of the four-cylinder o.h.c. *190SL* engine in saloon bodywork almost identical externally to that of the *180* saloon, but capable of 85 m.p.h. compared with the under-75 m.p.h. maximum of the *180*.

It was goodbye to side-valves in 1957 when the *180a* was given an o.h.c. engine with a lower compression-ratio than that of the *190* and 10 b.h.p. less power, and it was also goodbye to the famous gull-wing doors of the *300SL* when this model became available in open roadster form only. To make up for this the *190SL* was put on sale with a hardtop for those who wanted it. Slight alterations had to be made to the multi-tube space frame chassis of the *300SL* to take the different body with normal opening doors.

1958 saw two new models, the *220SE* which was the same as the *220S* but with fuel injection in place of carburettors (the *E* being for *Einspritzen*—German for injection), and the *190D*, the compression ignition version of the *190* saloon.

Turning to the competition successes of the touring cars discussed so far, 1956 saw the Mercedes drivers Schock and Moll winning the European Rally Championship through being victors in the Acropolis and Sestrières rallies on a *300SL* and second in the Monte Carlo rally on a *220*. They were also tenth in the Geneva rally on a *300SL*.

A *300SL* driven by Mairesse and Genin won the Liège–Rome–Liège, whilst Paul O'Shea, also *300SL*-mounted, won the sports-car championship in America.

O'Shea was again sports-car champion of America in 1957 with his *300SL*, and other *300SL* successes this year were a victory in the thousand-mile Caracas–Cumana–Caracas road race (Dos Santos and Huertas) and in the fifth Spanish rally (Andres and Portoles).

1958 was not such a successful year in the major rallies. The Sestrières was run in heavy snow and was a small-car benefit for Abarths, Alfa-Romeos and Porsches, but Crone Rawe and Peemoeller won the over 2600 cc. Grand Touring class with their *300SL*. On the Coronation Safari in East Africa over a 3000-mile route starting and finishing in Nairobi, K. Savage and C. J. Manussis were second in the class for cars costing over £850 retail in Nairobi driving a *219* Mercedes, and finished sandwiched between two Ford Zephyrs. *190* successes were a Grand Touring Class win in the Norwegian Viking rally (Gulbrandsen and Stensrud) and an overall win in a rally in Hong Kong (W. Sulke). Cotton and Simon won the minor French Snow-and-Ice rally on a *300SL*.

1959 saw impressive performances on the African continent. In January the Mediterranean-to-the-Cape rally was held from Algiers to the Cape via the Sahara, French Equatorial Africa and the Belgian Congo, a distance of 8700 miles. This was won by Karl Kling and Gunzler driving a *190D*, a fine vindication of the diesel-engined private car which went through without a single repair or change of tyres. Second was a Citroën *ID19* driven by Olivier and Mme. Gendebien, whilst third was a 1956 Land-Rover driven by Peter Riviere and Gyde Horrocks.

In March the East African Coronation Safari was an outright win for a Mercedes *219* driven by W. A. Fritschy and J. Ellis from two Ford Zephyrs, whilst the less important Union of South Africa Winter rally was an overall win for a *190* driven by Paulsen and Sommens.

It came as quite a shock in Britain a few years after the war when those deadly rivals Morris and Austin joined forces to form the British Motor Corporation in November 1951. An equivalent shock occurred in Germany in 1959 when Daimler-Benz purchased their traditional opponents on the race track Auto-Union, manufacturers of the D.K.W. Five years later further peaceful co-existence in the West German car market was promised in October 1964 when an armistice was signed between the former competitors Volkswagen and D.K.W. This came about with the announcement that Daimler-Benz A.G. would concede to Volkswagenwerk A.G. approximately equal shares in Auto-Union, whose production and business would thenceforth be run jointly by the two firms.

1959 was a notable year in Mercedes-Benz design for, broadly speaking, the present range of cars dates back to that year when the new 'squared-off' shape made its first appearance. The new models in 1959 were the *220b*, the *220S* and the *220SE* with longer, lower, wider bodies of integral construction. Engines and transmissions remained substantially the same, but improvements were made to the front and rear suspensions.

The *300* de luxe saloon at £5221 was available with Saginaw power-steering built under licence by ZF and operated from an engine-driven Vickers pump. An air-conditioning and refrigeration unit could be housed in the boot. This was capable of maintaining a temperature of 75 degrees Fahrenheit inside when the outside temperature was 90 degrees. The *300* still maintained the tubular cruciform frame, but the space frame *300SL* roadster remained the most expensive model at £5313.

Throughout the years Mercedes cars had often been criticized for braking deficiencies despite the firm's vast competition experience of braking problems. Such criticisms did not apply to the drum brakes of the new *220* models of 1959 which were described as being very light, apparently without fade, and with no vacuum-servo woolliness.

The road holding of these new models was remarked on as being of a high order, there being extremely little cornering roll, although there was still some dipping and rising of the nose under braking and acceleration. The recirculating ball steering was very light and sensitive to such things as raised white lines, yet the car was invulnerable to crosswinds and would only wander on the straight if the driver gripped the wheel too hard. The steering lock was excellent.

In February 1961 Herr Walter Hitzinger, who started his career with Steyr in Austria, was appointed Chairman of the Board of Directors and Daimler-Benz celebrated its Jubilee —75 years of Car Production 1886–1961. This was marked by the opening of the new Daimler-Benz Museum in Stuttgart at which a new model, the *220SE* coupé/convertible, made its first appearance. This was a handsome, prestige version of the *220SE* saloon with two-door four-seater sporting bodywork and refinements such as disc front brakes, a floor change and a wood and matt-leather fascia complete with rev. counter and easily readable instruments. No alteration was made to the engine output. The coupé cost over £1300 more than the saloon and the convertible over £1600 more, although the saloon also shared the refinement of German Dunlop disc brakes at the front as, indeed, do all present-day Mercedes models that do not have discs all round.

At the end of December 1961, Jack Brabham, the Grand Prix driver and constructor, drove a *220SE* Mercedes for nearly 500 miles and wrote in the *Sunday Pictorial* that it came nearer to being his ideal car than anything he had previously driven.

The *300d*, introduced in 1957, was in production until March 1962 and was the last model to use the old tubular cruciform frame. It was succeeded by the *300SE* saloon, a very advanced fuel-injected car with unit construction, air suspension, disc brakes on all four wheels operated through a hydraulic servo, automatic transmission and a limited-slip differential adapted from the Mercedes racing-cars. The *300SE* also became available in coupé/convertible form. The 2996 cc. o.h.c. engine developed 185 S.A.E. h.p. at 5200 r.p.m., and the claimed top speed was 109 m.p.h. or 124 m.p.h. in Special Equipment form with an average fuel consumption of 11½ to 16½ m.p.g.

October 1962 saw the withdrawal of the last of the old rounded-shape cars, the *180* and *180D* 1·8-litre petrol- and diesel-engined cars. The reason given was that the works wanted the productive capacity to turn out more of the very popular *190* models which, even in 1965, were still in short supply in Germany. The *190* was re-vamped in 1961 to get away from the old rounded shape, and the *190D* was given a completely new 55 b.h.p. single o.h.c. diesel engine. The old criticism of high pedal pressures was sometimes applied to the drum-braked *190* models, but was corrected for on the later cars with disc brakes at the front. Despite having a big *220* body shell, the 90 b.h.p. of its 1·9-litre engine gave the *190* adequate acceleration and a top speed of nearly 90 m.p.h. which was also its cruising speed. At £1727 it was the least expensive model in the range.

In diesel form as the *190D* it cost £1868 with an 87 mm. bore 1988 cc. engine with single o.h.c. and 4 cylinders (the petrol *190* still had the 85 mm. bore) and a 21 to 1 compression ratio. Maximum speed of the *190D* was a genuine 80 m.p.h., at which speed it could be cruised all day, but acceleration was naturally on the slow side compared with the petrol-engined version, 0–60 m.p.h. taking over 38 secs. compared with half that time for a petrol *190* with Daimler-Benz automatic transmission. However, the *190D* gave 30–35 m.p.g. compared with about 25 m.p.g. for the petrol *190*, and on small throttle-openings the engine was so smooth and refined that it was quite indistinguishable from a petrol-driven unit. It is not surprising that the *190D* was popular as a taxi. For cold starts there had to be a wait of 20 to 30 seconds whilst the glow-plugs warmed up, but once it was started the engine pulled away from cold without a trace of snatch, though initially with reduced power.

In March 1963 the *190SL* and the famous *300SL* bowed out to be replaced by the two-seater *230SL*, which made its debut at the Geneva show. This new fuel-injected six-cylinder sports car fitted roughly in between the prices and performance of the two models it replaced. At the time the *230SL* Mercedes was undoubtedly one of the best looking sports cars on the road, with a lightness and grace that had not always been a distinguishing feature of previous Mercedes models.

As its title implies the *230SL* engine was a slightly enlarged version of the *220SE*, the stroke remaining the same at 72·8 mm. but the bore being increased from 80 mm. to 82 mm. This increased the capacity from 2195 cc. to 2306 cc. In addition a number of modifications were made to the fuel injection system, which had a six-plunger pump, and to the camshaft, valves and inlet manifold. The compression ratio was increased from 8·7 to 1 to 9·3 to 1 resulting in a power output of 170 b.h.p. gross at 5000 r.p.m. as against the 134 b.h.p. at 5000 r.p.m. of the *220SE* engine.

The *230SL* was sold as an open roadster, a closed coupé, or a combination of the two called a coupé/convertible with a removable hardtop. The coupé was distinguished by having what was described as a 'concave roof' which caused not only the windscreen and rear window to slope towards the centre of the car, but also the side windows. This made for exceptionally good visibility and it was claimed that occupants under the coupé roof almost had the impression of driving in an open car. Easily read instruments were fitted, including a rev. counter, and a short gear-lever was mounted on the transmission tunnel. Daimler-Benz automatic transmission and power-steering were optional extras. Maximum speed was officially given as 124 m.p.h., with 84 m.p.h. in third gear. Prices in 1966 ranged from £3481 for the roadster to £3667 for the coupé/convertible, tax paid.

The greatest Mercedes was the supremely luxurious *600* which was introduced just before the Frankfurt Show of 1963 and came in two versions, the Saloon and Pullman limousines. The Saloon 'Grand Mercedes' held 5 to 6 people, but owners of the Pullman could entertain 7 or 8 people in it. The engine was a 103 × 95 mm. fuel-injected 90-degree V8 of 6329 cc. with single overhead camshafts to each bank of cylinders. Output was 300 b.h.p. gross at 4100 r.p.m. with a maximum engine-speed of 4800 r.p.m. Compression ratio was 9 to 1.

The specification included D-B automatic transmission and power-steering, self-levelling air suspension, disc brakes on all four wheels and a limited-slip differential. Inside the car there was hydraulic press-button operation for adjusting the front seats and seatbacks, opening and closing the windows and glass partition and the sliding roof, bonnet and boot lid. The rear-view mirrors, which were external, could be adjusted from inside. The doors never had to be slammed as hydraulic pressure closed them when they were pushed lightly to.

Despite a weight of around 2½ tons, a 0–100 m.p.h. time of 26 secs. was claimed by the makers. It was a sign of the times that this vast limousine was 4 m.p.h. faster than the sports *230SL* with a maximum of 128 m.p.h. The saloon cost £8926 and the Pullman £9994, over £1500 of which went into purchase tax.

The more recent cars had been proving themselves in international rallies and races since 1960, particularly the *220SE*. In that year Walter Schock and his partner Moll became European Rally Champions having been *220SE*-mounted throughout the season. They won the Monte Carlo rally on a works car after the Mercedes team had carried out pre-rally preparation over the route reminiscent of their preparations before the French Grand Prix at Lyons in 1914. In 1960, though, they are said to have practised using D.K.W. cars. To gain the Championship Schock and Moll also won the Acropolis, were second in the Viking, third in the Tulip, fourth in the German and fifth in the Geneva.

Another *220SE* victory in 1960 was on the Nürburgring, where von Zedlitz and Golderer were overall winners of the A.D.A.C. six-hour touring-car race, whilst for the second year running Fritschy and Ellis won the East African Safari on a *219*.

In 1961 Mercedes achieved the hat-trick in the Safari when Manussis, Coleridge, and Beckett won on a *220SE* and Fritschy and Ellis came second on a similar car. *220SE* cars also came first and second in the Algiers–Central African rally, the winner being that experienced pair Kling and Gunzler, whilst Bettoja and Eger were second. In this year there was also a splendid *220SE* performance in the tough Argentine Road Race for touring cars over a total distance of nearly 2900 miles, with Schock and Schiek the winners and Herrmann and Gunzler second. In the U.S.A. a Mercedes lady driver, Helen Hough, was announced as being National American Rally Champion.

Back in 1960 the runner-up to Walter Schock in the Monte Carlo rally had been a driver having his first outing as a Mercedes works driver. He later won a Coupe des Alpes in the Alpine rally. His name was Eugen Böhringer, and he was destined to become one of the finest rally drivers of all time. Böhringer was born in Stuttgart in 1923 and he only returned to West Germany in the late 'forties after many years of hardship and imprisonment in Siberia. Short and rotund, his quiet good nature has made him extremely popular in the rallying world. Before driving for Mercedes he drove Porsches and Alfa Romeos for two seasons in hill-climbs and circuit races.

A Stuttgart hotelier by trade, he runs the Rotenburg Hotel on a hill overlooking the Untertürkheim works, and his hobbies are cooking and stamp-collecting. In 1961 he had won the Polish rally with Rauno Aaltonen after his regular co-driver, Socher, had suddenly been taken ill. In 1962 he became

The Swedish girls Ewy Rosqvist (now Baroness Korf) and Ursula Wirth, who have won just about every rally that there is with Mercedes. *(Mercedes-Benz)*

European Rally Champion driving a *220SE*, his score being three wins (in the Acropolis, Polish and Liège–Sofia–Liège), two seconds (in the Monte Carlo and German) plus a fifth in the Midnight Sun and a seventh in the Tulip. On the Liège–Sofia–Liège he was partnered by Hermann Eger, but in all the other events his partner was Peter Lang, the son of the great Mercedes Grand Prix driver Hermann Lang.

Other 1962 Mercedes successes included one of the finest performances ever by lady drivers when Ewy Rosqvist and Ursula Wirth were overall winners of the extremely tough Argentine Road Race on a *220SE*. A *220SE* also won the Tour d'Europe, driven by Becker and Golderer, and Mercedes driver Rolf Kreder was named as the German Rally Champion.

In 1963 the *300SE* started to come into the picture and the brand new *230SL* had its first taste of victory. On the rally scene a *300SE* won the Acropolis (Böhringer and Knoll) and the German (Böhringer and Kaiser). Driving a *220SE* Glemser and Braungart won the Polish and were second in the German, whilst Ewy Rosqvist and Ursula Wirth won the Coupe des Dames in the Monte Carlo rally on a *220SE*. The *230SL* victory was in the Liège–Sofia–Liège with Böhringer and Kaiser as the drivers.

The first four cars in the 1963 Argentine Road Race were all Mercedes. Eugen Böhringer and Klaus Kaiser were the winners on a *300SE*, Dieter Glemser and Martin Braungart on a similar model were second, Ewy Rosqvist and Ursula Wirth were third on a *220SE* and fourth were Bordeu and Winter on another *300SE*.

Two *300SE* saloons in the hands of Böhringer and Herbert Linge and Hans Herrmann and Peter Lang took part in the *Motor* 6-Hours Race at Brands Hatch in June 1964, the first works Mercedes appearance in Britain since Moss's win in the British Grand Prix at Aintree in 1955. Though winning their class they finished third and fourth overall behind two Lotus Ford Cortinas. A fortnight later Böhringer turned the tables on Ford by beating two Lotus Cortinas to win the Nürburgring Six-Hour Touring-Car Race with a *300SE*. The privately entered *220S* of Schiek and A. Kling was fourth.

The biggest Mercedes win of 1964 was in the Argentine Road Race for the fourth year running. *300SE* saloons came first, second and third in the hands of Eugen Böhringer and Klaus Kaiser, Dieter Glemser and Martin Braungart and Baroness Ewy von Korff (née Rosqvist) and Eva-Maria Falk. Part of the course was washed out by torrential rain causing the race to be postponed for a week, and sections of the 474-mile final leg were flooded. On a 2983-mile course varying from rough tracks and steep mountain roads to fast main-road sections Böhringer averaged 85·9 m.p.h.

In August 1965, Mercedes-Benz released details of a new range of 1966 models due to be presented to the public for the first time on the eve of the Frankfurt Show in September. Altogether there were fourteen distinct models in the new range (making it the most comprehensive passenger-car programme in the long history of the company), and these will be described starting with the lowest-powered and least expensive cars.

## The 1966 Range

1. The *200*.

This was the successor to the *190*, and carried the familiar *190/220* body-shell. Recognition points from the front were the round headlamps and combined sidelamps and indicators.

The four-cylinder engine, fitted with two Solex single-choke carburettors, was slightly larger than that fitted to the previous *190*, the bore having been increased from 85 mm. to 87 mm. as on the *190D* compression-ignition engine. Thus the 87 ×

83·6 mm. engine had a capacity of 1988 cc. and, with a 9 to 1 compression ratio, had a gross S.A.E. output of 105 b.h.p. at 5400 r.p.m. It had a new five-bearing crankshaft in place of the former three-bearing, a claimed maximum speed of 100 m.p.h. and a fuel consumption of 25·9 m.p.g. A price of £1875, including purchase tax, was quoted for 1966.

2. The *200D*.

All that was said about the diesel *190D* really applies to this car, which had the latest single o.h.c. four-cylinder five-bearing crankshaft diesel engine with a 21 to 1 compression ratio producing a gross output of 60 b.h.p. S.A.E. at 4200 r.p.m.

3. The *230*.

This was an interesting new model combining the *200* bodywork, round headlamps and short bonnet (106·3-inch wheelbase) with the enlarged *220* six-cylinder engine (82 × 72·8 mm., 2306 cc.) of the same dimensions as that first fitted to the *230SL*. Price for 1966, including tax, was £2157.

4. The *230S*.

This had similar bodywork to the previous *220S* with the combined head- and sidelamp glasses, plus the longer bonnet giving a wheelbase of 108·2 in. Claimed maximum speed was 110 m.p.h. and fuel consumption 25·2 m.p.g. Kerb weight was 2975 lb., and the 1966 price, including tax, was £2395.

5. The *250S*.

With the *250S* we enter the luxury range, the restyled bodywork being the immediately noticeable feature. There was a lower waist line and a larger glass area, with curved glass in the side-windows, whilst the whole car was nearly 2½ in. lower than its predecessor and the roof was flatter.

The *250S* weighed 3175 lb. and the claimed maximum speed was 112 m.p.h. with a 24·1 m.p.g. fuel consumption. The fuel tank held 18 gallons compared with the 14 gallons of the *200* and *230* chassis. The price for 1966, including tax, was £2575.

6. The *250SE*.

There was no *230SE* in the 1966 range, and the *250SE* was identical to the *250S* except for its engine having fuel injection. This had a 9·3 to 1 compression ratio producing 170 b.h.p. gross at 5600 r.p.m.

The *250SE* weighed 3263 lb. and the manufacturers claimed a maximum speed of 118 m.p.h. and a fuel consumption of 24·1 m.p.g. Maximum speeds in the intermediate gears were given as 29, 50 and 81 m.p.h. Price, including tax, was £2865 for 1966.

7. *220SE* Coupé/Convertible.

This prestige car, already described, with the 2195 cc. engine incorporating the two-plunger injection pump, still remained in production for 1966 with its specification unaltered. The price for 1966 was £3858 for the coupé and £4165 for the convertible, tax included. Claimed maximum speed was 106 m.p.h. with a fuel consumption of 26·4 m.p.g.

8. *250SE* Coupé/Convertible.

This had the same mechanical specification as the *250SE* saloon, the weight of the coupé being 3284 lb. and of the convertible 3472 lb. Claimed maximum speed was 118 m.p.h. with a fuel consumption of 24·1 m.p.g. The prices for 1966 were £4484 for the coupé and £4883 for the convertible, including tax.

9. *300SEb.*

The *300SEb* had the same body and components as the *250* series although it had powered steering as a standard fitting. The engine was the bigger 3-litre unit with the classic bore and stroke figures of 85 × 88 mm., 2996 cc., as on the first *300* introduced in 1951. Power on the 1966 model, however, was 195 b.h.p. at 5500 r.p.m. with a compression ratio of 8·8 to 1 and all the latest refinements such as the six-plunger injection pump were fitted. 118 to 124 m.p.h. and 22·6 m.p.g. were claimed. The price was given as £4086, tax included, for 1966.

10. *300SEL.*

The *300SEL* had four inches of extra length in the region of the rear door, bringing the wheelbase to 112·2 in. and making the car roomier for rear-seat passengers. It also had powered steering, automatic transmission and full air-suspension.

11. *300SE* Coupé/Convertible.

Similar to the *300SEb* in specification, the coupé weighed 3638 lb. and the convertible 3781 lb. A maximum speed of 124 m.p.h. was claimed with a fuel consumption of 23·9 m.p.g. Prices for 1966 were £4968 for the coupé and £5330 for the convertible, tax included.

12. *230SL.*

This model has already been described. It was the lightest car in the range at 2855 lb. which may account for the good claimed fuel consumption of 27·7 m.p.g. 124 m.p.h. was the maker's maximum speed.

13, 14. *600* and *600* Pullman.

These models, already described, continued in production for 1966. Claimed fuel consumption was 15·9 m.p.g. The normal *600* weighed 5445 lb. and the Pullman 5820 lb. with 18 ft. 2 in. and 20 ft. 6 in. wheelbases respectively.

In 1966 the Competition Department of Mercedes-Benz was very small, consisting in the main of former Grand Prix driver Karl Kling and a small office staff. Car preparation was done in the experimental workshops under the aegis of the great Rudi Uhlenhaut.

Alfred Neubauer had now definitely retired from the Company at the age of 74 after a number of years in semi-retirement when he came to work in his office in the Mercedes Museum for half a day each week. Even in his eighties, although rather frail, he is still tremendous fun, and even today still capable of the famous Neubauer practical jokes. Quite recently I was at the receiving end of one. He was nominally in charge of

Rennleiter Alfred Neubauer on March 29, 1966, his seventy-fifth birthday. (*Mercedes-Benz*)

compiling and completing the Company's racing records, but in fact he spent a great deal of his time on speaking tours in various European countries. He should have retired on December 31, 1964, but this was extended to February 1, 1965, to enable him to come to London to open the Racing-Car Show in January of that year.

## THE NEW GENERATION 1966–1979

To ME personally, it was a great sadness when Mercedes bowed out of Grand Prix racing. But I suppose, looked at objectively, it was a wise decision that the directors took, for it released their best brains on research and development to concentrate on safety. They must have been one of the first firms, as long ago as the late nineteen thirties, whose design department were safety conscious. Already in the early nineteen fifties they were running test cars into a wall at ever increasing speeds: after the 'accident', the dummy driver was examined for injuries. From then to 1956 cars were built on the principle of the passengers being protectively enclosed in a rigid box, while front and rear absorbed the shock, as far as possible, by folding up. As the years went by, more and more internal safety factors were developed. Among these were an impact-absorbing steering wheel, with padded boss and telescopically collapsing steering column, laminated glass windows, safety locks on all doors, yielding instrument panel, and, of course, padding everywhere that the crash tests showed it might be needed. They did not just leave it at that. Up to this day, the research and development boys are beavering away improving the safety of the occupants in the event of a crash.

It would take pages to list the safety factors developed in the last couple of decades. But there is one great leap forward which I see as of paramount importance. We oldsters, in the days when motor-cars were stark, fast and pretty basic, had, of necessity, our own techniques. One of them was the technique for braking on a treacherous surface. If one just put on the brakes, the wheels locked and one slid all over the place, possibly finishing the less usual way up in a ditch. What one did was to apply the brakes in a series of dabs so that one got the maximum retardation and then released the pressure just before the wheels locked. This called for very considerable virtuosity on the part of the driver, and, of course, the brakes had to be synchronized spot-on. Mercedes have now produced a braking system with which the driver, however big a clot he is, cannot lock his wheels. This was developed in conjunction with a firm called Teldex.

Very briefly this is how it works. Each wheel has a sensor which warns a mini computer when an individual wheel is about to lock, and pressure on the disc brake calipers is eased. The system is, of course, derived from aircraft practice. Boeings are much too expensive to tip over on one corner every time one wheel hits a skid patch and others do not. Those drivers who have, at some time, had front wheels lock on ice, will appreciate the inestimable boon of the non-locking brakes because one can steer and brake at the same time.

One interesting method of test is used in the development of safety devices. The test car is driven at given speeds on a test track where various surfaces can be simulated. Suddenly, without warning, dummy 'suicidal pedestrians' pop up at random on its path. The behaviour of the components under test are recorded by a 'black box', as in aircraft. The data is then fed to the engineers responsible.

The *versuchtsabteilung*, as the research and development

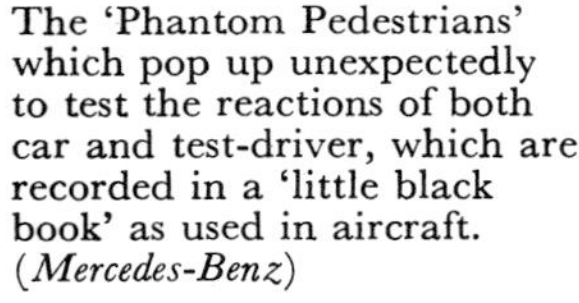

The 'Phantom Pedestrians' which pop up unexpectedly to test the reactions of both car and test-driver, which are recorded in a 'little black book' as used in aircraft. (*Mercedes-Benz*)

department is known, has always given a high priority to the compression ignition engines. That is to say an engine, as patented by Rudolf Diesel in December 1892, in which the piston squeezes the mixture until it goes pop. This beautifully simple idea, in practice, was full of too many snags and problems to list. It was not until 1923 that Mercedes had developed it sufficiently to put one in a heavy lorry. Thirteen years later I reviewed, for an English paper, their first production diesel-engined private car. I don't remember much about it except that its performance was more than somewhat pedestrian, but it was, at certain engine speeds, far smoother than I expected it to be. They have come a very long way since then and are now the largest producers in the world of diesel cars. And very good they are.

Twice of recent years Mercedes have pushed up world records in class 8 for supercharged diesel-engined cars. This was accomplished at Nardo, in Italy, in 1976, with drivers Dr. Hans Liebold, Erich Waxenburger and Joachim Kaden. They beat earlier records by 60 kilometres an hour, establishing sixteen class records, three of which were world records. The car was the 'mobile test bed', the experimental coupé *C111*, built of carbon glass reinforced plastic and the result of some very hard work by the wind-tunnel boffins. The end product of this latter effort was nothing less than sensational. The air resistance value was 0·195. For purposes of comparison the air resistance of a vertical plate is 1·1, a sphere 0·45 and an aeroplane wing 0·2.

The second attempt was also made at Nardo, with Paul Frère, Rico Steineman and Guido Moch, one of the car's designers, following on in the footsteps of Rudi Uhlenhaut who liked to do his own testing. More new world records were taken this time with slight body modifications and basically the same engine, a single-cam, five-cylinder, 3-litre diesel, turbo charged by Garrett and with fuel injection by Bosch. The average speeds were only a cat's whisker off 200 m.p.h. and speeds of 202 m.p.h. were frequently attained. And, even more remarkable, 0–60 m.p.h. in 6·5 seconds! A respectable enough figure for a sports car today. The refuelling and servicing stops ranged between 20 and 30 seconds, which shows that even if Alfred Neubauer was not there physically then he was certainly there in spirit.

It does seem possible that these 3-litre turbo-charged diesels might be the shape of things to come. Firstly, in view of the world's dwindling oil resources, there is the matter of fuel consumption. To do twelve hours at 200 m.p.h. giving 17·7 m.p.g. does point to most commendable consumption figures

The *C111* 'Flying Testbed' as it looked taking sixteen International Class Records powered by a five-cylinder diesel engine. (*Mercedes-Benz*)

by the *300SD* model, determined to give 115 b.h.p. instead of the 230 b.h.p. of the record breaking *C111*. As I write I learn that the *300SD* is due to go on sale in the U.S.A. in the near future.

The other factor which may make the Mercedes diesel the prototype of engines to come, as Maybach's 1901 Mercedes influenced automobile design for two decades, is air pollution. Most of us who have been stuck behind a diesel truck and forced to inhale its fumes may think this suggestion a little fanciful. But look at these figures given by a Mercedes type *OM402* V.8 truck engine. Carbon monoxide emission is 3·8g/BHph and the permitted emission in California, where they take their smog very seriously, is 40g/BHph. Nitric oxides and unburned hydrocarbons puff out at around half the permitted figure. The point I would like to make is this, the Mercedes diesel is only doing what comes naturally, it does not need any of the various costly exhaust controls necessary for petrol engines to pass the regulations. These are said to increase the cost of building a car by 5% to 10%. Certainly, the popularity of diesel cars has increased by leaps and bounds, and other large continental producers such as Peugeot-Citroen have jumped on the band wagon. Mercedes, the largest makers of diesel cars, have had to step up their output enormously.

Germany has not one drop of oil of her own, so it is only natural that their premier motor factory should be heavily involved in research into alternative fuels. There is not enough space to discuss them all, but so far hydrogen seems the most promising. It is cheap to produce, supplies can't run out and, when burned, it leaves no noxious gases in the air. The problem, up to relatively recently, was storage, which had to be in bulky, extremely heavy cylinders. Now, the backroom boys have come up with a new material called hydride which absorbs hydrogen like a sponge at one temperature and releases it at another. There are still plenty of problems, especially that the dual tanks of hydrides, heavy tank to start, light tank to run, still weigh, together, four times as much as a tank of petrol for an equivalent distance. The research team who have been beavering away at this in conjunction with the University of Karlsrühe, have come a long way since 1972. So there is a possibility that you may see fleets of hydrogen powered trucks in the nineteen eighties. And, of course, a lovely pipe dream that one might, one day, be able to fill one's car up via a tube and filter from the gas cooker—for what is domestic gas but rather dirty hydrogen?

Diesel car production has burgeoned of recent years. The popular *190Dc* 1·9-litre four-cylinder giving 55 h.p. notched up a production of over a quarter of a million, 1961–5. The 2-litre, four-cylinder *200D* sold three-quarters of a million between 1965 and 1976, while the 2·2-litre four-cylinder which followed it, now giving 57 h.p., sold 420,270 from 1958 to 1976. This was followed by the 2·4-litre, four-cylinder which now gave 62 h.p. and of which 131,319 were sold in the three years between 1973 and 1976. Now we come to the most exciting diesel car built since the *260D* that I tried forty-four years ago, of which they built and sold nearly two thousand up to the outbreak of war. This is the four-cylinder, 3-litre *300D*, giving 77 h.p., from whose engine the record breaking *C111* was developed and which is the direct parent of the *300SD*, far and away the most advanced diesel car produced today. During the four years between the first *300D* going into production and the *300SD* a great many modifications were made, including a modified cylinder block and sodium-cooled valves. The latter, of course, are nothing new to Mercedes: my SSK, built in 1929, had them! The great leap forward was the addition of a Garrett Ai Research TA 0301, which produces 11 pounds per square inch at 2000 revolutions. It is lighter in weight than the turbo chargers which they have used for so long on their commercial vehicles. At high engine speeds, boost pressure is maintained at constant level by the 'wastegate', which uses pressurized air from the compressor to activate a spring-loaded bypass valve to divert exhaust gas from the turbine wheel into the exhaust system.

The effect of this turbo charger is sensational. Between 1936 (*260D*) and 1974 (*300D*) they had only managed to increase the horsepower from 45 to 77, through thirteen models. The *300SD* has produced, in one go, a horsepower of 110. This gives a speed of 103 m.p.h. This is, of course, very little use to the Americans, where the car is on sale, with their 50 m.p.h. speed limit enforced by cops in helicopters. But what is really remarkable, and remember, the *300SD* is a big car weighing around 4000 lb., are the consumption figures—24 m.p.g. in town, 29 on the highway, and an overall average of 26 m.p.g. This is even better than the *300D*, which although a lighter car had not as good a performance. The *300SD*'s acceleration figures compare well with the less sporting petrol-driven car at 0–60 m.p.h. in 14 seconds. The noxious emission figures are minimal, and these are achieved naturally, without costly added devices. With all the suspension, steering, braking, safety and other features developed for the petrol-driven cars it is a most desirable vehicle for these hard times.

I have devoted, some readers may think, too much space to the diesel-engined cars, but it must be realized that diesel-powered Mercedes account for 41·3% of their annual passenger car production.

Mercedes have been building cross-country vehicles for some time, so have Steyr-Daimler-Puch incorporating Steyr who make firearms, Austro-Daimler who make cars, and Puch who make bikes, mopeds and motorbikes. The Stuttgart firms have linked up with the Austrian combine based in Graz to produce an all-purpose cross-country vehicle. Although only introduced in 1979, this rugged go-anywhere car with four-wheel drive and differential locks, fore and aft, all of which can be engaged at will, looks, in spite of stiff opposition from Britain and Japan, like being a winner. It is available, long or short, with six styles of bodywork, ranging from pick-up truck to four-door station wagon and van. There is a choice of four engines: four-cylinder, 2·4-litre, or five-cylinder, 3-litre diesels, or four-cylinder, 2·3-litre, or six-cylinder, 2·8-litre petrol. One ingredient for success is that it is being supplied 'CKD', for assembly abroad.

This book must, of necessity, be restricted to passenger vehicles. To discuss the trucks and buses built over the years by Mercedes-Benz would take a large book on its own. But mention must be made of the '*O Bahn*' now being developed by Mercedes in conjunction with civil engineers Ed. Zublin AG. This forward-thinking concept might go a long way to solving the appalling traffic problems in our cities. Very briefly this is the system. The 'O Bus' running on normal pneumatic tyres can travel either free-steering on the road or with its wheels in prepared reinforced concrete troughs, on the surface, or in precast concrete tunnels, according to traffic density and road conditions. A rough parallel would be if a London Underground train were able to continue on the road as a bus! A great advantage of this system is its flexibility, as anything from a minibus to a six-module bus-train can be used on the same tracks, according to the traffic at different hours of the day. And, of course, due to the greater adhesion of pneumatic tyres, much steeper slopes are possible to take the 'O Buses' above or below ground. There are of course tremendous pros and cons for this revolutionary concept. Mercedes, however, seem to think well of it, for they are spending huge sums on its development. A pilot scheme is expected in a German city within the next year or two. It is sad that Britain will be unable to afford the large capital outlay. We must go on forming in queues or being packed like little sardines in our inadequate public transport. But it will be extremely interesting to see how it works out.

Now, let us take a look at the passenger cars of 1966, the year with which we start this chapter, namely the *230S*, *250S*, *250SE*, *300SE*, *300SEL*, *600* (long and short) and the *200D*. That ever popular type *220* which remained in production from 1951 to 1965 was replaced by the *230S* and *250S* of 2·3-litres and 2·5-litres respectively, both with six cylinders. The *220* was a four-cylinder, but some *230*s were also built with four cylinders. These *230*s and *250*s were great little work-horses and nearly half a million of them were built. Of course as modifications to springing, steering, braking etc. appeared, they were, over the years, incorporated. The *230SL* and *250SL* were powered by engines of the same dimensions as the saloons and fitted with Bosch fuel injection. This increased their horse-powers from 100 h.p. to 115 h.p. and 130 h.p. to 150 h.p. The 3-litre models, the *300SE* and *300SEL*, were equipped with light alloy cylinder blocks and air-suspension. They were powerful cars giving 170 h.p. at 5400 r.p.m. and attaining speeds well over 100 m.p.h. They were also available with custom-built coupé and cabriolet bodies. These, indeed all type *300*s, are much sought-after collector's pieces, commanding very high prices. They were also available in long chassis for formal limousine coachwork. Special coachwork was also available on the type *220*.

In 1964 Mercedes had come back into the *Prunkwagen* market where, earlier, the *Grosser* Mercedes had held undisputed sway in Germany. *Prunkwagen* was a German term applying to the magnificent carriages of the High Nobility, to whom the peasantry respectfully doffed their caps. Today it applies to the grandest of motor-cars that only heads of state and pop stars can afford and can be translated, for lack of a better word, as 'prestige'. I was once allowed to drive a *Grosser* in 1935. I did not like it at all. It felt enormous, like a bus and, although this may have been my fault, when I took it up to around 90 m.p.h. I did not feel I had it under proper control, that is to say I did not feel 'all of one piece with the car' as one should. I discussed this with a senior engineer who, having made quite sure no one was listening, replied, '*Naturlich*, it is a politically motivated car.'

The new *600* Mercedes is a very different kettle of fish. Like the Phantom Rolls it gives you the feeling that you are not driving a big car, it has a surprising amount of urge, and it handles beautifully. The V.8 engine, single o.h.c. of just over 6 litres, with petrol injection by Bosch gives (at the clutch, taking into account driving all the auxiliaries) 300 h.p. This propels the quite heavy car, which weighs around 7000 lb., briskly up to over 120 m.p.h. The high axle ratio of 3·23 gives a very pleasant 60 m.p.h. cruising at only 2485 r.p.m. Acceleration through the gears to 62 m.p.h. in 9·7 seconds is brisk for a large, heavy car, but this can be expected with a power weight ratio of 18·2 lb. per S.A.E. horsepower. Front suspension is as always by Mercedes coil and wishbone, devised by Dr. Nallinger so long ago, with all the refinements which the firm have since developed. The same goes for the swing axle aft. Both fore and aft suspension are supplemented by air bags which are controlled both automatically and manually. There is a limited slip differential, servo steering, and caliper brakes with vacuum servo at both ends. The chauffeur will be delighted to learn that he does not have to do any chassis lubrication at all.

As far as coachwork goes, the *600* can be had as a saloon or limousine. The longer chassis permits top-up seats. A car in this price range does not tie down the design team to rigid cost controls. They can and do equip it with everything for the man who has everything. As in aircraft practice, much use is made of hydraulic controls. Windows, sun roof, glass partition, boot lid, horizontal vertical movement and backrest angles of seats, and other luxurious refinements are all controlled hydraulically by push buttons. Full air-conditioning, electronically controlled, sets itself to any predetermined temperature. Few, if any, cars built today are so luxuriously equipped. It is certainly a worthy flagship for the Mercedes fleet. It is sold, in Germany, for 57,600 D.M.

A type *280S* photographed in Czechoslovakia. (*Mercedes-Benz*)

There were many detail improvements in 1967, but no new models. Perhaps the most exciting innovation was the installation, for customers who wanted more performance, of the 6-litre V.8 engine in the *300SEL*. This certainly delivered the goods. It must have been a popular car as it stayed in production till 1972, and nearly 7000 of this model were built.

1968 produced a crop of new models, the six-cylinder 2778-cc *280S*, *280SE*, *280SEL* and *280SE* with custom-built cabriolet coachwork. The *280SE* and *SEL* had Bosch fuel injectors, and the *280S* Zenith carburettors. This year also saw the birth of the new *250E*, replacing some earlier models. Its engine was developed from the *250S*, born in 1965 and phased out by early 1969. This dating also applies to the *250SE*. The modified injection engine gave 146 h.p. and a speed of 112 m.p.h. was claimed. There were two new four-cylinder models, the *200* and the *220*. The former 1988-cc engine gave 105 h.p. and the latter 2197-cc 116 h.p. Speeds of 99 and 104 m.p.h. were claimed. A great many new safety devices were incorporated in these cars. By now, virtually all models could be equipped with the extremely efficient Mercedes automatic transmission.

The type *280SL*. Note negative curve to roof. (*Mercedes-Benz*)

The *200* and *220* were reasonably priced at 11,500 and 12,000 D.M. One of the prettiest cars that Mercedes ever built was the *190SL*, which ceased production early in 1963. I can't say that the performance thrilled me a lot. Neubauer said to me, 'You expect too much, this is just a car for pretty girls.' This was probably a sly reference to 'les girls' of Frankfurt, all of whom drove them. The *190SL* was replaced by the *230SL*, and in 1968 by the *280SL*. This was quite a useful performer and was one of those pretty, flat-topped, almost concave, fixed-head 'glass-house' coupés which, ever since, have been so popular. 1968 was quite an *Annus Mirabilis* for no less than fifteen new

The *C111* in the form that was used to test Wankel engines. (*Mercedes-Benz*)

models, or old ones updated, appeared.

After this, of course, nothing very much in the way of new models came out in 1969. Improvements, especially those affecting safety, naturally went on being steadily incorporated into production. But one car was shown to the public for the first time which will undoubtedly have great influence on the shape of motoring to come. This was the world famous *C111* experimental car, developed under closest secrecy, by Rudi Uhlenhaut's team. At that time this immensely important 'mobile test bed' was powered by a Wankel engine. This vehicle was built both for engine testing and to evaluate body stresses. It is an aerodynamic resin-base fabrication, strengthened with glass fibre and equipped with a steel frame floor unit. Few cars have ever provided so much invaluable data. When, at a later date, it cracked so many diesel-engined car records, it was wearing a modified *300SD* motor. Also in 1969, a *250* coupé with a 2·75-litre engine made its first appearance in

Cross-section of a Wankel-engined *C111*. (*Mercedes-Benz*)

July and stayed in production till 1976. In 1970 the mixture was much as before except for the introduction, in the summer, of an improved *250*, which remained in production till 1976.

In 1971 Germany was well and truly booming and everyone had spending money in their pockets. So, it was only natural that the Mercedes directors should go for the top end of the market by fitting more powerful engines to the *280* range, which were very good cars already. At the same time, of course, they also appealed to the American market, where, until the 1979 energy crisis, the more powerful engine the better. This gave a new range of *280SE* 3·5, *280SEL* 3·5, *280SE* 4·5 and *280SEL* 4·5. There was also a *300SEL* 4·5, presumably for people not brave enough for the hairy *300SEL* 6·3 litre. The 3·5- and 4·5-litre engines were short stroke, long bore V.8s with twin overhead camshafts, electronically controlled fuel injection and transistorized ignition. They gave 200 h.p. and 225 h.p. respectively. The 3·5 did 130 m.p.h. and the 4·5, although no figures are quoted, presumably exceeded this. These big-engined models only remained in construction for a year when their success encouraged the makers to produce a complete new range based on them.

1972 saw the arrival of the new *280*, *280C* and *280E* and *280CE*. They were powered by a brand new six-cylinder in-line twin overhead cam engine. The carburettor models *280* and *280C* developed 160 h.p. and the *280E* and *CE*, with electronically controlled fuel injection, gave 185 h.p. The

Sectional model of the twin overhead cam *280E*, which now gives 185 h.p. (*Mercedes-Benz*)

The extremely pretty new coupé shape on a *280CE* with electronically controlled fuel injection. (*Mercedes-Benz*)

designers felt that acceleration for passing other traffic was of far greater importance than a very high top speed. So maximum speed was 115 m.p.h. and 125 m.p.h. respectively. But the acceleration figures to 62 m.p.h. were impressive: 10·6 seconds for the models with normal ignition and only 9·9 seconds for the injected cars. The road holding reserves of the existing chassis were so outstandingly good that the only changes they felt were necessary were larger brake discs and brake-operating cylinders and high-speed radial tyres. All these models were also available with custom-built coupé coachwork. There were a number of detailed improvements fitted to the 1972 cars. Among these were some interesting innovations available as optional extras. One of these was a washer and wiper for the headlamps controlled by a button on the dashboard. Another was an intermittent windscreen wiper halting for five seconds between wipes. Opticians say that this is very beneficial to eye strain on long drives. As well as the *280*s, two new models were introduced with the big engines. Both 3·5- and 4·5-litre motors were available in the *350SE* and *450SE*. Normal or automatic gear boxes were optional.

After such a spate of very splendid new models, 1973 was a year of consolidation. A luxury car—the *350SEL*, a new diesel—the *240D*, and a new four-cylinder version of the six-cylinder *220*—the *230/4* were the only new models in 1973. And these were only variations on earlier true and tried themes. The *230/4* 2·4-litre four-cylinder engine was more powerful than anything Mercedes had produced in that range. The intake valves had been enlarged and breathing redesigned, so that it gave 110 h.p. at 4800 r.p.m. The new

*240D* was basically a development of the very successful *200D* and *220D*. Any explorer will tell you that in the very last outpost before the desert or the jungle, one invariably finds a general store kept by a Greek with a model T Ford. Nowadays he drives a battered but indestructable *200D*. The *240D* had a new head with larger inlet and exhaust valves. This improved breathing helped it to give 65 h.p. at 4200 r.p.m. with a compression ratio of 21 to 1. As a direct result of this it could wind itself up to the very respectable speed of 86 m.p.h. With a diesel engine, of course, one can put one's foot down on the *autobahn* at Frankfurt and keep it there till the Austrian frontier. Cooling was much improved, giving this long-life engine an even longer one. The *240D* had all the goodies associated with its petrol-driven counterpart, particularly in suspension and brakes. The fuel consumption was, of course, excellent: 29·7 m.p.g. at 64 m.p.h.

In 1974 the *240D* engine had one cylinder added, thus giving it five and increasing its capacity from 2376 cc to 2971 cc. Known as the *240D/3·0*, it gave 80 h.p. and its top speed was increased by 10 km. per hour. The acceleration was much improved, 19·9 seconds to 62 m.p.h. Fuel consumption was given at 31·2 to 34·5 m.p.g., much the same as its predecessor. The only other innovation in 1974 was the *280SL*. This was a very attractive and sporty 118 m.p.h. two-seater, the *280SL* and the *280SLC* coupé. The fuel-injected version was some 6 m.p.h. faster. In my personal opinion, the petrol-driven *280SL* is one of the most desirable cars Mercedes have built since the war. It has excellent performance, looks good and is comfortable. It has first-class braking, steering and road holding, and, so important in these hard times, has a supportable fuel consumption of around 20 m.p.g. Frankly I would trade the extra performance of any of the super playboy cars for the economy of the *280SL* and its freedom from constant maintenance problems. Let's face it, how often does one use that extra 45 m.p.h. giving one 165 m.p.h.?

In 1975, Mercedes offered a very comprehensive range, most of which have been described earlier, but with modifications.

*200D* 2·0-litre diesel 55 h.p.
*220D* 2·2-litre diesel 60 h.p.
*240D* 2·4-litre diesel 60 h.p.
*240D3·0* 3-litre diesel (5-cylinder) 80 h.p.
*200* 2-litre 4-cylinder 94 h.p.
*230/4* 2·3-litre 4-cylinder 110 h.p.
*230/6* 2·3-litre 6-cylinder 120 h.p.
*280* and *280C* 2·8-litre 6-cylinder 160 h.p.

*280E* and *280SE* 2·8-litre 6-cylinder injected 185 h.p.
*280S* 2·8-litre 6-cylinder 160 h.p.
*280SE* and *280SEL* 2·8-litre 6-cylinder 185 h.p.
*350SE* and *350SEL* 3·5-litre 8-cylinder 200 h.p.
*450SE* and *450SEL* 4·5-litre 8-cylinder 225 h.p.
*450SEL* 6·9-litre 8-cylinder 286 h.p.
*600* 6·3-litre 8-cylinder 250 h.p.

There was also new bodywork on the luxury models *280SLC*, *350SLC*, and a very important newcomer, the *450SEL* 6·9, replacing the *220SE*, *250SE* and *280SE*. 33,000 of them were built. Besides being extremely elegant, these new coupés had a good deal more room both inside the car and in the luggage boot. 1975 was also the year when Mercedes celebrated having built one and a half million cars since 1968. The new models were designed to incorporate a number of new safety devices. The *450SEL* 6·9 also featured a limited slip differential. It had a nice big 6·834 cc engine which lolloped along at an effortless 2500 r.p.m. at 60 m.p.h. When you put your foot down in this car, things really happen. The acceleration is terrific and the top speed exceeds 140 m.p.h. It is a worthy

A lovely car in a lovely setting. The *450SEL* with 6·9 litre engine. (*Mercedes-Benz*)

successor to my beloved old *SSK*, even though one must contrast the stark hoodless discomfort of cart springing with the really sybaritic super luxury of the *450SEL*.

A major introduction in 1976 was that of the so-called *W123* series of compact-bodied saloons, replacing the New Generation cars introduced in 1968 and since further developed. These have a slightly wedge shape, and the less powerful versions are distinguished from the 'top-of-the-range' *280* and *280E* by having circular instead of rectangular headlights. There was also a parallel development of petrol with diesel, thus: *200* (petrol)—*200D* (diesel); *230* (petrol)—*240D* (diesel); and *250* (petrol)—*300D* (diesel). Later the same year, elegant coupé versions were added to the range, called the *230C* and *280CE*.

The *versuchtsabteilung*, together with the production engineers, had not been idle over the last two years, for 1977 produced a whole batch of exciting new models. There were two really outstanding cars, the *300SD* turbo diesel and the *450SLC5·0*. The five-cylinder engine of the *300SD* was, as we have seen, developed in turbo charged form on that wonderful 'mobile test bed', the *C111*. This model was designed with the American market in mind. It was thought that to Americans, the luxurious 'S' coachwork combined with economy, superclean exhaust emission, and very useful performance, would be irresistible. The directors were quite right: it was an unqualified success. With the ever increasing fuel shortage and stringent exhaust regulations, it is providing a lot of Americans with the answer to their problems.

The other winner unveiled in this year was the *450SLC5·0*, which was introduced at the Frankfurt show. The engine, developed from the earlier *M117* is constructed largely of light alloys and now gives 240 h.p. at 5000 r.p.m. The crankcase is made of a siliconized aluminium alloy and is produced by a low pressure chill-casting progress. Special electrochemical treatment of the cylinder block exposes the silicon crystals in the surface of the bores. In the course of the process, the aluminium particles are pushed back far enough from the piston rings for the chrome-plated or iron-coated light alloy pistons to make contact only with the silicon crystals, which are about 0·02 mm. to 0·05 mm. large. Thus it is now possible to do without steel or grey cast iron cylinder liners. The light alloy cylinder head has much larger exhaust valves and parts. These exhaust valves are fitted with natrium. There is nothing new about this: my 1929 *SSK* had its exhaust valves filled with sodium to keep them cool. The effect of 'adding lightness' is dramatic; the 5-litre engine weighs over 80 lb. less than the

This is the view one tends to get of a *450SLC* 5-litre! (*Mercedes-Benz*)

earlier $4\frac{1}{2}$-litre. Bonnet, boot lid, etc., are all made of light metal and the weight saving, comparing the bodies of the two cars, is no less than 225 lb. Spoilers have been added fore and aft and considerable wind tunnel work has been carried out to give the car a better drag coefficient. Performance figures are most satisfactory, 0–62 m.p.h. in 8·5 seconds, and maximum speed is 130 m.p.h. Of course, the consumption would increase higher up the scale, but the makers give a figure of 18·7 to the gallon at 62 m.p.h. A friend of my son's has one of these highly desirable luxury sports cars and tells me that he prefers it to his three previous cars which were all very upmarket and Italian.

Let us now look at the Company's fortunes in the rally world in recent years. For Mercedes, the tradition of rallying goes back to the Herkomer trials early in the century, and indeed even earlier. Their successes over three-quarters of a century have been legion. When the company gave up racing, it retained competition staff to back up rallying, both works teams and selected private entrants, giving massive support to the latter. One of their most spectacular recent successes was to gain first and second places on the rough, tough London–Sydney Rally of 1977.

Success does not come easy on this month-long, 30,000 km. marathon. Both Neubauer and Enzo Ferrari have told me that they like to have Englishmen on their teams, and here it certainly paid dividends. A lot of very knowledgeable people were tipping the superbly suspended Citroens for a second win, especially because one of these was driven by the redoubtable Paddy Hopkirk. But two British teams of works prepared *280Es* got their cars home first, beating two Citroens into third and fourth position. The winner was Andrew Cowan, a 41-year-old farmer from Berwickshire, with Colin Malkin and Mike Broad. The runner-up was Tony Fowkes with Peter O'Gorman. German drivers Alfred Kling, Klaus Kaiser and Jorg Leiningen got sixth place, and Herbert Kleint, Gunther Klapproth and Harry Vormbruck were eighth. The sports preparation department say that they owe a great deal to Tony Fowkes for his preparation experience with his privately entered *450SLC* in British rallies.

The regulations restrict to within fairly narrow limits the modifications that are permitted on the rally cars. But Mercedes were permitted to lower the compression on the *280Es* to

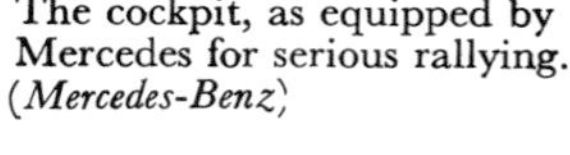
The cockpit, as equipped by Mercedes for serious rallying. (*Mercedes-Benz*)

prevent the very inferior petrol of the Asian section damaging the engines. Tank capacity was increased to 180 litres. Other permitted modifications included roll bars and extra strong front and rear bumpers with quick-release locks, which can be released and used as 'traction mats' in difficult country. Coil springs were modified and special Bilston gas-filled shock absorbers were installed. The four-speed gearbox and power steering were as standard. Four separate halogen headlamps with two more under the grille were fitted. This is just as well because Andrew Cowan was able to carry on after a head-on right-of-way dispute with a kangaroo. And of course there were all the little extras that the inexperienced rally driver does not consider, until he needs them and then it is too late. These are things like cans of drinking water, a comprehensive first aid kit, axes, shovels, ropes and a spare radiator.

It was a glorious victory, not just because of the appalling road conditions once Western Europe was left behind, but because of the gruelling challenge set to the two drivers in Australia. Cowan was a sound choice by Mercedes, as, among many other rallies, he had won the 'Southern Cross' six times and so must know Australian rallying as well as anyone. But even he said, 'The Australian stages were the hardest I have ever come across in my career.'

The following year, 1978, saw another 30,000 km. challenge, the round South American rally. This went through Argentina, Uruguay, Paraguay, Brazil, Venezuela, Colombia, Ecuador, Peru, Bolivia and Chile. There were around 6000 km. which had to be covered at racing speeds in order to clock in on time. Some eighty teams from Europe, Africa and the Americas were competing, and it says a good deal for the severity of the rally that only nineteen cars finished. Mercedes fielded seven Stuttgart-prepared cars, four *450SLC*s and three *280E*s. The four former were driven by Cowan and Malkin, the mercurial Timo Makinen with a Frenchman Jean Todt, two Poles—Zasada and Zemvrzuski, and two Argentinians—Daray and Aranzo. The *280E*s were driven by Fowkes and Kaiser, Kleint and Klapproth, and Caballero from Paraguay partnered by an Argentinian, Nathan. There was a privately entered *280E* from Germany driven by Pfung and Kling.

Regulations did not allow any boosting of engine power or improvements to transmission or body. But a duralumin undershield and front and rear rebound stops on springs were permitted. Other modifications were a roll cage, bucket seats, a special container for tools and accessories replacing the two back seats, a two-way intercom between driver and navigator, fire extinguisher, medical kit, two spare wheels, distress flares to notify break down, and absolutely essential oxygen masks and bottles for crossing the high Andes. There were two back-up teams, each consisting of six mechanics with three vehicles. 120-litre petrol tanks were fitted. It is interesting that, to conform with the regulations, the *450SLC*s had to run with their standard three-speed automatic transmissions and these behaved impeccably throughout. In fact it proved a great boon to poor Zasada who had twisted his left knee so badly in a fall that he had to drive in a cast. And, indeed, it helped him, in spite of this disability, to gain second place in the overall results.

Trouble started fairly early on in the steamy Argentinian jungles. There was a 12-km. stretch consisting of mud so deep that all competitors had to be pulled out by a bulldozer. Trouble hit the impetuous Finn Timo Makinen quite early on. He rolled his *450* coupé four times over. This creased the bodywork very considerably, but does not seem to have harmed the going ability of the car. To make up the time he had lost, Makinen clocked up 'best time' on almost every successive stage. In the end, in spite of his difficulties, he finished fourth, a very creditable achievement for both car and driver.

By the time the Andes and the Cordillera Central mountains were reached, only forty cars were left in the running. These high mountains, rising to over 15,000 feet, produced a fresh hazard. The crews were continually reaching for their oxygen masks and bottles and also suffered from an unsuspected side effect. The altitude impaired concentration quite badly, and if there is one thing you need on a long-distance rally, it is just that.

By mid-September less than thirty cars were left in the running for the leg through the snow and ice of Tierra del Fuego at the southern tip. The exhausted drivers said that the final 5000 km. from here to Buenos Aires seemed as if they would never end. And, just before the finish, the weather pulled a final dirty trick out of the bag. Torrential rains turned the rally route into a sea of mud. The cars, now reduced to only twenty-two, had to be pushed and pulled through the mire that had, prior to the rains, been a dust road.

Motor sport has a far greater number of fans in the Argentine than in most countries, and a crowd of football dimensions, numbering hundreds of thousands, was waiting in the Buenos Aires Autodrome to welcome the nineteen weary teams in battered cars who had survived the ordeal. The first four were all Mercedes: Cowan/Malkin the winners, the Poles Zasada/Zembrzuski second, and Fowkes/Kaiser third. The first two drove *450*s and Fowkes a *280E*. Makinen/Todt finished fourth with a very crumpled *450* and Kleint/Kapproth were fifth in a *280E*. A brace of Renaults and a Toyota separated them from the privately entered *280E* of Pfung/Kling in ninth place, followed by another *280E* driven by South Americans Nathan and Caballero who were tenth. I think one can say without any fear of contradiction that Mercedes-Benz dominated this very tough rally.

It seems to be the policy of Daimler-Benz to pick the toughest rally each year and compete. In the year I am writing this, 1979, they chose the East African Safari Rally. This is a four-day event covering 3250 miles over three loops in Kenya, comprising some of the worst roads in the country. The conditions range from blinding, impenetrable dust to ankle-deep mud and swollen river crossings. In this rally, the new 5-litre *450SLC5·0* was to receive a baptism of fire, being motored competitively for the first time, and it was thus an important event for the Company. Six Mercedes were entered: three *450SLC*s, driven by Hannu Mikkola, Bjorn Waldegaard and a young Kenyan of great promise, Vic Preston, jnr.; and three *280E*s, driven by Andrew Cowan, Sobieslan Zasada and the

It is not surprising that a Mercedes driver at speed on a Safari Rally through Africa excites the natives more than somewhat. (*Mercedes-Benz*)

Kenyan ace and former Safari winner, Joginder Singh.

In the first two stages, Mikkola set up an impressive lead in the new *450SLC* and it seemed as if victory was well within his reach. But then, in the third and decisive stage, his chances were ruined by an owl. The bird flew into the front of the car, and the time taken to make the necessary repairs meant that he lost the leadership to Shekar Mehta in a Datsun *160J*. Mercedes were philosophical about the outcome, pointing out that victory often depends upon incalculable risks and mishaps. In fact, they had every reason to be delighted with the performance of their cars. Of the six that started, four Mercedes finished within the first nine places, Joginder Singh coming ninth, Waldegaard sixth, Cowan fourth and Mikkola second to Mehta.

At the end of 1977, Mercedes launched a completely new series of bodywork, the 'T' series. For once, the Company was not much ahead of the rest of the industry. Other makers, in other countries, had been coming out for several years with 'station waggons', that is to say high volume cars with folding or removable back seats and tail gate loading. These are called by a number of names including 'estate cars', which imply ownership of a large country estate, or an even worse misnomer, 'shooting brake'. These are usually driven by people who have never even shot a sitting rabbit in their lives. Admittedly Mercedes were late in the day with their 'station waggon', but

The top model in the new Mercedes-Benz 'T' series: the six-cylinder, 2·8-litre *280TE*. (*Mercedes-Benz*)

when it did appear, it was an absolute winner. It carries, with the back seat removed, a very large volume indeed and accommodates anything up to 6 feet long. With half the front seat folded back, one half of the cargo space is increased to 9 feet in length. Load carrying capacity is up to 1,400 lb. Automatic self levelling on the back axle to cope with extra weight is standard. A whole gamut of special equipment has been developed for the new 'T' range. Special rails are incorcorporated in the roof which can take roof racks with aerodynamically styled luggage containers, ski and ski boot containers. There are also special racks available to carry small boats, surf boards and even bicycles. Two 'T' station waggons are available in diesel form, the *240TD* and *300TD*. These two models have everything that the *240D* and *300D* have, including a reasonably adequate performance, fabulously low running costs and all the built-in steering suspension and safety features developed over the last decade. Three petrol-motivated versions are available, the *230T*, *250T* and *280TE*. The first is a four-cylinder and the other two six-cylinders, all true and tried basic designs, developed over a number of years. When in the post-war years the British motor industry was not taking the export trade very seriously, Mercedes were pulling out all the stops and by now they have a huge, very well established, global market. There is no doubt that the 'T' series holds great appeal both in the less developed countries and in those, such as Brazil, where distances are vast, roads poor, and there is no indigenous oil production. I have little doubt that they have made no mistake in putting their rugged, economical, load-carrying cars on the market. I would say that they are on to a very good thing.

As will have been seen, a large number of new models have gone into production over the last few years. As inevitably as night follows day, a new model going into production is followed by problems of varying magnitude euphemistically called 'Teething Troubles'. Such problems are not only wasteful, but make the customers hopping mad, especially if replacement spares are not readily obtainable. With this in mind, Mercedes-Benz built what they call a 'Pilot Plant'. Started in 1968 and in action by 1975, this quite separate plant puts new models, not yet on the market, into production. Its function is to iron out all the mistakes, eliminating the time lag at the beginning of a normal production run. So, when a new model goes on the production line proper, it has already 'played itself in'. From a financial view, this pilot plant demanded a frighteningly heavy capital investment, but, they tell me, it pays handsome dividends. At the same time, a brand new skill-teaching technique was brought in, using audio and visual cassettes and aimed mainly at the Company's large contingent of 'guest workers' who are mostly from Eastern Europe. These audio video film cassettes are made, not by actors, directors and all the other film paraphernalia, but by three chaps off the shop floor who really know what it's all about. The instructor plays them over to the learners through a machine which translates the script into the appropriate language. The actual lessons are confined to twenty minutes, so as not to confuse the pupils. It is a very good idea, and, over a period of years, has been found to work very well indeed. As far as automation goes the works are well ahead. When I was there in 1954, the Company was well on to automated transfer of body panels from one press to the next. At home, 'untouched by human hand' transfer from one press to the next had hardly got off the drawing board. As I write this, Fiat are showing an excellent public relations film of how the welding is done by robots, the latest, greatest up-to-datest. Mercedes are no stranger to this: their welding has been automated for a number of years. Today 29% is done by machines.

This year, 1979, no less than thirty-seven different models of Mercedes-Benz are on offer. They range from the economical type *200* to the lordly *prunkwagen*, the type *600* limousine. None of them are particularly cheap, and some are very, very expensive. But they all have one thing in common, for which they have always striven since the days of Gottlieb Daimler and William Maybach—quality.

# APPENDIXES

## APPENDIX I

# ROBERT BOSCH

THE house of Robert Bosch has grown up with the factories of Daimler and Benz, and its history is so intimately connected with these two firms as to be virtually integral with theirs. It is, therefore, only right that it should have a section to itself.

First of all, let us examine the various ways of igniting the highly inflammable mixture of petrol and air, admitted by the inlet valve and compressed by the piston:

(1) *Compression Ignition.* This, as the name suggests, is the simple principle of compressing the gas till it detonates. Diesel, Prosper L'Orange, and much later a team headed by the younger Nallinger have done great work in this field with the result that compression-ignition engines for marine use, for trucks since 1930, and latterly for private cars, have long been the main product of Mercedes and Benz.

(2) *Hot-tube Ignition.* This might be described as a development of Leo Funk's system of 1879 (patent No. 7408 of March of that year), but Daimler abolished the slide valve that Funk used and made it self-timing and far simpler. Funk's system, however, was an advance on Otto's more complicated method. In Daimler's tube ignition a short platinum tube, its outer end closed, projected horizontally from the cylinder head, heated by a petrol burner. The piston, having sucked in the fresh gas, compressed it into the tube, when it exploded. According to early motorists who regularly drove cars so equipped, this arrangement was fairly reliable, unless, of course, the burner or burners blew out or stopped up. This system became obsolete after the turn of the century.

(3) *Low-tension Ignition* is of considerable antiquity. The first successful attempt to ignite the gas electrically was made by Lenoir on a gas engine in about 1861, but it may well have been done earlier. Certainly drawings exist showing that people at least had the idea. Lenoir's method was not truly low tension, but a trembler coil with a contact between the coil and the sparking plug wiped in passing by the connecting rod. As the engine revolved eighty times a minute, no very serious technical difficulties were involved. The first time low-tension magneto ignition was used, involving the actual making and breaking of the circuit inside the cylinder, was in the Siegfried Marcus engine of 1875. Benz, however, favoured the Lenoir principle. In his case, however, he operated the break in the low-tension circuit; there was no need for a distributor until Benz began to make twin-cylinder engines. There was only one cylinder to which the current could be distributed. The battery, however, was the weakest point, for storage batteries of seventy-five years ago were unreliable, and Robert Bosch, therefore, was forced to return to the Siegfried Marcus system, and develop something

more reliable than the two methods already in use, battery and hot tube.

But, going deeper into the question of low-tension magneto ignition, let us just take a quick look at Robert Bosch himself. In 1886, while still a very young man, he established his own workshop at the back of a block of flats in Rotebuhlstrasse in Stuttgart. His first advertisement in the local paper *Der Beobachter* set forth his accomplishments. He was a specialist in telephones and private telegraph lines. He tested and installed lightning conductors with fine craftsmanship, installed and repaired electrical apparatus, and undertook all fine mechanical work. He had hardly been in practice a year when, in the summer of 1887, the proprietor of a small machine shop came to him and asked him to build a low-tension magneto apparatus for his petrol-driven stationary engine, similar to one he had seen on a gas engine built by Otto & Langen, who had been building them with ignition on the Siegfried Marcus principle since 1884. The gas was ignited by the opening of contacts inside the cylinder by a system of cams and springs to ensure that they sprang apart. This action is described very nicely by the German word for the machine, *Abschnappzündung*. The current was supplied by a small positively driven armature rotating in an electric field created by a permanent magnet.

Bosch wrote to Otto & Langen, the gas-engine makers at Deutz, to inquire if this device had been patented, but they did not even trouble to reply to his letter. He could find no evidence of such a patent, so he went ahead and started to build. He built one for a Swiss firm, F. Martini & Co., in that year, and he also showed one to Gottlieb Daimler, who does not appear to have been very interested. These experiments with a form of low-tension magneto would have been quite unsuitable for any fast-running internal combustion engine used for a road vehicle, and it is not at all surprising that Daimler failed to be impressed with what Bosch put before him. It was at this stage in the proceedings that F. R. Simms became involved in this system of ignition.

As an engineer, Simms was not impressed with any form of ignition then in vogue; tube ignition, although a great advance on Otto's original system, was both dangerous and very limited in its scope of application. High-tension ignition of the battery-and-coil type, as used by de Dion-Bouton on their motor-tricycles, was also faulty, due largely to the poor coils, batteries and contact-breakers then used. Simms foresaw an increase in the speed of the car engine as time progressed, but battery-and-coil ignition was not progressing in harmony. He was convinced that some different method would have to be introduced which would be independent of coils and batteries.

He could find nothing in this country that answered his requirements, but when he was stopping in Germany, he was introduced to Robert Bosch by the President of the Berlin Automobile Club.

He called on Bosch and inspected the work that had been accomplished so far on low-tension magneto ignition. Nothing he saw impressed him in the least; it was merely suitable for heavy low-speed gas engines. Just as he was about to leave, Bosch informed him that one of his employees had lately devised a magneto machine in which the armature was stationary and a shield oscillated between two highly-magnetized pole-pieces. On examination, Simms saw nothing more than the germ of what he had in mind; it was a ponderous machine, with a back spring arrangement for operating the shield in one direction, but it at least was a finger-post pointing in the right direction.

Simms at once gave Bosch a sketch and measurements of the type of magneto he required, and then and there, placed an order with him for three such machines. This magneto was the subject of patent No. 15411 of 1897, and it was ultimately agreed—Simms being an extraordinarily fair-minded man—that all patents in future in connexion with magnetos should be taken out in the joint names of Simms and Bosch. For many years, the names of Simms-Bosch in ignition circles signified what Rolls-Royce does today in car manufacture.

The stationary armature system was soon abandoned in favour of a revolving armature and the abolition of the sleeve between the two pole-pieces. Tests with these prototypes enabled Simms to draw up a specification for low-tension magneto ignition as it was used from 1899 to 1901 or thereabouts.

It will probably never be decided who 'invented' magneto ignition, nor whether the lion's share of the credit is due to Simms or Bosch. As stated above, the germ of the idea was introduced by one of Bosch's employees and it was adapted by Simms—it is an arguable point whether Robert Bosch personally ever invented anything; he was an industrialist, not an inventor—but it is beyond question that when Simms first opened up negotiations with Bosch, the latter had nothing which would in any way be suitable for a high-speed internal combustion engine, even of that day.

The sweeping victories of the first Mercedes of 1901 set the seal of success on Simms-Bosch low-tension ignition and Emile Jellinek was enthusiastic about it. By the time that Jenatzy won the Gordon Bennett race in Ireland in 1903, Simms-Bosch magneto ignition had already become a household word. This win was of particular satisfaction to Robert Bosch, as Jenatzy had been a friend of his for some time. It was, in fact, in his honour that the firm of Bosch ran the 'Red Devil' advertisements, so well known in the early days of motoring. Next year, in the Gordon Bennett race, all the first five cars were equipped with Simms-Bosch magnetos. Low-tension ignition continued for a year or two but was gradually superseded by Bosch high-tension, first fitted to a Mercedes car in 1902.

Low-tension magneto ignition was fairly satisfactory when it was new and unworn, but the large number of moving parts, their delicacy, and the fact that as wear took place, the timing was thrown out, all served to show that a magneto machine, which could be used with the ordinary type of sparking plug, instead of mechanically-operated igniters inside the cylinder, was required.

(4) *High Tension.* Shortly after the turn of the century Bosch decided to combine the advantages of magneto and coil ignition. He therefore arranged a low-tension magneto to send impulses through a coil to the plug points. This was the beginning, for which he and his foreman Zähringer were responsible, of high-tension magneto ignition. In 1901, Gottlob Honold rejoined the firm. Honold had been apprenticed to Bosch and had left to go to the Technical High School at Stuttgart. Professor Dietrich recommended him to Bosch who inquired if he (Honold) would care to come to him and develop his new high-tension ignition project. In eighteen months Honold had a high-tension magneto sufficiently

far advanced to fit to a Mercedes. Although the patent was applied for in January 1902, because of many difficulties it was not granted till 1904. Then Otto & Langen of Deutz produced Winand's patent of 1887. They had never done anything to develop it, but it was likely to prove the basis for very profitable litigation. Bosch was able to sidestep this by letting his own patent lapse in 1909, by which time he was so firmly established that he had little to fear from competition. The real father of the high-tension magneto ignition was Gottlob Honold, who remained in continuous charge of the development of this field till his death at the early age of forty-seven in 1923.

From the high-tension magnetos, as a natural result of their close association with Mercedes, the next step was to make self-starters, electric lights, and dynamos. Then, in due course, every kind of electrical fitment for the car, from cigarette lighters to traffic indicators, followed. When Mercedes were working on the Diesel engine, they were glad to have the firm of Bosch, who had worked hand-in-hand with them for so long, to develop the injection pumps fitted to the Mercedes lorries which appeared in the early nineteen-thirties.

The association between the two firms in racing has now lasted for over half a century. The racing department of Mercedes and that of Bosch work in close collaboration, and for any race of importance a technician from Bosch always travels in the Mercedes équipe.

## APPENDIX II

## KARL BENZ'S FIRST CAR OF 1885

*(This account first appeared, as did the description of Gottlieb Daimler's first engine of 1885 in Appendix III, in that famous classic of the veteran car,* Motor Vehicles and Motors, *2nd edition, by W. Worby Beaumont, published by Archibald Constable & Co., Ltd. in 1902. The authors and publishers are indebted to Messrs. Constable & Co., Ltd. for their kind permission to reproduce these two invaluable extracts from that book.)*

Karl Benz, of Mannheim, took out a patent (No. 5789 of 1886) for an oil spirit motor tricycle carriage which he had made in 1885. In this a single horizontal cylinder water jacketed engine with a vertical crankshaft was used. It must be looked upon as the embryo of the Benz cars now known so well, and made in very large numbers. The specification shows two principal forms of it. Figs. 1 and 2 are from the specification, but with modifications.

In these the piston in the cylinder A is connected to the vertical crankshaft B, having a flywheel C running in a horizontal plane. On the top end of the crankshaft is a bevel pinion gearing with a bevel wheel of double its size on a short horizontal shaft, which thus runs at half the speed of the crank, and, by a crank pin at the end, communicates motion to the exhaust valve. At the other end of this valve-motion shaft is a pulley D, which by belt communicates

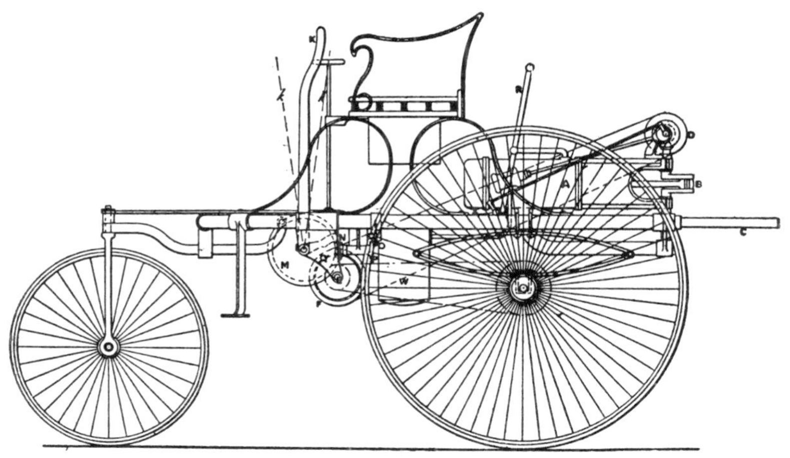

FIG. 1.—Benz car of 1885

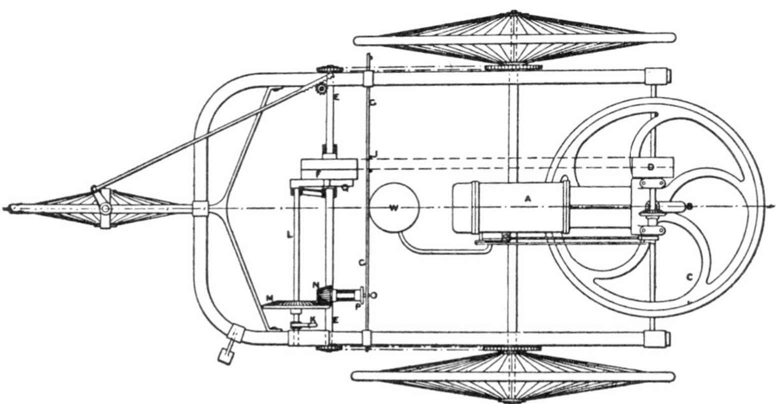

FIG. 2.—Plan of Benz car of 1885

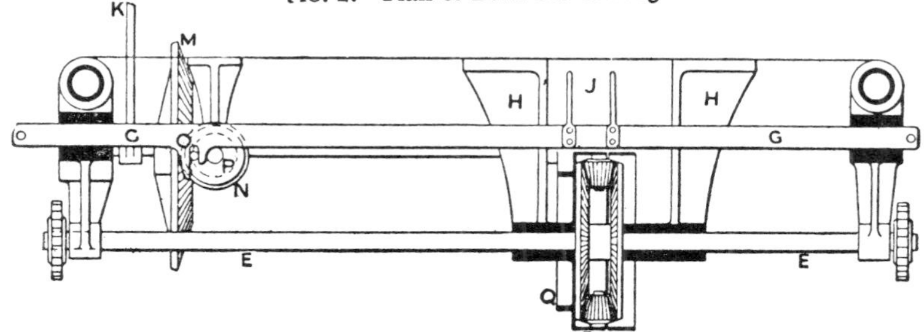


FIG. 3.—Benz car: transverse section at countershaft

motion to the second motion shaft E E, which is in two parts, by a fast pulley F, the valve-motion shaft being used for conveying the power of the engine. F′ is a loose pulley, and within F′ and F is the balance or differential gear. The shaft E E is divided between the fast and loose pulleys, as shown by Fig. 3, which is a transverse section near the bar G of Fig. 2. Two bracket bearings H H carry these inner ends of the shaft E E. The bar G is for shifting the belt by the fork J. It is actuated by the lever K on the spindle L, on which is a bevel wheel M, which moves a bevel pinion N on a short spindle. At one end of this short spindle is a crank pin O, which engages with the fork P formed on the bar G. By pushing the lever forward the pin O is pushed against the longer line of the fork, and the strap put on the tight pulley. When the lever is pulled backward the pin O pushes against the shorter line of the fork, and then misses or gets past it, the bar having by this time been moved far enough to have pushed the belt on the loose pulley. No further motion of the bar G takes place upon a further backward movement of the handle K; but its movement to *k′* puts a brake block at the end of the spindle L into contact with the brake pulley Q on the side of the fast pulley. The steering was effected by a link and rack and pinion.

For cooling the jacket water, Benz described in 1886 the natural circulation arrangement shown by Figs. 2 and 4, in which R is a grid of pipes arranged above the cylinder with internal baffles, so

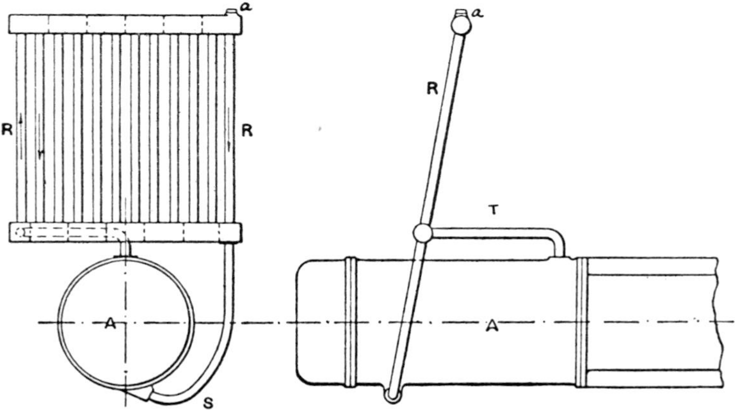


FIG. 4.—Water-cooler for Benz car

that the hot water which passed from the top of the cylinder A by the pipe T traversed the consecutive tubes in series, and finally descended cooled, or cooler, down the pipe S to the bottom of the cylinder. Steam formed escaped at *a*. In 1885, this was not used, a small tank being then, as now, used by Benz.

A carburettor or vaporizer was placed at W, spare petrol being carried in a separate tank above. The vaporizer is of considerable interest even now, and is shown by Figs. 5–10, as described in the English patent of 1886. It consists of a vessel F, containing the light oil, with means for heating it slightly to encourage evaporation. For this purpose some of the exhaust is admitted by the pipe *p* into the chamber U. Air is admitted through an adjustable valve *r* into the annular chamber Q, which is of very small width at the bottom part, where the inner wall of the chamber Q dips into the petrol. The air is thus forced or drawn through the petrol at considerable speed, and converts it into a spray. To prevent spray from passing upwards with the vapour, layers of thin metallic plates snipped all round, as in Fig. 10, were used. At the top of the vapour vessel

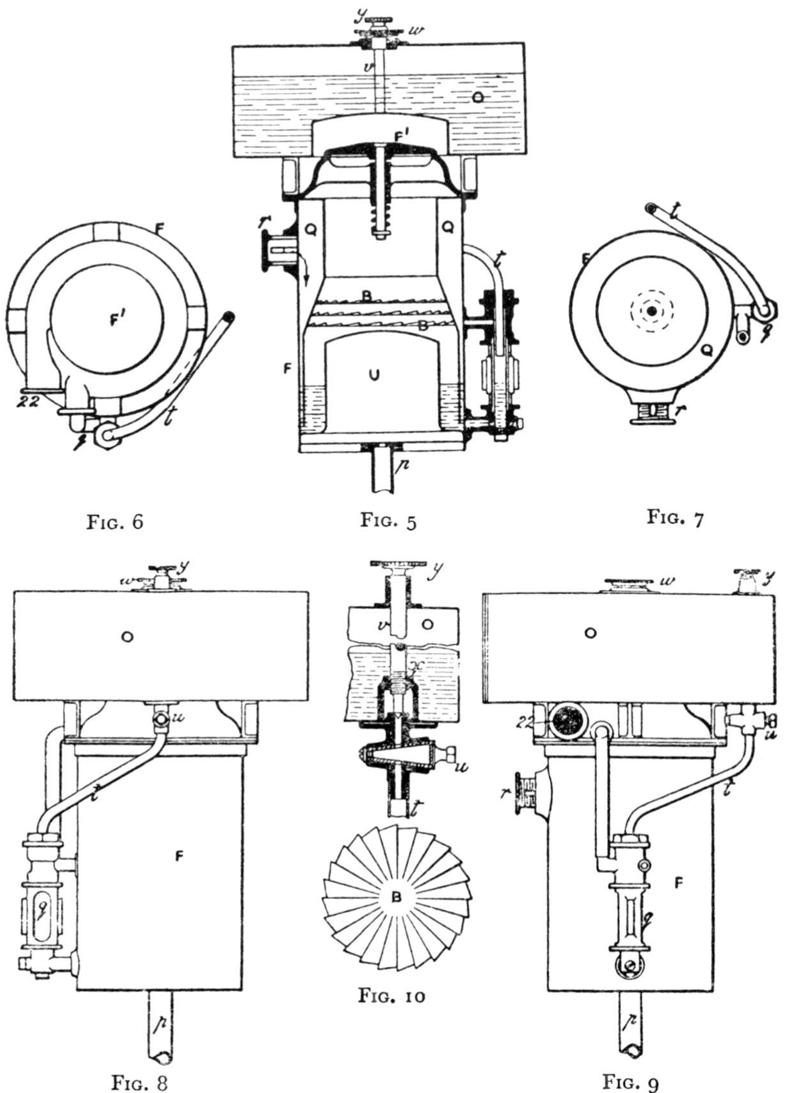


FIGS. 5–10.—The Benz vaporizer of 1886

was a safety valve F′, held down by a light spring. Over the vaporizer was a petrol supply tank O, from which a pipe *t*, with a cock *u*, led petrol to the bottom of the vaporizer through a glass gauge *g*. As well as the cock *u* there was a regulating valve *v*, with a screw at *x* and milled head at *y*. The valve *r* was usually set so that a non-explosive mixture of air and vapour or carburetted air was formed. The carburetted air passed away by the pipe 22, taken off tangentially from the top of the generator.

Between the inlet valve on the engine and the vaporizer there was a 'mixer', shown by Fig. 11. In this A is the pipe leading to the inlet

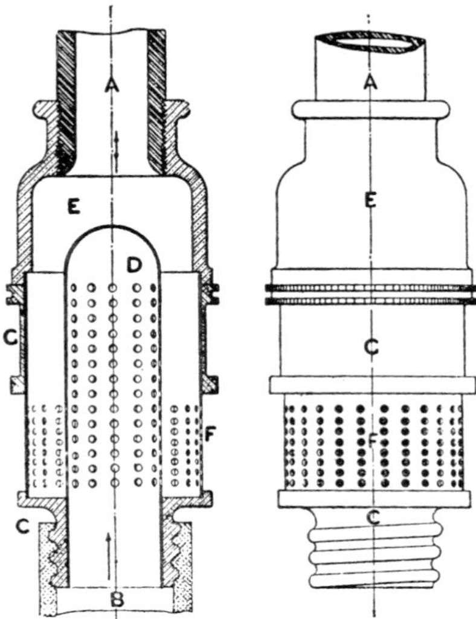


Fig. 11.—The Benz 'mixer'

valve on the cylinder, and B the pipe from the vaporizer. G is a socket carrying internally a thin pipe D, finely perforated. It also carries the larger pipe, which extends upward into the socket E, and is perforated at the lower part F. The air thus enters at F in numerous fine streams, and meets the finer streams of carburetted air coming out of the pipe D. G is a separate movable shutter tube, which may be placed where shown, allowing the most air to enter the holes in F, and thus give the weakest mixture; or it may be anywhere between that position and C, so as to vary the air let in, and thereby the strength of the mixture.

It was thought that by having the stronger mixture or incombustible carburetted air brought up to within a little of the cylinder, an accidental ignition during the admission or compression strokes would not result in explosion or back ignition beyond the mixer. Inasmuch, however, as the carburetted air, as it came from the vaporizer, was not always incombustible, back ignitions did occur, and it became necessary to place a pad of several layers of wire gauze in the socket of the mixer on the vaporizer side. This pad is held between two flanges in the mixer, as will be seen hereafter with reference to the Benz vehicles.

The product of the carburettor may be lowered in richness by the following causes, which may vary the working of the motor or necessity for air adjustment:

(*a*) Failure to keep supply of petrol in the vessel, and thus reducing the quantity through which the air passes, and also its volatility—heavy oil remaining.

(*b*) Fall in temperature of outer air, and insufficient heating from exhaust.

(*c*) Change in the hygrometric state of the air, as in fog.

(*d*) Unintentional adjustment of air admission, or accidental change by vibration and other origin.

In another part of the specification referred to, Benz illustrated and described a very ingenious arrangement of two-speed and free running gear for the motor, all with consecutive movements of the same handle, part of the gear being similar to that used in the later Benz cars for slowest motion for hill climbing. Altogether this is a most interesting specification, taken either as a precursor of a great business in its subject, or as containing numerous things of mechanical interest.

## APPENDIX III

# GOTTLIEB DAIMLER'S ENGINE OF 1885

(*From* Motor Vehicles and Motors, *2nd edition, by W. Worby Beaumont. Archibald Constable & Co., Ltd. 1902.*)

Gottlieb Daimler, who had for some years been occupied on gas engine construction, turned his attention to the production of small light petrol motors, made highly powerful by their capability of running continuously at very high speeds of rotation.

As a result of much labour and experiment, he produced and patented (No. 9112, 1884) a small high-speed gas engine, with cylinder small in proportion to the stroke of its piston, running at a sufficiently high speed to ignite the charge by the heat of compression, aided by an ignition tube for maintaining the regularity of ignition, when the walls of the combustion space became too cool either by lowering of speed or by the infrequency of the charges when on light work. The ignition tube, or 'priming cap' as he called it, was of course required for starting, and until the cylinder was hot.

Early in the following year he patented (No. 4315, 1885) his well-known single cylinder, enclosed crank and flywheel engine, which has been the parent of all the Daimler engines of the many forms now made under so many different names. In this engine the inlet and exhaust valves were brought together, one immediately over the other, the inlet being automatic, as in the first engine, and the exhaust actuated by a rod worked by a double cam groove in the outer face of one of the enclosed fly wheels. This cam groove is the equivalent of the peripheral double cam groove used in the Peugeot-Daimler of today. Daimler, however, fitted it with a switch, actuated by a simple governor, also in the side of this fly wheel, by means of which the feather running in the groove was shunted so as to run in a nearly circular path, and thus give no motion to the exhaust valve. Thus, when the speed exceeded the normal, the exhaust valve remained closed, no new charge entered, and the speed again falling, the governor shifted the switch and allowed the exhaust valve to be opened. For starting, the exhaust valve was held open by a support easily moved out of position when the engine had started, so as to allow the valve to be worked. The cylinder was cooled by an enclosed fan wheel, which sent air round the cylinder within a jacket. The crank-chamber was practically air-tight, and acted as a pump chamber, with the piston as plunger. A small inlet valve was provided in the case, and a valve was fitted in the centre of the piston, as shown in Figs. 12 and 13, which in this respect is similar. When the piston descended, the piece *t*, sliding on

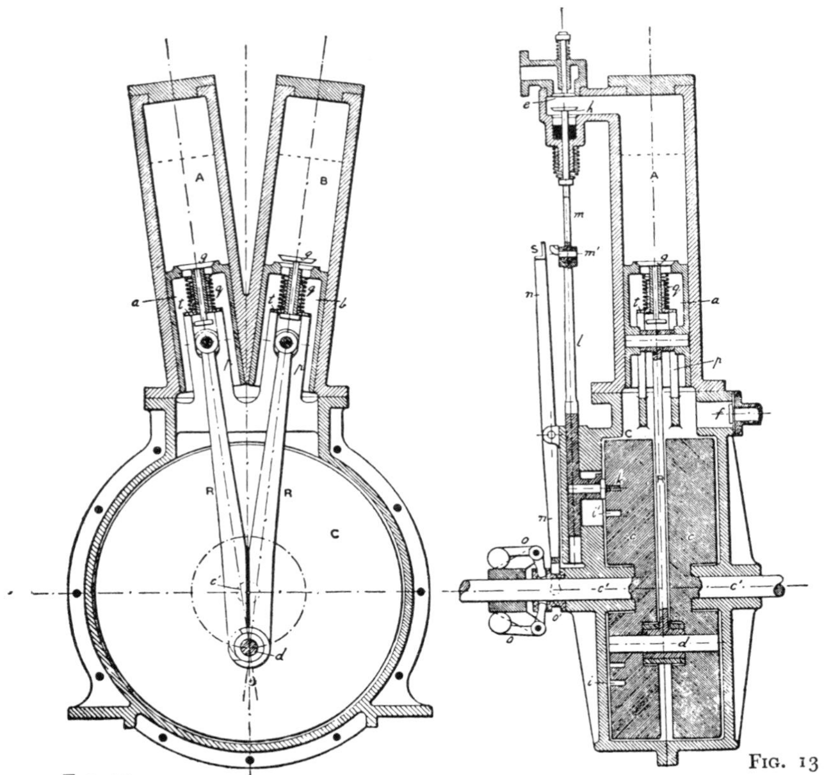


FIG. 12

FIG. 13

FIGS. 12–13.—Daimler's single-cylinder engine of 1885

the stem of the valve *g*, and surrounded by the spring which kept the valve ordinarily on its seat, came into contact with the upper part of a fork *p*, formed by an upward projection from the centre of the crank-chamber casting. If the exhaust valve were open, the superior pressure of the air in the crank-chamber could open the valve *g* against the resistance of the spring *q*, and the consequent inrush of air helped to give a complete discharge of the products of combustion of the previous stroke. This latter arrangement is, however, not found necessary, as will be seen from a description of the latest engines.

Six months after patenting this single-cylinder engine, Daimler patented an application of it to a bicycle (No. 10786, 1885) as shown in side view in Fig. 14, and thus gave the first suggestion of its applicability for motor-cycle purposes. The bicycle was not beautiful in appearance, but it contained several points of much interest. In it a little high speed motor similar to that one just described was used, and for it he devised the first of the carburettors, of which there are now so many for carburetting air with mineral and other spirit for motor purposes. The cylinder L was air-cooled in the manner already described. In the illustration M is the crank-chamber of the motor, N the rod for giving motion to the exhaust valve in the box H, which also contained the air admission valve A, E being the exhaust valve spring. At P was the carburettor, a pipe F from which allowed the passage of the oil vapour to inlet valve A, a regulating valve at D admitting more or less air and controlling admission of the mixture to the valve A. The pipe C, not connected to H, as appears, admitted air to the carburettor. At B was a petrol lamp burner for heating the ignition tube. The exhaust passed from below the exhaust valve into a silencer, and thence

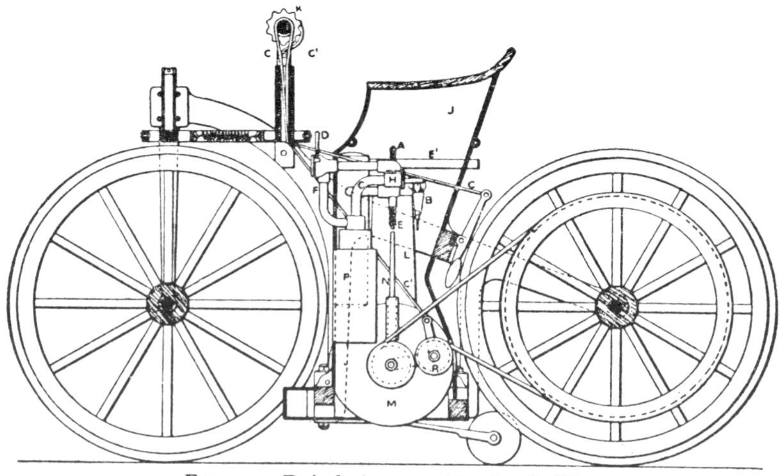

FIG. 14.—Daimler's motor-bicycle of 1885

away to the rear by the pipe E′. The motor, driven by a round leather band running over a small pulley on the crankshaft, tightened by the jockey pulley R, which was dropped by the cord C′, when the roller K on the steering handle was turned for the purpose of putting the brake on by pulling on cord C. Thus as the brake was put on the motor ceased to drive. There were two rollers, one on either side, as seen on the ground near the driving wheel. Normally they were off the ground, but could be one or both depressed by the foot for standing or for aid in steering. The pulley on the crankshaft was driven by a frictional drive which was adjustable as to frictional hold, and would slip when the resistance became sufficient to be likely to stop the engine.

They may be understood in their action from Fig. 15, which shows the carburettor designed by Daimler, and patented in 1885, for use with motors of the motor bicycle which the patent covered, and for the engines which soon began to be largely used as fixed engines and launch engines.

The lighter oils, such as petroleum spirit, now called petrol, or gasolene, or benzoline, will all evaporate readily in presence of air, and the more readily in presence of air moving more or less rapidly. In presence of dry air it will evaporate into and be taken up by that air until the air is saturated, which at 50° F. is when the air contains 17·5 per cent of the hydro-carbon vapour, that is, a mixture of one volume of oil vapour to about 6·7 per cent of air. This mixture will burn and give a very good white light. It is a rich mixture, of oil vapour and air, which, diluted with a considerable quantity of air, will burn with explosive rapidity under the circumstances of its combustion in a gas or oil cylinder.

For the production, then, of this carburetted air, Daimler invented the apparatus shown in Fig. 15 and described it in his patent, No. 10786 of 1885, for a motor bicycle, and in No. 7286 of 1886. It consists of a vessel A, which is about two-thirds filled with petrol. In this is a float D, cylindrical in exterior, and a conical central opening forming a basin, in which the petrol rises through a small hole B, to the level of the petrol outside the float. In the centre of the float is fixed a tube E, which fits freely in the tube F above, fixed to the cover of the petrol vessel. The float is thus free to rise or fall with the level of the petrol. The lower end of the tube E is perforated where it is immersed in the petrol in the conical basin C. Above the oil vessel A is a small vessel I, which forms a reservoir for carburetted air. From this, by attachment to the pipe G, this

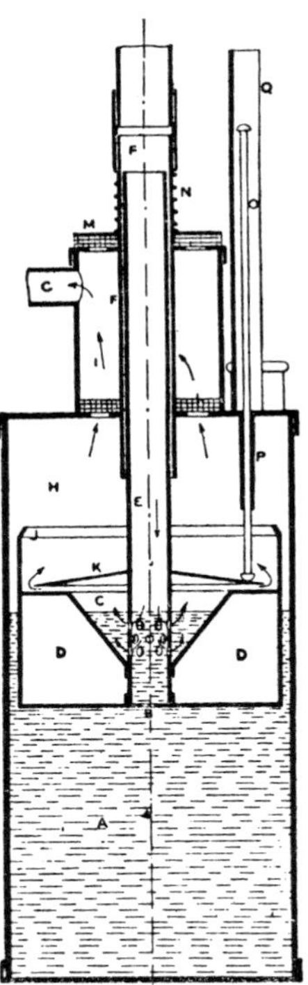


Fig. 15.—Daimler's surface carburettor of 1885

carburetted air is drawn by the piston of the motor cylinder. When this is drawn out there is a corresponding inrush of air from without down the pipe F. This new air bubbles through the petrol in the basin C, any petrol in the form of heavy spray being caught by the baffle plate K and lip, and caused to fall back into the basin. The air, now heavily charged with petrol, is drawn from the space H into the reservoir I through the holes in the top of the petrol vessel, and through the wire gauze at L, nothing but carburetted air passing. On the top of the reservoir I is a safety valve M, held down by a light spiral spring N. The object of this was, in the event of a back ignition from the cylinder from any cause striking back through the pipe G, to prevent a flame extending beyond the gauze partition L by providing an easy outlet for any rise in pressure. At P is a tubular guide for O, a small rod which rests in the baffle plate K of the float, and extends upwards to form an indicator of the level of the oil in the vessel. The upper part of the rod is surrounded by a U-shaped guard and guide Q, of a sufficient length to register the whole range of the rise and fall of the float, and thus show the quantity of oil at any time present in the vessel.

By this arrangement of carburettor, it will be seen that the main body of the petrol was not aerated, and that which was acted upon by the air was maintained at a uniform level in its basin, and kept sufficiently separate from the other. It will be seen also that this apparatus provided for an engine a supply of carburetted air always ready, and prevented the entrance of petrol not vaporized into the cylinder.

APPENDIX IV

# THE FIRST MERCEDES CAR

(*This detailed account is quoted verbatim from the issues of* The Autocar *for May 10, May 17, May 31 and June 14, 1902, and the authors and publishers take this opportunity of thanking the editor of* The Autocar *and Messrs. Iliffe & Sons, Ltd. for their kind permission to reprint these articles.*)

In common with others who saw the Cannstatt flier at the Automobile Club Show, the writer was impressed with its many good points, both in design and construction, and therefore proceeded with a good deal of interest to carry out the editor's instructions, which were to make a complete examination of the *chassis*, and note such points as would be of interest and use to manufacturers. The appearance of the car when the bonnet and body were removed fully bore out the impression gained at the show that every detail had been thoroughly considered in the original design, and there was an absence of makeshifts or afterthoughts in the details, which is more than can be said of many other well-known makes.

In the first instance, it is intended to deal with the general arrangement of the car, mentioning the special features, and subsequently to go more fully into the engine, transmission, and control gear, giving some particulars of the adjustments and proportions.

The wheelbase of the car is 2450 mm. by 1450 mm., and the wheels are 910 mm. by 90 mm. and 920 mm. by 120 mm., shod with

Fig. 16—Alfred Harmsworth's 1901-2 40-h.p. Mercedes, which is described fully in Appendix IV

Fig. 17—The chassis of the same car

Continental tyres. The axles are of weldless steel tube, with the ends brazed and pegged on, and the steering pivots of the front wheels are inside the hubs, which are of large diameter. All four wheels run on ball bearings of liberal dimensions, the balls being 15 mm. diameter.

The plan view (Fig 17) shows the general arrangement very clearly. The frame, of which dimensioned drawing is given (Fig 21), is of very special construction, and has evidently had very careful consideration on the part of the designer. The longitudinal members are of channel section steel 110 mm. deep in the middle, and tapering to 50 mm. at the back and 35 mm. in front. They are formed by flanging a steel plate 4 mm. in thickness, and are a very fine sample of work. To avoid the use of long dumb irons in the front, the frames themselves extend beyond the cooler, and terminate in small forgings, which take the spring links. The engine arms form the cross pieces for the front of the frames, while at the back a channel is used, and there is another cross member immediately behind the countershaft to carry the end of the gear-case.

It has been noticeable in many channel frames which have been used by motor-car makers that the section has been considerably weakened by putting bolts through the flanges instead of the web, but in this case the drilling of the flanges has been studiously avoided. The frame has evidently been designed with the object of removing any possibility of deflection, even under the severe conditions of road racing, so that the engine and transmission gear may be lined up and fixed into position without any flexible connexions or universal joints. The crankshaft of the engine, first and second shafts of the speed gear, and the countershaft are all in the same horizontal plane, and the underframe, such as is used on the Panhard and other similar cars, is dispensed with altogether, the crank chamber and speed gear-case being furnished with carrying brackets sufficiently long to extend to the main frame. The cooler, which is fixed in a vertical position in front of the engine bonnet, is of the marine condenser type which is now well known, but improvements have been made in its construction, so that its efficiency is greatly increased. It consists of a very large number of square tubes 5 mm. × 5 mm. in section, which are grouped together, so that the

Fig. 18—The engine of Alfred Harmsworth's 40-h.p. Mercedes, seen from the left-hand side

A. Cylinder heads
B. Induction pipe
C. Float chamber
D. Vaporizer
E. Induction valve spindles
F. Cooler
G. Water pipe from pump
H. Water pipe to cooler
I. Camshaft casing
J. Adjustable stop over nipple
K. Throttle valve spindle
L. Fork lever to governor sleeve
M. Throttle lever
N. Nut from hand throttle
O. Governor arms
P. Governor spring
Q. Camshaft gear-wheel
R. Wayshaft for advance ignition
S. Lever for advance ignition
T. Cross-shaft from levers steering wheel
U. Sight feed lubricators
V. Reducing valve for pressure feed
W. Flanges carrying igniting trip gear

Fig. 19 The engine of Alfred Harmsworth's 40-h.p. Mercedes, seen from the right-hand side

A. Cylinder heads
B¹. Exhaust pipe
C¹. Camshaft casing
D¹ Pump
E, E¹. Exhaust valve spindles
F. Cooler
F¹. Hot-air box for carburettor
G. Water pipe from pump
H. Water pipe to cooler
I¹. Exhaust pipe opener
J¹. Compression cocks
K¹. Bridges to hold cups over valves
L¹. Valve cups
M¹. Magneto
N¹. Spur wheel on camshaft driving magneto pinion
O¹. Magneto pinion
U. Sight feed lubricators

space between them is exceedingly small. The air is drawn through the tubes in a horizontal direction, while the cooling water occupies the interstices between them. A large centrifugal pump, run at a moderate speed off the magneto shaft, produces circulation of the water, while a fan (the vanes of which are formed by the arms of the flywheel) draws the air through the tube. The bonnet, which is fitted between the dashboard and the cooler, has no openings, except the inspection doors, and there is a sheet of aluminium, which passes under the engine, and is secured to the frame on each side. It will therefore be seen that all the air which is drawn by the flywheel must pass through the cooler. The aluminium sheet, which also serves to protect the engine from mud and dust, extends back beyond the gear-case, so that the whole of the mechanism is well protected.

The engine will be dealt with in detail later, although the leading features will be mentioned here. It is of the four-cylinder type, but has its admission valves, as well as its exhaust valves, actuated. The admission valves are all on one side of the engine, and the exhaust valves on the other, so that two camshafts are required, and these are operated by spur gearing from the crankshaft. Low-tension magneto ignition is used with wiping contact in the cylinder head on the admission valve side. These are operated by cams on the lay shaft below, and the time of firing may be varied by a mechanism similar to that used on the Simms engines. A single float chamber and jet supplies all the four cylinders, and the vaporizer contains a throttle valve consisting of a sliding sleeve, which is operated by the governor. The governor itself is carried in the spur wheel of the camshaft, which operates the admission valves, and a small lever on the steering wheel is used in place of a foot accelerator. The advance ignition lever is also carried on the steering wheel.

When the car is standing and the engine's throttle is right down, the latter runs at about two hundred revolutions per minute, and the sound is scarcely perceptible. For silence of running, the car is certainly unique, and is surprising having regard to the high power of the engine. The throttle control is also said to be very effective in traffic, allowing the car to be driven on high gear, even through towns.

The flywheel is of large diameter, and its arms, as has already been remarked, are suitably shaped to produce a powerful current of air through the cooler and engine bonnet. It is a mild steel casting, and by reason of its large diameter is comparatively light in weight. The clutch is extremely small, and it is fitted inside the boss of the flywheel. It consists of a spiral spring, one end of which is anchored to the flywheel, while the other is connected to a small lever, also carried on the flywheel boss. When this small lever is operated, the spring is tightened on to a cylindrical drum, which is connected to the first shaft of the change speed gear, and there is sufficient frictional grip to drive the car. One arm of the lever referred to carries a roller, which, when the clutch is disengaged, lies on the shaft, and a sliding cam pushed forward by a spring engages with it and puts the clutch into operation. This cam is withdrawn against the spring by a clutch foot pedal of the ordinary form, but when the foot is removed from the pedal it moves forward, and, having a quick rise on its face, the roller on the end of the lever runs up it on to a conical part, where the rise is more gradual. So long as

Fig. 20—Chassis detail of Alfred Harmsworth's 40-h.p. Mercedes

A. Flywheel rim
B. Flywheel arm
C. Fibre spur wheel on admission valve camshaft
D. Flywheel boss containing clutch
E. Clutch pedal
F. Footbrake pedal
G. Footbrake pedal
H. Sleeve moved by lever I on steering wheel
I. Accelerator lever
J. Advance ignition lever
K. Sprocket-brake lever
L. Change-speed lever
M. Sleeve of change-speed lever
N. Toothed segment
O. Key to interlock gear shifters
P. Rod to cam which takes clutch out of gear during change
Q. Lever which takes clutch out of gear when handbrake is on
R. Brakeshaft
S. Valve for water to cool brake
T. Third brake
U. Counter-shaft brake
V. Case over spring which holds reverse pinion out of gear
W. Countershaft
X. Countershaft brackets
Y. Petrol tanks
Z. Aluminium plate under gear

there is any relative movement between the flywheel and the first shaft of the speed gear, the roller will continue to mount the cam until the clutch is sufficiently tight to drive.

Passing on to the change speed gear, we find an invention which the late Gottlieb Daimler worked out in very practical form. This enables the driver to change speed without applying his foot to the clutch pedal, by automatically holding the clutch out of gear when the wheels are not fully in mesh. The gear-case is comparatively short, owing to the use of two separate sliding sleeves, each of which carries a pair of spur wheels. A broad reverse pinion is moved into engagement with the low speed wheels to give the backward movement. To obtain these three separate motions, there are three sliding bars in the gear-case, and these are each cut in the form of a rack, which projects from the case. The teeth of the racks are well pointed, and the way shaft of the control lever carries a toothed segment, whose teeth are also well pointed on the ends, so that it may be moved into engagement with one or other of these racks. The control lever itself, besides its fore and aft movement, is also capable of being moved sideways, so as to give the necessary movement to the toothed segment on its way shaft, and this side movement also operates a sliding key, which locks one pair of racks, while the other one is being operated. A connecting link from

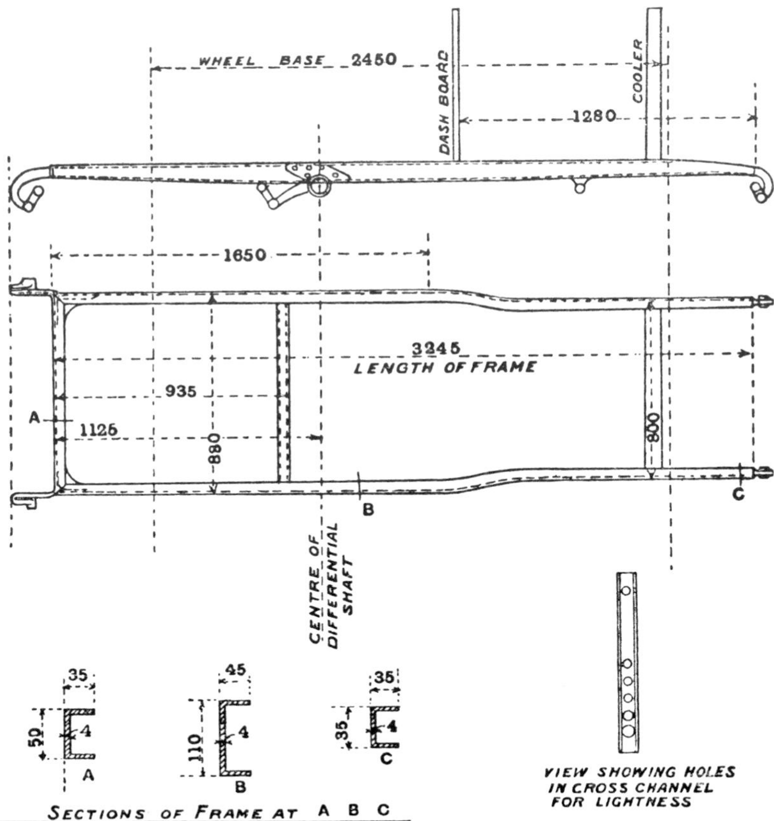


FIG. 21.—Dimensional drawing of the frame

the toothed segment operates the cam, which throws the friction clutch out of gear when the spur wheels are not fully engaged.

Ball bearings are used throughout the transmission gear—in fact, everywhere except in the engine. Ample brake power is provided by expanding toggle brakes inside the sprockets, operated by a hand lever—an ordinary double action brake, lined with cast iron on the countershaft, and a third brake on the forward end of the second shaft of the speed gear. These two latter are operated by foot pedals, and all are cooled by water, which is automatically turned on when the brakes are applied. This water is not drawn from that which cools the engine, but from a separate tank carried below the frame. The petrol is carried in two large tanks below the frame at the back, and the lubricating oil in a small tank, also below the frame. Exhaust pressure is used to bring the petrol to the float chamber, also to bring the oil to the sight feed lubricator on the dashboard and the water to the brakes, so that in no case is there gravity feed, and the body itself is quite free from tanks of any description, and can easily be detached.

The dimensions, which will be given later, will show that, in some cases at any rate, material of very high quality must be employed, as some of the parts are no larger than those used at present on cars of one-fourth the power.

The engine, which is nominally 40 h.p., has four cylinders, each 118 mm. bore, with the stroke 150 mm. The cylinders are cast in pairs, as will be seen from the Figs. 18 and 19. No attempt is made to use aluminium for the water jackets, but as these only extend a very short distance down the cylinders very little saving of weight could be looked for in that direction. Referring to Fig. 18, which shows the admission valve side, the method of actuating the admission valves will be clearly seen. The camshaft passes right along the side of the engine, the cams being covered by the caps I I. The valves themselves, whose stems project vertically downwards over the camshaft, are lifted by the same method as that usually employed to actuate exhaust valves when no cut-out governor is used. The valves have flat seats of 50 mm. diameter.

Although it is by no means a new idea to actuate the admission valves, the method of doing so in this particular car excited a good deal of interest by reason of the fact that their lift is stated to be variable, and to be controlled by the governor, which caused the variation to synchronize with the action of the throttle in the carburettor. The Cannstatt people, who were down at Nice with the car, were originally responsible for this statement, and it was generally accepted, but it appears necessary to take some of their claims with a pinch of salt, for not seeing any advantage in throttling the mixture in two places, we measured the lift of the valves with the governor sleeve in different positions, with the result that no variation could be discovered, and we have since heard from Mr. Harmsworth's engineer (who, feeling wrath at being misled, readily undertook to remove the cover and examine the mechanism at the first opportunity) that the admission valves were simply operated by plain cams giving a constant lift.

The ignition cams, which move the rods operating the make and break device in the cylinder, are not encased, and the lower ends of the rods are guided by swing links carried from the ends of short levers on the small wayshaft R. By rocking this wayshaft, which is connected to a lever on the steering wheel, the lower ends of the

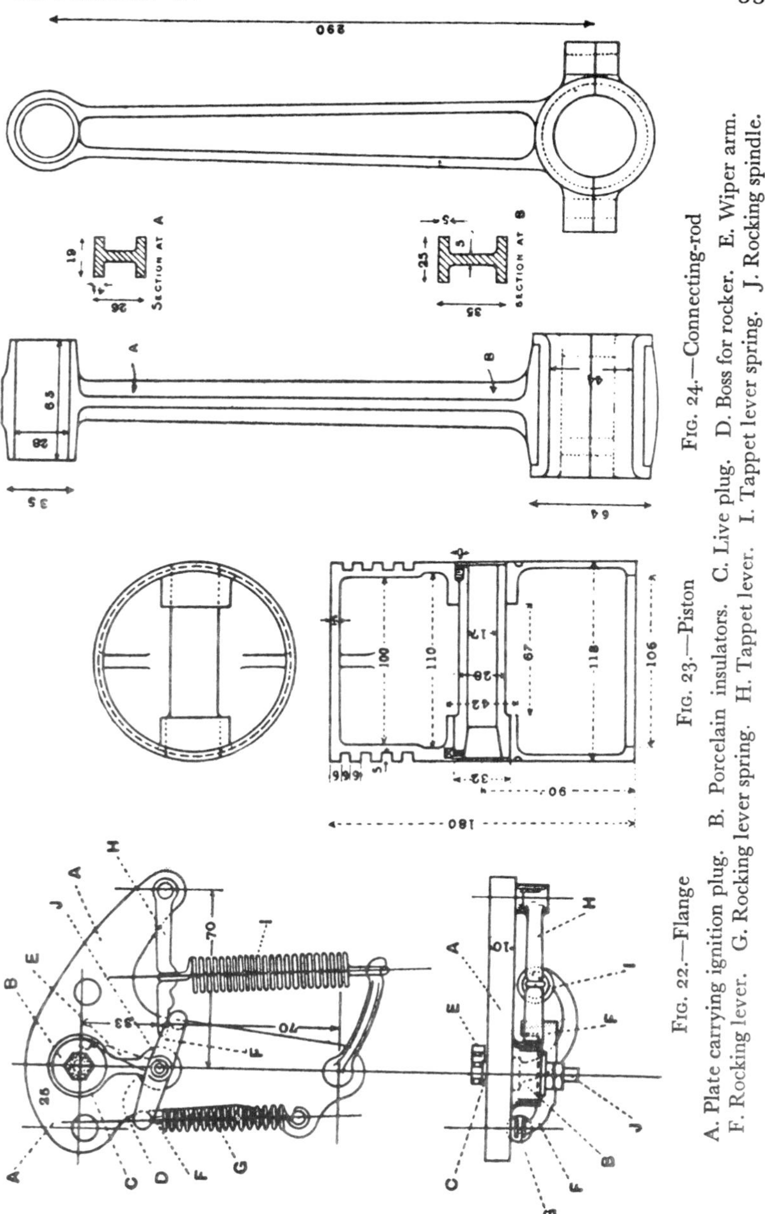

Fig. 22.—Flange

Fig. 23.—Piston

Fig. 24.—Connecting-rod

A. Plate carrying ignition plug. B. Porcelain insulators. C. Live plug. D. Boss for rocker. E. Wiper arm. F. Rocking lever. G. Rocking lever spring. H. Tappet lever. I. Tappet lever spring. J. Rocking spindle.

rods are moved in a plane at right angles to the camshaft, thus causing the cams to lift the rods earlier or later in the stroke. Fig. 22 shows the flange, which is bolted to the cylinder head, and which carries the make and break arrangement. The plug C is connected with a live wire from the magneto, and is insulated from the plate A by porcelain bushes. The dotted lever E, whose end is normally in contact with C, is capable of rotation about the spindle J, and when the contact is broken a low tension or wipe spark takes place at C. The spindle J is rocked by the lever F F on its end, which in its turn is moved by the lever H. The lever H is normally held up by the rod from the cams, but at the firing point this falls, and the end of the lever H comes in contact with the lever F, and as the spring I is sufficiently strong to overcome the spring G the spindle J is rocked, and the contact broken in the cylinder.

The carburettor (Fig. 25) is placed fairly high, thus permitting the use of short induction pipes. The vaporizer consists of a horizontal tube, into which the spray nozzle projects vertically. This tube is surrounded by a rectangular box, which is fed with hot air from a casing round the exhaust pipe, and the hot air has a free passage into the tube and past the nipple, after which the mixture passes

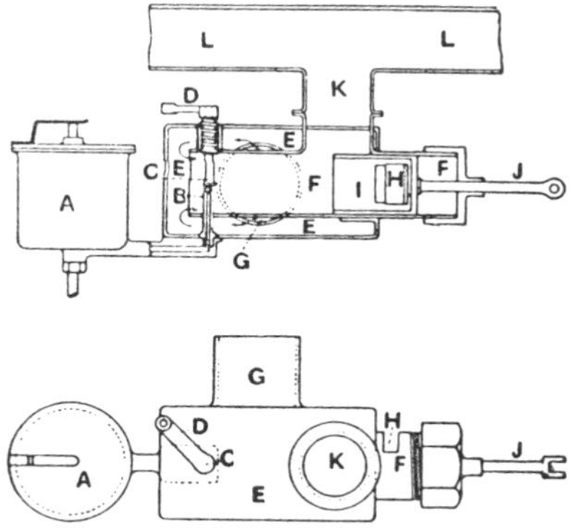


Fig. 25.—Carburettor

A. Float chamber. B. Spray nozzle. C. Adjustable stop. D. Lever operated from dashboard. E. Hot-air box. F. Tube containing throttle sleeve. G. Hot-air supply. H. Cold-air supply. I. Sliding throttle sleeve. J. Rod actuated by governor. K. Passage to induction pipe. LL. Induction pipes.

by a vertical branch into the induction pipe. Cold air from the other end of the horizontal tube passes through the cylindrical sleeve, which forms the throttle valve, and dilutes the mixture as it passes into the vertical branch leading to the induction pipe. When the throttle valve sleeve is moved along by the governor or the hand lever on the steering wheel it reduces the area of the vertical branch, and at the same time reduces the cold air supply, thus increasing the richness of the mixture. An adjustable stop J is fitted over the nozzle, and it is connected to a lever on the dashboard, by which its height can be varied. This stop has a function similar to that on the carburettor of a de Dion voiturette, and regulates the amount of oil flowing from the nozzle.

On the exhaust side of the engine, which is shown in Fig. 19, it will be seen that the valve gear is similar to that on the admission side. The exhaust valves themselves are of the same diameter as the admission valves, but have conical seatings, and the lift in both cases is 8 mm. A single exhaust pipe is used, from which it would appear that the makers do not attach much importance to the interference between the exhaust of one cylinder and another. A spur wheel on the middle of the camshaft drives the pinion on the magneto-shaft, and also the pump, which is of the centrifugal type, and of large size. A valve is fitted in the exhaust pipe just before it reaches the silencer, which can be opened by a lever I′

on the dashboard, and allow the exhaust to pass directly into the atmosphere. This was fitted for racing purposes, but when we inspected the car it was opened when the engine was throttled down for quiet running, and from the weakness of the explosions it was clear that the silencer is not entirely responsible for the extremely quiet running of this engine when the car is standing. The silencer itself, which is at the side of the car between the wheels, is 700 mm. long and 195 mm. diameter. The exhaust pipe projects into it, the end being plugged and the pipe perforated. There are two baffle plates, which divide the silencer up into three compartments, and one long pipe passes to the rear of the car.

Figs. 23 and 24 show the piston and connecting rod, which were supplied amongst the spare gear for the car. The small end of the connecting rod is case hardened, and works on a hollow hardened steel gudgeon pin, shown in place in the piston. The large end of the connecting rod is fitted with white metal bearings.

The general arrangement of transmission and control gear is clearly shown in Fig. 20, which view also gives a good idea of the construction of the flywheel, whose light rim A and curved arms B (forming the fan) may be seen. The clutch is concealed, but some estimate of its size may be formed from the fact that it is wholly contained within the fly-wheel boss D. The regulating levers I and J, above the steering wheel, operate the throttle valve and advance ignition gear respectively. I is attached to a hollow spindle passing down inside the revolving steering column. This spindle has a quick-threaded screw and nut, the latter being connected through slots in the steering column to the outside sleeve H, from which the movement is taken by a forked lever. The ignition lever J has a solid rod, which passes right down the centre of the steering column and through the hollow worm, terminating in a screw and nut, from the latter of which the motion is conveyed to the advance ignition gear. The mechanism for change gear is based on Daimler's patent, No. 9805, 1899.

The first and second shafts of the speed gear, as well as the differential shaft, have their axis in the same horizontal plane, and the case itself is divided through the bearings into two halves. The lower portion has arms or carrying brackets, which are attached to the frame while the top is more readily removable. The first shaft, on which the sliding sleeves are mounted, is provided with four long feather keys, instead of being squared, and the sleeves are grooved to suit. There are two sleeves, each of which carries a couple of gear wheels. The width of the first and second speed wheels is 30 mm., the third 25 mm., and the fourth 22 mm. The spur wheels on the second shaft are fixed, and the cross shaft is driven by a pair of bevel wheels (50 mm. width of face) in the usual manner.

For reversing, a broad pinion mounted on a suitable arm is moved into engagement with the low speed wheels when they are in the out-of-gear position. The object of the special change speed mechanism is to automatically release the drive, by taking the friction clutch out during the changing of gear without the use of the foot-pedal. Its action may be traced by reference to Fig. 20, in which L is the control lever, which can be moved forward or backward in one of three quadrants, or when brought to its central position can be moved sideways from one to the other, a gap being provided in the dividing bars to admit of this. The control lever is keyed to one end of the sleeve M, which is free to rotate on, or slide along, the brake shaft R. At the other end of M is a lever carrying the toothed segment N, also a plain segment engaging with the key O. Three sliding bars are provided in the gear-case: two of these have shifting forks, which engage with the sliding sleeves on the first shaft, and the other is connected to the arm which carries the reverse pinion. By cutting slots in the top portion of the gear-case, these sliding bars are exposed for a portion of their length, and are cut to form racks, so that the toothed segment N may engage with them.

In Fig. 20 N is in engagement with the rack, which moves the sleeve carrying the first and second speeds, but by moving the control lever to the left the other racks may be operated. To remove the possibility of damage by two sets of gears engaging at the same time, an interlocking arrangement of a simple form is provided. The sliding bars are notched on their under sides, and a groove is cut in the gear-case, so that when they are all in their 'out-of-gear' positions a rectangular hole is formed through which the interlocking key O can slide freely when actuated by the side movement of the control lever. The key itself has a notch exactly under the toothed segment N, so that the particular rack with which N is engaged can be moved while the other two are securely locked in the out-of-gear position. The small connecting rod P has one end jointed to the lever carrying N, and the other to a cam under an extension of the clutch pedal lever. When the control lever is in the out-of-gear position this cam holds the clutch out, and does not allow it to grip again until the control lever has been moved sufficiently far to put the spur wheels right into gear.

The brake pedals F and G actuate brakes T and U, which are of ordinary construction, consisting of steel bands lined with cast iron. They are hinged at the top, and the operating levers are at the bottom in each case, so that they are double-acting.

The brake drums themselves are water-cooled by the dripping of water on the inside of the rim. A separate water valve is provided for each brake, and the water is only turned on to the brakes which are actually in use. The sprocket brakes are of special construction, as shown in Fig. 26. The sprocket wheel itself is quite a light shell, and is bolted to the spokes in the usual way. The expanding cast-iron ring H is anchored at the top by rod F, from the rear of the frame, and when not expanded is carried by the rollers on the fixed arms E. The wire rope from the hand-brake lever pulls the lever L, which acts through the link K on the powerful toggle formed by the arms J J. These sprocket brakes are encased as far as possible in order to keep out the mud and grit. To equalize the pull the wire rope passes up the short arm of the brake lever and through the hollow shaft R to the other brake.

We have described the engine, transmission gear, and other important parts of the mechanism, and it remains for us to illustrate the complete car in racing trim and to give a summary of the leading dimensions.

It will be readily understood that an inspection of the chassis, however thorough, did not enable us to obtain dimensions of some of the internal parts, which would only be accessible when the car was thoroughly stripped, but we have no doubt the dimensions we are able to give will be of interest to manufacturers:

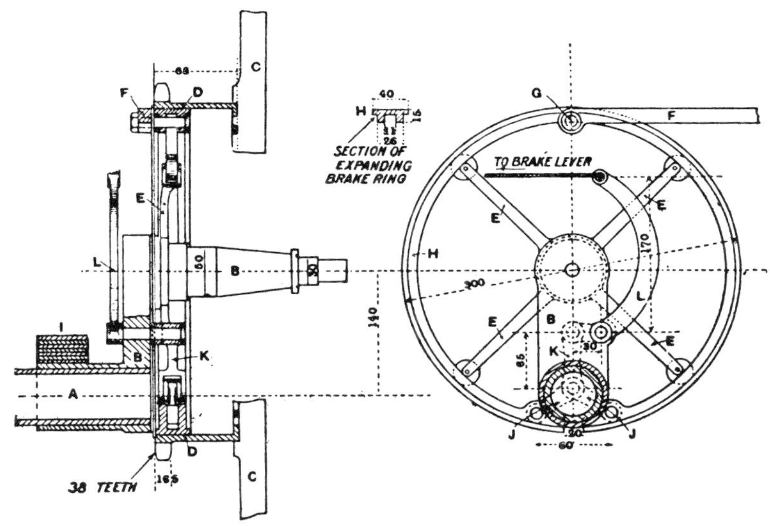


FIG. 26.—Sprocket brakes

A. Tubular back axle. BB. Forged axle ends. C. Back wheel spokes. D. Back wheel sprocket. E. Stationary arms carrying brake ring supporting rollers. F. Anchor rod from rear of frame. G. Anchor pin. H. Expanding brake ring. I. Back Spring. J. Toggle arms. K. Toggle link. L. Lever.

*Wheelbase.*—Length, 2450 mm.; width, 1450 mm.

*Size of Wheels.*—Front, 910 × 90; rear, 920 × 120mm.

*Tyres.*—Continental.

*Axles (hollow).*—Front and back, 55 mm. outside diameter; 45 mm. inside.

*Springs.*—Front, 900 mm. long, 45 mm. wide; two plates 8 mm. thick, four plates 6 mm. thick: back, 1100 mm. long, 50 mm. wide; two plates 8 mm. thick, five plates 6 mm. thick.

*Frame.*—See drawing, page 282.

*Radius Rods.*—18 mm. diameter.

*Engine.*—Number of cylinders, four; bore, 118 mm.; stroke, 150 mm.

*Length of Connecting Rod.*—290 mm.

*Length of Piston.*—180 mm.

*Diameter of Exhaust Valve.*—50 mm.

*Lift.*—8 mm.

*Flywheel.*—Diameter, 600 mm.; width of rim, 85 mm.; thickness of rim, 18 mm.

*Timing of Valves and Ignition.*—Admission valve opens at commencement of charging stroke and closes when piston has moved 13 mm. up the compression stroke. Early ignition when piston is 17 mm. from top of compression stroke. Late ignition when piston has moved 2 mm. down working stroke. Exhaust valve opens when piston is 33 mm. from bottom of working stroke, and closes at top of exhaust stroke.

*Silencer.*—Length, 700 mm.; diameter, 195 mm.; diameter of outlet (pipe to back of car), 25 mm.

*Transmission Gear.*—First shaft, 40 mm. diameter; second shaft, 37 mm. diameter; countershaft, 28 mm. diameter; width of gears, first speed 30 mm., second speed 30 mm., third speed 25 mm., fourth speed 22 mm.; sprockets, 28 and 38 teeth.

*Chain.*—35 mm. pitch; 20 mm. wide.

*Brakes.*—Sprocket brakes (see Fig. 26); countershaft brake, 240 mm. diameter, 80 mm. wide; extra brake (on second shaft of speed gear), 200 mm. diameter, 70 mm. wide.

The performances of the Mercedes-Simplex have been dealt with from time to time in the reports of the important races, and are no doubt well known to our readers. It is therefore unnecessary for us to refer to them in this article, which is purely a technical description of the mechanism. Nor do we propose to comment on its proportions or adjustments beyond remarking that manufacturers will do well to compare them carefully with the results of their own experience.

*Readers who are interested in more detailed descriptions than lie within the scope of this book of other notable Mercedes racing-cars are referred to Laurence Pomeroy's great work* The Grand Prix Car (*Motor Racing Publications, 1954*), *where in Vol. I pp. 136–142 they will find a description of the 1914 Grand Prix Car and in Vol. II descriptions of the* W25B, *the* W125 *and the* W163 *on pp. 205–213, 224–233 and 235–247 respectively.*

## APPENDIX V

## THE MODELS *33/180K, 36/220S, 38/250SS, SSK* AND *SSKL* SUPERCHARGED SUPER SPORTS MERCEDES-BENZ CARS

by R. H. Johnson

(*This article, by the Founder and Vice-President of the Mercedes-Benz Club, first appeared in* Motor Sport *of February, 1952, and the authors and publishers wish to express their gratitude to Mr. Johnson for revising his article for the purpose of this book, and to the Editor and Proprietors of* Motor Sport *for giving permission for its reproduction here.*)

Throughout the stirring history of motor sport few cars have quite achieved such fame nor aroused such intense enthusiasm as did the *38/250* Mercedes-Benz. It is almost unique in having acquired an idealism which finds expression in such emotionally charged descriptives as 'immortal' or 'legendary', so often used by writers and advertisers when referring to this car.

As regards the latter suggestion, unlike most legends, the facts are indisputable, for, on its first appearance in an International meeting in this country, the 1929 Irish T.T., a sensational victory was achieved in appalling conditions when Caracciola completed what is generally regarded as the outstanding drive of his career, and, often referred to as the greatest drive in motor racing history.

It was a sad day for the 'wearers of the green': three 'blower' $4\frac{1}{2}$ Bentleys failed to catch this screaming white production model sports-car which was destined to develop into a highly successful Grand Prix winner, perhaps the only production sports touring-car ever to achieve this distinction with such slight departure from production specification.

There was, however, something more about this car than its victories which fired the imagination of the sports-car world; this was a car simply breathing the indefinable as contained in that eternal question, 'What constitutes a sports-car?' The appeal lay in the embodiment of a refined balance between the symbolic artistry of speed, sleekness, and unlimited power, which no other design had succeeded in translating into a thing of beauty nor has been equalled since in the impressiveness of its lines.

Perhaps no more imposing looking sports-car has ever been conceived: it was the ultimate of its kind and to this day is regarded as the most classic sports-car of all times. In the words of 'Bunty' Scott-Moncrieff, 'Mention of the name *38/250* makes all true vintagents drool at the chops' and, as remarked by the editor of *Motor Sport* after his road test in November 1929, 'Words fail me —this is the most amazing motor-car it has ever been our fortune to drive.'

Information and data on this car is surprisingly rare, considering the tremendous impression it made on the motoring world. With this premise, the author hopes that the description which follows will contribute a little more information to the general knowledge.

## Evolution

The original conception of a six-cylinder supercharged production-car was produced in 1924 as the 4-litre model 15/70/100 with a bore of 80 mm. and stroke 130. It was immediately followed in the same year by the model 24/100/140 of 6·3 litres, usually known in Great Britain as the *33/140*, with the long-chassis 12 ft. 4 in. wheelbase. These two cars were not sports-cars as the term is now understood, particularly the high-chassis rear cantilever sprung heavy bodied *33/140*.

The first of the big six-cylinder sports models from which was evolved the *38/250*, was known as the model *33/180K*, with shortened wheelbase, 11 ft. 2 in., and semi-elliptic springs. The supercharged engine, bore 94 mm. × stroke 150 mm., was of 6245 cc., capacity of power 110/160 b.h.p. These models first arrived in England towards the end of 1926, being described by road test reports as the first genuine 100 m.p.h. touring-car. (N.B. for owners: The former *33/140* engine plate stating *24/100/140 P.S.* was fitted to all *33/180K* models in lieu of *110/160*.)

At the 1927 Olympia Motor Show, Mercedes-Benz exhibited for the first time since the close of World War I, and a sensational comeback was staged by introducing the model *36/220S*, which was bigger and better than the *33/180*, with a supercharged engine, 98 mm. × 150 mm. of 6789 cc. capacity, developing 120 b.h.p. unblown and 180 blown. This model had a lowered chassis and radiator and was a definite break-away from the upright vintage styling of its predecessor, but retained the 11 ft. 2 in. wheelbase. It was capable of speeds in excess of 100 m.p.h. and secured many victories in international road racing.

The opinion is held by some that the *36/220* is a more flexible car to drive than the *38/250*, and as Mr. Edward L. Mayer (who can well deserve to be described as the greatest Mercedes enthusiast still living, having owned over 100 different examples of this marque, after a lifetime crammed with experience of Daimler-Benz Aktiengesellschaft products), chose to run an immaculate touring *36/220* until quite recently, while keeping an equally handsome 2-seater as a spare car, I am convinced this opinion is not unwarranted. Another excellent example of the *36/220*, still with us today, is the ex-Earl Howe maroon 2-seater now owned for many years by H. E. Rohll, which is frequently seen competing at V.S.C.C. and B.D.C. Silverstone meetings.

The *38/250* model *SS* (Super Sports) had already demonstrated its capabilities during 1929 in the Irish T.T. and Grand Prix races, so that when the British public had their first opportunity to view this car at close quarters in the 1929 Olympia Motor Show, it was with profound respect. Production of the *SS* model was commenced late in 1928 (but not in time to be included in the 1928 Olympia Motor Show), and continued until late in 1929, by which time some 114 cars had been manufactured (excluding *SSK*s), ready for export mainly to Britain and the Americas during the years 1930–34. Although this model was catalogue listed up to 1934, the great majority were sold in 1930 and 1931.

The following nomenclature was used in English language catalogues:

| | |
|---|---|
| 1929 and 1930 | *38/250 SS* (Super Sports) and *SSK* (Super Sports Kurz*) |
| 1931 | Grand Prix Sports *SS* and *SSK* |
| 1932 | *SS* and *SSK* |
| 1933 | *SSK* only |
| 1934 | Super Sports *37/225* |

Daimler-Benz terminology for the Model *SS* is *27/140/200 WO 6/13*. The price complete ranged from £2,500 in 1930 to £3,085 in 1934. The *SSKL* (L for 'Leicht') which had a lightened, copiously drilled short chassis, was not a production model in the full sense of the term. The few examples of this type were 'Works team cars' but some were supplied to very special order from early 1930 onwards. The author has not as yet traced any example in Britain or the U.S.A., and has been informed that no true *SSKL* ever came to this country in private hands.

The car in which Caracciola won the 1930 Irish Grand Prix, again soundly beating the Bentley team in the process, although frequently referred to as an *SSKL* model, does not appear in photographs of the race to have a lightened chassis. This description probably refers to the engine which will be mentioned later.

Following upon the success of the *36/220* model it is surprising that its successor was not considerably larger. One would have expected something in the region of 8-litre capacity, as was seen in the development of the 6½-litre Bentley to the 8 litre, although it must be remembered that these were unblown engines. The 36/220 engine capacity was merely increased by 280 cc. by enlarging the bore from 98 to 100 mm., the new capacity being 7069 cc.

* *Kurz*—short.

The extra brake horse power obtained was assisted by a larger supercharger and slightly different valve lay-out, the extra urge being taken care of by a more robust crankshaft.

The sleek low lines of the *36/220* were subtly transformed by a higher chassis and radiator, giving the *38/250* a more formidable appearance. A design feature which could have been greatly improved was the braking system. An improvement over the *36/220* was achieved and in theory the extremely large diameter drums were considered adequate without servo assistance, but the weight-velocity factor proved greater than had been foreseen. There is no denying that the lack of braking power of the *38/250* constitutes a serious drawback to the enjoyment of anything approaching full performance on roads in this country.

Standard production body-styling by Karosserie Mercedes consisted in the 4-seater open tourer, and the 2-door drophead coupé or cabriolet, all with left- or right-hand drive to order. In 1931, production 2-seater sports bodies were made for the long chassis *SS*, but not the stripped body, which was only made for the *SSK*. Some excellent examples of 2-seater bodywork were provided on the *SS* by specialist coachbuilders. One outstanding example which springs to mind is the ex-Rothschild, ex-Eccles, maroon 2-seater with massive chromed external three branch exhaust cowling. This car has not been seen in the post-war years and it is earnestly to be hoped that it escaped the ravages of war.

Practically all the leading coachbuilders of the time produced striking examples of contemporary styling on this chassis. Amongst these were Saoutchik of Paris, Erdmann & Rossi, Million-Guiet, von Castagna, Kellner of Berlin, Van den Plas, Corsica, Mulliner, Freestone & Webb, etc. The well-known black drop-head coupé *SSK* recently owned by G. Crozier, often seen at Prescott and other meetings, has a Corsica body, and was the only drop-head *SSK* in this country. This car has now gone to enrich the eyes and ears of our friends in America, and is another example of the serious depletion which is taking place by the loss to this country of our finest examples of vintage sports-cars. We have, however, some consolation in the knowledge that they are going to owners who will cherish them with equal respect.

## Chassis

The overall length of the *SS* chassis is 15 ft. 5 in. The wheelbase is 11 ft. 1⅞ in., track 4 ft. 7⅞ in., road clearance 6 in. The chassis is of deep channel section with an extra-strong transverse box section member about mid-length. It is deeply curved at both ends, obtaining a low centre of gravity. At the front, long semi-elliptic overslung leaf springs are fitted and the same, but underslung, at the rear.

It is known for certain chassis to possess a tendency for front end whip, which in an extreme case caused a slight contact of fan blade tip with the radiator. This phenomenon is fortunately rare, but that it was appreciated is evidenced by the wire bracing and bottle screws which were a feature of Caracciola's 1929 Irish TT. car, which was still in place when last seen by the writer some years ago.

Wheels are 20 in. diameter for 6·50 tyres all round, or 7·00 on rear wheels. Construction is of 3-spread wire spokes with detachable rim guards and heavy duty knock-on hub caps.

The transmission is flange mounted to engine, through a dry multiple plate clutch to a four-speed gear-box with chrome nickel steel gears and centrally mounted ball joint control rod, which can be locked in neutral to prevent unauthorised use. The standard gear-box ratios are 8·72; 5·0; 3·76 and 2·76 to 1. The gear-box is in unit with engine, necessitating displacement of transmission aft before removal. Reverse gear is engaged by lifting ball socket and moving to the left forward.

Rear-end drive, via universal joint in ball housing in which terminates the torque tube, is by spiral bevel gears and differential to the rear axle, housed in pressed steel. The standard rear axle ratio is 2·76, with special ratios of 2·5 or 3·09 supplied to order. The 2·5 ratio is well suited for high-speed track work but noticeably impairs acceleration in sprints. (Speeds in each gear, and with varying axle ratios, will be found under the section on Performance Characteristics.)

Steering is high-geared via deep worm and nut, and although heavy in manoeuvring becomes the acme of precision at high speeds. This is one of the chief joys in the handling of the *38/250*, a point which was spontaneously remarked upon by the late Pierre Marechal as the most perfect he had ever experienced, when on one occasion driving the author's car. Turning circle to the left is 50 ft. 9 in. and to the right 49 ft. 10 in.

Shock absorbers were Houdaille hydraulic both front and rear, but triple Hartford friction dampers at the front were favoured by racing owners. The semi-elliptic suspension, hard by modern standards, is just right for a car of this character. Brakes have already been commented upon, regretting the lack of servo-assistance. Adjustment by the hand-wheel regulators on each leading rod is frequently required, and in this respect improvement can be obtained, in catching up with the lost movement in the linkages, by cutting quarter turn notches in the rods in way of the hand-wheels, great care being taken not to overweaken the cross-sectional area.

A large fuel tank (*benzin enthalten*) of 27 gallons capacity is situated behind the rear axle, supplying an Autovac or gravity tank on the engine bulkhead with the air pressure system. Two spare wheels were usually mounted behind the petrol tank providing useful weight compensation aft.

Chassis weight is 25 cwts., weight with 4-seater bodywork 37½ cwts., and total laden weight with two people is 47 cwts.

The overall length with 4-seater bodywork is 16 ft. 8 in. and width 5 ft. 8 in.

## Engine

The engine has an R.A.C. rating of 37·2 h.p., and is a six-cylinder of 100 mm. bore × 150 mm. stroke or 428 cubic inches piston displacement, capacity 7069 cc. Total power developed at 3200 maximum safe revolutions (*undrehungen in der minute*) is 140 b.h.p. unblown, later increased to 160, and 200 blown: b.h.p. to piston area ratio is 3.3 for the *SS* model. The *SSK* model, with larger supercharger, obtained 170 unblown and 225 blown, and the *SSKL* with racing camshaft and 'elephant' blower is reputed to have developed 300 brake horse-power.

Of monobloc design with detachable head, the upper portion of the crankcase and the cylinder block is manufactured from a single piece of silumin. The lower half of the crankcase and the cylinder head cover is of cast aluminium. The sump casing and overhead valve cover are metal to metal fit with the block, the only gasket used being the copper-asbestos cylinder head. The block is fitted with sleeves of grey casting on the wet-liner principle, and light metal pistons, each with three compression rings and one scraper ring, are used. Connecting rods are of high tensile steel, circular section, drilled to pass oil up to the gudgeon pins. Later engines had beam section forgings machined all over in lieu of circular. The only case of conn-rod failure known to the author in a *38/250* was the unfortunate one of the owner who forgot to turn off his Ki-gass pump. Whilst the *36/220S* had separate bronze shell conn-rod bearings, the *38/250SS* had the bearing metal bonded direct to the rod.

The crankshaft is of chrome nickel steel, fully balanced, with four main bronze backed poured bearings, as also are the six big-end bearings. All engines had a friction type crankshaft vibration damper. The engine needs this damper, for there exists an unbalanced couple (dynamic) in the *S* at about 1400 r.p.m., and in the *SS* at 1600 to 1700 r.p.m., varying between cars according to gear ratios. The vibration is audible and exists both $\pm$ 75 to 100 r.p.m. The overhead camshaft is driven, by a flexible construction vertical shaft at the rear end, from the crankshaft through silent helical gears. Valves, two per cylinder, are operated by rocker arms. Tappet clearances when warm should be 0·005 inch for inlet valves and 0·007 inch for exhaust valves.

The oil-pump is likewise driven by the same vertical shaft, drawing oil from a gauze enclosed trap in the sump. There is also a special piston pump which meters fresh pre-heated oil from an auxiliary tank to preserve the maximum sump level. A glass sight is provided in the side of the block to observe the level of fresh oil in the auxiliary tank. This is a very excellent idea for long distance high-speed work, but in normal conditions it has a tendency to provide too much oil with consequent fouling of sparking plugs. On right-hand drive models, where the autovac is on the left-hand side of the engine bulkhead, it is found that the auxiliary oil tank filler cap is inaccessible and the glass level sight half obscured. This is entirely due to transpositioning of the steering column, and not in any sense attributable to oversight in the layout.

Provided normal routine check on the sump level is made, the auxiliary oil tank need never be used. The sump level is ascertained by the use of a three-way tap mounted on the base of the block, under the forward carburettor. The first position, moving the hand lever forward, drains off any excess oil over the maximum level (two gallons capacity), the second position, moved forward again, is the minimum safe level and if there is no discharge at this position —you have been warned! The third position, again forward, empties the sump. At the position moved aft of the closed position, the whole tap can be withdrawn for cleaning. It is not clear what advantage the designers had in mind over the normal dipstick procedure, as the latter at least indicates the amount consumed. One snag about this patent tap is the great care necessary when replacing the sump chamber, in order not to jam the housing on its valve seating. Crankcase ventilation is also embodied in the bell housing of the tap.

The oil filter is contained in the rear end engine casting crankcase and is reached by unscrewing a large cap. It consists of an unbelievable length of spiral spring steel, the release of which, even whilst cleaning, is to be avoided at all cost. Once let slip it will encircle the garage twice and attempt to choke the well meaning liberator.

Standard oil pressure when hot should be 42 lb. per square inch (3 kilogrammes per square centimetre for those with gauges thus calibrated). Maximum oil sump content is two gallons.

Standard compression ratio is 5 to 1 and high compression pistons were available which gave 5·75 to 1. Valve timing is checked by observation of a number of letters on the flywheel for each position of the 4-stroke cycle in No. 1 cylinder.

## Supercharger

The supercharger is a Roots type two-vane, two-lobe, vertically mounted centrally at the front end of the engine. It is geared to the crankshaft to run at three times engine revs and blows air through the carburettors, unlike its normal British counterpart which sucks the mixture from the carburettor. Dimensions of the standard 8½ lb./square inch blower fitted to the *SS* model are, height 283 mm., inlet port 64 × 107 mm., and circular outlet to carburettors. In effect it provides an eight speed transmission, as follows: first gear unblown, first gear blown, and so on up the range of the box. Normally it is out of use, being braked by a special clutch assembly with eight pairs of discs.

To operate, the foot throttle is depressed hard down to the floor board, throwing over a trip-stop which is positioned at the normal full throttle opening (to prevent misjudged use of the blower). The movement is transmitted through rod controls to the driving clutch which consists in pairs of discs. It is extremely important that the foot throttle be held hard down all the time whilst using the supercharger, as it is the foot applied pressure which holds the clutch in engagement. A powerful spring returns the throttle pedal immediately it is released.

The noise of a Mercedes blower is, to the occupants of the car, bloodcurdling and diabolic. Nothing approaching it has ever been fitted to a sports-car. After the first terrifying bursts of boost have been attempted and it is found that the engine does not blow up, the experience becomes extremely exhilarating. The noise rises like an air-raid siren and becomes quite as demented as a pack of Irish banshees. One literally feels the seat pushing one in the back nd the wheelspin on a greasy or wet road can produce a complete volte-face. It should be emphasized for the benefit of the unimpressed, who have only heard the blower cutting in and out whilst spectating on track or airfield, that a full appreciation can only be obtained whilst in the car. From a distance the Merc blower does not sound all that impressive, but if a mean advantage be taken of the unsuspecting passenger, his first impulse is to bail out.

An incident illustrating another aspect which should be allowed for, occurred after an informal sporting race to Salisbury one Sunday morning, when the author by a chance meeting overtook Dr. W. A. Taylor of 'Alfi-Capa Cæsar Special' fame who was driving his 3-litre Bentley (in commendable manner), conveying a friend to Salisbury station to catch a train they had already decided was lost.

Having the advantage of surprise, we cheerily waved on passing, but the Bentley, true to its finest traditions, sensed that a gauntlet had been dropped and gave chase. The shriek of a Teutonic blower echoed over the Plain that morning and the Druids stirred uneasily in their '*unterwelt spuken*'. The pace was so hot it transpired that the Doctor's passenger caught the train.

The incident referred to is that after a good few minutes stop in Salisbury Square, and when just on the point of climbing up into the Merc, we were indignantly accosted by a most enraged couple whose car, it appeared, we had passed on the road by using a siren to clear the way, and did we not know this was illegal? Tempers were rising after the lady passenger declared it was obvious I had never been taught to drive; calm, however, was obtained when the bonnet was lifted and a short lecture delivered on the ABC of supercharging.

To return to the technical description. Whilst blowing, the autovac is converted to a vacuum tank by automatic operation, in order to balance float chamber pressure, and a butterfly valve in the air intake of the carburettors, actuated by the blower clutch rod, is closed whilst under compressed air. A glass sight petrol reservoir is mounted on the dashboard to indicate excess petrol in the autovac, through which sight it is free to overflow; when petrol is observed in the glass, blowing should be discontinued at once.

A point usually ignored or unknown in this country is that the instruction manual expressly states the supercharger must not be used on gasolene only. A mixture of benzole in equal proportion is essential in order to avoid the dire consequences of excessive cylinder head temperature. It is also not the manufacturer's intention for the blower to be used continuously. Fifteen to twenty seconds is quite long enough for the purpose for which it is designed, namely, to increase speed in each gear when hill-climbing. It should not be used at low speed nor brought in at high speed in top gear.

The popular opinion is held by many that the *38/250* Mercedes is notorious for blowing the cylinder head gasket. The answer is that any supercharged car will do this if the head is not thoroughly tightened down, and when unsuitable fuel is used. The gasket should embody reinforcing around the water holes, not merely punched through, but even without such refinements it is not a weakness in the design. The author's car, fitted with high-compression pistons, only once blew the cylinder head gasket, when the blower was used in bottom gear up a very steep hill. This was done in the initial exuberance which first ownership brings, and sure enough, the head was found to have been insufficiently tightened down after a recent de-coke by the previous owner. To this day, it has yet to be proved that the lone *38/250* driven by Caracciola in the 1930 Le Mans Race was forced to retire by reason of a blown gasket. The best evidence to the contrary, given in the words of Sir Henry (Tim) Birkin, whose job it was to force the Mercedes pace with that object in view, is quoted from *Full Throttle** as follows: 'The Mercedes second battery was exhausted, the engine would not start nor the lights work, so Caracciola admitted defeat with no shame to car or driver. They had run alone for 10 hours and held more than their own against a meticulously prepared team of 5 Bentleys—to have lasted as long as that was miraculous. I retired after 20 hours with a

* Foulis, 1932.

broken conn-rod.'

A slightly larger blower, compressing at 10 lb./square inch, was fitted in the *SSK* model whilst the *SSKL* had an even larger one, known as the 'elephant' blower in England, producing 12 lb./square inch, with dimensions of 317 mm. height and an inlet port 70 × 111 mm. The rotor diameter remained the same in all three sizes. It is not generally realized that three sizes were available for the *38/250*, and many cars which are mistakenly described as fitted with the 'elephant' blower have in fact got the medium one. Within recent years only three genuine 'elephant' blowers were known to exist in this country, and now that the ex-Caracciola 1929 Irish T.T. car and the ex-Crozier *SSK* have gone to the U.S.A. only one remains.

It will be recalled that the fitting of one of these large blowers in Caracciola's car for the 1930 T.T. resulted in his disqualification by the scrutineers, who contended it was a non-standard fitting, although a few had in fact been used on the Continent that year, admittedly in racing events. The main issue was that the 'elephant' blower was not fitted to the production *38/250* Mercedes exhibited for sale in the Park Lane showrooms, but it was available to special order. It was certainly a border-line case over which most people agreed the scrutineers were scrupulously fair to other competitors.

This system of supercharging 'at will' has much to commend in preference to the continuously engaged method. It has the advantage of economy in fuel consumption, great reliability due to less use, improved flexibility at low speed and an instant acceleration 'on tap' which is extremely useful when in a tight spot.

## Carburettors

Normal aspiration is by two huge Pallas carburettors fitted on the near side of the engine, provided with a hot-air cross over down-draught duct from the exhaust manifold to the inlet manifold. The rear carburettor has a choke device operated from the dashboard. A Ki-gass pump is however usually found to be indispensable for easy cold starting.

The carburettors rarely give trouble provided the correct combination of jets are used. These, for the information of present-day owners who have no instruction manual, are as follows:

| *Fuel* | *Main Jet* | *Compensating Jet* | *Idling Jet* |
|---|---|---|---|
| Petrol | 145 | 90 | 65/28 |
| Petrol/Benzole | 140 | 90 | 60/28 |
| Benzole | 135 | 90 | 60/27 |

A box containing a full range of spare jets with special carburettor tools was provided with each car. A choice of petrol system was permitted to order, Autovac or air-pressurized petrol tank; for the latter a hand-priming pump is fitted on the dashboard with pressure gauge and release cock. A small air pump is provided at the rear end of the camshaft to maintain pressure whilst running.

Petrol consumption is not quite as staggering as most present-day comments would lead one to believe. Used as a normal touring car a genuine 12 m.p.g. can be relied upon and with deliberately careful driving 14 m.p.g. is possible, but the man who really drives this car to attain high average speeds and uses the blower between the change-ups must be prepared for a consumption of alarming proportions. The *38/250*, one must remember, was designed at a time when petrol was cheap and a few m.p.g. here and there was of absolutely no consequence to those who demanded power and performance.

As a point of interest, there exists in this country one *38/250* fitted with an experimental petrol injection system of carburation, but whilst some improvement was obtained in the power curve little, if any, was found in the consumption.

## Cooling System

The water pump is located under the exhaust side engine portable cover plate. An automatic grease stuffing box is provided with a spring-loaded piston combining an indicator with red and white diagonal sections. This indicator is observed through a peephole window in the cover plate; when red comes into view it is an indication that the grease cup mounted on the floor of the cab requires refilling.

A drain tap is fitted on the pump inlet pipe through which the entire content of the cooling system can be emptied, including the radiator. The fan is fitted at the front end of the overhead camshaft and is provided with a slipping clutch which reduces drive-gear chatter at low revs. This unusual feature, which also has its value in the case of a front end 'prang', was first brought to the writer's attention in a startling manner by Mr. W. E. Morley, a well-known Mercedes specialist, who nonchalantly grabbed the fan in order the better to pick out which erring tappet was causing the noise. Emulation is not recommended, but use the left hand when trying!

The massive vee-pointed radiator mounting the classic Mercedes star pedestal, combining temperature gauge and mascot, is the crowning glory of the *38/250*. It is of true honeycomb section, the core being cast, costing around £50 pre-war. The capacity of the water-system is six gallons, which produces a tendency towards over-cooling. It will be found advisable to blank off about one-third of the radiator in cold weather. The implications of this large capacity are only fully realized when the purchase of anti-freeze solution is made!

Most of the competition type models are adorned with very elaborate stoneguards of striking design. Various badges have been fitted by the works at different times. The earlier model *S* (*36/220*) had only an embossed star (not enamelled) on each side of the radiator header casing. Early *SS* and *SSK* models had a coloured red and black centre badge in addition to the embossed stars, whilst later models have only the coloured centre badge which was altered to blue and gold. Many of the cars exported to the U.S.A. carried a written name scroll attached to the honeycomb of the radiator.

## Electrical System

Bosch equipment is fitted throughout.

Engine firing order is 1, 5, 3, 6, 2, 4.

The ignition system is dual, using coil and magneto; the coil-supplied sparking plugs are on the exhaust side and magneto-supplied plugs on the inlet side. In the event of failure of either means of ignition or derangement of either, the faulty member can be switched off from the dashboard. A marked falling off in performance is noticeable on single source ignition but smoothness and pulling remain satisfactory. Distributor contact points gap: fully open not more than ·016 inch. Although using a dual distributor head mounted on the magneto, the coil spark timing is set slightly in advance of the magneto timing. Advance and retard is manually controlled from the steering wheel boss. When using the supercharger the ignition should be fully advanced. Full advanced ignition takes place at 45° for coil and 40° for magneto before T.D.C. Starter motor, Bosch, type BJG 1·5/12 L11 is on the forward moving armature principle. Starting, by a handle of staggering length, is not so hazardous as would appear to be the case as the compression only allows of one pull up per swing from 9 to 12 o'clock which, on full retard, and with the help of coil ignition plus two shots of Ki-gass when cold, rarely fails. De-compression taps are fitted on each cylinder with spring-loaded valves, but require constant finger pressure, having no positive lock for securing open. They are useful as a quick check on combustion conditions but of no help in starting on the handle.

The recommended sparking plugs for normal touring conditions using petrol only are: Coil, Champion 16; Magneto, Champion 7. For more strenuous work with frequent use of the blower, Champion R3V should be used with the coil, and for flat racing, Champion R1V on both sides. These are the plugs recommended in the instruction manual alongside the equivalent Bosch grading. Electrode gap: ·017 to ·020 inch.

The dynamo, supplying automatic regulated current to the high capacity 12-volt battery, is mounted under the cast aluminium engine cover plate on the offside of the engine and driven in tandem with the magneto and water pump.

Zeiss 10-inch diameter headlamps are fitted using Bilux bulbs. Dimming is operated by pressure on the inner ring mounted on the steering wheel; pressure on the opposite side of this ring operates the electric Bosch horn which also has a duo-tone control switch on the dashboard.

## Miscellaneous Equipment

The dashboard is certainly an enthusiasts delight and is strictly functional. The numerous fittings and gauges comprise the following, with pride of place to a centrally mounted huge revolution counter boldly proclaiming '*Undrehungen in der minute*': a smaller speedometer which really agrees with the r.p.m. and is converted from kilometres to m.p.h. on export models; oil-pressure gauge in kilogrammes per square centimetre, kg./cm.$^2$ being approximately equivalent to 14 lb./square inch; oil and water temperature thermometers, Bosch ignition and lighting switch box, electric clock, pneumatic fuel capacity gauge, reeled self-returning inspection lamp, dual ignition selector switch, dual dashboard lights, Ki-gass pump, air-pressure petrol tank priming pump with pressure test gauge, fuel overflow sight glass, carburettor choke lever, etc., etc.

Other standard fittings comprise dual blade windscreen wipers by Bosch, trafficators on closed models, driving mirror, cigar-lighter, ashtray, bumpers front and rear and a tyre inflating air pump mounted on the gear-box with flexible hose supply line, fitted on left-hand drive cars only. The steering wheel is of very large diameter, well notched on the underside, with an inner ring for dimming and horn operation. Mounted on the central boss plate are two antennae, the left hand for throttle opening setting, the right hand for ignition timing control. Direction of movement is indicated by zig-zag arrows, black for throttle, red for ignition, and the central boss covering plate surmounted with a large red and black Mercedes badge.

An outfit of tools and spare parts was provided in portable cases.

## *SSK MODEL*

Daimler-Benz terminology for the *SSK* is *27/170/225 WO6/17*.

The following description covers the major differences as compared with the long chassis model *SS*.

The suffix *K* is the German word 'Kurz' or short chassis. The shortening consists in a reduction of 1 ft. 5¾ in., resulting in a wheelbase of 9 ft. 8⅛ in. This was effected behind the mid-length cross-member, bringing the rear wheels well forward. In the driving position the elbow can actually rest on the mudguard. The chassis weight was thus reduced to 24 cwt. Most of these chassis were fitted with the stark competition-type body, low cut sides with no doors, and the passenger's seat set slightly behind the driver's. A short stub hand grip is mounted behind the driver for passengers use in case of his ejection in right hand corners.

The standard blower was stepped up to deliver 10 lb./square inch, and with high compression pistons, b.h.p. increased to 225. Over 120 m.p.h. was obtainable within safe revs. Competition models are fitted with an exhaust cut-out slide valve, and tyre size increased to 7·00 on rear wheels. Power to weight ratio is 1 to 17 unblown, and 1 to 13 blown.

This model was designed specifically for competing in the Continental hill-climbs such as Mount Ventoux, Freiburg, Semmering, Kesselberg, Klausen, Monte Carlo, etc., and was attended by continuous success, winning the European Hill Climb Championship in 1930 and 1931. At the 1931 Mount Ventoux Climb, Caracciola established a new record for the hill of 15 minutes 22 seconds, averaging 52·4 m.p.h., and in July, 1930, at Shelsley Walsh, the same driver set up a new 'blown' sports-car record of 46·8 seconds, both records being gained in the *SSK* model.

It certainly proved much superior to the *SS* in cornering on hills and fast road courses, and from 1931 onwards was used exclusively in Grand Prix events, before the new Formula 1 commenced in 1934.

The *SSK* chassis was also fitted with a drophead coupé body to special order; mention of these models has already been made; for example, the ex-Crozier car.

The *SSK* has been aptly described in humorous vein as the largest motor car with the least luggage space.

## *SSKL MODEL*

This is the short chassis *SSK* with a lightened chassis. The suffix *L* is for the German 'Leicht'. This model was the ultimate development of this class or conception of sports-car.

The frame was copiously lightened in no half-hearted manner, even the dumb irons being perforated. The chassis weight was reduced to well under 24 cwt.

The *SSK* engine was highly tuned, embodying a lightened crankshaft, high-lift camshaft with special valves, even higher compression ratio, and fitted with the famous (or infamous) balanced 'elephant' blower boosting at 12 lb./square inch. The b.h.p. delivered was reputed to be close on 300, with a power to weight ratio of 1 to 12.

Many Grand Prix races were won by this car, which reached a speed of 147 m.p.h. on the Avus track, and a grand all-time ultimate for the developed *38/250* engine of 156 m.p.h. when fitted with streamlined body and in the hands of von Brauchitsch, at the same track in 1931, whilst in 1932 the same driver obtained the World Record for two hundred kilometres, averaging 121·6 m.p.h. on the Avus track.

A superb specimen was preserved in the Daimler-Benz Aktiengesellschaft Museum at Stuttgart before World War II dispersal, and is now believed to be in a Dresden Transport History Museum.

The *SSKL* will live in history as the only production sports-car ever to approach the performance of contemporary racing-cars in the pre-World War II era.

## *PERFORMANCE OF THE SS MODEL*

Speeds, based on the maximum safe revolutions of 3200, 6·5 × 20 inch rear tyres, and the 2·5 axle ratio, are theoretically 125 m.p.h., and using the 2·76 ratio, 112 m.p.h.

Speeds in the gears (on 2·76 axle ratio) are: 3rd, 93 m.p.h.; 2nd, 62 m.p.h.; 1st, 35 m.p.h.

Speed at 1000 r.p.m.: 2·5 axle ratio equals 41 m.p.h.; 2·76 axle ratio equals 35 m.p.h.

Power to weight ratio is 1 to 18 unblown and 1 to 15 blown.

An outstanding feature of the performance of this model is its ability to accelerate in top gear from a mere crawl, without snatch or pinking, by judicious use of the ignition control. Advertisement slogans by the manufacturers claimed '10 to 110 m.p.h. in top gear' which proved justifiable in practice. The real joy, however, lies in acceleration through the gears combined with an easy cruising speed of 80 m.p.h. with the engine turning at a (slow) comfortable 2000 r.p.m.

A brief period of flat spot can be detected in the power output between approximately 75 to 85 m.p.h. in top, but with continued throttle opening the acceleration comes in progressively up to peak revs.

Acceleration figures are, from a standing start to 90 m.p.h., 45 seconds; from 40 to 90 m.p.h. in top gear just over 30 seconds; from a standing start to 60 m.p.h. 17·9 seconds.

Brooklands test hill was climbed in bottom gear in 11⅗ seconds.

A Brooklands 120 m.p.h. certificate is held by Zehender driving a stripped *38/250*.

Roadholding is an outstanding attribute. Only in severe circumstances is there any tendency to break away on corners. An empty fuel tank can result in slight tail slip, but under normal loading cornering can be indulged in at high speed with confidence.

## Maintenance and Driving

Dependability is all that could be desired. The *38/250* is a sure starter (and in the coldest weather) with the minimum of fuss. It has a regular slow tick over quite free from oiling-up tendencies; carburation is even, requiring no choke assistance, and the transmission pulls smoothly without snatch even on the highest gear.

No tuning is required, year in year out, provided standard settings are maintained.

The following remarks are offered as points of interest and advice to the owner-driver, many of which, although elementary, are nevertheless important and have been brought to notice by experience of the model.

(*a*) The clutch is not the best component and must be treated with respect: 16 to 18 mm. free play in the pedal should always be present. Never slip the clutch or hold out whilst waiting for traffic lights, etc., and always depress pedal to floor board. It is advisable to have the plates slotted to relieve distortion.

(*b*) The supercharger should not be engaged at low speed nor at near maximum speed. The throttle must be held flat on the floorboard and kept there, slipping of the blower clutch either in or letting out must be avoided, but a momentary slip when engaging has the advantage of reducing the initial shock on the rotors. Ignition should be fully advanced during blowing. Avoid low-gear blowing on wet roads, or else expect to correct the wheelspin slide.

(*c*) Keep the brakes regularly adjusted by the handwheels provided. When relining, extreme care is necessary in bedding to suit the drum, and it must be done in situ. Brakes should be relined when the thickness is less than ·08 inch. The copperized brake drums should never be painted.

(*d*) A fast tick over is usually caused by the foot throttle linkage sticking. To slow, kick the throttle down, allowing it instantly to spring back. Normal tick over is 100 to 150 r.p.m.

(*e*) The sparking-plug cables from the dual distributor head to the magneto fired plugs pass through the cylinder block in one bunch. It is advisable to inspect for oil saturation and to replace worn rubber glands where cables thread through the runway below the plugs. Connexions to distributor head should be very carefully attached with no stray strands.

(*f*) Constantly observe water pump warning window and keep pressure on hand greaser cup.

(*g*) Shock absorbers should be regulated on the hard side.

(*h*) Engine oil should be always topped up to the maximum level of the three-way tap. Never allow to run down to minimum.

(*i*) With air-pressure fuel system, release blow-off tap under dashboard when pressure builds up to 3 lb./square inch.

Safety blow-off valve embodied in the air pump or the filler cap may be blocked. This needs watching with a full tank.

(*j*) Full retard when starting reduces risk of damage to starter motor by the severe high compression kick back.

(*k*) Special solid cylinder head gaskets cannot be used owing to a projecting lip on the cylinder liners.

It is beyond the scope of this appendix to attempt to describe procedure in tackling major maintenance operations such as decarbonization, clutch withdrawal, etc., which require skilled specialist attention. Few present day owner-drivers will possess the heavy tackle necessary or the special tools (for certain operations) which were originally supplied with the car.

Lastly, it should be kept constantly in mind that one is travelling much faster than realized. The change from the everyday run-about to a slow-revving, high chassis car of this type can be very deceptive, particularly when coming up behind slow traffic. It is then that full appreciation is realized of what it takes to stop two tons at velocity *x* without servo or any other assistance!

This illusory effect can best be portrayed in recalling Brooklands, when, after a longish race and approaching the pits, the mechanic was sometimes seen to hop out and go flying head over heels acting under the illusion that the car had slowed to a mere crawl.

## Racing History

A long series of successes were achieved by the *38/250*, the extent of which has never received full appreciation in this country.

These successes of the big six-cylinder Mercedes started with the *36/220* model *S* which came in first, second and third in the German Grand Prix in 1927.

In Great Britain 'Scrap' Thistlethwayte was the first driver to demonstrate the power of the *36/220S* to the British public, and he did this to good effect by achieving the fastest lap of 74·39 m.p.h. in the 1928 Irish T.T. The next year, May, 1929, he won the *Daily Dispatch* Trophy at Southport in the '100' using the same car.

With the advent of the *38/250*, it will be simpler to deal consecutively year by year over the period of the formule libre then in force.

### 1929

German Grand Prix. 3rd (Momberger).

Irish T.T. 1st (Caracciola) fastest lap 77·81 m.p.h. in Class B. Average speed 72·8 m.p.h. Defeated team of three 'blower' 4½-litre Bentleys.

Monaco Grand Prix. 3rd (Caracciola) *SSK*.

Monza Grand Prix. 3rd (Momberger). 1st in first heat winning from an eight-cylinder Maserati.

Irish Grand Prix. Fastest lap was by Thistlethwayte, 83·8 m.p.h. Retired with blown gasket.

1930

Mille Miglia. 1st in the over 6-litre Class (Caracciola and Werner) *SSK*. 6th in General Classification.
Irish T.T. Highest average speed of 71·53 m.p.h. was by Sir Malcolm Campbell driving the famous GP. 10.
Fastest lap of 77·2 m.p.h. was by Earl Howe driving the 1929 winning car acquired from Caracciola, UW. 302.
Irish Grand Prix. 1st (Caracciola) *SSK*. Lap record of 91·3 m.p.h. and averaged 85·88 attaining 137 m.p.h. beating Bentley team.
3rd (Earl Howe) *SS* 1929 Irish T.T. winning car.
Hill Climb Championship of Europe (*SSK*) 1st.

Before proceeding, mention should be made of the widely held conception that an intense rivalry existed between the official Bentley and Mercedes teams, whereas in actual fact they met in only three international events, namely the 1929 Irish T.T., 1930 Irish Grand Prix and the 1930 Le Mans race. Of these Mercedes won the first two races and Bentley the third. Over-confidence in only entering one car at Le Mans against six Bentley entries cost Mercedes their one and only failure in international competition with the Bentley marque.

1931

Avus. 1st (Caracciola) *SSKL*. Average speed 119 m.p.h. over 183 miles, maximum speed 147 m.p.h.
3rd (von Brauchitsch) *SSKL*. Average speed 115·39 m.p.h.
German Grand Prix. 1st (Caracciola) *SSKL*.
Belgian 24-hour Race. 1st (Prince Djordjadze and Zehender) *SSK*.
Circuit of Lwow. 1st (Stuck) *SSKL*.
Eifel Race. 1st (Caracciola) *SSKL*.
3rd (von Brauchitsch) *SSKL*.
Mille Miglia. 1st (Caracciola and Sebastian) *SSKL*. 1001 miles in 16 hours 10 minutes. Record average of 70 m.p.h.
Argentine National Grand Prix. 1st (Zatuszek) *SSK*.
Autumn Prize Argentine. 1st (Zatuszek) *SSK*.
Geneva Grand Prix. 3rd (Caflisch) *S*.
Le Mans. 2nd (Stoffel and Ivanowsky) *SSK*. Lap record 87·27 m.p.h.
Czechoslovak Grand Prix. 2nd (Stuck) *SSKL*.
Irish Grand Prix. 5th (Earl Howe) *SS*. Lap record 91·8 m.p.h., beating Caracciola's 1930 lap record of 91·3 m.p.h.
Hill Climb Championship of Europe. 1st (Caracciola) 5 wins.

1932

Avus. 1st (von Brauchitsch) *SSKL*. Achieved World Record

for 200 Kilometres averaging 121·6 m.p.h. with a maximum speed of 156 m.p.h.

Czechoslovak Grand Prix. 3rd (von Brauchitsch) *SSKL*.

Monte Carlo Hill Climb. Record for the Hill of 2 minutes $59\frac{2}{5}$ seconds by Prince Djordjadze driving an *SSK*.

Returning to appearances of the model in this country we find that between 1929 and 1932 a few *38/250*s frequently appeared at Brooklands but although always spectacular they did not have the consistency in private hands of the works-tuned cars on the Continent.

Amongst the more interesting of Brooklands meetings entries were as follows:

1930

Whitsun B.A.R.C. Mountain Speed Handicap won by Sir Malcolm Campbell driving an *SS* model at 64·8 m.p.h.

Autumn B.A.R.C. Earl Howe lapped at 118·3 m.p.h. in the ex-Caracciola T.T. car.

September. Mountain Speed Handicap. Sir Malcolm Campbell lapped at 71.39 m.p.h. whilst Earl Howe's best lap was 65·81 m.p.h.

1931

Whitsun B.A.R.C. 2nd Mountain Speed Handicap, Sir Malcolm Campbell broke the lap record at 73·86 m.p.h., finishing 3rd.

Autumn B.A.R.C. 2nd Mountain Speed Handicap. Campbell's best lap was 72·13 m.p.h., finishing 2nd.

October. 120 m.p.h. Badge Certificate won by Zehender.

1932

J.C.C. 1000 Mile Race. Staniland lapped at 93 and 97 m.p.h. despite having blown up his engine in practice and rebuilding.

Sir Malcolm Campbell on an *SS* (GP. 10) threw a blazing tyre.

In many of the lesser races held at Brooklands meetings private owners often had the misfortune to experience failure due to either blowing the cylinder head gasket or to supercharger faults. It must be admitted that the *38/250* has carried in the enthusiast's mind these labels to this day, and in addition to being voracious consumers of tyres due to the weight combined with a high b.h.p. thrust, the initial cost debarred the acquisition of such a car, except by the very wealthy. These, then, are the chief reasons why the *38/250* did not appear to be a popular choice of the leading drivers of those days despite their unassailable international reputation.

The record of motor sport history of the *38/250* will not be complete without reference to its appearances at British hill-climbs. In September, 1929, the first appearance was made at Shelsley Walsh when Earl Howe, driving the ex-Caracciola T.T. car registered 47·6 seconds, which was very creditable on the long-chassis model. At this meeting Thistlethwayte also entered an *SS* and recorded 49·6 seconds.

In July, 1930, Caracciola set up a new sports-car record for Shelsley of 46·84 seconds, and at the same meeting Jack Dunfee driving the Hon. Dorothy Paget's car went up in 50·4 seconds. In 1931 Earl Howe recorded 46·8 seconds, improving this in 1934 to 46·2 seconds, which remains the best time up Shelsley by a *38/250* Mercedes.

It will be of interest to Bentley enthusiasts to compare with the foregoing, Forrest Lycett's best time at Shelsley in the famous 8-litre, of 44·08 seconds, which without the kick from a big supercharger is a most impressive feat of sheer driving skill.

In these present times of vintage car enthusiasm a few notable examples of the *38/250* can still be seen in action. The best known of these has been Gerry Crozier's immaculate black drophead coupé on the *SSK* chassis, which contributed elegance to our beloved Prescott meetings. A car always impeccably handled, but, alas, to be seen no more on this side of the Atlantic.

Earl Howe's original *36/220*, now owned for many years by H. E. Rohll, with its beautiful sleek maroon 2-seater body and torpedo running boards, is also a well known competitor.

Another present day entrant, which is considered to be the only authentic German team-car in this country, is N. Powell's silver 2-seater *SSK* with left-hand drive. Its exact racing history is obscure, but is reputed to be one of the ex-Caracciola cars used in Continental events and first brought to this country in 1935, when it was owned by that great Mercedes enthusiast D. Conan Doyle, and later by Sir R. Gunther.

Other examples include a *38/250*, driven by D. Storr in the 1951 Bentley Drivers Club Silverstone Invitation Race, coming in 3rd behind the 8-litre Barnato Hassan and Tony Hartridge's *Speed Six*.

Brighton Speed Trial spectators will be familiar with Mrs. Lee Kennard's white competition-bodied 2-seater on the *SS* chassis. This car was tuned by the late R. Arbuthnot and has high-compression pistons and the 2·5 axle ratio. It is probably the most powerful sports-car to be seen handled by a lady driver in post war meetings, and was previously owned by R. H. Johnson.

In addition to Norman Powell's *SSK*, there are only two other examples remaining in Great Britain, namely, the well-known blue car GN. 66 (ex-Roy Lewis) now owned by Lord O'Neill and the red car GC. 96 (ex-J. Coates) now owned by G. E. Milligen.

The ex-Dorothy Paget tourer *SS* also still remains in Great Britain.

Of the famous examples well known in pre-war days only the maroon 2-seater *SS* ex-Roy Eccles remains untraced.

The famous ex-Sir Malcolm Campbell white *SS* 4-seater, GP. 10, is now in Canada.

## *SUMMARY*

The *38/250* is now becoming a rare specimen of the high-performance vintage sports-car. It is almost certain that a few were scrapped during the war, which partially accounts for their non re-appearance in the numbers we were accustomed to seeing. Let us rather hope that some are still stored away awaiting that liberation which only the hands of enthusiasts can bring about.

Strangely enough, there have been no reports from tourists nor correspondents of any examples having been seen on the Continent. It is ironic to contemplate that the country of origin must have been responsible for their extinction on the Continent as scrap metal.

The following table lists chassis and engine numbers of the total production of the models *36/220S*, *38/250SS* and *SSK*, giving the total numbers produced of each model. (With acknowledgment to Daimler-Benz A.G. Historical Archives Division.)

*Model 36/220S (26/120/180PS)*

| *Year* | *Quantity* | *Chassis Nos.* | *Engine Nos.* |
|---|---|---|---|
| 1927 | 80 | 35201–35225, 35251–35255, 35306–35355 | 60401–60425, 60485–60489, 66501–66550, |
| 1928 | 75 | 35901–35925, 35936–35985 | 68651–68675, 71801–71825, 72151–72175 |

Total 155, of which five were modified to *SS* and one to *SSK* specification. A remaining *S* total production of 149 cars.

*Model 38/250SS (27/140/200PS and 27/160/200PS)*

| *Year* | *Quantity* | *Chassis Nos.* | *Engine Nos.* |
|---|---|---|---|
| 1928 | 40 | 36201–36240 | 72311–72350 |
| 1929 | 62 | 36037–36046, 36261–36275, 36336–36365 | 76101–76110, 77631–77645, 78751–78780 |

Total 102, which was increased by five modified *S* models and seven modified *SSK* models, a remaining *SS* total production of 114 cars.

*Model 38/250SSK (27/170/225PS)*

| *Year* | *Quantity* | *Chassis Nos.* | *Engine Nos.* |
|---|---|---|---|
| 1928 | 11 | 36241–36250, 36083 | 72351–72360, 72215, |
| 1929 | 25 | 35986–35990, 36047–36056, 36251–36260 | 72181–72185, 76111–76120, 77621–77630 |
| 1931 | 1 | 36393 | 86031 |

Total 37, of which seven were modified to *SS* plus one *S* model modified to *SSK*, giving a total *SSK* production of 31 cars.

The writer has kept a record of all models noted to be in existence at the present time, the numbers being as follows:

| *Country* | *S 36/220* | *SS 38/250* | *SSK* |
|---|---|---|---|
| Great Britain | 29 | 25 | 3 |
| U.S.A. | 15 | 10 | 10 |
| Canada | — | 2 | — |
| Australia | — | 1 | — |
| South America | — | 2 | 1 |

Included in the above are three *S* models and six *SS* fitted with Diesel engines in this country. Only one genuine *SSKL* model is in existence and is reputed to be in a Dresden museum.

The above figures represent a mere residue of the total production, but it is considered that the numbers quoted for Great Britain are close to the ultimate. Numerous others probably exist in the U.S.A.

today, a supposition based on reports received from past owners.

## *CONCLUSION*

This chapter has been confined to the vintage models which above all others have given colour to the saga of Mercedes. Greater heights of fame were to be achieved later with the scintillating successes of the *pur sang* Grand Prix racing-cars; sleeker and more luxurious supercharged Mercedes production models took the limelight of the World's Salons, but to the true motor sportsman of those days nothing can ever take the place or attain the appeal of those full-blooded deep-throated super-sports supercharged *38/250*s.

At the 1939 Berlin Motor Show a new model was displayed called the *580K*, which owing to the war never went into production. A maximum speed of 140 m.p.h. was claimed, and as Mercedes have always been conservative in published performance figures this would have been the world's fastest pre-war production car.

In the post-World War II years, a resurgence of that genius of Gottlieb Daimler and Karl Benz for automobile design has been re-born on the drawing boards at Stuttgart-Untertürkheim. New models have appeared bearing the indefinable stamp of pedigree; with each new revelation the pulse beats faster; triumphs of the new Grand Prix cars once more stir the imagination — the three pointed star is in the ascendancy. The toast of International Motor Sport, as it was in the beginning, continues to be '*Hoch die Mercedes*'.

## APPENDIX VI

## BENZ CARS 1885 to 1926

(*Based on information kindly supplied by the Daimler-Benz Company*)

| *H.P.* (*German rating*) | *Number of cylinders* | *Details* | *Manufactured* |
|---|---|---|---|
| $\frac{3}{4}$ | 1 | 3-wheeler | 1885 |
| $1\frac{1}{2}$ | 1 | 3-wheeler | 1886–1887 |
| 2 | 1 | 3-wheeler. (With an occasional extra seat) | 1887–1888 |
| $3\frac{1}{2}$–6 | 1 | '*Vis-a-Vis*'. 4-wheeler. (With passengers facing the driver) | 1893–1899 |
| 3–6 | 1 | '*Victoria*' | 1893–1898 |
| $1\frac{1}{2}$, $2\frac{1}{2}$, 3 | 1 | '*Velo*' | 1893–1898 |
| 5 | 1 | '*Landau*' | 1894–1899 |
| 5 | 1 | '*Phaeton*'. 8-seater shooting brake, enclosed body, coupé | 1895 |
| $2\frac{1}{2}$–3 | 1 and 2 | '*Velo Comfortable*' | 1896–1898 |
| 5 and 9 | 2 | '*Dos-a-Dos*'. (Dog-cart) | 1897–1899 |
| 9 and 14 | 2 | '*Brake*'. For 8 and 12 people | 1897–1899 |
| 5 and 10 | 1 | '*Duc*'. 2-seater | 1898–1900 |
| 4, 5 and 9 | 1 and 2 | '*Ideal*'. 2-seater | 1898–1902 |
| 9 | 2 | '*Mylord*'. Coupê with folding head | 1899 |
| 10 | 2 | '*Spider*'. 2 seats with double dickey<br>'*Tonneau*'. 2 seats with single dickey | 1899–1901 |

| *H.P.* (*German rating*) | *Number of cylinders* | *Details* | *Manu- factured* |
|---|---|---|---|
| | | '*Phaeton*' | |
| 16 | 2 | Racing-car | 1899–1901 |
| 6 | 1 | '*Elegant-Tonneau*'. With horizontal engine | 1900–1902 |
| 15 and 20 | 2 | '*Phaeton-Tonneau*' | 1901–1902 |
| 8/10 | 2 | *'*Phaeton-Tonneau*' | 1902–1903 |
| 10/12 | 2 | *'*Phaeton-Tonneau*' | 1902–1903 |
| 12/14 | 2 | *'*Phaeton-Tonneau*'. (Open and closed) | 1902–1906 |
| 14/18 | 4 | '*Phaeton-Tonneau*'. (Open and closed) | 1903–1906 |
| 60 | 4 | Racing-car | 1903–1908 |
| 16/20 | 4 | '*Phaeton*'. Limousine | 1904 |
| 40 | 4 | '*Phaeton*'. Limousine. (Open and closed.) Chain-drive | 1905–1907 |
| 18/28 | 4 | '*Phaeton*'. Limousine. (Open and closed.) Live axle | 1905–1908 |
| 28/50 | 4 | '*Phaeton*'. Limousine. (Open and closed.) Chain-drive | 1906–1907 |
| 24/40 | 4 | '*Phaeton*'. Limousine. (Open and closed.) Chain-drive | 1906–1909 |
| 50 | 4 | Sports- and racing-car. Chain-drive | 1907–1909 |
| 70 | 4 | Racing-car. Chain-drive | 1907 |
| 80 | 4 | Racing-car. Chain-drive | 1907 |
| 120 | 4 | Racing-car. Chain-drive | 1908 |
| 25/35 | 4 | Sports-car. Live axle | 1908 |
| 50/80 | 4 | Sports-car. Chain-drive | 1908 |
| 75/105 | 4 | Sports-car. Chain-drive | 1908 |
| 35/60 | 4 | Open and closed. Chain-drive | 1908–1910 |
| 150 | 4 | Racing-car. Chain-drive | 1908–1912 |
| 10/18 | 4 | Open and closed. Live axle | 1908–1912 |
| 10/20 | 4 | Open and closed. Live axle | 1908–1912 |
| 20/35 | 4 | Sports-car and open and closed. Live axle | 1909–1911 |
| 40/70 | 4 | Sports-car. Chain-drive | 1909 |
| 75/110 | 4 | Racing-car. Chain-drive | 1909 |
| 200 | 4 | World's record car. ('*Blitzen*' Benz). Chain-drive | 1909–1913 |
| 22/60 | 4 | Sports-car. Live axle | 1910 |
| 28/80 | 4 | Sports-car. Live axle | 1910 |
| 14/30 | 4 | Open and closed sports-car. Droshky (public cab in Germany) | 1910–1920 |
| 25/45 | 4 | Open and closed. Live axle | 1910 |
| 29/60 | 4 | Open and closed. Live axle | 1910–1912 |
| 8/18 | 4 | Open and closed. Live axle | 1911 |
| 25/55 | 4 | Open and closed. Live axle | 1912 |
| 10/30 | 4 | Open and closed sports-car. Live axle | 1912–1925 |
| 10/30 | 4 | Streamlined racing-car with engine at rear: predecessor of the '*Teardrop*' Benz | 1912–1925 |
| 16/35 | 4 | Open and closed. Live axle | 1912 |
| 8/20 | 4 | Open and closed. Live axle | 1912–1920 |
| 16/40 | 4 | Sports-car. Live axle | 1912 |
| 39/100 | 4 | Open and closed. Live axle | 1912 |
| 33/75 | 4 | Open and closed. Live axle | 1912 |
| 28/100 | 4 | Sports-car. Chain-drive | 1912 |

* These three models were the first to have a vertical engine in front.

| *H.P.* (*German rating*) | *Number of Cylinders* | *Type* | *Manu-factured* |
|---|---|---|---|
| 12/30 | 4 | Open and closed. Live axle | 1913–1915 |
| 16/50 | 4 | Sports-car. Live axle | 1913 |
| 82/200 | 4 | Sports-car. Chain-drive | 1913 |
| 21/50 | 4 | Open and closed. Live axle | 1914 |
| 18/45 | 4 | Open and closed. Live axle | 1914–1921 |
| 25/65 | 4 | Open and closed. Live axle | 1915 |
| 27/70 | 4 | Open and closed. Live axle | 1918–1921 |
| 6/18 | 4 | Sports-car. Live axle Racing-car | 1918–1921 |
| 16/50 | 6 | Open and closed. Live axle. Sports-car | 1921–1926 |
| 11/40 | 6 | Open and closed. Live axle | 1923–1925 |
| 2-litre | 6 | '*Teardrop*' Benz: rear-engined racing-car. Live axle | 1925–1926 |

## APPENDIX VII

# CANSTATT-DAIMLER CARS

(*Based on information kindly supplied by the Daimler-Benz Company*)

| *H.P.* (*German rating*) | *Number of cylinders* | *Details* | *Manu-factured* |
|---|---|---|---|
| 1-2 | 1 | Motor-cycle | 1885 |
| 1½ | 1 | First motor-car | 1886 |
| 2 | 2 (V) | Fitted with metal wheels | 1889 |
| 2 | 2 | Chain-drive | 1892-1894 |
| 4-6 | 2 | Belt-drive. Types of body: '*Phaeton*', '*Victoria*', '*Laundalet*' | 1892-1898 |
| 4-9 | 2-4 | Chain-drive. '*Victoria*', '*Phaeton*', '*Charrette*', brake. Fitted with Phoenix engine | 1896-1899 |
| 28 | 4 | Racing-car with Phoenix engine | 1899-1900 |
| 4 | 2 | PD Car | 1900 |

From 1901, until the fusion with Benz et Cie. in 1926, all cars made by Daimler Motoren-Gesellschaft were called 'Mercedes'.

# APPENDIX VIII

## MERCEDES AND MERCEDES-BENZ CARS 1900–1979

A: 1900–1939

(*These details are based on the list of cars manufactured given in* Mercedes-Konstruktionen in fünf Jahrzehnten, *published by Daimler-Benz in 1951. The disparity between this record and details given in the text is due mainly to the fact that the latter is culled from the contemporary English motor press and refers to models available on the English market. A number of cars produced were sold only in Germany and on the continent of Europe. The difference between German and English horse-power ratings is, of course, another reason for variation. The details given below have been checked by Daimler-Benz and passed as correct to the best of their current knowledge.*)

| *H.P. (German rating)* | *Number of Cylinders* | *Type* | *Manu-factured* |
|---|---|---|---|
| WILHELM MAYBACH REGIME | | | |
| 30/35 | 4 | Racing and touring | 1900–1901 |
| 8/11; 12/16; 18/22; 28/32 | 4 | Touring | 1902–1903 |
| 18/22; 35/40; 40/45 | 4 | Touring | 1903 |
| 60; 90 | 4 | Racing | 1903 |
| 80 | 4 | Racing | 1904 |
| 10/20; 21/35. (Live axles) | 4 | Touring | 1905 |
| 26/45; 31/55; 36/65. (Chain-drive) | 4 | Touring | 1905 |
| 100 | 4 | Racing | 1905 |
| 37/70; 39/80 | 6 | Touring | 1906 |
| 120 | 6 | Racing | 1906 |
| 70 | 4 | Touring | 1907 |
| 75 | 6 | Touring | 1907 |
| PAUL DAIMLER REGIME | | | |
| 8/18; 10/20; 14/30; 22/40; 28/60. (All with live axles and poppet valves) | 4 | Touring | 1907–1913 |
| 130 | 4 | Grand Prix racing | 1908 |
| 10/30; 16/40; 16/45. (All with live axles and sleeve valves) | 4 | Touring | 1910–1913 |
| 22/50; 28/60; 38/70; 37/90 (chain-drive) | 4 | Touring | 1910–1913 |
| 4·5 litres; 115 | 4 | Grand Prix racing | 1914 |
| 28/95 | 6 | High-efficiency touring | 1914–1923 |
| 16/50. (Sleeve-valve engine and live axle. A development of the Knight engine —16/45 h.p.—of 1911–12) | 4 | Touring | 1916 |
| 2·6 litres; 10/35. (Live axle) | 4 | Touring | 1919 |
| 1·5 litres; 6/25/40. (Production model with live axle and supercharger) | 4 | | 1921–1922 |
| 2·6 litres; 10/40/65. (Production model with live axle and supercharger) | 4 | | 1921–1922 |

| H.P. (German rating) | Number of Cylinders | Type | Manu- factured |
|---|---|---|---|
| 2 litres; 125. (With super- charger) | 4 | Racing | 1921–1922 |
| FERDINAND PORSCHE REGIME | | | |
| 2 litres; 130/150 with super- charger | 8 | Racing | 1923 |
| 4 litres; 15/70/100 with supercharger | 6 | Touring | 1924 |
| 6 litres; 24/100/140 with supercharger. (This car was fitted with an engine of 6·5 litres in 1929) | 6 | Touring | 1924 |
| 2 litres; 8/38 | 6 | *200 Stuttgart* | 1926 |
| 3·1 litres; 12/55 | 6 | *Mannheim* | 1926 |
| Racing-car in accordance with Paul Daimler's de- sign of 1914 but fitted with supercharger | | | 1927 |
| 6·2 litres; 24/110/160. (Sports-car with super- charger but without the shortened chassis and a slightly larger bore, similar to the model 24/100/140 h.p.) | 6 | *K* | 1927 |
| 6·8 litres; 26/120/180. (Sports-car with super- charger) | 6 | *S* | 1927 |
| 7·1 litres; 170/225. (Touring models. A development of the 6·8 litre car of 1927) | 6 | *SS* and *SSK* | 1928 |
| 3·5 litres; 14/70 | 6 | *Mannheim 350* | 1928 |
| 2·6 litres; 10/50. (A further development of the 2- litre 8/38 h.p. model of 1926) | 6 | *Stuttgart 260* | 1928 |
| 4·6 litres; 18/80 | 8 | *Nürburg 460* | 1928 |
| HANS NIBEL REGIME | | | |
| 5 litres; 100. (Developed from the 4·6 litre '*Nür- burg 460*' of Porsche) | 8 | *Nürburg 500* | 1929 |
| 3·7 litres; 75 | 6 | *Mannheim 370* | 1929 |
| 7·7 litres; 150/200. (The *Grosser Mercedes.*) With or without supercharger | 8 | | 1930 |
| 3·7 litres; 75 | 6 | *Mannheim Sports 370S* | 1930 |
| 7·1 litres; 170/225. With supercharger. (A further development of the *SS* and *SSK* types) | 6 | *SSKL* | 1931 |
| 1·7 litres; 7/32 | 6 | *170* | 1931 |

| *H.P.* (*German rating*) | *Number of Cylinders* | *Type* | *Manu factured* |
|---|---|---|---|
| 2 litres; 40. (This was a development of the *170* of the previous year) | 6 | *200 Short* | 1932 |
| 2 litres; 40. (Also a development of the *170* of 1931) | 6 | *200 Long* | 1932 |
| 3·8 litres; 15/90/140. Sports-car with supercharger. (This was the first vehicle with I.F.S. and front spiral springing) | 8 | *380* | 1932 |
| 5 litres; 100/160. Sports-car with supercharger. (A development of the *380* of the previous year) | 8 | *500K* | 1933 |
| 2·9 litres; 68. (Later 3·2 and 3·4 litres under Sailer) | 6 | *290 Short* | 1933 |
| 1·3 litres; 26. (First Mercedes with engine at the rear) | 4 | *130* | 1934 |
| 1·7 litres; 38. (First car with an X-formed oval tubular frame) | 4 | *170V* | 1934 |
| 1·7 litres; 38. (Engine at the rear) | 4 | *170H* | 1934 |
| 2·9 litres; 68 | 6 | *290 Long* | 1934 |
| 3·3 litres (1935, 3·6 and 1937, 4 litres); 280. (A racing-car in accordance with the 750 kg Grand Prix formula for 1934–1937) | 8 | Racing | 1934 |
| 1·5 litres; 55. (Rear-engined model) | 4 | *150* | 1934 |
| MAX SAILER REGIME | | | |
| 2·6 litres; 45. (With Diesel engine) | 4 | *260D* | 1935 |
| 4 to 5·6 litres; 600 | 8 | Racing | 1935–1937 |
| 2·3 litres; 55. The *W143* | 6 | *230* | 1936 |
| 3·2 litres; 78. (This car was developed from the 2·9-litre model of 1932, and in 1938 was developed further into the 3·4 litre) | 6 | *320* | 1936 |
| 5·6 litres. (Record-breaking type) | 12 | | 1936 |
| 5·4 litres; 115/180. With supercharger. (This car was a development from the *500K* of 1933) | 8 | *540K* | 1937 |
| 7·7 litres; 155/230. With supercharger and oval tubular frame | 8 | The *Grosser Mercedes* | 1937 |
| 3 litres. (Racing-car in accordance with the Grand Prix formula for 1938 and 1939) | 12 Vee | Racing | 1937 |

| *H.P.* (*German rating*) | *Number of Cylinders* | *Type* | *Manu-factured* |
|---|---|---|---|
| 2·3 litres; 55. (This was a development of the *W143* of 1936, with a different chassis, and first fitted with an all-steel body) | 6 | *230* | 1938 |
| 1·5 litres. With two-stage supercharger | 8 Vee | Racing | 1939 |
| B: 1946–1965 | | | |
| 38 | 4 | *170V* (Resumed) | 1946 |
| 52 | 4 | *170S* | 1949 |
| 38 | 4 | *170D* | 1949 |
| 45 | 4 | *170Va* | 1950 |
| 40 | 4 | *170Da* | 1950 |
| 80 | 6 | *220* | 1951 |
| 115 | 6 | *300* | 1951 |
| 150 | 6 | *300S* | 1952 |
| 175 | 6 | *300SL*, carburettor | 1952 |
| 45 | 4 | *170Vb* | 1952 |
| 40 | 4 | *170Db* and *170DS* | 1952 |
| 52 | 4 | *170Sb* | 1952 |
| 45 | 4 | *170SV* | 1953 |
| 40 | 4 | *170SD* | 1953 |
| 52 | 4 | *180*, side valve | 1953 |
| 40 | 4 | *180D* | 1953 |
| 85 | 6 | *220a* | 1954 |
| 125 | 6 | *300a* and *b* | 1954 |
| 215 | 6 | *300SL*, fuel injection | 1954 |
| 300 | 8 | *300SLR*, sports racing car, fuel injection | 1954 |
| 280 | 8 | 2·5 litre formula car, fuel injection | 1954 |
| 105 | 4 | *190SL* sports car | 1955 |
| 125 | 6 | *300c*, automatic | 1955 |
| 175 | 6 | *300Sc*, fuel injection | 1955 |
| 75 | 4 | *190* | 1956 |
| 85 | 6 | *219* | 1956 |
| 100 | 6 | *220S* | 1956 |
| 65 | 4 | *180a*, overhead camshaft | 1957 |
| 160 | 6 | *300d*, mechanical and automatic | 1957 |
| 215 | 6 | *300SL* roadster, fuel injection | 1957 |
| 50 | 4 | *190D* | 1958 |
| 115 | 6 | *220SE*, fuel injection | 1958 |
| 68 | 4 | *180b* | 1959 |
| 43 | 4 | *180Db* | 1959 |
| 80 | 4 | *190b* | 1959 |
| 50 | 4 | *190Db* | 1959 |
| 95 | 6 | *220b* | 1959 |
| 110 | 6 | *220Sb* | 1959 |
| 120 | 6 | *220SEb*, fuel injection | 1959 |
| 68 | 4 | *180c* | 1961 |

| *H.P.* (*German rating*) | *Number of Cylinders* | *Type* | *Manu-factured* |
|---|---|---|---|
| 48 | 4 | *180Dc* | 1961 |
| 80 | 4 | *190c* | 1961 |
| 55 | 4 | *190Dc* | 1961 |
| 120 | 6 | *220SEb/c*, fuel injection | 1961 |
| 160 | 6 | *300SE*, fuel injection | 1961 |
| 160 | 6 | *300SE* (long wheelbase), fuel injection | 1963 |
| 150 | 6 | *230SL*, fuel injection, sports | 1963 |
| 250 | 8 | *600*, fuel injection, V8 | 1963 |
| 250 | 8 | *600* Pullman, fuel injection, V8 | 1963 |
| 95 | 4 | *200* | 1965 |
| 55 | 4 | *200D* | 1965 |
| 105 | 6 | *230* | 1965 |
| 120 | 6 | *230S* | 1965 |
| 130 | 6 | *250S* | 1965 |
| 150 | 6 | *250SE*, petrol injection | 1965 |
| 170 | 6 | *300SEb*, petrol injection | 1965 |
| 170 | 6 | *300SEL*, petrol injection | 1965 |
| C: 1967–1978 | | | |
| 150 | 6 | *250SL* | 1967 |
| 55 | 4 | *200D* | 1968 |
| 60 | 4 | *220D* | 1968 |
| 95 | 4 | *200* | 1968 |
| 105 | 4 | *220* | 1968 |
| 120 | 6 | *230* | 1968 |
| 130 | 6 | *250* | 1968 |
| 140 | 6 | *280S* | 1968 |
| 160 | 6 | *280SE*, petrol injection | 1968 |
| 160 | 6 | *280SE* convertible and coupé, petrol injection | 1968 |
| 170 | 6 | *280SL*, petrol injection | 1968 |
| 250 | V8 | *300SEL* 6·3, petrol injection | 1968 |
| 130 | 6 | *250C* coupé | 1968 |
| 150 | 6 | *250CE* coupé, petrol injection | 1968 |
| 170 | 6 | *280SEL*, petrol injection | 1968 |
| 200 | V8 | *280SEL* 3·5, convertible and coupé, petrol injection | 1969 |
| 200 | V8 | *300SEL* 3·5, petrol injection | 1969 |
| 200 | V8 | *280SE/SEL* 3·5, petrol injection | 1970 |

| *H.P. (German rating)* | *Number of Cylinders* | *Type* | *Manu-factured* |
|---|---|---|---|
| 200 | V8 | *350SL*, petrol injection | 1971 |
| 200 | V8 | *350SLC* coupé, petrol injection | 1971 |
| 160 | 6 | *280* | 1972 |
| 185 | 6 | *280E*, petrol injection | 1972 |
| 160 | 6 | *280C* coupé | 1972 |
| 185 | 6 | *280CE* coupé, petrol injection | 1972 |
| 160 | 6 | *280S* | 1972 |
| 185 | 6 | *280SE*, petrol injection | 1972 |
| 200 | V8 | *350SE*, petrol injection | 1972 |
| 225 | V8 | *450SE*, petrol injection | 1974 |
| 225 | V8 | *450SEL*, petrol injection | 1974 |
| 225 | V8 | *450SLC* coupé, petrol injection | 1974 |
| 225 | V8 | *450SL*, petrol injection | 1974 |
| 286 | V8 | *450SEL* 6·9, petrol injection | 1975 |
| 55 | 4 | *200D* | 1976 |
| 65 | 4 | *240D* | 1976 |
| 80 | 5 | *300D* | 1976 |
| 94 | 4 | *200* | 1976 |
| 109 | 4 | *230* | 1976 |
| 129 | 6 | *250* | 1976 |
| 185 | 6 | *280E*, petrol injection | 1976 |
| 109 | 4 | *230C* coupé | 1977 |
| 185 | 6 | *280CE*, coupé, petrol injection | 1977 |
| 109 | 4 | *230T* estate | 1978 |
| 65 | 4 | *240TD* estate | 1978 |
| 80 | 5 | *300TD* estate | 1978 |
| 185 | 6 | *280TE* estate, petrol injection | 1978 |

# APPENDIX IX

## SOME OF THE MAJOR SUCCESSES ACHIEVED BY CANNSTATT-DAIMLER, PHOENIX-DAIMLER, BENZ, MERCEDES AND MERCEDES-BENZ CARS FROM 1894

When the make of a car is other than one of the above, the engine used was either a Daimler or one manufactured under the Daimler patents.

(*The authority for the information given, covering the period 1894 to 1939, is* Die Renngeschichte der Daimler-Benz A.G., *published by the Daimler-Benz Company during the late war. This book is encyclopædic in character and a mine of information. Very few copies exist, as almost the entire stock was destroyed through bombing.*)

Abbreviations

Cannstatt-Daimler . . . . C-D
Phoenix-Daimler . . . . P-D
Benz . . . . . . . B
Peugeot . . . . . . Pe
Mercedes . . . . . . M
Mercedes-Benz . . . . . M-B
Panhard . . . . . . Pa

| *Date* | *Event* | *Car* | *Place* | *Drivers* | *Distance* | *Time Hrs :mins :secs* | *Speed k.p.h.* |
|---|---|---|---|---|---|---|---|
| 1894 July 22 | Paris-Rouen (Reliability trial) | Pe | 2 | Kreutler and Clément | 126 km | | |
| | | Pe | 3 | Lemaître and Giffard | | | |
| | | Pa | 4 | Panhard | | | |
| 1895 June 11–14 | Paris-Bordeaux-Paris | Pa | 1 | Levassor | 1192 km | 48:47 | 24·4 |
| | | Pe | 2 | Koecklin | | 54:35 | 21·8 |
| | | Pe | 3 | Rigoulot | | 59:48 | 19·9 |
| 1896 Sept 24 –Oct 3 | Paris-Marseilles-Paris | Pa (8 h.p., four cylinder) | 1 | Mayade | 1728 km | 67:42:58 | 25·2 |
| | | Pa (two cylinder) | 2 | d'Hostingue | | 68:11:05 | 24·6 |
| | | Pa (two cylinder) | 3 | de Knyff | | 71:23:22 | 23·9 |

| *Date* | *Event* | *Car* | *Place* | *Drivers* | *Distance* | *Time Hrs :mins :secs* | *Speed k.p.h.* |
|---|---|---|---|---|---|---|---|
| 1898 May 11–12 | Paris-Bordeaux | Pa | 1 | de Knyff | 573 km | 15:15:44 | 37·6 |
| May 25–27 | Berlin-Leipzig-Berlin | C-D (7½ h.p.) | 1 | Greiner | 387 km | 15:57:30 | 24·3 |
| July 15–17 | Paris-Amsterdam-Paris | Pa (Phoenix) | 1 | Charron | 1500 km (approx.) | 32:44:34 | 44·4 |
| | | Pa | 2 | Girardot | | 33:25:19 | 42·6 |
| 1899 May 24 | Paris-Bordeaux | Pa (Phoenix) | 1 | Charron | 565 km | 11:43:20 | 48·2 |
| | | Pa | 2 | de Knyff | | | |
| | | Pa | 3 | Girardot | | | |
| July 16–24 | Tour de France | Pa | 1 | de Knyff | 2300 km | 44:43:39·2 | 51·3 |
| | | Pa | 2 | Girardot | | | |
| | | Pa | 3 | Comte Chasse-loup-Laubat | | | |
| Sept 20 | Berlin-Leipzig | B (12 h.p.) | 1 | Held and R. Benz | 187 kı | 5:19:15 | 35·2 |
| 1901 March 25 | Nice Speed Trials | M (35 h.p.) | 1 | Werner | 392 km | 6:45:48 | 58·1 |
| March 29 | La Turbie Hill-Climb | M (35 h.p.)* | 1 | Werner | 15·5 km | 18:06·8 | 51·4 |
| | | M (35 h.p.) | 2 | Lemaître | | 18:49·6 | 49·4 |
| Sept 22 | Semmering Hill-Climb | M (35 h.p.)* | 1 | von Stern | 10 km | 12:30·8 | 47·9 |
| | | M (35 h.p.) | 2 | Werner | | 13:42 | 43·8 |
| 1902 April 7 | La Turbie Hill-Climb | M (40 h.p.) | 1 | Stead | 15·5 km | 16:37·6 | 55·2 |
| | | M (40 h.p.) | 2 | Lemaître | | 18:25·2 | 50·4 |
| | | M (40 h.p.) | 3 | Werner | | 18:30·2 | 50·2 |

| | | | | | | | |
|---|---|---|---|---|---|---|---|
| April 10 | Nice Speed Trials | M (40 h.p.) | 1 | Degrais and Werner equal | One mile (Standing start) | 1:09·6 | 83·2† |
| June 26–29 | Paris-Vienna (Gordon Bennett Race) | M (40 h.p.) | 2 | Zborowski | 1120 km | 16:13:29·6 | 69 |
| Sept 7 | Semmering Hill-Climb | M (40 h.p.)*<br>M (40 h.p.) | 1<br>2 | Werner<br>von Stern | 10 km | 10:37·2<br>10:46·6 | 56·5<br>55·7 |
| 1903 April 1 | La Turbie Hill-Climb | M (60 h.p.)*<br>M (60 h.p.)<br>M (60 h.p.) | 1<br>2<br>3 | Hieronymus<br>Werner<br>Degrais | 15·5 km | 14:26·8<br>14:45·8<br>16:56·4 | 64·4<br>62·9<br>54·9 |
| April 7 | Nice Speed Trials | M (60 h.p.) | 1<br>2 | Braun<br>Werner | One mile (Standing start) | 1:03·7<br>1:04 | 90·9<br>90·5 |
| July 2 | Gordon Bennett Race (Ireland) | M (60 h.p.) | 1 | Jenatzy | 368 miles (592·7 km) | 6:39:0 | 89·2 |
| July 4 | Phoenix Park, Dublin Speed Trials | M (60 h.p.) | 1 | Hutton | One mile (Standing start) | 1:28·4 | 65·5 |
| Sept 17 | Semmering Hill-Climb | M (60 h.p.)*<br>M (60 h.p.) | 1<br>2 | Braun<br>Werner | 10 km | 8:47·6<br>9:04·2 | 68·2<br>66·2 |
| 1904 Jan. 27–30 | Daytona Speed Trials | M (90, 60 and 40 h.p.) | | (Many American records captured) | | | |
| May 19 | Ostend Speed Trials | M (90 h.p.) | 1 | de Caters | One km (Flying start) | 23 | 156·5† |
| June 17 | Gordon Bennett Race (Germany) | M (90 h.p.) | 2<br>4 | Jenatzy<br>de Caters | 564 km | 6:01:28<br>6:46:31 | 93·6<br>83·4 |

* Racing-car. † World record.

| *Date* | *Event* | *Car* | *Place* | *Drivers* | *Distance* | *Time* *Hrs :mins :secs* | *Speed* *k.p.h.* |
|---|---|---|---|---|---|---|---|
| Sept 4 | Brescia-Verona-Brescia | M (60 h.p.) | 3 | Florio | 370 km | 3:18:09·2 | 112 |
| Sept 17 | Semmering Hill-Climb | M (90 h.p.) | 1 | Braun | 10 km | 8:11·6 | 73·2 |
| 1905 Jan 26 | Daytona Speed Trials | M (90 h.p.) | | Thomas | Ten miles | 6:31·8 | 147·9† |
| Aug 10–17 | Herkomer Trials | M (40 h.p.) | 1 | Ladenburg | | | |
| Aug 12 | Kesselberg Hill-Climb | M (120 h.p.)* | 1 | Hieronymus | 6 km | 5:34·6 | 64·5 |
| Sept 17 | Semmering Hill-Climb | M (100 h.p.)* | 1 | Braun | 10 km | 7:50·4 | 76·5 |
| Oct 15 | Gaillon Hill-Climb | M (120 h.p.)* | 1 | de Caters | 1 km | 31 | 116·1 |
| 1906 June 5–13 | Herkomer Trials | B (40 h.p.) | 2 | Erle | | | |
| Sept 23 | Semmering Hill-Climb | M (100 h.p.)* | 1 | Braun | 10 km | 7:47 | 77 |
| 1907 June 4–13 | Herkomer Trials | B (50 h.p.) | 1 | Erle | | | |
| July 27 | Ardennes Circuit | M (130 h.p.)<br>M (130 h.p.) | 1<br>3 | de Caters<br>Jenatzy | 600 km | 6:29:10<br>6:49:40 | 92·6<br>87·9 |
| Sept 1 | Coppa Florio | B (60 h.p.)<br>B (60 h.p.) | 2<br>3 | Héméry<br>Hanriot | 486·4 km | 4:49:49<br>4:57:47 | 100·7<br>98 |

| | | | | | | | |
|---|---|---|---|---|---|---|---|
| Sept 22 | Semmering Hill-Climb | M (130 h.p.)* | 1 | Poege | 10 km | 7:29·2 | 80·1 |
| Oct 20 | Gaillon Hill-Climb | M (130 h.p.)* | 2 | Sir Ralph Gore | 1 km (Flying start) | 31·6 | 114 |
| 1908 March 3–4 | Florida 100-Miles Race | B (60 h.p.) | 1 | Bergdoll | 100 miles | 1:53:30·2 | 85 |
| June 1 | St. Petersburg-Moscow | B (120 h.p.) | 1 | Héméry | 686 km | 8:30:48 | 80·6 |
| July 7 | French Grand Prix (Dieppe) | M (140 h.p.)<br>B (120 h.p.)<br>B (120 h.p.) | 1<br>2<br>3 | Lautenschlager<br>Héméry<br>Hanriot | 769·88 km | 6:55:43<br>7:04:24<br>7:05:13 | 111·1<br>108·9<br>108·7 |
| Sept 20 | Semmering Hill-Climb | M (150 h.p.)*<br>M (150 h.p.) | 1<br>2 | Salzer<br>Poege | 10 km | 7:23·6<br>7:29·4 | 81·2<br>80·1 |
| Nov 26 | American Grand Prize | B (150 h.p.)<br>B (150 h.p.) | 2<br>4 | Héméry<br>Hanriot | 688·4 km | 6:10:47<br>6:26:16 | 111·4<br>106·9 |
| 1909 March 24 | Daytona Beach Meeting | B (150 h.p.)<br>B (150 h.p.)<br>B (150 h.p.) | | Bruce-Brown<br>Robertson<br>Bruce-Brown | One mile<br>Five miles<br>Ten miles | 33<br>2:45·2<br>5:14·2 | 175†<br>175·5†<br>184† |
| Aug 19 | Indianapolis | B (150 h.p.) | 1 | Oldfield | One mile (Standing start) | 43·1 | 134·4† |
| Sept 19 | Semmering Hill-Climb | M (150 h.p.)*<br>M (150 h.p.)<br>B (200 h.p.) | 1<br>2<br>3 | Salzer<br>Poege<br>Erle | 10 km | 7:07<br>7:13·4<br>7:28·8 | 84·3<br>83·1<br>80·2 |
| Oct 17 | Brussels World Championship Meeting | B (200 h.p.) | 1 | Héméry | 1 km (Standing start) | 31·2 | 115·4† |

* Racing-car. † World record.

| *Date* | *Event* | *Car* | *Place* | *Drivers* | *Distance* | *Time Hrs :mins :secs* | *Speed k.p.h.* |
|---|---|---|---|---|---|---|---|
| Nov 8 | Brooklands | B (200 h.p.) | | Hémery | Half-mile (Flying start) | 14·1 | 205·7† |
| | | B (200 h.p.) | | Hémery | 1 km (Flying start) | 17·8 | 202·6† |
| 1910 March 16 | Daytona | B (200 h.p.) | | Oldfield | One mile (Flying start) | 27·3 | 211·4† |
| June 26 –July 13 | Russian Trials (St. Petersburg-Moscow-St. Petersburg) | M (16/50 h.p.)<br>M (16/50 h.p.)<br>M (16/50 h.p.) | 1<br>2<br>3 | Poege<br>Fritsch<br>Luede | 3000 km | Awards on | points |
| Oct 2 | Gaillon Hill-Climb | B (200 h.p.)<br>M (180 h.p.) | 1<br>2 | Erle<br>Jenatzy | 1 km (Flying start) | 23<br>26·4 | 156·5<br>136·4 |
| Nov 12 | American Grand Prize (Savannah) | B (150 h.p.)<br>B (150 h.p.) | 1<br>2 | Bruce-Brown<br>Hémery | 668 km | 5:53:05<br>5:53:06 | 113·5<br>113·5 |
| 1911 April 23 | Daytona | B (200 h.p.) | | Burman | One mile (Flying start) | 25·4 | 228·1† |
| May 14 | Targa Florio | M (model unknown) | 3 | Soldatenkoff | 446·5 km | 10:23:23·4 | 43 |
| May 30 | Indianapolis | M (140 h.p. 1908 Grand Prix type) | 4 | Wishart | 500 miles | 6:52:57 | 116·9 |
| Oct 9 | Fairmount Park Races, U.S.A. | B (150 h.p.)<br>M (140 h.p.) | 1<br>2 | Bergdoll<br>Wishart | 324 km | 3:18:41·3<br>3:20:11·4 | 97·8<br>97·1 |

| | | | | | | | |
|---|---|---|---|---|---|---|---|
| Nov 27 | Vanderbilt Cup | M (140 h.p.)<br>M (140 h.p.) | 2<br>3 | de Palma<br>Wishart | 468 km | 3:58:11·9<br>4:06:20·3 | 117·9<br>114 |
| Nov 30 | American Grand Prize (Savannah) | B (150 h.p.)<br>M (140 h.p.) | 2<br>3 | Hearne<br>de Palma | 661 km | 5:33:39<br>5:34:40 | 118·9<br>118·5 |
| 1912<br>Aug 30–31 | Elgin Races, U.S.A. | M (140 h.p.)<br>B (150 h.p.) | 1<br>2 | de Palma<br>Bergdoll | 490·7 km | 4:25:36<br>4:30:28 | 112·7<br>108·9 |
| Oct 2 | Vanderbilt Cup | M (140 h.p.)<br>M (140 h.p.) | 1<br>3 | de Palma<br>Wishart | 481·5 km | 4:20:31<br>4:36:35·7 | 108·5<br>104·4 |
| Oct 5 | American Grand Prize | B (150 h.p.) | 2 | Bergdoll | 660 km | 6:14:51 | 110·6 |
| Oct 6 | Gaillon Hill-Climb | B (200 h.p.)* | 1 | Erle | 1 km | 22 | 163·6 |
| 1913<br>May 30 | Indianapolis | M (16/45 h.p. Knight) | 5 | Pilette | 500 miles | 7:19:25 | 110·1 |
| June 9 | St. Petersburg Grand Prix | B (29/60 h.p.) | 1 | Suvorin | 204·8 km (approx.) | 2:23:57 | 93·4 |
| Aug 4–5 | French Grand Prix (Le Mans) | M (140 h.p.)<br>M (75 h.p.) | 3<br>4 | Pilette<br>Salzer | 540·6 km | 4:27:53·6<br>4:34:53·6 | 121·1<br>117·9 |
| Aug 24–25 | Belgian Grand Prix | M (16/45 h.p.) | 3 | Elskamp | 800 km | 8:30:51 | 88 |
| Nov 9 | Santa Fé, Mexico Race | B (29/60 h.p.) | 1 | Pica | 420 km | 5:42:00 | 73·7 |
| Dec 22 | Brooklands | B (200 h.p.) | | Hornsted | Half-mile (Standing start) | 25·5 | 113·8† |
| | | B (200 h.p.) | | Hornsted | 1 km (Standing start) | 30·4 | 118·4† |

† World record. * Racing-car.

| *Date* | *Event* | *Car* | *Place* | *Drivers* | *Distance* | *Time Hrs :mins :secs* | *Speed k.p.h.* |
|---|---|---|---|---|---|---|---|
| 1914 Feb 26 | Vanderbilt Cup | M (37/95 h.p.)<br>M (140 h.p.) | 1<br>2 | de Palma<br>Oldfield | 473 km | 3:53:41<br>3:55:01 | 123·2<br>120·7 |
| Feb 28 | American Grand Prize | M (37/95 h.p.) | 4 | de Palma | 648·4 km | 6:09:08 | 105·4 |
| May 31 | St. Petersburg Grand Prix | B (150 h.p.) | 1 | Scholl | 204·8 km (approx.) | 1:47:32·4 | 115·2 |
| July 4 | French Grand Prix (Lyons) | M (4½ litre 115 h.p.)<br>M (4½ litre 115 h.p.)<br>M (4½ litre 115 h.p.) | 1<br>2<br>3 | Lautenschlager<br>Wagner<br>Salzer | 752·6 km | 7:08:18·4<br>7:09:54·2<br>7:13:15·8 | 105·6<br>105·1<br>104·3 |
| Aug 21 | Chicago Cup | M (4½ litre 115 h.p.) | 1 | de Palma | 482·9 km | 4:05:01 | 118·3 |
| Aug 22 | Elgin Trophy of Chicago | M (4½ litre 115 h.p.) | 1 | de Palma | 482·9 km | 4:06:18 | 117·6 |
| Sept 5–7 | Brighton Beach, U.S.A. | M (4½ litre 115 h.p.) | 1 | de Palma | 100 miles | 1:40:15 | 96·3 |
| | | M (4½ litre 115 h.p.) | | de Palma | Wins over | 10, 25 and 50 | miles |
| 1915 May 31 | Indianapolis | M (4½ litre 115 h.p.) | 1 | de Palma | 500 miles | 5:35:55 | 144·6 |
| 1916 July 22 | Kansas City Race, U.S.A. | M (4½ litre 115 h.p.) | 1 | de Palma | 100 miles | 1:42:54 | 93·8 |
| 1921 May 29 | Targa Florio | M (28/95 h.p.) | 2 | Sailer | 432 km | 7:27:16·2 | 57·9 |
| | Coppa Florio | M (28/95 h.p.) | 1 | Sailer | 432 km | 7:27:16·2 | 57·9 |
| Aug 7–15 | Italian Alpine Trophy | M (28/95 h.p.) | 1 | Minoia | 2305·2 km | 48:02:00 | 47·9 |
| Sept 11 | Italian Grand Prix (Brescia) | M (4½ litre 115 h.p.) | 1 | Masetti | 432·5 km | 3:44:15·2 | 115·7 |

| | | | | | | | |
|---|---|---|---|---|---|---|---|
| 1922 April 2 | Targa Florio | M (4½ litre 115 h.p.) | 1 | Masetti | 432 km | 6:50:50·4 | 63·1 |
| Sept 24 | Semmering Hill-Climb | B (200 h.p.)* | 1 | Hoerner | 10 km | 7:35 | 79·1 |
| 1923 June 17 | Solitude Hill-Climb | M (2 litre super-charged)* | 1 | Salzer | 6 km | 3:43 | 96·9 |
| Sept 9 | European Grand Prix (Monza) | B (2 litre 'Teardrop') | 4<br>5 | Minoia<br>Hoerner | 760 km<br>710 km | 5:34:02<br>5:31:40·6 | 136·5<br>128·3 |
| 1924 April 27 | Targa Florio | M (2 litre super-charged) | 1 | Werner | 432 km | 6:32:37·4 | 66 |
| | Coppa Florio | M (2 litre super-charged) | 1 | Werner | 540 km | 8:17:13 | 65·2 |
| May 18 | Solitude Hill-Climb | M (2 litre super-charged)* | 1 | Merz | 6 km | 3:28·4 | 103·4 |
| July 13 | Coppa Acerbo (Castellamere) | M (28/95 h.p.) | 3 | Bonmartini | 255 km | 2:31:42·2 | 100·8 |
| July 19 | Eifel Races | M (1½ litre super-charged) | 1 | Caracciola | 330 km | 5:27:50 | 60·4 |
| Aug 16–17 | Klausen Hill-Climb | M (2 litre super-charged)* | 1 | Merz | 21·5 km | 18:48·6 | 68·6 |
| | | M (1½ litre super-charged)‡ | 1 | Caracciola | 21·5 km | 20:29·2 | 63 |
| Aug 31 | Mugello Circuit (Florence) | M (28/95 h.p.) | 3 | Cesaroni | 398·4 km | 5:58:36·4 | 66·7 |

* Racing-car. ‡ Sports-car.

| *Date* | *Event* | *Car* | *Place* | *Drivers* | *Distance* | *Time* *Hrs :mins :secs* | *Speed* *k.p.h.* |
|---|---|---|---|---|---|---|---|
| Sept 14 | Semmering Hill-Climb | M (4½ litre 115 h.p.)* | 1 | C. Werner | 10 km | 6:55·6 | 86·6 |
| Sept 24 | San Sebastian Meeting | M (28/95 h.p.) | 1 | Gaertner | 426 km | 5:10:23 | 82·4 |
| 1925 May 16–17 | Solitude Races | M (2 litre super-charged) | 1 | Merz | 223 km | 2:22:09 | 94·1 |
| May 24 | Coppa della Perugia | M (33/140 h.p.) | 3 | Cesaroni | 295·2 km | 3:01:55 | 97·3 |
| Aug 16 | Freiburg Hill-Climb | M (2 litre eight cylinder super-charged)* | 1 | C. Werner | 12 km | 11:3·41 | 62·5 |
| | | B (2 litre 'Teardrop')‡ | 1 | Walb | | 11:49·3 | 61 |
| 1926 July 11 | German Grand Prix (Avus) | M (2 litre eight cylinder super-charged) | 1 | Caracciola | 392·3 km | 2:54:17·8 | 135·2 |
| Aug 1 | Freiburg Hill-Climb | M (2 litre eight cylinder super-charged)* | 1 | C. Werner | 12 km | 10:24·2 | 69·2 |
| Sept 12 | Solitude Races | M (2 litre eight cylinder super-charged) | 1 | Merz | 446 km | 4:50:24·2 | 92·2 |
| Sept 12 | Semmering Hill-Climb | M (4½ litre 115 h.p.)* | 1 | Caracciola | 10 km | 6:40·8 | 89·8 |
| 1927 June 4 | Southport Races | M (2 litre eight cylinder super-charged) | 1 | Mays | 100 miles | | 100 (approx) |

| | | | | | | | |
|---|---|---|---|---|---|---|---|
| June 19 | Opening Nürburgring | M (2 litre eight cylinder supercharged)* | 1 | C. Werner | 396·2 km | 4:17:07 | 92·5 |
| | | M-B (*S*)‡ | 1 | Caracciola | 359·6 km | 3:33:21 | 101·1 |
| | | M-B (*S*) | 2 | Rosenberger | | 3:50:24 | 93·6 |
| July 17 | German Grand Prix (Nürburgring) | M-B (*S*) | 1 | Merz | 509·4 km | 4:59:35·6 | 102 |
| | | M-B (*S*) | 2 | C. Werner | | 5:02:54·6 | 101 |
| | | M-B (*S*) | 3 | Walb | | 5:10:49·4 | 98·4 |
| Aug 6–7 | Freiburg Hill-Climb | M (4½ litre 115 h.p.)* | 1 | Rosenberger | 12 km | 10:10·1 | 70·8 |
| | | M-B (*S*)‡ | 1 | Caracciola | | 10:23 | 69·3 |
| | | M-B (*S*) | 2 | Kimpel | | 10:23·1 | 69·3 |
| Aug 13–14 | Klausen Hill-Climb | M (4½ litre 115 h.p.)* | 1 | Rosenberger | 21·5 km | 17:17 | 74·6 |
| | | M-B (*S*)‡ | 1 | Caracciola | | 17:35·4 | 73·3 |
| Sept 11 | Semmering Hill-Climb | M-B (*S*)‡ | 1 | Rosenberger | 10 km | 7:02·8 | 85·1 |
| Sept 24 | Shelsley-Walsh Hill-Climb | M (2 litre eight cylinder supercharged)* | 2 | Mays | 1000 yds | 48·2 | 68·3 |
| Dec 25 | Pergameno Circuit, Argentine | M-B (*K*) | 2 | Zatuszek | 305 km | 3:05:09 | 98·8 |
| 1928 April 15 | Caserta Circuit | M-B (*K*) | 2 | Caflisch | 248 km | 3:01:02 | 82·2 |
| April 15 | Herbstpreis (Autumn Prize), Argentine | M-B (*K*) | 3 | Zatuszek | 400 km | 3:22:28·6 | 118·5 |
| May 12–17 | Wiesbaden Races | M-B (*S*) | 1 | von Wentzel-Mosau | 100 km | 1:21:21·4 | 73·7 |

* Racing-car. ‡ Sports-car.

| *Date* | *Event* | *Car* | *Place* | *Drivers* | *Distance* | *Time Hrs :mins :secs* | *Speed k.p.h.* |
|---|---|---|---|---|---|---|---|
| May 27 | Argentine 500 Mile Race | M-B (*K*) | 3 | Zatuszek | 804 km | 6:04:01 | 132·5 |
| June 10 | Kesselberg-Hill Climb | M-B (*S*)‡ | 1 | Prince Hohenlohe | 5 km | 4:47·3 | 62·6 |
| July 15 | German Grand Prix (Sports cars) | M-B (*SS*) | 1 | Caracciola and C. Werner | 509·4 km | 4:54:24·4 | 103·9 |
| | | M-B (*SS*) | 2 | Merz | | 4:56:02·4 | 103·3 |
| | | M-B (*SS*) | 3 | C. Werner and Walb | | 5:04:23·6 | 100·5 |
| July 28 | Shelsley-Walsh Hill-Climb | M-B (*S*)‡ | 1 | Clay | 1000 yds | 53·6 | — |
| Aug 5 | Freiburg Hill-Climb | M-B (*SSK*)* | 1 | Caracciola | 12 km | 9:51·4 | 73 |
| Aug 25 | Grand Prix de la Baule | M-B (*SS*) | 2 | von Wentzel-Mosau | 100 km | 48:10·4 | 124·5 |
| Sept 16 | Semmering Hill-Climb | M-B (*SSK*)* | 1 | Caracciola | 10 km | 6:40·3 | 89·9 |
| Nov 4 | Cordoba (Argentine) Circuit | M-B (*K*) | 3 | Zatuszek | 405 km | 4:38:40·4 | 87·2 |
| Nov 12 | Avellanda Races, Argentine | M-B (*K*) | 3 | Berndt | 506 km | 4:32:54 | 111·2 |
| Nov 18 | Buenos-Aires 300 Mile Race (Chivilkoy Circuit) | M-B (*K*) | 2 | Zatuszek | 480 km | 3:30:22·8 | 136·8 |
| Dec 23 | Buenos-Aires Production Car Race (Twelve Hours) | M-B (*K*) | 1 | Zatuszek | 1096 km | 12:00:00 | 106·1 |

| | | | | | | | |
|---|---|---|---|---|---|---|---|
| 1929 April 14 | Monaco Grand Prix | M-B (*SSK*) | 3 | Caracciola | 318 km | 3:58:33·6 | 79·9 |
| May 18 | Southport Races | M-B (*S*) | 1 | Thistlethwayte | 100 miles | | 109 (approx) |
| June 2 | Argentine 500 Mile Race (Rafaela Circuit) | M-B (*SSK*) | 2 | Zatuszek and Berndt | 804 km | 5:40:02·4 | 141·9 |
| July 7 | Piemonte Race (Avellino Circuit) | M-B (*S*) | 3 | Caflisch | 240·6 km | 2:58:35·4 | 80·8 |
| July 14 | Grand Prix of the Nations, Nürburgring | M-B (*SSK*) | 3 | Momberger and Count Arco-Zinneberg | 508·7 km | 5:00:37·8 | 101·6 |
| July 21 | Kesselberg Hill-Climb | M-B (*SSK*)‡ | 1 | Count Arco-Zinneberg | 5 km | 4:34·4 | 65·6 |
| Aug 7–12 | Alpine Trials | M-B (various) | | | Eight Alpine | Cups | |
| Aug 17 | Tourist Trophy, Belfast | M-B (*SS*) | 1 | Caracciola | 410 miles | 5:37:40 | 117·2 |
| Sept 8 | Gaisberg Hill-Climb | M-B (*SSK*)‡ | 1 | Count Arco-Zinneberg | 11·9 km | 8:50·9 | 80·7 |
| Sept 15–16 | Monza Grand Prix | M-B (*SSK*) | 3 | Momberger | 99 km | 34:17·4 | 173·2 |
| Sept 15 | Shelsley-Walsh Hill-Climb | M-B (*SS*)‡ | 1 | Lord Howe | 1000 yards | 47·6 | 69·5 |
| Sept 15 | Semmering Hill-Climb | M-B (*SSK*)‡ | 1 | Count Arco-Zinneberg | 10 km | 7:04·4 | 84·8 |

* Racing-car. ‡ Sports-car.

| Date | Event | Car | Place | Drivers | Distance | Time Hrs:mins:secs | Speed k.p.h. |
|---|---|---|---|---|---|---|---|
| Oct 20 | Cordoba Grand Prix, Argentine | M-B (*SSK*) | 1 | Zatuszek | 505·4 km | 4:33:34·4 | 111 |
| 1930 Jan 12 | Buenos-Aires Grand Prix (Chivilkoy Circuit) | M-B (*S*)<br>M-B (*SSK*) | 1<br>2 | Malcolm<br>Zatuszek | 409 km | 4:24:08·8<br>4:31:41·2 | 92·9<br>90·3 |
| Jan 25 | Gran Premio Nacional (Moron-Cordoba-Moron) | M-B (*SSK*) | 2 | Zatuszek | 1480 km | 18:16:06 | 87·4 |
| May 11 | Königsaal-Jilowischt Hill-Climb | M-B (*SSK*)‡ | 1 | Caracciola | 5·6 km | 2:52·7 | 116·7 |
| May 18 | Caserta Circuit | M-B (*S*) | 1 | Caflisch | 304·4 km | 2:55:19 | 104·2 |
| June 14–15 | Kesselberg Hill-Climb) | M-B (*SS*)‡ | 1 | Spandel | 5 km | 4:24·2 | 68·1 |
| June 29 | Cuneo Colle della Maddalena (Hill-Climb) | M-B (*SSK*)‡ | 1 | Caracciola | 66·5 km | 41:24·2 | 96·4 |
| July 12 | Shelsley-Walsh Hill-Climb | M-B (*SSK*)‡ | 1 | Caracciola | 1000 yards | 46·8 | 70·3 |
| July 18–19 | Irish Grand Prix and Eireann Cup | M-B (*SSK*) | 1 | Caracciola | 300 miles | 3:28:24 | 139 |
| | Eireann Cup | M-B (*SS*) | 3 | Lord Howe | | 3:39:53 | 131·7 |
| Aug 9–10 | Klausen Hill-Climb | M-B (*SSK*)‡ | 1 | Caracciola | 21·5 km | 17:04·6 | 75·5 |
| Aug 17 | Freiburg Hill-Climb | M-B (*SSK*)‡ | 1 | Caracciola | 12 km | 9:38 | 74·7 |
| Aug 24 | Mont Ventoux Hill-Climb | M-B (*SSK*)‡ | 1 | Caracciola | 21·6 km | 15:02 | 86 |

| | | | | | | | |
|---|---|---|---|---|---|---|---|
| Aug 31 | Gaisberg Hill-Climb | M-B (*SS*)‡ | 1 | Spandel | 11·9 km | 8:23·4 | 85·1 |
| Sept 14 | Semmering Hill-Climb | M-B (*SSK*)‡ | 1 | Caracciola | 10 km | 6:35·4 | 90·9 |
| Sept 21 | Schwabenberg Hill-Climb | M-B (*SSK*)‡ | 1 | Caracciola | 4·64 km | 3:21·1 | 83·1 |
| | | | | Caracciola—European Hill-Climb champion | | | |
| Oct 20 | Cordoba Grand Prix Argentine | M-B (*SSK*) | 1 | Zatuszek | 505 km | 4:33:34·4 | 110·8 |
| Dec 19 | Frühlingspreis (Spring Prize), Argentine | M-B (*SSK*) | 1 | Zatuszek | 400 km | 3:04:43 | 129·9 |
| 1931 Feb 7–8 | Gran Premio Nacional (Moron-Cordoba-Moron) | M-B (*SSK*) | 1 | Zatuszek | 1480 km | 15:44:40·2 | 94 |
| April 12 | Herbstpreis (Autumn Prize), Argentine | M-B (*SSK*) | 1 | Zatuszek | 400 km | 2:54:43·2 | 137·4 |
| April 12–13 | Mille Miglia | M-B (*SSKL*) | 1 | Caracciola and Sebastian | 1635 km | 16:10:10 | 101·1 |
| May 17 | Rabassada (Spain) Hill-Climb | M-B (*SSKL*)*‡ | 1 | Caracciola | 4·9 km | 3:45·4 | 78·2 |
| May 31 | Königsaal-Jilowischt Hill-Climb | M-B (*SSKL*)* | 1 | Stuck | 5·6 km | 2:42·8 | 123·8 |
| | | M-B (*SSKL*)‡ | 1 | Caracciola | | 2:42·7 | 123·9 |
| June 7 | Eifel Races | M-B (*SSKL*) | 1 | Caracciola | 312 km | 2:50:47·2 | 109·6 |
| | | M-B (*SSKL*) | 3 | Brauchitsch | | 3:00:22·3 | 103·8 |
| June 7 | Lemberg (Lwow, Poland) Grand Prix | M-B (*SSKL*) | 1 | Stuck | 150 km | 1:56:46·7 | 77·1 |
| June 7 | Geneva Grand Prix | M-B (*S*) | 3 | Caflisch | 250 km | 2:01:16 | 123·7 |

* Racing-car. ‡ Sports-car.

| *Date* | *Event* | *Car* | *Place* | *Drivers* | *Distance* | *Time* *Hrs :mins :secs* | *Speed* *k.p.h.* |
|---|---|---|---|---|---|---|---|
| June 13–14 | Le Mans Grand Prix D'Endurance | M-B (*SSK*) | 2 | Stoffel and Ivanowsky | 2905·1 km | 24 hours | 121·1 |
| June 14 | Kesselberg Hill-Climb | M-B (*SSKL*)‡ | 1 | Caracciola | 5 km | 4:03·4 | 73·8 |
| July 6 | Touring-Car Grand Prix of Belgium (Spa Circuit) | M-B (*SSK*) | 1 | Djordjadze and G. Zehender | 2544 km | 24 hours | 105·9 |
| July 11 | Shelsley-Walsh Hill-Climb | M-B (*SSK*)‡ | 1 | Lord Howe | 1000 yards | 46·8 | 70·8 |
| July 19 | German Grand Prix | M-B (*SSKL*) | 1 | Caracciola | 501·8 km | 4:38:10 | 108·3 |
| July 26 | Freiburg Hill-Climb | M-B (*SSKL*)‡ | 1 | Caracciola | 12 km | 8:51·2 | 81·3 |
| Aug 2 | Avus Races | M-B (*SSKL*)<br>M-B (*SSKL*) | 1<br>3 | Caracciola<br>Brauchitsch | 294·4 km | 1:35:07·6<br>1:42:32·2 | 185·7<br>172·3 |
| Aug 9 | Gaisberg Hill-Climb | M-B (*SSKL*)‡ | 1 | Brauchitsch | 11·9 km | 7:45·4 | 92 |
| Aug 16 | Tatra Hill-Climb | M-B (*SSKL*)*‡ | 1 | Caracciola | 7·5 km | 5:29·9 | 81·9 |
| Aug 30 | Mont Ventoux Hill-Climb | M-B (*SSKL*)* | 1 | Caracciola | 21·6 km | 15:22 | 84·4 |
| Sept 20 | Drei-Hotter Hill-Climb | M-B (*SSK*)*‡ | 1 | Caracciola | 4 km | 2:44·8 | 87·4 |
| | | | | Caracciola— | European Hill- | Climb champ | ion |
| Sept 27 | Masaryk Circuit | M-B (*SSKL*) | 2 | Stuck | 495·4 km | 4:26:10·2 | 111·6 |
| 1932 Feb 28 | Hill-Climbing Championship of Brazil | M-B (*SSKL*) | 1 | Stuck | 43 km | 23:14·4 | 110·9 |

| | | | | | | | |
|---|---|---|---|---|---|---|---|
| May 8 | Finnish Grand Prix | M-B (*SSK*)<br>M-B (*SSK*) | 1<br>3 | Widengren<br>Ebb | 101·5 km | 1:08:41·6<br>— | 88·7<br>— |
| May 8 | Herbstpreis (Autumn Prize), Argentine | M-B (*SSK*)<br>M-B (*SSK*) | 1<br>2 | Zatuszek<br>Estanguet | 400 km | 2:47:40·2<br>3:01:27·2 | 143·1<br>132·2 |
| May 22 | Avus Races | M-B (*SSKL*) | 1 | Brauchitsch | 294·4 km | 1:30:52·4 | 194·4 |
| May 29 | Eifel Races | M-B (*SSKL*) | 3 | Brauchitsch | 319·3 km | 2:57:50·6 | 107·7 |
| June 12 | Kesselberg Hill-Climb | M-B (*SSKL*)‡ | 1 | Stuck | 5 km | 4:03 | 74·4 |
| June 19 | Lemberg (Lwow, Poland) Grand Prix | M-B (*SSK*) | 2 | Broscheck | 225·1 km | 2:34:25 | 87·4 |
| July 24 | Gaisberg Hill-Climb | M-B (*SSKL*)‡ | 1 | Stuck | 11·9 km | 8:17·7 | 86·2 |
| July 25 | Shelsley-Walsh Hill-Climb | M-B (*SSK*)‡ | 1 | Lord Howe | 1000 yards | 47·2 | 69·7 |
| Aug 6–7 | Klausen Hill-Climb | M-B (*SSKL*)‡ | 1 | Stuck | 21·5 km | 17:00·6 | 75·8 |
| Aug 21 | Freiburg Hill-Climb | M-B (*SSKL*)‡ | 1 | Stuck | 12 km | 9:13 | 78·1 |
| Aug 28 | Stelvio Hill-Climb | M-B (*SSKL*)*‡ | 1 | Stuck | 14 km | 15:23 | 54·6 |
| Sept 4 | Mont Ventoux Hill-Climb | M-B (*SSKL*)‡ | 1 | Stuck | 21·6 km | 15:48·6 | 81·9 |
| | | | | Stuck—Alpine champion | | | |
| 1933<br>May 7 | Finnish Grand Prix | M-B (*SSK*) | 1 | Ebb | 100 km | 1:03:18·7 | 94·8 |
| May 28 | Eifel Races | M-B (*SSKL*) | 2 | Brauchitsch | 342·1 km | 3:06:54·6 | 109·8 |
| June 18 | Kesselberg Hill-Climb | M-B (*SSKL*)‡ | 1 | Brauchitsch | 5 km | 4:01·2 | 74·6 |
| July 16 | Freiberg Hill-Climb | M-B (*SSKL*)‡ | 1 | Brauchitsch | 12 km | 9:24·1 | 76·6 |

* Racing-car. ‡ Sports-car.

| *Date* | *Event* | *Car* | *Place* | *Drivers* | *Distance* | *Time* *Hrs :mins :secs* | *Speed* *k.p.h.* |
|---|---|---|---|---|---|---|---|
| 1934 May 13 | Finnish Grand Prix | M-B (*SSK*) | 3 | Ebb | 100 km | 1:01:47·2 | 97·1 |
| June 3 | Eifel Races | M-B (750kg Grand Prix formula car) | 1 | Brauchitsch | 342·1 km | 2:47:36·4 | 122·5 |
| July 15 | German Grand Prix | M-B (750kg Grand Prix formula car) | 2 | Fagioli | 570·2 km | 4:40:26·1 | 122·2 |
| Aug 5 | Klausen Hill-Climb | M-B (750kg Grand Prix formula car)* | 1 | Caracciola | 21·5 km | 15:22·1 | 83·9 |
| Aug 15 | Coppa Acerbo (Pescara) | M-B (750kg Grand Prix formula car) | 1 | Fagioli | 513 km | 3:58:56·8 | 129·6 |
| Sept 9 | Italian Grand Prix (Monza) | M-B (750kg Grand Prix formula car) | 1 | Caracciola and Fagioli | 501 km | 4:45:47 | 105·2 |
| Sept 23 | Spanish Grand Prix (San Sebastian) | M-B (750kg Grand Prix formula car) | 1<br>2 | Fagioli<br>Caracciola | 519·5 km | 3:19:14<br>3:20:24 | 156·3<br>155·5 |
| Sept 30 | Masaryk Circuit | M-B (750kg Grand Prix formula car) | 2 | Fagioli | 495·4 km | 3:56:24·5 | 125·7 |
| Oct 30 | Gyon, near Budapest | M-B (750kg Grand Prix formula car) | | Caracciola | One mile (Standing start) | 30·71 | 188·6† |
| 1935 April 22 | Monaco Grand Prix | M-B (750kg Grand Prix formula car) | 1 | Fagioli | 318 km | 3:23:49·8 | 93·6 |
| May 12 | Tripoli Grand Prix | M-B (750kg Grand Prix formula car) | 1 | Caracciola | 524 km | 2:38:47·6 | 198 |
| | | M-B (750kg Grand Prix formula car) | 3 | Fagioli | | 2:41:03·8 | 195·3 |

| | | | | | | | |
|---|---|---|---|---|---|---|---|
| May 12 | Finnish Grand Prix | M-B (*SSK*) | 1 | Ebb | 100 km | 59:34 | 100·7 |
| May 26 | Avus Races | M-B (750kg Grand Prix formula car) | 1 | Fagioli | 195·7 km | 49:13·4 | 238·5 |
| June 16 | Eifel Races | M-B (750kg Grand Prix formula car) | 1 | Caracciola | 250·9 km | 2:08:02·6 | 117·8 |
| June 23 | French Grand Prix | M-B (750kg Grand Prix formula car) | 1 | Caracciola | 500 km | 4:00:54·6 | 124·6 |
| | | M-B (750kg Grand Prix formula car) | 2 | Brauchitsch | | 4:00:55·1 | 124·6 |
| June 30 | Barcelona Grand Prix | M-B (750kg Grand Prix formula car) | 1<br>2 | Fagioli<br>Caracciola | 265 km | 2:27:40<br>2:28:28 | 107·8<br>107·2 |
| July 14 | Belgian Grand Prix | M-B (750kg Grand Prix formula car | 1<br>2 | Caracciola<br>Fagioli and Brauchitsch | 506·6 km | 3:12:31<br>3:14:08 | 157·5<br>156·1 |
| July 28 | German Grand Prix | M-B (750kg Grand Prix formula car) | 3 | Caracciola | 501·8 km | 4:11:32 | 119·9 |
| Aug 8 | Argentine 500 Mile Race (RafaelaCircuit) | M-B (*SSK*) | 1 | Zatuszek | 804 km | 5:43:41·2 | 140·5 |
| Aug 25 | Swiss Grand Prix | M-B (750kg Grand Prix formula car) | 1 | Caracciola | 509·6 km | 3:31:12·2 | 144·3 |
| | | M-B (750kg Grand Prix formula car) | 2 | Fagioli | | 3:31:48·1 | 143·4 |
| Sept 22 | Spanish Grand Prix | M-B (750kg Grand Prix formula car) | 1 | Caracciola | 519 km | 3:09:59 | 164 |
| | | M-B (750kg Grand Prix formula car) | 2 | Fagioli | | 3:10:42 | 163·2 |
| Sept 29 | Tucuman Race, South America | M-B (*SSK*) | 1 | Zatuszek | 318 km | 3:06:01·4 | 102·6 |

* Racing-car. † World record

| Date | Event | Car | Place | Drivers | Distance | Time Hrs:mins:secs | Speed k.p.h. |
|---|---|---|---|---|---|---|---|
| Dec | Urquiza Circuit, South America | M-B (*SSK*) | 1 | Zatuszek | 162 km | 2:17:37·2 | 71·1 |
| 1936 Feb | Swedish Winter Grand Prix | M-B (*SSK*) | 2 | Ebb | 373·3 km | 3:51:52 | 96·5 |
| April 13 | Monaco Grand Prix | M-B (750kg Grand Prix formula car) | 1 | Caracciola | 318 km | 3:49:20·4 | 83·2 |
| May 10 | Tripoli Grand Prix | M-B (750kg Grand Prix formula car) | 3 | Fagioli | 524 km | 2:33:38·4 | 204·6 |
| May 17 | Tunis Grand Prix | M-B (750kg Grand Prix formula car) | 1 | Caracciola | 381·42 km | 2:22:44·6 | 160·3 |
| May | Cordoba Race (San Francisco Circuit) | M-B (*SSK*) | 1 | Zatuszek | 450 km | 3:05:29·6 | 145·6 |
| June 7 | Barcelona Grand Prix | M-B (750kg Grand Prix formula car) | 2 | Caracciola | 303·5 km | 2:43:13 | 111·6 |
| Sept–Oct | | Further extensive wins for Zatuszek on his model *SSK* in America | | | | | |
| Nov 11 | Frankfurt a. M.-Darmstadt autobahn | M-B (750kg Grand Prix formula car) | | Caracciola | 10 miles (Flying start) | 2:53·73 | 333·5† |
| Dec 13 | La Tablada Circuit, South America | M-B (*SSK*) | 1 | Zatuszek | 339·2 km | 2:45:52 | 122·7 |
| 1937 Feb 21 | Llavallol Circuit, Argentine | M-B (*SSK*) | 1 | Zatuszek | 227 km | 1:45:11 | 129·5 |

| | | | | | | | |
|---|---|---|---|---|---|---|---|
| May 9 | Tripoli Grand Prix | M-B (750kg Grand Prix formula car) | 1 | Lang | 524 km | 2:27:57 | 212·5 |
| May 30 | Avus Races (final) | M-B (750kg Grand Prix formula car) | 1 | Lang | 154·8 km | 35:30·4 | 261·7 |
| June 13 | Eifel Races | M-B (750kg Grand Prix formula car) | 2 | Caracciola | 228·1 km | 1:43:01·4 | 133 |
| | | M-B (750kg Grand Prix formula car) | 3 | Brauchitsch | | 1:43:56·4 | 131·9 |
| July 5 | Vanderbilt Cup, U.S.A. | M-B (750kg Grand Prix formula car) | 2 | Seaman | 300 miles | 3:38:51 | 132·3 |
| June 11 | Belgian Grand Prix | M-B (750kg Grand Prix formula car) | 3 | Lang | 506 km | 3:04:07 | 164·7 |
| July 25 | German Grand Prix | M-B (750kg Grand Prix formula car) | 1 | Caracciola | 501·8 km | 3:46:00 | 133·2 |
| | | M-B (750kg Grand Prix formula car) | 2 | Brauchitsch | | 3:46:46·3 | 132·7 |
| Aug 1 | Freiburg Hill-Climb (German Hill-Climb championship) | M-B (750kg Grand Prix formula car)* | 3 | Caracciola | 12 km | 8:17·7 | 86·9 |
| Aug 8 | Monaco Grand Prix | M-B (750kg Grand Prix formula car) | 1 | Brauchitsch | 318 km | 3:07:23·9 | 101·8 |
| | | M-B (750kg Grand Prix formula car) | 2 | Caracciola | | 3:08:48·2 | 101·1 |
| | | M-B (750kg Grand Prix formula car) | 3 | Kautz | | — | — |
| Aug 15 | Coppa Acerbo (Pescara) | M-B (750kg Grand Prix formula car) | 2 | Brauchitsch | 412·8 km | 2:57:20·9 | 139·7 |

* Racing-car. † World record.

| Date | Event | Car | Place | Drivers | Distance | Time Hrs :mins :secs | Speed k.p.h. |
|---|---|---|---|---|---|---|---|
| Aug 22 | Swiss Grand Prix | M-B (750kg Grand Prix formula car) | 1 | Caracciola | 364 km | 2:17:39·3 | 158·6 |
| | | M-B (750kg Grand Prix formula car) | 2 | Lang | | 2:18:28·7 | 157·7 |
| | | M-B (750kg Grand Prix formula car) | 3 | Brauchitsch | | 2:18:45·7 | 157·4 |
| Sept 12 | Italian Grand Prix (Coppa Ciano) | M-B (750kg Grand Prix formula car) | 1 | Caracciola | 360·9 km | 2:44:54·4 | 131·3 |
| | | M-B (750kg Grand Prix formula car) | 2 | Lang | | 2:44:54·8 | 131·2 |
| Sept 12 | Argentine 500 Mile Race, Rafaela Circuit | M-B (*SSK*) | 1 | Zatuszek | 804·7 km | 5:03:42·6 | 158·9 |
| Sept 26 | Masaryk Grand Prix | M-B (750kg Grand Prix formula car) | 1 | Caracciola | 437·1 km | 3:09:25·3 | 138·4 |
| | | M-B (750kg Grand Prix formula car) | 2 | Brauchitsch | | 3:10:01·7 | 138 |
| Oct 2 | Donington Grand Prix | M-B (750kg Grand Prix formula car) | 2 | Brauchitsch | 250 miles | 3:01:40 | 132·9 |
| | | M-B (750kg Grand Prix formula car) | 3 | Caracciola | | 3:02:18 | 132·4 |
| 1938 April 10 | Pau Grand Prix | M-B (3 litre Grand Prix formula car) | 2 | Caracciola and Lang | 276·9 km | 3:10:50 | 87·1 |
| May 15 | Tripoli Grand Prix | M-B (3 litre Grand Prix formula car) | 1 | Lang | 524 km | 2:33:17·1 | 205·1 |
| | | M-B (3 litre Grand Prix formula car) | 2 | Brauchitsch | | 2:37:55·6 | 199·1 |
| | | M-B (3 litre Grand Prix formula car) | 3 | Caracciola | | 2:38:20·7 | 198·6 |

| | | | | | | | |
|---|---|---|---|---|---|---|---|
| July 3 | French Grand Prix | M-B (3 litre Grand Prix formula car) | 1 | Brauchitsch | 500·9 km | 3:04:38·5 | 162·8 |
| | | M-B (3 litre Grand Prix formula car) | 2 | Caracciola | | 3:06:19·6 | 161·3 |
| | | M-B (3 litre Grand Prix formula car) | 3 | Lang | | 3:04:54·3 (One lap behind) | 159·9 |
| July 24 | German Grand Prix | M-B (3 litre Grand Prix formula car) | 1 | Seaman | 501·8 km | 3:51:46·2 | 129·8 |
| | | M-B (3 litre Grand Prix formula car) | 2 | Caracciola | | 3:55:06·2 | 128 |
| Aug 7 | Coppa Ciano (Livorno) | M-B (3 litre Grand Prix formula car) | 1 | Lang | 232 km | 1:40:35·2 | 138·4 |
| Aug 14 | Coppa Acerbo (Pescara) | M-B (3 litre Grand Prix formula car) | 1 | Caracciola | 412·8 km | 3:03:45·6 | 134·8 |
| Aug 21 | Swiss Grand Prix | M-B (3 litre Grand Prix formula car) | 1 | Caracciola | c. 364 km | 2:32:07·8 | 143·6 |
| | | M-B (3 litre Grand Prix formula car) | 2 | Seaman | | 2:32:33·8 | 143 |
| | | M-B (3 litre Grand Prix formula car) | 3 | Brauchitsch | | 2:32:11·6 (One lap behind) | 140·6 |
| Aug 28 | German Hill-Climb Championship (Grossglockner) | M-B (750kg Grand Prix formula car) | 2 | Lang | 25·2 km | 20:19·4 | 74·4 |
| | | M-B (750kg Grand Prix formula car) | 3 | Brauchitsch | | 20:41·8 | 73·1 |
| Sept 11 | Italian Grand Prix | M-B (3 litre Grand Prix formula car | 3 | Caracciola and Brauchitsch | 419·6 km | 2:42:39·4 (Three laps behind) | 146·7 |
| Sept | Rafaela Race, South America | M-B (*SSK*) | 1 | Brosutti | 500 miles | 4:52:52 | 164 |

| *Date* | *Event* | *Car* | *Place* | *Drivers* | *Distance* | *Time Hrs :mins :secs* | *Speed k.p.h.* |
|---|---|---|---|---|---|---|---|
| Oct 22 | Donington Grand Prix | M-B (3 litre Grand Prix formula car) | 2 | Lang | 250 miles | 3:08:00 | 128·4 |
| | | M-B (3 litre Grand Prix formula car) | 3 | Seaman | | 3:06:22 (One lap behind) | 132 |
| Oct 29 | Olavarria Grand Prix, Argentine | M-B (*SSK*) | 1 | Fermin | 224 km | 1:39:05 | 135·7 |
| | | M-B (*SSK*) | 3 | Olivari | | — | — |
| 1939 April 8 | Pau Grand Prix | M-B (3 litre Grand Prix formula car) | 1 | Lang | 276·8 km | 3:07:25·2 | 88·7 |
| | | M-B (3 litre Grand Prix formula car) | 2 | Brauchitsch | | 3:07:42 | 88·4 |
| May 7 | Tripoli Grand Prix | M-B (1½ litre car) | 1 | Lang | 393 km | 1:59:12·3 | 197·8 |
| | | M-B (1½ litre car) | 2 | Caracciola | | 2:02:49·6 | 191·9 |
| May 21 | Eifel Races | M-B (3 litre Grand Prix formula car) | 1 | Lang | 228·1 km | 1:40:57·1 | 135·5 |
| | | M-B (3 litre Grand Prix formula car) | 3 | Caracciola | | 1:41:28·4 | 134·8 |
| June 11 | Vienna Hill-Climb | M-B (3 litre Grand Prix formula car) | 1 | Lang | 8·2 km | 4:38·6 | 106·3 |
| June 25 | Belgian Grand Prix | M-B (3 litre Grand Prix formula car) | 1 | Lang | 507·5 km | 3:20:21 | 152 |
| | | M-B (3 litre Grand Prix formula car) | 3 | Brauchitsch | | 3:22:14 | 150·5 |
| July 23 | German Grand Prix | M-B (3 litre Grand Prix formula car) | 1 | Caracciola | 501·8 km | 4:08:41·8 | 121·9 |
| Aug 6 | German Hill-Climb Championship (Grossglockner) | M-B (750kg Grand Prix formula car) | 1 | Lang | 25·2 km | 20:07·9 | 75·1 |

| | | | | | | | |
|---|---|---|---|---|---|---|---|
| Aug 20 | Swiss Grand Prix | M-B (3 litre Grand Prix formula car) | 1 | Lang | 218·4 km | 1:24:47·6 | 154·6 |
| | | M-B (3 litre Grand Prix formula car) | 2 | Caracciola | | 1:24:50·7 | 154·4 |
| | | M-B (3 litre Grand Prix formula car) | 3 | Brauchitsch | | 1:25:57·5 | 152·5 |
| Sept 3 | Belgrade City Race | M-B (3 litre Grand Prix formula car) | 2 | Brauchitsch | 139·7 km | 1:04:11·4 | 130·4 |
| 1951 | | | | | | | *m.p.h.* |
| Feb 18 | Peron Cup, Buenos Aires Grand Prix | M-B (3 litre Grand Prix formula car) | 2 | Lang | 98 miles | 1:35:35·3 | 61 (approx) |
| | | M-B (3 litre Grand Prix formula car) | 3 | Fangio | | 1:36:10·4 | — |
| Feb 25 | Grand Prix Eva Peron, Buenos Aires | M-B (3 litre Grand Prix formula car) | 2 | Kling | 98 miles | 1:37:53·1 | 60 (approx) |
| | | M-B (3 litre Grand Prix formula car) | 3 | Lang | | (Two laps behind) | |
| 1952 May 4 | Mille Miglia | M-B (*300SL*) | 2 | Kling | 971·8 miles | 12:14:17 | 78 (approx) |
| | | M-B (*300SL*) | 4 | Caracciola | | 12:40:25 | — |
| May 18 | Prix de Berne | M-B (*300SL*)<br>M-B (*300SL*)<br>M-B (*300SL*) | 1<br>2<br>3 | Kling<br>Lang<br>Riess | 81 miles | 54:08·4<br>54:46·4<br>(One lap behind) | 89·9<br>— |
| June 14–15 | Grand Prix D'Endurance, Le Mans | M-B (*300SL*) | 1 | Lang and Riess | 2320 miles (277 laps) | 24 hours | 96·6 |
| | | M-B (*300SL*) | 2 | Helfrich and Niedermayer | 276 laps | | — |
| Nov 19–23 | Pan-American Race, Mexico | M-B (*300SL*)<br>M-B (*300SL*) | 1<br>2 | Kling<br>Lang | 1932 miles | 18:51:19<br>19:26:30 | 102·8<br>— |

| Date | Event | Car | Place | Drivers | Distance | Time Hrs :mins :secs | Speed m.p.h. |
|---|---|---|---|---|---|---|---|
| 1954 July 4 | French Grand Prix | M-B ($2\frac{1}{2}$ litre Grand Prix formula car) | 1 | Fangio | 311 miles | 2:42:47·5 | 115·6 |
| | | M-B ($2\frac{1}{2}$ litre Grand Prix formula car) | 2 | Kling | | 2:42:48 | — |
| Aug 1 | German Grand Prix | M-B ($2\frac{1}{2}$ litre Grand Prix formula car) | 1 | Fangio | 312 miles | 3:45:45·8 | 82·7 |
| Aug 22 | Swiss Grand Prix | M-B ($2\frac{1}{2}$ litre Grand Prix formula car) | 1 | Fangio | 280 miles | 3:00:34·5 | 99·1 |
| | | M-B ($2\frac{1}{2}$ litre Grand Prix formula car) | 3 | Herrmann | | (One lap behind) | |
| Sept 5 | Italian Grand Prix | M-B ($2\frac{1}{2}$ litre Grand Prix formula car) | 1 | Fangio | 313 miles | 2:47:47·9 | 111·9 |
| Sept 19 | Avus Races | M-B ($2\frac{1}{2}$ litre Grand Prix formula car) | 1 | Kling | c. 313 miles | 3:39:59·8 | 132·5 |
| | | M-B ($2\frac{1}{2}$ litre Grand Prix formula car) | 2 | Fangio | | 3:40:00·3 | — |
| | | M-B ($2\frac{1}{2}$ litre Grand Prix formula car) | 3 | Herrmann | | 3:40:00·7 | — |
| Oct 24 | Spanish Grand Prix (Barcelona) | M-B ($2\frac{1}{2}$ litre Grand Prix formula car) | 3 | Fangio | 313 miles | 3:14:17·8 (One lap behind) | — |
| 1955 Jan 16 | Argentine Grand Prix | M-B ($2\frac{1}{2}$ litre Grand Prix formula car) | 1 | Fangio | 233 miles | 3:00:38·6 | 75·1 |
| Jan 30 | Buenos Aires Grand Prix | M-B ($2\frac{1}{2}$ litre Grand Prix formula car) | 1 | Fangio | 175·2 miles | 2:23:18·9 | 73·4 |
| | | M-B ($2\frac{1}{2}$ litre Grand Prix formula car) | 2 | Moss | | 2:23:30·8 | — |
| May 1 | Mille Miglia | M-B (*300SLR*) | 1 | Moss | 992 miles | 10:07:48 | 97·9 |
| | | M-B (*300SLR*) | 2 | Fangio | | 10:39:33 | — |

| | | | | | | | |
|---|---|---|---|---|---|---|---|
| May 29 | Eifel Races | M-B (*300SLR*) | 1 | Fangio | 141·7 miles | 1:44:52·9 | 81 |
| | | M-B (*300SLR*) | 2 | Moss | | 1:44:53 | 81 |
| June 5 | Belgian Grand Prix | M-B (2½ litre Grand Prix formula car) | 1 | Fangio | 315 miles | 2:39:29 | 118·4 |
| | | M-B (2½ litre Grand Prix formula car) | 2 | Moss | | 2:39:37·1 | — |
| June 19 | Dutch Grand Prix (Zandvoort) | M-B (2½ litre Grand Prix formula car) | 1 | Fangio | 260 miles | 2:54:23·8 | 89·6 |
| | | M-B (2½ litre Grand Prix formula car) | 2 | Moss | | 2:54:24·1 | — |
| July 16 | British Grand Prix (Aintree) | M-B (2½ litre Grand Prix formula car) | 1 | Moss | 270 miles | 3:7:21·2 | 86·5 |
| | | M-B (2½ litre Grand Prix formula car) | 2 | Fangio | | 3:7:21·4 | — |
| | | M-B (2½ litre Grand Prix formula car) | 3 | Kling | | 3:8:33 | — |
| Aug 7 | Swedish Grand Prix | M-B (*300SLR*) | 1 | Fangio | 129·9 miles | 1:18:13·7 | 100·4 |
| | | M-B (*300SLR*) | 2 | Moss | | 1:18:14 | — |
| Sept 11 | Italian Grand Prix | M-B (2½ litre Grand Prix formula car) | 1 | Fangio | 313 miles | 2:25:4·4 | 128·42 |
| | | M-B (2½ litre Grand Prix formula car) | 2 | Taruffi | | 2:25:5·1 | — |
| Sept 17 | Tourist Trophy (Dundrod Circuit, Northern Ireland) | M-B (*300SLR*) | 1 | Moss and Fitch | 623 miles | 7:3:11 | 88·32 |
| | | M-B (*300SLR*) | 2 | Fangio and Kling | | 1 lap behind | — |
| | | M-B (*300SLR*) | 3 | Von Trips and Simon | | 2 laps behind | — |
| Oct 16 | Targa Florio | M-B (*300SLR*) | 1 | Moss and Collins | 581·63 miles | 9:43:14 | 59·8 |
| | | M-B (*300SLR*) | 2 | Fangio and Kling | | 9:47:55 | 59·25 |

At the end of 1955, Mercedes-Benz withdrew from Grand Prix racing.

# INDEX